STRUCTURED FORTRAN WITH WATFIV

TEXT AND REFERENCE

ALTERNATE EDITION

STRUCTURED FORTRAN WITH WATFIV

TEXT AND REFERENCE

ALTERNATE EDITION

John B. Moore

Leo J. Makela

RESTON PUBLISHING COMPANY, INC., Reston, Virginia

A Prentice-Hall Company

Library of Congress Cataloging in Publication Data

Moore, John B

    Structured FORTRAN with WATFIV.

    Includes index.
    1. FORTRAN (Computer program language)
2. Structured programming. I. Makela, Leo J.,
joint author. II. Title.
QA76.73.F25M65 1980   001.64'24   80-23006
ISBN 0-8359-7104-X
ISBN 0-8359-7103-1 (pbk.)

    1981 by
RESTON PUBLISHING COMPANY, INC.
A Prentice-Hall Company
Reston, Virginia

10 9 8 7 6 5 4 3 2

Printed in the United States of America.

Preface

The Fortran programming language continues to be used extensively in North America as an aid in solving a wide variety of scientific and mathematical problems. Until recently however Fortran did not provide the programmer with many of the tools necessary to take advantage of the problem-solving approach which has come to be known as structured programming. Structured programming is primarily a method of organizing the task of algorithm development so that correct and efficient programs result. Its methods, along with those of hierarchical or top-down design, have helped transform the "art of computer programming" to the "science of computer programming". Several versions of Fortran now exist which contain the cornerstones of structured programming -- the IF-THEN-ELSE construct and the WHILE-DO construct. These, along with many other enhancements to standard Fortran, are now an integral part of the Fortran language processed by the WATFIV compiler developed at the University of Waterloo.

The purpose of this book is to provide a comprehensive description of the structured programming approach to problem-solving using the Fortran language processed by the WATFIV compiler. The authors believe it is the most complete and up-to-date book on the subject yet published.

The content is organized into four parts. Part I describes the statements in the language which define and manipulate fixed-point and floating-point values. In Part I the output device is always a printer, the input device, always a card reader. Unlike most programming texts which present new topics in the sequence: "Here's another statement in the language."; "Here's how it is used."; "Here's some examples.", the approach taken in this book is: "Here's what we are trying to do."; "Here's how we could do it using our existing knowledge."; "Here's an easier way of doing it.". In other words, the approach is to present the language in terms of purpose or function.

Part II describes the use of non-INTEGER, non-REAL values. Chapter 11 presents the concepts. Chapters 12 thru 16 each deal with a specific type of value. Chapter 17 concludes Part II with a summary of the rules for statements which may contain references to more than one type of value.

Part III describes the non-card input, non-printer output features of the language. Separate chapters describe punched output, magnetic tape input-output, direct access input-output, and simulated input-output using CHARACTER variables. Two chapters describing NAMELIST input-output and unformatted READ-WRITE statements conclude Part III.

Part IV contains ten appendices. Aside from the standard topics usually found in programming texts, they include hints for program "debugging" and efficiency (Appendix G) and a comparison of the Fortran language processed by the WATFIV compiler and that processed by the IBM Fortran compilers (Appendix F). Flowcharting conventions and symbols are described in Appendix B. Flowcharts are used to define and illustrate the logic of the decision-making elements of the language. Appendix J describes how the structured language elements can be coded using the conventions of standard Fortran.

The text does not contain a description of how computers work. Many suitable books are available to the teacher who wishes to present these topics in parallel with a course on Fortran programming.

Use as a text. Because of the detailed nature of the explanations and example problems, the text can be used in a self-study environment. It is also appropriate for a one or two semester course. At Waterloo, first year students cover the material in Parts I and II in twenty-five lecture hours. They have an additional twenty-five hours of laboratory time during which tutorial help is available for assisting them with their assignments. Topics in Part I which are marked with an asterisk are omitted in this one semester course. The approach taken in lecture periods is to present one or two programming problems, introducing new language features as needed, but leaving the student to learn the details of the new statements on his own. More than five-hundred-and-fifty exercise, drill-type questions are included in the text. These provide the student with the opportunity for intensive practice on specific features of the language.

Use as a reference. Most introductory texts are unsuitable as a reference because the content is organized so that so-called "advanced" topics are presented toward the end of the book or as part of an appendix. This means that information on a particular topic may be found in two or more places thus necessitating much page-flipping and searching to find the required information. The fragmentation of topics is not present in this book. The index contains over 1000 references.

vi

The text material was prepared, modified and printed using the SCRIPT text-editing system at the University of Waterloo. Texts, like programs, are not usually error-free. All programs used as examples have been carefully checked. Please accept our apologies for any undetected errors.

We acknowledge the contributions of the Computer Systems Group and the University of Waterloo -- the developers of the WATFIV compiler. Specific thanks go to Sandra Ward and Bruce Hay for providing us with details of the most recent changes to the WATFIV language. Thanks also the many helpful suggestions from those who used the predecessor of this book, "WATFIV: Text and Reference", by John B. Moore.

To you the reader, We hope that you will find this a useful and enjoyable book. We have tried to keep your needs in mind from start to finish.

Waterloo, Ontario, Canada
John B. Moore
Leo J. Makela

Preface to the Alternate Edition

Since the original publication of this book a number of improvemements have been made both in standard Fortran and in the version of Fortran processed by the WATFIV compiler. The alternate edition of Structured Fortran with WATFIV reflects the most recent changes made to WATFIV. These include the addition of the four new statements ELSEIF, QUIT, UNTIL and ADMIT, and the constructs GUESS-END GUESS and LOOP-END LOOP.

The ELSEIF statement is now part of standard Fortran. Consequently its description and use has been integrated into the presentation. The other new constructs and statements are not part of the standard Fortran language. In keeping with our objectives of providing a reference on WATFIV as well as a Fortran text, new sections providing detailed descriptions and examples of the other new constructs and statements have been added.

The widespread use of the book is naturally gratifying to us. Writing a text is a very speculative venture. Your acceptance of our efforts to help develop more knowledgable and productive programmers and problem solvers is appreciated.

Waterloo, Ontario, Canada
John B. Moore
Leo J. Makela

To

Kelly, Jay, Greg, Mike,
the Koskinens and the Rivetts

Preface To The Student

This is a book that teaches you how to speak a language -- a language which permits you to use a computer to perform the numerical calculations necessary to solve problems. The language is one member of the Fortran family of languages. It was developed at the University of Waterloo to make using a computer easy for students. Some of you will learn to speak the language well -- others just enough to get by or to solve a specific problem. The more exercises and programming problems you do, the more fluent you will be in the use of the language. Good luck and good programming.

TABLE OF CONTENTS

PART I   THE STATEMENTS IN THE LANGUAGE

CHAPTER 1 SO YOU WANT TO USE A COMPUTER

CHAPTER 2 NUMBERS, ARITHMETIC AND VARIABLES

CHAPTER 3 DECISION AND CONTROL

CHAPTER 4 LOOPS AND LOOP CONTROL

CHAPTER 5 INPUT

CHAPTER 6 OUTPUT

CHAPTER 7 SETS OF VARIABLES

CHAPTER 8 REMOTE BLOCKS

CHAPTER 9 SUBPROGRAMS -- THE BASICS

CHAPTER 10 SUBPROGRAMS -- THE DETAILS

PART II   OTHER TYPES OF VALUES

CHAPTER 16 CHARACTER VALUES

CHAPTER 17 MIXED-TYPE STATEMENTS -- A SUMMARY

PART III   OTHER TYPES OF INPUT OUTPUT

CHAPTER 18 PUNCHED OUTPUT

CHAPTER 19 MAGNETIC TAPE INPUT-OUTPUT

CHAPTER 20 DIRECT ACCESS INPUT OUTPUT

CHAPTER 21 CHARACTER "DEVICES"

Part I

THE STATEMENTS
IN THE LANGUAGE

CHAPTER 1   SO YOU WANT TO USE A COMPUTER

Questions Answered In Chapter 1.

1. What can a computer do?

2. If that's all it can do, why do we use them?

3. What steps are necessary to solve a problem using a computer?

4. O.K. - How about an example?

5. What happens when you make a mistake?

1.1 What Can A Computer Do?

Computers are attributed with many remarkable powers. However, all computers, whether they are the large ones which control the space flights or ones that look more like a desk-top calculator, are simply collections of electronic components which have three basic capabilities.

First: Every computer has circuits which can do arithmetic. What kinds of arithmetic can be done? There are circuits for performing the following five kinds of arithmetic operations: + - * / **. That is: addition, subtraction, multiplication, division, and exponentiation. The asterisk or star symbol "*" is used to indicate multiplication to avoid any confusion with the letter X which we often like to use as a variable. The "/" symbol for division should cause no problem since we often write fractions such a three-sevenths as 3/7. The double asterisk "**" is used to describe the operation of exponentiation (raising a number to an exponent). For example, two-to-the-fifth is written as 2**5.

Second: Every computer has a means of communicating with you and me. After all, if we couldn't put numbers in and get results back, these machines wouldn't be much use, would they? A common method of inputting information is to use "punched cards". By using a machine called a keypunch which resembles a big typewriter, we can put holes in a card. Each different letter or symbol has its own unique little pattern of holes. Although the keypunch machine prints a line across the top of the card showing the symbols corresponding to the holes punched below them, with a little practice, you can learn to "read the holes". Fortunately this ability is not necessary to successfully use computers. The computer's input device, called a card reader, reads the holes punched in the card using a set of wire brushes which close a circuit when a hole is detected.

For outputting information, the most common computer device is a printer. Small hammers push the paper into type slugs which are located on a rapidly rotating chain. This chain contains a large number of slugs, one (or more) for each of the symbols which can be printed.

Third: Computers   have   circuits   which   can   make decisions. The kinds of decisions which computer circuits can make are not of the type: "Who would win a war between Russia and China?",   or "What is the largest city in North America?".   Unfortunately,   the computer can only   decide three things, namely: Is one number less than another?; Are two numbers equal?; and, Is one number greater than another?

Since all computers have only these three limited capabilities -- simple arithmetic, input-output, and trivial decision-making, it is only natural to ask the following question.

1.2 Why Do We Use Them?

There are perhaps three good reasons why we use these machines in spite of their limited capabilities.

1. Speed.   Computers are capable of doing all   three things (arithmetic,   input-output,   decision-making)   at tremendous speeds. For example, a very powerful machine can do as many as 20*10**6 additions per second. By the way, if you thought this value might be 64000000000000 instead of twenty-million, you can look ahead to Section 1 of Chapter 2 to find out why it can only be twenty-million. To gain some appreciation of this speed, it would probably take you or me (working a 40 hour week) about seventeen years to do this many additions. Speeds for doing other types of arithmetic and decision-making are comparable to that for addition. Input and output operations however, involve mechanical motion of cards and paper and hence the speeds for these operations are much slower. On a typical computer system, cards are read at about 1000 cards per minute and lines are printed at an average speed of 1000 lines per minute.

2. Accuracy and Reliablility. In spite of newspaper headlines such as "Computer Fails Student", these machines are very accurate and reliable -- especially when you

consider the number of operations they can perform every second. Because they are man-made machines they do occasionally break down and have to be repaired. However the mistakes that are made are almost always due to the people who use them, you and I.

3. **A Big Problem = A Set Of Little Problems.** The most important reason computers are so widely used today is that almost all big problems can be solved by solving a bunch of little problems -- one after the other. Moreover, solutions to these little problems can be obtained using the very limited capabilities possessed by all computers. For example, the problem of producing the federal civil service payroll is indeed a big problem. But to solve that problem we need only do the following kinds of things for each employee on the payroll. First: Input information about the employee such as his wage rate, hours worked, tax rate, past pension deductions, etc. Second: Do some simple arithmetic and decision making. Third: Output a few printed lines on a check. By repeating this process over and over again the payroll will eventually be finished. Since computers can do all these things accurately and at high speeds, the reason for using them is obvious.

Having seen what these machines can do and having stated the reasons for using them, let's find out what steps are necessary to have them assist us in solving a problem.

1.3 What Are The Five Steps In Problem Solving?

There are five steps which must be followed before a computer can be used to solve a problem.

Step 1. Define the problem. Unless the problem is well-defined there is no sense in even thinking about using a computer to help solve it. The people who get paid the highest salaries in the data processing business are those who are trying to answer the question: "What, precisely, is it that we want to use the computer to do?". Glib answers such as "do inventory control" are no good. The problem must be well-defined. Before you write any program, ask yourself: "Do I know exactly what the problem is?".

Step 2. Develop a procedure for solving the problem. A word which means "a procedure for solving a problem" is algorithm. The algorithm takes the form of a sequence of instructions which, if followed by a moron, will solve the problem. There are several different ways of describing an algorithm. One method is called

flowcharting and is described in Appendix B. This
second step is the key to using a computer successfully.
You should closely study the example algorithms
presented later in the chapter and try to develop
algorithms for all the problems suggested in the
exercises. If you can determine a procedure for solving
a problem, programming is easy.

Step 3. Translate the steps in the algorithm into a language
which the computer understands. The set of instructions
in the new language is called a computer program. There
are literally hundreds of languages which can be
"understood" by a computer. The language described in
this book is called WATFIV. This language is widely
used in North America for describing algorithms which
frequently solve problems of a scientific or
mathematical nature. Although we may think of the
computer as being able to understand WATFIV, all
computers actually understand only one language which is
made up of long strings of ones and zeros. Some of
these strings represent instructions, others represent
the data or numbers which are manipulated according to
the instructions. The "thing" that performs the
translation of the WATFIV language statements into
machine language (the ones and zeros), is a special
program called a compiler. More will be said about the
compiler when we come to Step 5.

Step 4. Keypunch the program. Once the procedure for
solving the problem has been written in a language the
computer understands, it is necessary to punch this
information into cards which will then be input into the
computer via the card reader. Information about punched
cards and keypunches can be found in Appendix A. Rules
for "where things go" on the cards will be given later
in this chapter. The set of cards produced is called a
source deck. As well as the cards which contain the
instructions in the program, two special cards are
required -- one at the beginning called the JOB card,
and one at the end called the ENTRY card. These cards
are used to separate your source deck from other source
decks.

Step 5. Run the job. The final step is to have the computer
perform the calculations which are necessary to solve
the problem. This is accomplished by giving the deck of
cards to the computer operator who puts the deck in the
card reader and presses a button which causes the cards
to be read into the memory of the computer.

Running a job is a two-stage process. As mentioned previously, the instructions and numbers in your program must first be translated into bits (ones and zeros) by a compiler.   This compiler is   already "inside" the computer at the time your deck is being entered via the card reader.   The cards in your deck are read in under the control of the compiler.   As each card is read, the information punched in the card is   analyzed and translated into the appropriate strings of ones and zeros. As well as producing the required bit strings, the compiler also outputs a line on the printer showing the information punched in   the card and messages regarding any errors detected.   The interval during which this translation process takes place is called the compile time of the job.

The second stage of running a job is to have the computer actually perform the calculations described in the program.   The order and type of calculations performed are those defined by the strings of ones and zeros (the machine language program) produced by the compiler.   The interval during which the calculations specified by the program are being done is called the execution-time of the job.   Any error such as dividing by zero which occurs during the execution-time of the job causes the execution to be stopped and an error message to be printed.   The two stages which occur when any WATFIV job is run are shown in the following diagram.

Stage 1 - Compile

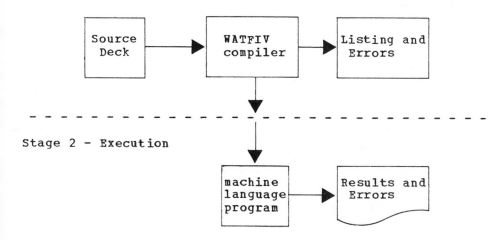

Stage 2 - Execution

1.4 How About An Example?

Step 1. Problem Definition.

For each value of x=0,1,2,...,9,10, calculate the corresponding value of y using the formula:

$$y = \frac{x^2 - x + 2}{x + 3}$$

Hopefully this is a well-defined problem. We are to take each of the eleven different values of x and produce the eleven corresponding values of y using the given formula.

Step 2. Develop a procedure for solving the problem.

One procedure which would solve the problem is shown below.

Algorithm A

        1. Set x = 0
        2. Calculate y using the formula
        3. Write down the values of x and y
        4. Set x = 1
        5. Calculate y using the formula
        6. Write down the values of x and y
        7. Set x = 2
        8. .
        9. .

            .

            .

            .

       31. Set x = 10
       32. Calculate y using the formula
       33. Write down the values of x and y
       34. Stop

If a robot were to follow this set of instructions, one after the other, the required eleven pairs of values of x and y would be produced. Using this algorithm, each step in the algorithm is executed once. Observe that any algorithm which solves the problem will require a minimum of thirty-four instructions to be executed.

Is this a good algorithm? In one sense it is the best because by using this algorithm the minimum number

of steps necessary to solve the problem will be
executed.   Suppose, however, the problem required us to
use values of x=0,1,2,...,9999,10000.   The algorithm
would then contain 30004 instructions!   The
disadvantage of Algorithm A, then, is due to fact that
three instructions must be written down for every value
of x used. Furthermore, following the first instruction

            Set x = 0

which gives x its initial value, the following group of
three instructions is repeated over and over

        Calculate y using the formula
        Write down the values of x and y
        Generate the next value of x

How long do we go on repeating this group of
instructions?   The answer is "as long as x has a value
less than or equal to 10". In other words:

    while x≤10 do the following

        1. Calculate y

        2. Print the values of x and y

        3. Generate the next value of x

When x is no longer less than or equal to 10 what should
we do?   Well, by then we've done everything required to
solve the problem, so we stop.   Thus an alternate
algorithm is the following:

Algorithm B

    1.   Set x = 0

    2.   While x ≤ 10 do the following

            .1 Calculate y using the formula

            .2 Write down the values of x and y

            .3 Add 1 to the value of x

    3.   Stop

If you are a first-time programmer it may seem peculiar to set x=0 in Step 1 and then immediately test if x≤10. in Step 2. You're absolutely right but this test is wasted only the first time and takes an inconsequential amount of time to execute. From then on it's necessary to test to determine if we are finished.

Note that generating the next value of x is accomplished by adding 1 to the current value of x. You should satisfy yourself that this algorithm does indeed solve the problem by following the instructions in a robot-like manner.

How many instructions did you execute when using Algorithm B? Step 1 is executed 1 time; the test for x ≤ 10 is made when x=0, x=1, x=2, ..., x=10, and x=11, twelve times in all. Eleven of those times x is ≤ 10 and so instructions 2.1, 2.2 and 2.3 are executed 11 times each. The stop instruction is executed once. Therefore using Algorithm B we execute (1+12+11+11+11+1) = 47 instructions. Recall that Algorithm A on the other hand only required that 34 instructions be executed to solve the problem. However, to describe Algorithm A we had to write down all 34 instructions, whereas to describe Algorithm B we only had to write down 6 instructions. Looking ahead and realizing that these instructions will be executed by a high-speed computer which can execute hundreds of thousands of instructions every second, the difference in execution times of the two algorithms becomes insignificant, (certainly less than 1/1000th of a second).

Since there is such an insignificant difference in the execution times of the two approaches and for several other reasons which will become apparent shortly, almost all algorithms are written using the type B approach instead of the "brute force" method of Algorithm A. Algorithms such as B possess a "looping" or "iterative" property. With a little practice, you will find it easy to think "iteratively".

A flowchart is a picture of an algorithm. Different shapes of symbols are used to represent different types of steps in the procedure. A flowchart of Algorithm B is shown in the diagram below.

Flowchart Of Algorithm B

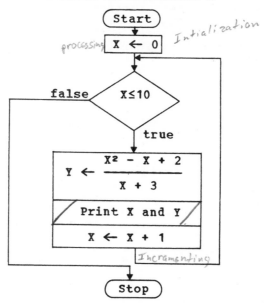

In flowcharts, only three basic shapes are required. These are:

oval shapes: used to   denote entry   and exit points

rectangles: used   to denote   actions not involving decisions

diamond shapes: which denote decisions to be   made.   The   decision   is   usually expressed as a true-false statement.   The path   to   be   followed in   each   case   is labelled TRUE or FALSE.

Straight lines with arrowheads   connect the symbols.   A complete   description   of flowcharting   symbols   can   be found in Appendix B.

Most   of   the   algorithms   you   will   use   to   solve problems   in the   first   part of   this   book   are   simple enough that the steps in the algorithm can be written using English-like statements as we have done in this example. For algorithms which involve a number of interrelated decisions, a flowchart is often a real help in seeing the solution procedure.

Step 3. Translate the Algorithm Into WATFIV.

Shown in the next diagram are the steps in the algorithm and the results of translating the steps into WATFIV to produce a WATFIV program. Each line on the right represents what would be punched into a single card.

Algorithm	WATFIV Program
	$JOB WATFIV
	C EXAMPLE PROGRAM 1
1. Set x = 0	X = 0.
2. While x ≤ 10	WHILE (X .LE. 10.)
.1 Calculate y	Y=(X**2-X+2.)/(X+3.)
.2 Print values of x and y	PRINT,X,Y
.3 Add 1 to x	X = X + 1.
	END WHILE
3. Stop	STOP
	END
	$ENTRY

Let's see how each of the six steps in the algorithm has been translated into WATFIV.

Step 1.   The translation of step 1 is straightforward. To assign X a value of zero, we simply write "X=0.".

Step 2.   The translation of the WHILE instruction needs some comment. First, the condition x≤10 being tested is enclosed in parentheses. Secondly, the type of test is indicated by the symbols .LE., the "LE" of course denoting less-than-or-equal-to. In WATFIV there are a total of six types of relationships which can be tested. These are:

    .LT.   less than
    .LE.   less than or equal to
    .EQ.   equal to
    .NE.   not equal to
    .GE.   greater than or equal to
    .GT.   greater than

Within step 2 there are three substeps. In the program they have been indented to the right to make it easy to see they are part of the WHILE loop.

Step 2.1 The translation of "Calculate y" shows that arithmetic expressions are written according to rules of arithmetic. For the "=" symbol you should read "is assigned the value of".

Step 2.2 The translation of step 2.2 is straightforward. Note that PRINT,X,Y means print the value of the variables X and Y. It does not mean print the symbol 'X' and the symbol 'Y'.

Step 2.3 The translation of step 2.3 looks a little weird at first. It should be interpreted in the following way. Evaluate the expression on the right hand side of the equal sign and assign that value to the variable on the left hand side of the equal sign. Statements such as these are called "Assignment" statements. An Assignment statement is used to assign a value to a variable. It is the most frequently used type of statement in almost all WATFIV programs.

Step 3.   The meaning of "STOP" in WATFIV is simply to stop executing any more instructions. It is used to indicate the job has been finished.

What of the other five lines in the program which are not translations of any step in the algorithm? These are:
```
$JOB    WATFIV
$ENTRY
C EXAMPLE PROGRAM 1
END WHILE
END
```

i) The "$JOB WATFIV" statement indicates that the program has been written in the WATFIV language instead of some other programming language.

ii) The "$ENTRY" statement follows the last statement of every WATFIV program. The $JOB and $ENTRY cards (they are written here but the information will subsequently be punched into cards), are called job control cards. Both must be present in every WATFIV program you write.

iii) The second line of the program, namely

C EXAMPLE PROGRAM 1

is called a comment and is identified by a "C" in the first position. Comments can be included anywhere in a program and their purpose is simply to make remarks which can be helpful to understanding or identifying the program. Good programmers generally use a lot of comments, especially in very large programs which may contain thousands of statements.

iv) The END WHILE statement follows the last statement of the group which is executed repeatedly while the condition is true. Every time a WHILE statement is used, there must be an END WHILE statement to delimit the statements which are part of the WHILE loop. The fact that the three statements are indented provides no information because statements can be placed anywhere on the card. Indentation however does greatly improve a reader's understanding of a program.

v) The "END" statement is also included in every program. Unlike the $ENTRY statement however, there may be more than one END statement in a program. This occurs if programs are written in pieces or segments. In such cases, an END statement is used to end each segment. For the time being however, we will only be writing programs which require one END statement and we should automatically place it ahead of the $ENTRY statement.

A couple of small points about the program. You will have noticed that capital letters have been used when writing the statements in the program. Most keypunches only contain symbols for the capital letters. This is fortunate since using small letters in WATFIV will produce error messages. You must always use upper case letters. The second point concerns whether or not it is necessary to use a decimal point after numbers such as 2, 10, etc. A complete answer will be given in Chapter 2. For the work in this Chapter, no problems will arise if decimal points are used when writing numbers used in a program.

Step 4. Keypunch the program.

Each line in the program is punched on a single card. A punched card contains enough room to punch 80 symbols -- one in each of the eighty columns of the card. The hole pattern for each symbol appears directly underneath it. Shown below are the symbols appearing in each column of the cards in the program.

```
                  one        ten        twenty      thirty
                   ↓          ↓           ↓           ↓
       card      {            1          2           3
       columns   {1234567890123456789012345678901 23456789

                 $JOB    WATFIV  acct.# your name
                 C EXAMPLE PROGRAM 1
                     X = 0.
                     WHILE (X .LE. 10.)
                        Y=(X**2-X+2.)/(X+3.)
                        PRINT,X,Y
                        X = X + 1.
                     END WHILE
                     STOP
                     END
                 $ENTRY
```

```
┌──────────────────────────────────────────────────────────┐
│                                                            │
│          *** RULES FOR KEYPUNCHING PROGRAMS ***            │
│                                                            │
│   1. Job Control Cards.                                    │
│                                                            │
│        Job control cards, (JCL  cards -- if you  want to   │
│   sound like a  professional),  are identified by  a  $    │
│   sign in card column 1.   These cards are usually pre-    │
│   punched and  available in  the keypunch  area.    You    │
│   will require  an account  number to  run your  jobs.     │
│   This account number is used  by the computing center     │
│   to charge the cost of  running your job against some     │
│   budget   account.   Leave  a  blank  space after  the    │
│   account number and  then punch your name.    At some     │
│   computing centers  it may  be necessary  to identify     │
│   the model of  the keypunch used to  punch the cards.     │
│   If so, the JOB card will look like:                      │
│                                                            │
│          $JOB    WATFIV  acct.#,KP=26 your name            │
│                         or                                 │
│          $JOB    WATFIV  acct.#,KP=29 your name            │
│                                                            │
└──────────────────────────────────────────────────────────┘
```

Ask your computer center which model of keypunch (26 or 29) is available.

The $ENTRY card always contains the symbols "$ENTRY" punched in columns 1 to 6.

Other Job Control cards can be used in WATFIV programs. These are described in Appendix E.

2. Comment Cards.

Comment cards are identified by a "C" in column 1. The comment can be punched anywhere in columns 2 thru 72. If the comment is too long for one card, punch a "C" in column 1 of the next card and continue the comment using whatever columns from 2 thru 72 that you wish. There is no limit on the number of comment cards which can appear in a program.

3. WATFIV Statements.

Cards which are not job control cards or comment cards are called Statement cards. The rules for "what goes where" in statement cards are as follows:

columns 1-5. The statement number. The statement number is optional. (In the example, no statements had a number. Chapter 3 contains the first examples requiring statement numbers.) If present, it can be any integer value from 1 thru 99999. The number may be punched anywhere in the first five columns. Statement numbers are only required if it is necessary to reference the statement somewhere else in the program.

column 6. The continuation indicator. Normally this column is left blank. It will contain something other than a zero or a blank only if the information punched in columns 7 to 72 of the card is to be considered a continuation of the statement punched in the previous card. Continuation cards are used whenever a statement is too long to fit on one card. There is no limit to the number of continuation cards which can be used for a single statement. A statement requiring several cards will have a non-zero, non-blank character punched in column 6 of all cards

but the first. Columns 1 thru 5 of
continuation cards must be blank.

columns 7-72. The statement. When punching
   WATFIV statements, blanks may be inserted
   anywhere to improve the readability of the
   statement. If the statement is such that it
   would go beyond column 72 then it should be
   continued on the next card as described
   above. Columns 7-72 of the continuation card
   can be considered as being placed on the
   right of column 72 of the previous card.

columns 73-80. Program identification area. As
   yet no use has been suggested for the last
   eight columns of the card. If desired, these
   columns may be used to identify the program
   and/or number the cards in the deck. When
   writing programs which contain several
   hundred cards, it is a good idea to number
   your cards sequentially so that if the deck
   is accidentally dropped, the problem of
   getting the cards back in their proper order
   will be easy. The symbols punched in columns
   73-80 are ignored by the compiler and are
   simply available for you to use if you wish.

*4. Multiple Statements In One Card.

   WATFIV permits more than one statement to be
punched on a single card. The details of this
technique can be found in Appendix E. All example
programs in the book, however, will be punched
according to the rules described above.

            *** END OF KEYPUNCHING RULES ***

Step 5. Run the job.

      As described earlier, running a job is a two stage
process -- compilation followed by execution. Shown
below is the output produced on the printer during the
two stages when the example program is run.

Stage 1. <u>Output</u> <u>Produced</u> <u>By</u> <u>The</u> <u>Compiler.</u>

```
     $JOB    WATFIV
     C EXAMPLE PROGRAM 1
1          X = 0.
2          WHILE (X .LE. 10.)
3              Y=(X**2-X+2.)/(X+3.)
4              PRINT,X,Y
5              X = X + 1
6          END WHILE
7          STOP
8          END

     $ENTRY
```

Note that the WATFIV compiler places a number beside
each <u>statement</u> in the program.   This is done so that
errors can be identified by the statement containing the
error.

Stage 2. <u>Output</u> <u>Produced</u> <u>During</u> <u>Execution.</u>

The output below is produced by executing the
machine   language instructions   which   the   compiler
produced when it   translated the WATFIV program into
strings of   ones and zeros.   This   output begins
immediately below the line "$ENTRY" which was printed by
the compiler.

0.0000000	0.6666667
1.0000000	0.5000000
2.0000000	0.8000000
3.0000000	1.3333333
4.0000000	2.0000000
5.0000000	2.7500000
6.0000000	3.5555550
7.0000000	4.3999990
8.0000000	5.2727270
9.0000000	6.1666660
10.0000000	7.0769220

```
STATEMENTS EXECUTED=       46
CORE USAGE- (data on amount of memory used by the progra
DIAGNOSTICS- (number of errors, warnings and extensions)
COMPILE TIME=...SEC,EXECUTION TIME=...SEC.
```

There are two points of interest concerning the
output produced during the execution time of the job.

First, following job execution, four lines of
statistics are printed. The first statement shows the
number of statements executed. For reasons which are
beyond the scope of this book, the STOP statement is not
included in the count. Thus the statement count appears
as 46 rather than 47. The second statement shows the
amount of memory used. The third statement gives
information on the number of errors, warnings and
language extensions. (Extensions are features of WATFIV
not found in other versions of the language.) The
fourth statement gives the times to compile and execute
the program.

The second point of interest concerns the way the
values of X and Y are printed. Each value of X and Y is
displayed with seven digits to the right of the decimal
point. Note that small round-off errors are evident in
some of the Y values. For example when X is 7, the true
value of Y is 4.4000000 but it is shown as 4.3999990.
Accuracy of numbers in a computer and round-off errors
are discussed in Chapter 2.

In some versions of WATFIV values are displayed in
the form

$$0.dddddddE \ ee$$

where the d's are the significant digits in the number
and the ee denotes the power of 10 by which the fraction
is to be multiplied in order to obtain the value. For
example 0.1234567E 03 means .1234567x10³ or a value of
123.4567.

The discussion above has described in some detail
the steps which are necessary to solve <u>any</u> problem using
a computer. The five steps are:

1. Define the problem
2. Develop a procedure for solving the problem.
3. Translate the algorithm into WATFIV
4. Keypunch the program.
5. Run the job.

<u>Exercise 1.1</u>

1. Keypunch the example program and run it.

2. What change or changes would be required in the example
   algorithm and program if the values of x to be used with
   the given formula for y were:

a) 0., 0.5, 1.0, 1.5,...,9.5, 10.0 (1 change
   required)
b) 0., 2., 4., 6.,...,20. (2 changes required)
c) 15.,14.,13.,12.,...,0. (3 changes required)
   Solve problem (c) by running it on the computer.
d) For each of the above, decide what changes would
   be required if you were using the brute-force
   approach of Algorithm A. By doing this the
   advantage of the iterative approach of Algorithm
   B should become more evident.

3. Use the computer to tabulate (compute and print out)
   values of the function

$$y = \frac{x^3 - 4x + 1}{3x^2 - 12}$$

for values of x= 3,4,...,12. What problem would be
encountered if x was allowed to have the value 2? Ways
of avoiding one or more values of x will be given in
Chapter 3.

4. Use the computer to tabulate values of the square and
   the square root of the first 20 natural numbers. Note
   that the square root of a number can be obtained by
   raising the number to an exponent of .5 .

1.5 What Happens When An Error Is Made?

We all make mistakes. Errors may occur in the
algorithm, in the translation of the algorithm into WATFIV,
or in keypunching. The program below contains at least one
obvious error.

```
$JOB   WATFIV acct.#
C EXAMPLE PROGRAM WITH ERRORS
      X=2.
      Y=X**2-3X
      Z= (Y+X)/ Y+2.)
      PRINT X,Y,Z
      STOP
$ENTRY
```

Suppose the program was punched as written and run on
the computer. The output appearing on the printer is shown
below.

```
          $JOB WATFIV
          C EXAMPLE PROGRAM WITH ERRORS
     1          X=2.
     2          Y=X**2-3X
 ***ERROR***   MISSING OPERATOR.UNEXPECTED X
     3          Z= (Y+X)/ Y+2.)
 ***ERROR***   UNMATCHED PARENTHESIS
 ***ERROR***   ILLEGAL QUANTITY ON RIGHT OF EQUALS SIGN
     4          PRINT X,Y,Z
 ***ERROR***   VARIABLE FORMAT MUST BE AN ARRAY NAME.
                         X IS INVALID
     5          STOP
 **WARNING**   MISSING END STATEMENT;END STATEMENT GENERATED
          $ENTRY
 STATEMENTS EXECUTED=          0
 CORE USAGE (information on memory used by the program)
 DIAGNOSTICS          NUMBER OF ERRORS=.        4,
                      NUMBER OF WARNINGS=       1,
                      NUMBER OF EXTENSIONS=     0
 COMPILE TIME= ... SEC,EXECUTION TIME= 0.00 SEC,
```

Observe that when an error is detected by the compiler, an error message is printed under the line containing the error.

The first error occurs in the line Y=X**2-3X and the message "MISSING OPERATOR, UNEXPECTED X" indicates that the symbol for some arithmetic operation was expected after the three. Since by "3X" we mean "three times X", we can easily correct the statement by writing it as "Y=X**2-3*X".

The second error, "UNMATCHED PARENTHESIS" is due to our carelessness in omitting the left bracket in the denominator.

The third error message, "ILLEGAL QUANTITY ON RIGHT OF EQUALS SIGN" was also generated because of the missing left bracket.

The fourth error message, "VARIABLE FORMAT MUST BE AN ARRAY NAME, X IS INVALID" is not too meaningful to us at this point. The clue comes from the phrase "X IS INVALID". The reason for the error is that we left out the comma after the word PRINT.

Just ahead of the $ENTRY a warning message is printed, indicating that the END statemnt is missing. The compiler assumes you wanted to put an END statement just ahead of the $ENTRY and has inserted one for you. Before running the job

again we should punch up an END card and include it in the
proper place.

    If any errors are detected by the compiler, no attempt
is made to execute the job as the print-out shows. (The
execution time was 0.).   If the only messages are warning
messages however, an attempt _is_ made to execute the job.
These warning messages should be examined carefully to make
sure the reason for the warning does not cause the output to
be different from that which was wanted.

    There is a third type of message which is sometimes
printed by the compiler.   It is called an EXTENSION message
and is used to indicate statements which are perfectly valid
in WATFIV but may not be valid in some members of the
Fortran family of languages.   Since our purpose is to learn
the WATFIV language, the existence and meaning of these
messages can be ignored.

    Suppose we corrected the errors and added an END
statement to the orginal program.   The output appearing on
the printer when the job is run is:

```
              $JOB    WATFIV acct.#
              C EXAMPLE WITH NO COMPILE-TIME ERRORS
       1          X=2.
       2          Y=X**2-3*X
       3          Z=(Y+X)/(Y+2.)
       4          PRINT,X,Y,Z
       5          STOP
       6          END

              $ENTRY
  ***ERROR*** LIMIT EXCEEDED FOR FLOATING POINT DIVISION BY
  ZERO. PROGRAM WAS EXECUTING LINE 3 WHEN TERMINATION OCCURRED
```

    This example shows that even though there are no
compile-time errors in the program, the job could not be
executed successfully because an _execution_ _time_ error
occured when performing the calculations defined in line 3.
The reason for the error is that the denominator has a value
of zero in the division described. The meaning of the words
"LIMIT EXCEEDED FOR FLOATING POINT DIVISION BY ZERO", will
become clear in Chapter 2. For the time being we will
simply avoid problems in which this type of error could
occur.

Consider the following program.

```
$JOB
C EXAMPLE OF UNDEFINED VARIABLE
      PRINT,A
      STOP
      END
$ENTRY
```

When this job is run no error messages are printed either at compile-time or during the execution of the job. However, the value printed for A will look like UUUUUUUUUUUUUUUUU. The reason for this is that no value has been given to the variable A. Its value is undefined and a string of 'U's is printed to indicate this fact.

A second example program containing an undefined variable is the following.

```
$JOB
C  EXAMPLE OF AN UNDEFINED VARIABLE
      B=A**2
      A=7.
      PRINT,B
      STOP
      END
$ENTRY
```

In the foregoing example, the job would terminate at execution time because of the operations specified by the statement "B=A**2". The error message would be "VALUE OF A IS UNDEFINED". Recall that a computer does not have circuits for doing algebra, only arithmetic. Since no value had been assigned to A, no value can be assigned to B. This example further emphasizes the fact that instructions are executed sequentially. No attempt is made to look ahead and see what the program is trying to do.

In order to detect undefined values at execution time, the compiler must generate instructions to see if each variable used in a statement has previously been assigned a value. Checking for undefined values slows down the execution of a job. If a program is known to work, this checking feature can be bypassed. Details of how this is done can be found in Appendix E.

One of the reasons the WATFIV language is so widely used is that its diagnostics (error and warning messages) are very extensive and thus make the job of correcting

programming mistakes very easy.   For this reason you
shouldn't hesitate to try something to see if it will work.
The confidence you have in your ability to write programs
will increase more rapidly if you experiment with different
ways of accomplishing the same thing.

It's sad but true, however, that if you make a mistake
in the algorithm, WATFIV can't help you. The ability to
correct algorithms is not one of the capabilities of a
compiler.

1.6 A Second Example

Step 1. Problem definition. Suppose we are required to find
the sum of the first 50 positive integers. That is, the
value of the sum 1+2+3+...+50.   The total is to be
obtained without using any formula.

Step 2. Develop an algorithm.   The required total could be
obtained by finding successively the totals: 1, 1+2,
1+2+3, 1+2+3+4, ..., and stopping when 50 has been
added to the previous total.   The initial total would
have to be zero and the first number to be added to this
total would be one.   A brute force algorithm would be:

```
1. Set Sum = 0
2. Set Number = 1
3. Add Number to Sum
4. Set Number = 2
5. Add Number to Sum
6. Set Number = 3
7.  .
      .
100. Set Number = 50
101. Add Number to Sum
102. Write down the value of Sum
103. Stop
```

For reasons discussed in the previous example, namely,
ease of writing the algorithm, and more important, the
flexibility of the algorithm, we should attempt to write
the algorithm above using a looping technique.

Looking at the brute force algorithm we realize
that after giving the sum an initial value of zero and
setting the first number to be added to the sum equal to
one that we are doing the same two thing over and over
-- first, increasing the total and second, generating
the next value to be added to the total.   This process

of add and generate is repeated as long as the number
generated is less than or equal to 50.   When it is not,
we print the result and stop.   Our iterative algorithm
is therefore:

    1.   Set Sum = 0
    2.   Set Number = 1
    3.   While Number ≤ 50
          .1 Add Number to Sum
          .2 Increase Number by 1
    4.   Write down the value of Sum
    5.   Stop

Step 3. Translate the algorithm into WATFIV.   A translation
of the algorithm is shown below.

```
$JOB   WATFIV  acct.# JOHN MOORE
C EXAMPLE PROGRAM 2
C CALCULATE THE SUM OF THE FIRST 50 NATURAL NUMBERS
      SUM = 0.
      NUMBER = 1
      WHILE (NUMBER .LE. 50)
         SUM = SUM + NUMBER
         NUMBER = NUMBER + 1
      END WHILE
      PRINT,'THE SUM IS',SUM
      STOP
      END
$ENTRY
```

Examine the PRINT statement in the program. It contains the
words "THE SUM IS" enclosed in single quotes.   It means the
phrase "THE SUM IS" is to be printed ahead of the value of
SUM. This technique can be used to print any phrases, words
or symbols which help to   make the   output   easier to
understand.

Step 4. Keypunch the program.   The deck will contain 12
cards, one for each line in the program.   The cards
should be punched according to the rules given earlier
and will appear as shown in the program.   In the deck
there will be: 2 job control cards; 2 comment cards; and
9 WATFIV statements.

Step 5. Run the job. When the job is run, the compiler will
list the information punched in the cards. When the job
is executed, the line printed is "THE SUM IS 0.1275000E
04". The answer to our problem is therefore 1275.

Exercise 1.2

1. Modify the algorithm of example 2 to find the sum $1^2 + 2^2 + 3^2 + \ldots + 50^2$. Write a program and run it to find the answer.

2. Find the sum of $2^3 + 4^3 + 6^3 + \ldots + 20^3$ using the computer.

3. Find the sum of $3^1 + 3^2 + 3^3 + \ldots + 3^8$ using the computer.

4. Find the sum of $1 + 2 + 4 + 8 + 16 + \ldots + 512$ using the computer. Print out all intermediate totals.

5. Find the average of all odd integers from 17 thru 83. Use the computer to obtain the result. A counter should be used to determine how many numbers have been added to the total. You will have to initialize three values: Sum, Number and Count.

6. Explain the difference between "PRINT,'X'" and "PRINT,X".

1.7 A Third Example.

Step 1.   Problem definition.   One method of finding the square root of a number is the following. Make an initial estimate of the value of the square root, say one-half the number. Call this initial estimate X_0. If the number is A, we would have $X_0 = A/2$. Given this initial estimate, X_1 will be a better estimate of the square root where X_1 is obtained using the formula:

$$X_1 = X_0 - \frac{X_0^2 - A}{2X_0}$$

An even better estimate, X_2, can be obtained using the previous estimate X_1 and the same formula. That is:

$$X_2 = X_1 - \frac{X_1^2 - A}{2X_1}$$

In general, by repeating this process over and over, one can obtain increasingly accurate estimates of the square root of any positive value. Suppose we want to use the computer to find the square root of 79.358. We are to make six improvements to our initial guess.

Step 2. Develop an algorithm.

How can we use a looping technique in our algorithm? To answer this question we must ask the following two questions. "What is it that we are doing over and over again?", and "What is changing each time we do this thing over and over again?". The answer to the first question is , "We are using the same formula six times to get successive improvements of the estimate of the square root.". The answer to the second question is, "We are changing a value in the formula each time.". Thus if we want to execute the formula six times and change the value used in the formula each time, we will need a counter which starts at 1 and goes up to 6. We must also insure the correct value is used in the formula each time. Our algorithm will therefore look like:

1.   Set A= 79.358
2.   Set Estimate = A/2
3.   Set Counter = 1
4.   While Counter ≤ 6
            .1 Set Estimate = improved value
            .2 Add 1 to the Counter
5.   Write down the value of the Estimate
6.   Stop

Note that the first three instructions are simply used to set up for the loop.

Step 3. Translate the algorithm into WATFIV. The result is:

```
$JOB    WATFIV  acct# JOHN MOORE
C EXAMPLE PROGRAM 3
C PROGRAM TO FIND THE SQUARE ROOT OF 79.358
        A=79.358
        ESTMAT=A/2.
        COUNT=1.
C       OBTAIN IMPROVED ESTIMATE
        WHILE (COUNT .LE. 6)
            ESTMAT=ESTMAT-(ESTMAT**2-A)/(2.*ESTMAT)
            COUNT = COUNT + 1.
        END WHILE
        PRINT,ESTMAT
        STOP
        END
    $ENTRY
```

Step 4. Keypunch the program.

Step 5. Run the job. The value printed as a result of executing the program is 0.8908311E 01, that is, 8.908311 . This result is accurate to the sixth decimal place. You should check this out by making ten improvements and printing the result.

The following point is illustrated by this example. In the example program the names ESTMAT and COUNT are used instead of ESTIMATE and COUNTER. The reason for this is that a maximum of six symbols can be used in a name. Complete details will be given in the next chapter.

Problems and Exercises 1.3

1. Use the computer to find eight improvements to an initial estimate of the square root of 4059.26. Print the value of each improved estimate.

2. Suppose rather than making a specific number of improvements to an initial estimate, it is desired to continue making improvements only until the next estimate differs from the previous one by less than .0001. This means that the decision to improve on an estimate will be based on whether or not the change (either an increase or decrease) is less than .0001. That is, while the improvement is greater than .0001 we should continue to obtain a better estimate. To determine the magnitude of the improvement it is necessary to "remember" what the previous estimate was in order to compare it with the most recent estimate. This means we will need two variables, OLDEST (the previous estimate), as well as ESTMAT (the current estimate).

   a) Using the method of obtaining successively increasingly accurate approximations, develop an algorithm to find the square root of 3.0. Continue making improvements while the change in estimates is greater than .0001.

   b) In WATFIV, the absolute value of the difference of two numbers X and Y say, can be found by writing "ABS(X-Y)". Using this feature of the WATFIV language, translate the algorithm you have developed in (a) into WATFIV and run the job.

3. Examine the following program before answering the
   questions which follow.

```
$JOB
      J=5
      WHILE (J .LE. 100)
          K=J**2
          PRINT,K
          J=J+5
      END WHILE
      STOP
      END
   $ENTRY
```

a) What is the first value printed?
b) How many values are printed?
c) In words, what does the program do?
d) What changes would be necessary in the above
   program to have it print the values:
      25,36,49,64,81,100,121,144 ?

4. a) Develop a brute-force algorithm to determine which,
      if any, of the numbers 8,15,22,29,36 divide evenly
      into a number N. Print only those numbers for which
      the division is even (leaves no remainder).   In
      this algorithm you will have to use a statement of
      the type "If N divides evenly by ___, then ____".

   b) How many instructions are executed in solving the
      problem using this method?

   c) Convert this brute-force algorithm to an   iterative
      algorithm   by   asking   yourself   the   following
      questions: (i) What operation is being repeated over
      and over again?; (ii) What is changing each time the
      operation is repeated?;   (iii) What   is the rule for
      generating the the values   which change?;   (iv) What
      is the rule   for deciding that no   more repetitions
      are required?

   d) In the algorithm developed in (c), how many times is
      each step in the algorithm   executed in solving the
      problem?   What is the total number of instructions
      which must be executed to   solve this problem using
      this algorithm?

   e) Although the total found in (d)   is somewhat larger
      than that found in (b),   why are   most algorithms
      executed on a computer written using a looping
      approach?

5.   Consider the following algorithm.

   1. Set Number = 78
   2. Set T = 1
   3. While T² < Number
       .1 Add 1 to T
   4. Write (T-1)², "is less than", Number
   5. Write T², "is greater than", Number
   6. Stop

a) How many times is each step executed?
b) What problem is solved by this algorithm?
c) What advantage results from making the first instruction "Set Number = 78" instead of using 78 every place the word "Number" appears?
d) Although the output (results produced) by the algorithm are correct for a value of 78, the statement in step 5 would be mathematically incorrect for some values of Number. Correct the wording so that it will be correct for any positive value of Number.
e) Translate the corrected algorithm into WATFIV and run it on the computer.

6. Shown below are 4 programs none of which will run without errors. Explain why.

a)
```
$JOB    WATFIV
        X = 1
        WHILE(X .LE. 10)
            PRINT,X
            PRINT,3*X+2
        END WHILE
        STOP
        END
$ENTRY
```

b)
```
$JOB    WATFIV
        WHILE(X*2 .GT. 5)
        PRINT,X
            X = X - 1
        END WHILE
        STOP
        END
$ENTRY
```

c)
```
$JOB WATFIV
        X = 10
        WHILE(X**2.GE.100)
            X = X + 1
        END WHILE
        PRINT,X,X**2
        STOP
        END
$ENTRY
```

d)
```
$JOB WATFIV
        X = 1
        WHILE(X .LE. 10)
            PRINT,X
            X = X + 1
        STOP
        END
$ENTRY
```

7. The programs in Problem 6 illustrate the three requirements for using a WHILE loop correctly, namely:

   1. The condition tested in the WHILE statement must be initialized before entering the loop.

   2. The condition tested in the WHILE statement must be set to false during some execution of the loop. If it remains true, then loop execution would never terminate.

   3. An END WHILE statement must follow the last statement in the loop.

   Which of the three rules above were violated by each the programs in question 6?

1.8 Summary

   1. The computer has circuits and components for performing simple arithmetic; getting information in and printing results out; making simple decisions.

   2. A computer is a valuable aid in solving problems because: it is fast; it is accurate and reliable; big problems can be solved by solving a set of little problems -- one after the other.

   3. To use the computer to assist in problem solving, five steps are necessary.

           1. Define the problem
           2. Develop an algorithm
           3. Translate the algorithm into a
                  programming language
           4. Keypunch the program
           5. Run the job (compilation then execution)

   4. Although you can describe a brute force procedure which will solve a problem it is desirable to write algorithms which have a looping or iterative property. The chief reason is that the saving in execution time using a brute force algorithm is more than compensated for by the ease and flexibility of using an iterative approach to solve a problem.

5.   Errors may occur during either the compile time of
     a job or during the execution time of the job.
     Correcting programming errors is relatively simple:
     Correcting errors in algorithms may or may not be
     simple depending on the complexity of the problem.

6.   All WATFIV programs must contain a $JOB card, an
     END card, and a $ENTRY card.

7.   Some of the important vocabulary of this chapter:
     algorithm, keypunch, source deck, program, job, job
     control cards,   WATFIV statements,   comments,
     compiler, compilation, compile time, execution,
     execution time, machine language, bit string, error
     message, warning message, iterative algorithm.

CHAPTER 2   NUMBERS, ARITHMETIC AND VARIABLES

Questions Answered In This Chapter

1. Why does WATFIV distinguish between numbers
    with, and without decimal points?

2. What are the rules governing the way in which
    arithmetic expressions are evaluated?

3. What are variables and how are they defined
    and used?

4. How can we obtain values of commonly required
    functions such as sines, logarithms, and
    absolute values?

    After completing this chapter you will be able to
translate a large number of algorithms into WATFIV. You
will have learned about ten of the most frequently used
WATFIV statements.

2.1 INTEGER Values

    In WATFIV, a number which is written without a decimal
point is called an INTEGER constant. Thus -7, 24569, +25, 0
are examples of INTEGER constants. Note that commas are not
used to separate successive groups of digits in the number.
If the number is positive it is not necessary to put a plus
sign in front of the number.

    Since we frequently want to perform operations such as
multiplication and division with pairs of INTEGERS, the
computer must have circuits for performing INTEGER
arithmetic. You will recall that the computer can only
manipulate strings of ones and zeros and that before your
program is executed, the instructions and numbers appearing
in your program are translated into bit strings by the
WATFIV compiler. The bit string produced by the compiler
for INTEGERS represents the value of the number in the base
two instead of the base 10 or decimal number system.
Details of the base two number system can be found in
Appendix C. On the computer systems which process WATFIV
jobs, a total of thirty-two bits (ones and zeros) are used
to represent each INTEGER value. For example, a value of 89
is stored as:

        00000000000000000000000001011001

Because only thirty-two bits are used to store INTEGER values, there is a limit to the size of INTEGER values which can be used in WATFIV.   Any INTEGER value used in a WATFIV program must be in the range -2147483648 thru +2147483647 or roughly between plus and minus 2.1 billion.

Operations With INTEGERS.

The five arithmetic operations that can be performed with pairs of INTEGER values are + - * / **.   What then are the values of the following expressions?

    i) 3+2*4

   ii) 5+2**3*7

  iii) -4**2

   iv) 4**2**3

    v) 5/2

   vi) 5/-2

  vii) 3*5/4*2

 viii) 1234**50

We can learn all that is necessary to know about INTEGER arithmetic by studying the eight examples above. In most of the examples it might appear that more than one answer could be given depending on the order in which the operations are performed.   To avoid any ambiguity there are rules which define the priorities of each operation. The rules will be summarized following a discussion of each case.

Consider (i).   The   result   must   be   11   since multiplication has a higher priority than addition and therefore is done first.

In the second example, the result is 61. Exponentiation is done before any multiplication and therefore the sequence of intermediate results is (5+2**3*7)=(5+8*7)=(5+56)=61.

The value of -4**2 is -16.   The rule is that a unary plus or minus (a + or - symbol preceding a value) is treated as though there were a zero in front of the sign.   Thus -4**2 is considered to be 0-4**2 and since exponentiation has a higher priority than addition or subtraction,   the result -16 is obtained.

The fourth example, namely 4**2**3, is evaluated by doing the rightmost exponentiation first. The expression is therefore equivalent to 4**8 which has a value of 65536.

The value of 5/2 is 2. This value is obtained because the result of an arithmetic operation with a pair of INTEGERS must be an INTEGER value. The rule for INTEGER division is to ignore any remainder and use the quotient as the answer.

The sixth example is perhaps a little unfair because this type of expression is not permitted in WATFIV. The reason is that two arithmetic operators cannot appear in succession. If your program included an expression such as 5/-2, the compiler would print an error message below the line containing the expression and you would have to change the expression to 5/(-2) to correct the problem. This points out a further important point -- expressions in brackets are evaluated before any arithmetic operations are done. (The value of 5/(-2) is of course -2.)

The seventh example 3*5/4*2 has a value of 6 since multiplication and division have equal priorities and are performed in the order in which they appear -- left to right.

The last expression, 1234**50, would produce a result which is much larger than the largest INTEGER value allowed in WATFIV. When this happens no error message is printed. You, the programmer, are responsible for avoiding situations where the result of an INTEGER calculation is outside the permitted range. Since the number produced is incorrect, weird results may be obtained if the result is used in subsequent calculations. In some sophisticated problems, a programmer may genuinely desire this "overflow" condition. This is the reason no error message is printed.

```
┌─────────────────────────────────────────────────────┐
│                                                       │
│  Order Of Evaluation Of Arithmetic Expressions        │
│                                                       │
│    1. Expressions in brackets, innermost first        │
│    2. Exponentiation, right to left                   │
│    3. Multiplication and division, equal              │
│         priority, left to right                       │
│    4. Addition and subtraction, equal                 │
│         priority, left to right                       │
│                                                       │
└─────────────────────────────────────────────────────┘
```

Later on, we shall want to add one item to the top of the list and several operations having lower priorities to the bottom of the list.

Exercise 2.1

1. Calculate the value of each of the following INTEGER expressions.

   a) 3*5-3   f) 4-2**3/2*2

   b) 3-5*3   g) 4-2**3/(2*2)

   c) 10*5**2   h) -2**4/3

   d) 10**2/5   i) 6/9/(-4)

   e) 3/2**2   j) 3**(1/2)-14*2/30

2. Correct the error in each of the following expressions.

   a) +2*-3
   b) (-16+2/(7-(+6))

3. Rewrite the expression below removing as many pairs of brackets as possible. Do not change the value of the expression.

$$((-(5*2)**3)+(14/(2**(-3))))$$

4. For each of the following write one INTEGER expression which has a value of 20 using the operations indicated.

   a) One multiplication and one subtraction operation
   b) Three divisions
   c) One exponentiation, one addition and one division
   d) Two pairs of brackets which are both necessary
   e) Two exponentiations and a division

2.2 REAL Numbers (Numbers with decimal points)

Numbers which have decimal points can be written in many different but equivalent ways. For example, three different ways of writing a single number having a value of seven-and-three-eights are:

7.375   .007375 x 10^3 737500.0 x 10^{-5}

In mathematics these numbers are frequently called "floating-point" numbers since the decimal point can "float" along the line of digits by multiplying by an appropriate power of ten. In WATFIV, numbers written with decimal points are called REAL constants. The computer stores REAL values so that decimal point precedes the first non-zero digit in the number. Some examples of REAL numbers are:

Value of Number	Value Stored In Computer
7.375	0.7375000×10^1
-.00621	$-0.6210000 \times 10^{-2}$
897524.	0.8975240×10^6
-0.	-0.0000000×10^0

To define REAL numbers in WATFIV the letter "E" is used to indicate "times 10 to the exponent ...".
If the E is omitted, it is understood the number is to be multiplied by ten-to-the-zero which of course is 1. Some examples follow.

Number Appearing In WATFIV Program	Value Stored In Computer
.236	0.2360000E+00
236.74E+02	0.2367400E+05
.0023674E-2	0.2367400E-04
-1234567.	-0.1234567E+07
-123.45E18	-0.1234500E+21
123E02	0.1230000E+05

These examples illustrate the following points when using REAL numbers in WATFIV programs.

i)   The number can be written with or without an exponent. If an exponent is used, it is indicated by putting an E after the last digit of the number and then writing the value of the exponent.

ii)   The computer stores the number so that the decimal point precedes the first significant digit.

Sufficient zeros are added to the right of the last digit so that seven significant digits are stored for all REAL values.

iii) You can be somewhat sloppy in the way the exponent is written. If the exponent is positive, the sign may be omitted. Thus 2.0E2, 2.0E+2, 2.0E+02, and 2.0E02 are equivalent. Similarly, 2.0E-03, and 2.0E-3 are equivalent.

iv) If the decimal point is omitted, it is assumed to precede the "E" symbol.

The magnitude of any REAL value used in WATFIV must be in the range .7237005 x 10^{76} and .5397605 x 10^{-78}. The reason for these peculiar limits is due to the bit pattern scheme used to store REAL values. It is usually sufficient to remember that the limits are roughly ten to the plus or minus seventy-five. If the result of some arithmetic operation lies outside these limits an error message is printed and the job stopped.

Examples of some invalid REAL numbers are:

-2,675.3	(comma not permitted)
1.25E	(no exponent value)
10.0E81	(too large)
12345678.	(too many digits, value will be rounded to seven digits)

Computers store REAL values using a string of thirty-two bits for each value. The circuits which must be used to perform arithmetic with numbers having decimal points are different from those used for INTEGER operations. For this reason the bit patterns representing the INTEGER value 2 and the REAL value 2.0 are different. Details of the pattern of ones and zeros used to represent REAL values can be found in Appendix C.

Operations With REAL Numbers.

The priorities of the five arithmetic operations are identical to those which apply to arithmetic operations with INTEGERS.

Some examples of simple REAL expressions and their values are shown below.

REAL Expression	Value of the Expression With and Without E Notation	
10./5.+3.46	5.46	0.5460000E 01
6.25-3.**2.	-2.75	-0.2750000E 01
30./8./100.	.0375	0.3750000E-01
-2.**6.	-64.	-0.6400000E 02
2.25/15.*(-.6)	-.09	-0.9000000E-01
3.*(5.**2./8.-1.)	6.375	0.6375000E 01

There are three important points you should be aware of when working with REAL values.

First. Consider the pair of expressions:

      a) 2.**3
      b) 2.**3.

As you would expect, the value of both expressions is 8.0.   However the values are calculated in different ways. Expression (a), in which the exponent is an INTEGER, is calculated by successive multiplications,   namely 2.*2.*2. Expression (b), containing a REAL exponent, is evaluated by finding the antilog of 3log2.   Since the second approach is more complicated, it takes longer to obtain the result. Not only that, but values of logarithms often have small round-off errors leading to slight inaccuracies in the result. For example, 3.**2. gives a value of 8.999999.   Thus, for reasons of accuracy and efficiency,   exponents should be written as INTEGERS.

Consider the expressions:

      c) (-2.)**3
      d) (-2.)**3.

Expression (c) results in a value of -8. as expected but expression (d) causes an error message to be printed! Recall that (d) will be evaluated by finding the antilog of 3log(-2.).   Since logarithms of negative numbers (and zero) are undefined, the error message is printed. This means you must avoid raising negative REAL numbers to REAL powers.

Second. The computer only stores 7 significant digits for each REAL value.   To see what can happen because of this, consider the pair of expressions below.

      a) 5.0E+10 - 5.0E+10 + 1.

      b) 1. + 5.0E+10 -5.0E+10

The value of (a) is 1. and the value of (b)   is 0.!
Remember that addition and subtraction have equal priorities
and are performed left to right. The steps in the evaluation
of each expression are shown below.

```
a)   50000000000.              b)               1.
    -50000000000.                 +50000000000.
              0.                  5000000.E+3
            +1.                  -5000000.E+3
              1.                            0.
```

<u>Third</u>. Numbers inside the computer are stored using the
binary number system.   It is a fact that many fractions in
the decimal number system require an infinite string of
decimal digits to represent a value accurately, (for example
the value 1./3. = .333333...).   The same fact is true in the
binary number system.   That is, there are many fractional
values which would require an infinite string of ones and
zeros to accurately represent the number.   For example a
value   of 1./5.   in the   binary   system looks   like
.001100110011... .   Since the computer can only store a
finite number of digits for each value, the value stored for
some fractional   values is really   only a   very good
approximation to the actual number.   This means that tiny
errors may result when performing REAL arithmetic.   For
example the value of .2+.2+.2+.2+.2 turns out to be .999999
instead of 1.   The point to remember is that if one is
performing a large number of calculations with REAL values,
the final result may have some small error.   REAL values
which do not have digits to the right of the decimal point
are always stored accurately.

2.3 <u>Operations Combining REAL And INTEGER Values</u>

Expressions such as: 2.+3 , 3./4, 5.**2*10, are called
<u>mixed-mode</u> expressions since each expression contains at
least one operation which combines a   REAL and an INTEGER
value.   The rule for determining the result of a mixed-mode
operation is:

Perform the calculation as if both values were REAL
and leave the result as a REAL value.

The order in which the operations are performed is identical
to that for expressions involving values which are all of
the same type.   Consider the following examples.

i) 2+3.

ii) 2/3*4.

iii) 4.*2/3

iv) 4.*(2/3)

v) 123456789 + 1.0E2

vi) 2.**3

In example (i) the result is 5.0 and the 2 is converted to 2.0 before the addition takes place.

In (ii) the division is done before the multiplication and since the division involves two INTEGERS the remainder is ignored and so the expression reduces to 0*4.. This means the value of the expression is the REAL value 0..

In (iii) the result is 2.666667.   The sequence of intermediate results is: 4.*2/3 = 8./3 = 2.666667.

Example (iv)   produces a different result from example (iii). Why? Since there are brackets, the INTEGER division is done first and produces a value of 0 which is then multiplied by 4. giving the result 0..

Example (v) is of interest since the INTEGER value 123456789 contains 9 digits.   When this number is converted to a REAL value before performing the addition, only 7 decimal digits are stored and so the addition is effectively 1234567.E+2 + 1.0E+2.   That is 1234568.E+2.

The last example has already been discussed in some detail.   It illustrates the one exception to the rule that INTEGER values are converted to REAL values when combined in an arithmetic operation. If an exponent is an INTEGER it is left as an INTEGER and the calculation is done by successive multiplications.

2.4 Variables

Thus far we have only considered specific numbers or constants.   If we merely wanted to use the computer as a desk calculator, it would not really be necessary to go beyond a discussion of constants.   In many problems however we are doing such things as adding to totals, counting inputs, finding increasingly accurate approximations to roots of equations, etc.. In such cases, the value of the total, the count, or the approximation will vary. Quantities whose values may change during the execution of a program are called variables and names such as TOTAL, COUNT and APPROX can be given to these quantities.

If variables are used in a program it is necessary to do three things.

(i) Use a valid name for the variable.

(ii) Tell the compiler the type of value which will be taken on by the variable. (INTEGER or REAL)

(iii) Cause the variable to be assigned or to "take on" the desired value.

Before seeing how each of these things is done we should state the restrictions on the names a variable may have. These rules are easy to learn and are stated below.

```
Valid WATFIV Names

1. A maximum of six symbols may be used in
   a name.

2. The first symbol must be a letter of the
   alphabet or a $ sign. (The $ sign is
   considered to be an alphabetic character
   in WATFIV.)

3. None of the special symbols such as + -
   ) . ' , ( & = may be used in a name.

4. Blanks may be used but are ignored in
   determining if two names are the same.
```

Examples

Valid Names	Invalid Names
MOTHER	9D
IF	A (I
NET PAY	RR#2
NETPAY	MOTHERS
$$$$8A	J=I
A 9A 9$	4 YOU
GO TO 8	NET-PAY
DO 10 I	LONG TIME
REAL	INTEGER
PRINT6	$AND¢

Remarks on the Examples.

1. Each of the invalid names violates one or more of the rules stated above. Examine each to determine which rule is being violated.

2. The valid variable names NETPAY and NET PAY are considered identical. (See Rule 4.)

3. Although words like REAL, PRINT and GO TO may be used as variable names, using them for this purpose makes a program harder to understand.

If a variable name has more than six symbols, the compiler prints a warning message and considers the first six non-blank symbols to be the name of the variable. Using variable names containing more than six symbols is unnecessary and should be avoided.

Declaring The Type (REAL or INTEGER) of Variables

The WATFIV compiler must know whether a variable is to take on REAL or INTEGER values. This is necessary so that the appropriate bit strings and instructions can be generated by the compiler. There are two commonly used ways of providing this information.

i) Default Typing. In the absence of other information, if the first letter of the variable name is one of I,J,K,L,M,N, the variable is assumed to take on INTEGER values. (Note that the first two letters of the word INTEGER define the range of the letters above.)

   If the first symbol in the name is any one of the remaining letters or a $ sign, the variable is assumed to take on REAL values. That is, in the absence of information to the contrary, a variable name beginning with a letter in the range A thru H, O thru Z, or a $ will take on REAL values.

   Thus, in the examples of variable names given previously, the variables IF, NET PAY, and NETPAY would be INTEGER variables and $$$$84, A9A9$, GO TO 8, PRINT6, DO 10 I, and REAL would take on REAL values. The phrase "first-letter rule" is a commonly used synonym for "default typing".

ii) <u>Explicit</u> <u>Declaration</u> <u>of</u> <u>Type.</u>   To   explicitly
declare certain variables to be of the REAL or
INTEGER type, one simply lists the variable
names of each   type at the beginning of the
program.   The variable names in the list are
preceded by either the word "REAL" or the word
"INTEGER". Consider the program below.

```
C EXAMPLE OF REAL AND INTEGER STATEMENTS
      REAL N,J96,I,BAF
      INTEGER A,OOPS,PRINT,$$,SUM
      ...
      ...
      ...
      END
```

In this example the variables N,   J96,   I and BAF will
take on REAL values.   The variables A, OOPS, PRINT, $$, SUM
on the other hand have been explicitly declared as being
INTEGER variables.   All other variables used in the program
will be typed using the default rule described above.   Note
that it was not necessary to include the variable BAF in the
REAL statement -- the first-letter rule would mean that BAF
was of the REAL type anyway. The compiler does not consider
this an error.

The REAL and INTEGER declaration statements are used to
override the first-letter rule.   In the absence of either or
both of these statements, variables are typed by default.

Two examples of invalid declaration statements are shown
below.

a) REAL,NUMBER,MAX   (comma after REAL)

b) INTEGER A,$NEXT
    REAL LOOP,A   (A cannot be both REAL & INTEGER)

*2.5 <u>Defining</u> <u>Your</u> <u>Own</u> <u>First-Letter</u> <u>Rule</u>

At the beginning of a program it is possible to define
your own first-letter rule by using an IMPLICIT statement.
The IMPLICIT statement specifies the set of letters which
determine if a variable will take on REAL values or INTEGER
values.

Here are a few examples using the IMPLICIT statement.

i) IMPLICIT REAL(I,J)

ii) IMPLICIT INTEGER(A-D,$),REAL(K,L,M)

iii) IMPLICIT REAL(A-H,O-Z,$),INTEGER(I-N)

iv) IMPLICIT REAL(I,M,N)
     INTEGER IPPSY,M64,M65,NINE

When considering the effect of an IMPLICIT statement, always begin by assuming the default rule is true, then examine the IMPLICIT statement to see what portions of the normal first-letter rule are changed.

In example (i) the first-letter rule applies to all variables except those beginning with the letters I and J. Variables beginning with either of these letters are to be considered as REAL variables.

In example (ii), variables beginning with the letters A thru D or the $ sign will be INTEGER variables and those beginning with K,L or M will be REAL. The first-letter rule will apply to all other variables used in the program.

The IMPLICIT statement of example (iii) defines the normal first-letter-rule and therefore could be ommitted from the program.

Example (iv) shows that the effect of an IMPLICIT statement can be overridden for specific names by using either a REAL or INTEGER declaration statement. In this example, variables other than IPPSY, M64, M65 and NINE which start with one of the letters I,M or N will be REAL. Those four have been specifically declared as being INTEGER variables.

There are two important points to keep in mind when using an IMPLICIT statement in a program.

i) Only one IMPLICIT statement can be used and it must be the first non-comment statement in the program.

ii) The IMPLICIT statement is used to override any part of or all of the first-letter rule and its effect can be negated for specific variables by using REAL or INTEGER declaration statements for those variables.

2.6 Giving Values To Variables

Remember that the computer can only do arithmetic and that <u>all</u> variables used in a program must be assigned a value before executing any statement in which they appear. There are essentially two ways that variables can be assigned values:

   a) Using an Assignment statement

   b) "Reading-in" the value of the variable

Method 1 -- The Assignment Statement

The general form of an Assignment statement is:

   variable name = arithmetic expression

The statement should be interpreted as meaning "The variable on the left side of the equal sign is to be given the value of the arithmetic expression on the right side of the equal sign." Thus

   i) A=3.*8./2.**4

   ii) JJ=MOM*(3**I)

   iii) A=10

   iv) LUCKY= 3.7

are examples of Assignment statements. Note that in (ii) it is assumed that the variables MOM and I have been assigned values earlier in the program. If either or both had not, the expression MOM*(3**I) could not be evaluated and the job would terminate with an execution-time error message.

In example (iii) the expression on the right is the INTEGER constant 10 whereas the variable on the left is REAL. Since A must take on a REAL value it is assigned the value 10.0. A similar case is shown in example (iv): LUCKY is an INTEGER variable and cannot be assigned the REAL value 3.7 . When this happens, the fractional part of the REAL value is ignored and so LUCKY takes on a value of 3.

Sometimes one wishes to assign a common value to several variables. This could be accomplished by writing a set of Assignment statements each of which assigned the value to a different variable or an <u>extended Assignment statement</u> could be used.

Here are some examples of extended Assignments.

  i) SUM1=SUM2=0.

 ii) JJ=NOPE=3.62E+1 +2.

iii) ·MM=X=I=123456789

When evaluating extended Assignment statements, the assignments are made beginning with the rightmost equal sign. Thus, in example (i), SUM2 is assigned the value 0. and then SUM1 is assigned the value of SUM2. Therefore both SUM1 and SUM2 are given a value of 0..

In example (ii) the expression 3.62E+1+2. is evaluated first, giving a value of 38.2. This REAL value is assigned to the INTEGER variable NOPE which results in NOPE having a value of 38 . The variable JJ is assigned the value of NOPE so both JJ and NOPE have values of 38.

In example (iii) I is given the value 123456789. Since X is REAL it can only store 7 significant digits and so X ends up with a value of 1234567.E+02. Since MM is assigned the value of X, it will have a value of 123456700. The last two examples illustrate that some caution must be exercised if you find it convenient to use extended Assignment statements.

Exercise 2.2

1. For each sequence of WATFIV statements below, determine the last value assigned to each variable used. Assume that the first-letter rule determines the type of each variable unless the variable appears in a type declaration statement.

   a) I=4-2*3.5

   b) I=6
       I=I+I

   c) A=3.**2/5
       B=A-A+3.**(2/5)

   d) REAL I,J
       J=2.5
       I=J*J-1

```
e) INTEGER X,AA,BOY
   Y=4.1
   I=55.2
   X=I/11
   AA=X*I/5
   BOY=Y*AA

f) REAL MOO
   INTEGER SUM
   SUM=MOO=1
   SUM=SUM+MOO/(SUM+1)
```

2. Identify the error in each of the following statements.

```
a) REAL,JACK
b) INTEGER A+10,XXX
c) REAL JAZZ,LONGNAME
d) XYZ=ABC,PQR=DEF
e) I+10=14
f) H=3.6=G
g) CAR=3*1.62E-99
```

Method 2 -- The READ Statement

Suppose one wishes to assign a value of factorial N to the variable FACTN where N is some positive integer. In other words, FACTN is to have the value of 1x2x3x4....xN. An algorithm which uses a looping technique is:

1. Set FACTN = 1

2. Set Multiplier =1

3. While Multiplier ≤ N do

    .1 Multiply FACTN by the Multiplier

    .2 Add one to the Multiplier

4. Print the value of N and FACTN

5. Stop

You should satisfy yourself that this algorithm will produce a correct result by taking a small value of N and following the procedure above. A program which is a translation of this algorithm is shown below. The program contains an error. What is it?

```
C EXAMPLE PROGRAM 2.1
      INTEGER FACTN
      FACTN=1
      MULPLR=1
      WHILE (MULPLR .LE. N)
         FACTN = FACTN*MULPLR
         MULPLR=MULPLR+1
      END WHILE
      PRINT,N,FACTN
      STOP
      END
$ENTRY
```

If this program is run,   an execution time error occurs
the first time the WHILE statement is executed.   Why?   The
reason is simply that   no value   has been   assigned to   the
variable N.   To   make the program work for a   value of N=5,
say, we could put the Assignment statement "N=5" immediately
following   the   INTEGER declaration   statement.   In   other
words, we   would have   to change   the program each time   a
different value of N   was to be used.   It would   be nice if
the   program could   be left   unchanged and   we could   simply
punch the desired value   of N on a card and   then somehow --
when the   job is executed --   cause the desired value   to be
assigned to N.   The following program shows how to do this.

```
C EXAMPLE 2.2 USE OF A READ STATEMENT
      INTEGER FACTN
      READ,N
      FACTN=1
      MULPLR=1
      WHILE (MULPLR .LE. N)
         FACTN=FACTN*MULPLR
         MULPLR=MULPLR+1
      END WHILE
      PRINT,N,FACTN
      STOP
      END
$ENTRY
   5
```

Observe that the value to be   assigned to the variable N
appears on a   card   which follows   the $ENTRY card.   The
instruction   which   causes   N   to   take   on   this   value   is
"READ,N".

The general form of a READ statement is:

```
┌──────────────────────────────────────────────┐
│                                                │
│              READ, input list                  │
│                                                │
│    where: input list is a set of one or more   │
│           variable names separated by commas.  │
│                                                │
└──────────────────────────────────────────────┘
```

Examples of valid READ statements are:
            READ,X
            READ,I,YY,VARNAM,KK

Examples of invalid READ statements are:
            READ X   (comma missing)
            READ,   (no input list)
            READ,10./A (expression in input list)

    The execution of a READ statement causes a card to be
read in at <u>execution time</u> and the values on the card are
assigned one-for-one to the variables in the input list.

```
┌──────────────────────────────────────────────┐
│                                                │
│          Rules For Values On Data Cards        │
│                                                │
│  1. The value(s) punched on the card(s) must be│
│     separated by a comma and/or blank columns. All│
│     eighty columns of a data card may be used. │
│                                                │
│  2. The numbers punched on the data cards should│
│     agree in type (REAL or INTEGER) with the   │
│     variables to which they are being assigned. The│
│     data values cannot be expressions, they must be│
│     valid constants.                           │
│                                                │
│  3. If there are insufficient values on a data card│
│     then another card is read in automatically and│
│     the values on it are used to continue the  │
│     assignment operation. This process continues│
│     until all variables have been assigned a value.│
│                                                │
│  4. If a data card contains more values than there│
│     are variables in the input list, these extra│
│     values are ignored and are not available for use│
│     by the next READ statement.                │
│                                                │
└──────────────────────────────────────────────┘
```

The examples which follow illustrate these rules.

i) One READ statement causing one data card to be read.

```
        READ,X,Y,I
        ...
    $ENTRY
      2.0E4, -7.1    67
```

When executed X=20000., Y=-7.1, I=67

ii) One READ statement causing 2 data cards to be read.

```
        READ,X,Y,I
        ...
        END
    $ENTRY
                2.0E4
      -7.1,                    67
```

When executed X=20000., Y=-7.1, I=67

iii) Two READ statements, the first causing three cards to be read, the second causing one data card to be read.

```
        READ, X,Y,I
        READ,J
        ...
        END
    $ENTRY
      2.0E4
        -7.1
    67,84,    25
        -18 ,    738
```

When executed, X=20000.,Y=-7.1, I=67, J=-18 .
The values 84,25, and 738 are unused.

iv) 'Out of Data' Two variables and only one data value.

```
        READ,I,X
        ...
        END
    $ENTRY
              3
```

When executed, an error message is printed and the job is terminated.

It remains to state the importance of assigning values
to variables by using a READ statement.   The primary
advantage is that programs can be written which are very
general in nature and which do not require changes to be
made to the program when different numbers are used in the
calculations.   For example a program can be written to find
the values of x which solve the equation:

$$Ax^2 + Bx + C = 0.$$

The required roots can be calculated from the values of
A,B and C.   The difference in the two approaches (Assignment
statements versus a READ statement) is illustrated below.

```
C WITH ASSIGNMENT STATEMENTS     C WITH A READ STATEMENT
         A=...                           READ,A,B,C
         B=...                           (statements to
         C=...                               find the roots)
         (statements to find          END
             the roots)           $ENTRY
         END                          values of A,B,and C
    $ENTRY
```

Using the method on the left,   three cards must be
changed each time a different equation is used.   Using the
READ statement to assign the values means only the data card
needs to be changed.   Furthermore, if the program is to be
used by someone else, instructions which you would give him
or her describing how to use the method on the right are
much simpler than those describing how to use the program on
the left.

A second and more significant point is evident if we are
required to write a program which would solve several
quadratic equations one after the other.   In this case using
a READ statement is far superior since a READ statement
could be placed inside of a loop.   Each time the loop was
executed the next set of values of A,B, and C would be read
in.   Using Assignment statements to assign values to the
variables would mean unique variable names would have to be
used for each set of coefficients.   It would be a messy
business.

Exercise 2.3

1. For each of the sequences below, determine what values
   will be assigned to the variables or the reason an error
   message will be printed. Assume the variables are typed
   by default.

a)   READ,II,JJ
                  ...
        $ENTRY
           2
                    -475

b)   READ,A,X,M
                  ...
        $ENTRY
        -2.64E+02,   -5.718643
                444   26.2

c)   READ,ROOT
                READ,OTHER,$,KLM,ROOT
                  ...
        $ENTRY
           -0.00064E-1, -2.5 3.46E20,10   17
        -0.00064E-1,-2.5   , 10   17.

d)   READ,A,B,C
                READ,D,E,F,G
                READ,H,I,J,K,L
                  ....
        $ENTRY
                1. 2. 3. 4. 5.
        6.
          7.,8.,9., 10.   11.
        12.   13.   14.   15.   16.
        17.

2.7 Built-In Functions

    Since the computer can only perform the five kinds of
arithmetic operations denoted by the symbols + - * / **, how
can commonly required calculations such as obtaining the
sine of an angle, or the logarithm of a number or the
absolute value be done?

    Many function values such as these can be obtained using
a formula.   For example, the sine of an angle of x radians
is given by:

$$\sin x = x - \frac{x^3}{3!} + \frac{x^5}{5!} - \frac{x^7}{7!} + \dots$$

where the exclamation mark denotes the factorial function.
Thus if you require the sine of an angle you could include a
sequence of WATFIV statements which would produce the
desired result as an intermediate step in the program.

Fortunately this is not necessary. The authors of the
WATFIV compiler have incorporated into the compiler the
ability to recognize such things as SIN(X), ALOG(X), and
ABS(X) when these "built-in functions" appear in statements
within a source program. When the built-in function is
recognized, the compiler automatically generates the
necessary machine language instructions to perform the
desired calculations. Each of the built-in functions
produces a value which is either INTEGER or REAL. The first
letter of the function name indicates the type of value
produced. The independent variables or "function arguments"
may also be either REAL or INTEGER depending on the function
being used. The general form of a built-in function is
shown below.

```
                    Built-in Functions

          name (argument1,argument2,....)

    where: name is the name of the function
           argument 1, argument 2, etc. are variables,
               constants or expressions specifying the
               values of the arguments.
```

In the table below the variables X,Y,Z,... represent
REAL-valued arguments and I,J,K,... represent INTEGER-valued
arguments. This table describes the commonly used built-in
functions available in WATFIV and the number and type of
arguments which they use. Examples of the result produced
by each of these functions can be found following this
information. A complete table of WATFIV built-in functions
can be found in Appendix J.

TABLE OF BUILT-IN FUNCTIONS

Purpose	Name And Arguments	Definition	Type of Result
Square Root	SQRT(X)	$\sqrt{X}$	REAL
Trigonometric Functions (angles in radians)	SIN(X) COS(X) TAN(X) COTAN(X)	sine cosine tangent cotangent	REAL REAL REAL REAL

Inverse trig Functions (result in radians)	ARSIN(X) ARCOS(X) ATAN(X) ATAN2(X,Y)	arcsine arccosine arctangent arctan(X/Y)	REAL REAL REAL REAL
Logarithms (X > 0)	ALOG(X) ALOG10(X)	log (base e) log (base 10)	REAL REAL
Exponential	EXP(X)	e^X	REAL
Absolute value	ABS(X) IABS(J)	$|X|$ $|J|$	REAL INTEGER
Transfer of sign	SIGN(X,Y) ISIGN(I,J)	$|X|$x sign of Y $|I|$x sign of J $sign= \begin{cases} +1 \ if \geq 0 \\ -1 \ if < 0 \end{cases}$	REAL INTEGER
Truncation	AINT(X) INT(X)	sign of X times largest integer ≤abs value of X	REAL INTEGER
Modular arithmetic	AMOD(X,Y)	remainder when X is divided by Y	REAL
	MOD(J,K)	remainder when J is divided by K	INTEGER
Positive difference	DIM(X,Y) IDIM(J,K)	X − min{X,Y} J − min{J,K}	REAL INTEGER
Largest value	AMAX0(I,J,K...) AMAX1(X,Y,Z...) MAX0(I,J,K...) MAX1(X,Y,Z...)	largest arg. largest arg. largest arg. largest arg.	REAL REAL INTEGER INTEGER
Smallest value	AMIN0(I,J,K...) AMIN1(X,Y,Z...) MIN0(I,J,K...) MIN1(X,Y,Z...)	smallest arg. smallest arg. smallest arg. smallest arg.	REAL REAL INTEGER INTEGER
Type Conversion	FLOAT(I)	value of I as a REAL number	REAL
	IFIX(X)	integer part of X, no round-off	INTEGER

Some examples of the results obtained when these built-in functions are used are shown below.

```
SIN(.5) = 0.4794255        ARSIN(0.4794255) = .5
COS(.5) = 0.8775826        ARCOS(0.8775826) = .5
TAN(.5) = 0.5463024        ATAN(0.5463024) = .5
COTAN(.5) = 1.830487       ATAN2(0.5463024,1.) = .5

ALOG10(100.) = 2.
ALOG(100.) = 4.605169      EXP(4.605169) = 100.

ABS(-24.3) = 24.3          IABS(-24) = 24

SIGN(-2.,24.3) = 2.        ISIGN(-2,24) = 2
SIGN(2.,-24.3) = -2.       ISIGN(2,-24) = -2

AINT(3.5) = 3.             INT(3.5) = 3
AINT(-3.5) = -3.           INT(-3.5) = -3

AMOD( 10., 2.7) = 1.9      MOD( 10, 3) = 1
AMOD( 10.,-2.7) = 1.9      MOD( 10,-3) = 1
AMOD(-10., 2.7) = -1.9     MOD(-10, 3) = -1
AMOD(-10.,-2.7) = -1.9     MOD(-10,-3) = -1

DIM(-3., 5.) = 0.0         IDIM( 3,-5) = 8
DIM( 4.,-2.) = 6.0         IDIM(-4,-1) = 0

AMIN0(-2,3,-8) = -8.       MIN0(-2,3,-8) = -8
AMIN1(-2.,3.,-8.) = -8.    MIN1(-2.,3.,-8.) = -8
AMAX0(-2,3,-8) = 3.        MAX0(-2,3,-8) = 3
AMAX1(-2.,3.,-8.) = 3.     MAX1(-2.,3.,-8.) = 3

FLOAT(-2) = -2.            IFIX( 2.7) = 2
FLOAT( 2) = 2.            IFIX(-2.7) = -2
```

Some examples of expressions and statements using built-in functions are shown below. These examples illustrate important points which you should know.

    i)   AMAX1(SIN(3.),COS(3.),TAN(3.))

   ii)   SQRT(EXP(2**ALOG10(ABS(-3.+FLOAT(I)))))

  iii)   I=FLOAT(I)

   iv)   A=IFIX(A)

    v)   L=I+J+K-MIN0(I,J,K)-MAX0(I,J,K)

   vi)   I=I+1-2*MOD(I+1,2)

vii) Y=SQRT(SQRT(X))

viii) A=X-AINT(X/Y)*Y

Example (i) produces a value which is the largest of the
the sine, the cosine and the tangent of an angle of 3
radians.   Note that if the value of 3 had been written
without a decimal point, an error would result since the
argument of the SIN function must be REAL.   This example
also shows that the arguments of built-in functions can be
expressions which involve built-in functions.

Example (ii) shows that one can evaluate functions of
functions.   In this example, the functions are nested to a
depth of five and the result is obtained by calculating the
value of the innermost function first and proceeding
outward.

Example (iii) produces no change in the value of I.   If
I is 2 for instance, FLOAT(I) will have a value of 2.0 and
when the assignment is completed I will again have the the
INTEGER value 2 .

Example (iv) causes the fractional part of A to be
truncated.   Suppose A is -3.671, then IFIX(A)=-3 and hence
A=-3.0 .   The same result could have been obtained by using
"A=AINT(A)".

Example (v) shows a single Assignment statement which
would produce a result equal to the value of the INTEGER
variable which is neither the maximum nor minimum of three
INTEGER values.   For instance if I=-8, J=12, and K=-1, then
L=-8 + 12 -1 -MINO(-8,12,-1) -MAXO(-8,12,-1)=3 -(-8)-12 =-1.

Consider example (vi).   Suppose the statement is
executed repeatedly.   The effect is to increase I by 1 if I
is odd and to decrease I by 1 if I is even.   Thus the value
of I would oscillate between a pair of adjacent INTEGER
values.   Quite often one can make use of a value such as
this which "flip-flops" between a pair of values, say 1 and
2, each time a sequence of statements has been executed.
This example shows one way of accomplishing this effect.

Example (vii) shows one way of obtaining the fourth root
of a REAL number.   (Others, of course, are X**.25, or
X**(1./4.), but not X**(1/4).)

Example (viii) shows the steps that are necessary to
obtain AMOD(X,Y) and hence could have been written
equivalently as A=AMOD(X,Y).

A Word About FLOAT And IFIX

Are the type conversion functions IFIX and FLOAT essential for writing programs in WATFIV? After all, isn't 2.*FLOAT(3) the same as 2.*3? There are two important reasons for having type conversion functions in WATFIV. First, each built-in function must have arguments of a specific type. This means, for example, to obtain the square root of an INTEGER value 25, say, that the expression SQRT(FLOAT(25)) must be used in order to use the built-in function SQRT. Second, some Fortran compilers do not permit both REAL and INTEGER values to appear in the same expression. For example, the expression "325.*10" which is valid in WATFIV would have to be written either as "IFIX(325.)*10" or as "325.*FLOAT(10)" to be acceptable. In this book, FLOAT and IFIX are sometimes used in examples even when the situation does not make their use necessary.

```
 _____
|                                                    |
|          Rules For Using Built-In Functions         |
|                                                    |
|   1. The type of function value produced is indicated |
|      by applying the first-letter rule to the name |
|      of the function.                              |
|                                                    |
|   2. The function arguments must be of the required |
|      type.  If not, an error message is produced.  |
|                                                    |
|   3. Functions may be nested to a depth of seven.  |
|                                                    |
|   4. The calculation of function values has the high- |
|      est priority in evaluating arithmetic expressions. |
|      That is, the values of any functions appearing in |
|      arithmetic expressions are calculated before any |
|      other operations are performed.               |
|                                                    |
 _____
```

Exercise 2.4

1. What is the value assigned to each of the variables appearing on the left sides of the following sets of Assignment statements?

   a) X=AMOD(10.,3.)
      Y=SQRT(49.)
      Z=-SIGN(X,Y)

b) A=ALOG10(100.)**MOD(7,4)

c) J=4
    J=SQRT(FLOAT(J))-(SQRT(FLOAT(9))**(-1))

d) I=J=K=1
    M=MINO(I+J-2*K,J-K)+MAXO(-MINO(2,-3),I)

e) K=IDIM(ISIGN(-2,4),IFIX(FLOAT(MOD(13,-5))))

2. What is the error in each of the following Assignment
    statements?

    a)   Y=SIN(3)
    b)   ABS(X)=10.
    c)   READ,J,MOD(J,2)
    d)   Y=IFIX(COS(ABS(X))
    e)   R=S+FLOAT(5.)

3. Write a single statement to achieve the same effect as
    Y=ABS(X) using:
                        a) the SQRT function
                        b) the SIGN function
                        c) the AMAX1 function

4. Write a single statement using the MOD function so that
    an INTEGER variable K which has an initial value of 1
    will take on succesive values of 2,3,4,1,2,3,4,1,2,...
    if the statement is executed over and over again.

2.8 Summary

    1. The WATFIV language distinguishes between numbers
       which are written with and without decimal points.

    2. The priority of operations in evaluating expressions
       is:
                   Functions (right to left)
                   Brackets (innermost first)
                   Exponentiation (right to left)
                   Multiplication and Division (left to right)
                   Addition and Subtraction (left to right)

    3. Variables may take on REAL values or INTEGER values.
       The type of value is determined:
                   1. By default. (the first-letter rule)
                  *2. Implicitly. (using the IMPLICIT statement)
                   3. Explicitly. (using a REAL or INTEGER
                                   declaration statement)

4.   Variables may be given a value in one of two ways.
     1. By using an Assignment (=) statement.
     2. By using a READ statement.

5. WATFIV has a library of built-in functions which are
   handy for obtaining the values of many frequently
   used functions.

2.9 Summary of WATFIV Statements Covered Thus Far

The types of statements discussed thus far, and their
purposes are:

1. Job Control Statements
   a) $JOB - the first card of any WATFIV job
   b) $ENTRY - separates the source program from
      the data cards

2. Comments - used to improve a reader's understanding
   the program

3. WATFIV statements

   a) Non-executable statements - used to provide
      information for the compiler.

      INTEGER - specifies variables which will
      have INTEGER values

      REAL - specifies variables which will have
      REAL values

      *IMPLICIT - defines part or all of a first-
      letter rule

      END WHILE - defines the end of a WHILE loop

      END - indicates the end of a program segment

   b) Executable statements - cause something to
      happen at execution time

      Assignment - assigns a value to a variable

      READ - assigns a value to a variable

      PRINT - displays values on the printer

> WHILE - begins a group of statements which are executed repeatedly as long as a specified condition is true.

> STOP - stops further execution of instructions

Full details of the READ and PRINT statements can be found in Chapters 5 and 6.

2.10 Programming Problems

2.1   Write a program to calculate the value of 12-(6-i) for values of i of 1, 2, 3, ..., 12. Twelve lines of output should be produced. The first value on each line should be the value of i, the second, the value of the expression.

2.2   Tabulate (calculate and print out) values of x and y given by the formula

$$y = \frac{x^3 - 4x^2 + x - 3}{|x + 2|}$$

for a) x = 0., .25., .5, .75, ..., 1.75, 2.0
    b) x = -1, -3, -5, ..., -11, -13
    c) x = 10, 9, 8, ..., -9, -10.

2.3   Read values of X and N. Print the values of X, X/2, X/4, ..., X/2**N.

2.4   The sum of successive powers of the INTEGER values one thru N are given by the following formulae.

a) Sum of values $\dfrac{N(N+1)}{2}$

b) Sum of squares $\dfrac{N(N+1)(2N+1)}{6}$

c) Sum of Cubes $\dfrac{N^2(N+1)^2}{4}$

d) Sum of Fourth Powers $\dfrac{N(N+1)(2N+1)(3N^2+3N-1)}{30}$

e) Sum of Fifth Powers $\dfrac{N^2(N+1)^2(2N^2+2N-1)}{12}$

Write a program to calculate the sum of the first, second, third, fourth and fifth powers of the numbers one thru twenty. That is, calculate the value of the five expressions above with N=20.

2.5   Write a program which reads in ten pairs of numbers, each pair representing a distance in millimeters and centimeters. After each pair of values is read, convert the distance to an equivalent distance in meters.

2.6   Write a program which reads six values, each representing a weight in killograms. After each value is read, convert it to an equivalent weight in grams and milligrams. For example, a weight of 3.56789 kilograms becomes 3567 grams and 890 milligrams. The results of this program will clearly demonstrate the errors which may result when working with fractional REAL values.

2.7   Read twelve values punched one per card each of which represents a number of hours. Express each value as the sum of weeks, days and hours. For example, 193 hours becomes 1 week + 1 day + 1 hour.

2.8   For integer values in the range 11 thru 77 print the number and the remainder when the number is divided by the number obtained by leaving off the last digit. For example, for 36, 12 0 would be printed.

2.9   An approximate value of the square root of x for x in the range .1 thru 10 is given by the formula $(1+4x)/(4+x)$. Write a program which calulates the value of the square root of .5, 1., 1.5, ..., 9.5, 10, using both the formula and the SQRT function. Print the value of each result and the percentage error resulting from using the formula.

2.10   For values of x in the range .1 thru 1 an approximate value of the logarithm of x is given by the formula

$$\log x = -.076 + .281x - \frac{.238}{x + .15}$$

Write a program which prints out the values of log x using the formula and the built-in function ALOG. Use values of x of .2, .4, .6, .8, and 1. For each print the absolute value of the difference of the two log values.

2.11 Write a program which reads in values of A,   B and C
      representing the lengths of three sides of a triangle.
      Calculate the area of the triangle using the formula

$$Area = \sqrt{S(S-A)(S-B)(S-C)}$$

      where S is one-half the perimeter of the triangle.
      Calculate the radius of the inscribed circle (given by
      Area/S).

2.12 A series circuit consists of a resistor of R ohms,   an
      inductance of L henries and a capacitor of C farads.   If
      the voltage across the circuit is E volts at F cycles
      per second,   the current in amperes flowing thru the
      circuit is given by the formula

$$i = \cfrac{E}{\sqrt{R^2 + \left(\cfrac{2\ FL - 1}{2\ FC}\right)^2}}$$

      Write a program which reads in values of R, L and C and
      computes the current thru the circuit at 60 cycles per
      second for values of E of 100, 200, 300, ..., 900 volts.

2.13 Suppose you borrow $X for a period of N months at a
      monthly interest rate of i (e.g. .01). The size of your
      monthly payment is given by the formula

$$i X \left(\frac{(1+i)^N}{(1+i)^N - 1}\right)$$

      Write a program which reads values of X, i and N and
      calculates the size of the monthly payment.

2.14 Tabulate the values of the sine, cosine and tangent of
      angles of 0 , 5 , 10 , ..., 60 (degrees). Note that the
      angles must be converted to radians before the built-in
      functions can be used.

2.15 The greatest common divisor (GCD) of two numbers M and
      N can be calculated in the following way (Euclid's
      Algorithm). Divide the larger by the smaller. If the
      remainder is zero, the GCD is the smaller. If not,
      divide the smaller by the remainder. If zero, the
      remainder is the GCD. If not, continue dividing the

remainder into the previous remainder until a remainder
of zero is obtained. The GCD is the value of the last
non-zero remainder. Write a program to find the GCD of
any two INTEGER values. Test your program by reading a
pair of data values punched on a card. Stop when a pair
of zeros is read in.

2.16 The input to the program consists of five pairs of
INTEGER values punched one pair per card. For each pair
calculate the   greatest common   divisor using   the
algorithm in problem 2.15.   To do this put the entire
program for   problem 2.15 (minus   the STOP and END
statements of course) inside the WHILE loop used to
process each pair of values.   This is an example of a
loop-within-a-loop -- more usually called a nested loop.

2.17 You are required to determine the smallest total
number of bills required to pay a sum of $1579.00 using
only fifties, tens and one dollar bills. Write a program
to do this. Note: No loop is required.

2.18 Modify the program for question 2.17 so that: the
amount to be paid is read from a card; the values of the
three denominations to be used in paying the bill are
read from a card.   (Assume   the values   of the
denominations are in decreasing order).   Why is the
programming problem much more difficult if you had to
read the number of different types of bills to be used
as well as the denomination of each?

CHAPTER 3   DECISION AND CONTROL

Questions Answered In This Chapter

1. In general, how do you determine if a relationship is
   true or false and take the appropriate action
   depending on the result?

2. If the result of an analysis falls into one of
   several distinct cases, how do you execute the
   appropriate set of instructions in each case?

3. How can you execute instructions in a non-sequential
   order?

4. What other decision making capabilities exist in
   Fortran and where should each be used?

3.1 Introduction

This is one of the most important chapters in the book.
It describes how you can base your actions upon the value of
a variable or the relationship of one value to another.   It
introduces the IF construct which says "under the following
conditions do ...".   A thorough understanding of sections
3.2 and 3.3 is a must if you want to be a good programmer.

Logical Expressions

Decision making in Fortran is usually done by testing
the truth of a relationship such as X.LE.3..   Expressions
which are   either true   or   false are   called logical
expressions and in Fortran are created by using one of the
six relational operators .LT., .LE., .EQ., .NE., .GE. and
.GT. between a pair of arithmetic expressions. For example
the truth value of a logical expression is tested to
determine if a WHILE-loop should be repeated.   Because
relational operators have lower priority than arithmetic
operations the logical expression is evaluated only after
the numeric values have been computed.   For example the
statement "WHILE(X+1.LE.2+3)" is equivalent to the statement
"WHILE((X+1).LE.(2+3))".

3.2 The IF-THEN-ELSE Construct

Until now, each example algorithm required no special
actions for particular values used in the calculations. All
programs had a straight-thru or sequential top-to-bottom
style. Consider, however, the following problem.

Example 1

Calculate and display values of $1/(x-2)$ for $x=0,1,2,...,10$. As you will realize, one of the values of x, namely 2, causes the division to be undefined because the denominator is zero. What are we to do? Well, what would be reasonable? One possibility would be to break the problem up into two sub-problems: the first taking care of $x=0$ and $x=1$, the second the values 3 thru 10. This might be fine for this simple example but what if there were many values that made the division undefined? Furthermore, it would be a good idea to let the person requesting the results know that the value is undefined when x is 2. That is, if $x=2$ then print "undefined for x=2", otherwise calculate and print the value of the expression. Shown below is an algorithm. The corresponding program follows the algorithm.

Example 1 Algorithm

```
1.    Set x=0
2.    While x ≤ 10
        .1 if x=2 then
              print "undefined for x=2"
           otherwise
              print 1/(x-2)
        .2 Add 1 to x
3.    Stop
```

Program for Example 1

```
C EXAMPLE 3.1 USING AN IF-THEN-ELSE CONSTRUCT
C
      X = 0.
      WHILE (X .LE. 10.)
         IF (X .EQ. 2.) THEN
            PRINT,'VALUE IS UNDEFINED FOR',X
         ELSE
            PRINT,X,1/(X-2.)
         END IF
         X = X + 1.
      END WHILE
      STOP
      END
```

This program contains a new feature called the IF-THEN-ELSE construct. It is called a construct because it involves more than one statement. In particular it includes an IF-THEN statement, an ELSE statement and an END IF statement. In the example, the IF-THEN statement

"IF(X.EQ.2.) THEN" tests the relationship (the logical expression) X.EQ.2. and indicates that if true, then the statement group immediately following should be executed. The ELSE statement precedes the group of statements to be executed when the relationship is false. The END IF terminates the construct. The general form of an IF-THEN-ELSE construct is shown below.

The IF-THEN-ELSE construct starts with an IF-THEN statement which contains the logical expression to be evaluated. Following the IF-THEN are one or more statements which are executed whenever the logical expression is true. The ELSE separates this group of statements from those which are executed when the logical expression is false.

The END IF statement is a non-executable statement and serves the same function for the IF-THEN-ELSE construct as the END WHILE does in a WHILE loop -- it indicates the end of the construct. It also means that the next statement executed, regardless of whether the THEN group or the ELSE group is executed, will be the statement following the END IF.

A flowchart description of the IF-THEN-ELSE logic is shown below.

IF-THEN-ELSE Logic

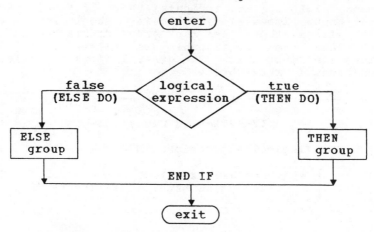

Note that there is only one entry point and one exit. Furthermore the THEN group and ELSE group can contain many statements or constructs including other IF-THEN-ELSE sequences (See Example 3 below.)

    In the examples which follow, the IF-THEN, ELSE and matching END IF statements are vertically aligned. The statements within the two groups are indented. This practice is highly recommended because it makes the program logic much easier to understand.

Example 2

What value is printed by executing the following sequence?

```
        C EXAMPLE 3.2
          I = 2
          IF(I*2 .LE. -2*I) THEN
              PRINT,I-3
          ELSE
              J = I + 5
              PRINT,J
          END IF
          STOP
          END
```

Result: Because the logical expression is false the ELSE group is executed causing a value of 7 to be printed. The THEN group is ignored.

Example 3

Four intervals have been defined along the REAL number line
as follows.

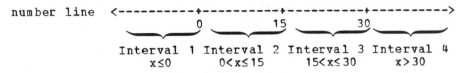

number line   <----------+----------+----------+---------->
                         0   15   30

Interval 1 Interval 2 Interval 3 Interval 4
   x≤0   0<x≤15   15<x≤30   x>30

Given any value of x, determine in which interval it lies.

     We could solve this problem in many ways.   One approach
is as follows.   First let us distinguish a value   which
belongs to either interval 1 or 2 from one in   intervals
3 or 4. Our partial algorithm is therefore as follows.

    1.   Get a value for x.
    2.   If x≤15 then
             .1 select Interval 1 or Interval 2
          otherwise
             .1 select Interval 3 or Interval 4
    3.   Print x and the interval
    4.   Stop

To complete the algorithm, the distinction between interval
1 and 2 and between 3 and 4 is made with another pair of if-
then-elses resulting in the following:

         1.   Get a value for x
         2.   If x≤15 then (interval is 1 or 2)
                  .1 if x≤0 then
                        interval = 1
                     otherwise
                        interval = 2
               otherwise (interval is 3 or 4)
                  .1 if x≤30 then
                        interval = 3
                     otherwise
                        interval = 4
         3.   Print x and the interval
         4.   Stop

Note that both interior "ifs" are labelled with the sub-step
number .1.   This is done because either the first or the
second but never both will be executed.   The resulting
program and flowchart are shown below.

```
C EXAMPLE 3.3 INTERVAL ANALYSIS
      READ,X
C     SELECT 1&2 OR 3&4
      IF(X .LE. 15.) THEN
C         CASE 1&2,NOW SELECT 1 OR 2
          IF(X .LE. 0.) THEN
              INTVAL = 1
          ELSE
              INTVAL = 2
          END IF
      ELSE
C         CASE 3&4,NOW SELECT 3 OR 4
          IF(X .LE. 30.) THEN
              INTVAL = 3
          ELSE
              INTVAL = 4
          END IF
      END IF
C     SHOW RESULT
      PRINT,X,' IS IN INTERVAL',INTVAL
      STOP
      END
```

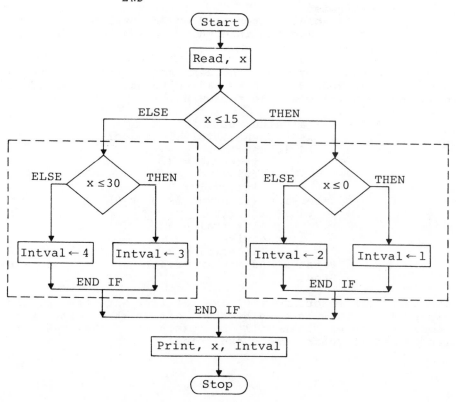

In the program the first IF statement separates the first two cases from the last two cases. If a value is in interval 1 or 2 another IF-THEN-ELSE construct separates interval 1 from interval 2. A similar decision is made for values in intervals 3 or 4. This is an example of nested (one-inside-the-other) IF constructs.

In the flowchart, large boxes have been drawn around the first-level THEN and ELSE groups to emphasize that from the point of view of the first IF statement, they can be viewed as single blocks of logic. It more clearly indicates the structure of the logic.

Example 4

An alternative way to solve the problem would be to first determine whether the value is in interval 1. If it is not, then check whether it is in interval 2. If not in 2 then check whether it is in interval 3. If it is not in 3, then it must be in the last interval, interval 4. The algorithm is shown below.

```
1. Get a value for x
2. If x≤ 0 then (must be interval 1)
   .1 interval = 1
   otherwise (must be 2, 3 or 4)
   .1 If x≤15 then (must be 2)
      .1 interval = 2
      otherwise  (must be 3 or 4)
      .1 If x≤30 then (must be 3)
         .1 interval = 3
         otherwise
         .1 interval = 4
3. Print x and the interval
4. Stop
```

The WATFIV program corresponding to the this algorithm is shown on the following page.

```
C EXAMPLE 3.4 SECOND METHOD FOR INTERVAL ANALYSIS
      READ,X
C       TEST FOR INTERVAL 1
      IF(X .LE. 0.) THEN
         INTVAL = 1
      ELSE
C          TEST FOR INTERVAL 2
         IF(X .LE. 15.) THEN
            INTVAL = 2
         ELSE
C             TEST FOR INTERVAL 3
            IF(X .LE. 30.) THEN
               INTVAL = 3
            ELSE
               INTVAL = 4
            END IF
         END IF
      END IF
      PRINT,X,' IS IN INTERVAL',INTVAL
      STOP
      END
```

In this example there is a staircase-like structure to the program' reflecting the test-within-test-within-test nature of the logic. The three END IF statements in a row need not be confusing. Each IF construct requires its own "END IF". It is that "END IF" which the program goes to after completing the "THEN" group of statements or the "ELSE" group of statements in the construct. Notice again that each triple -- "IF-THEN", "ELSE", "END IF" -- is vertically aligned in order to make the program structure more visible.

Example 5 (Missing ELSE group)

Suppose that you simply want to read and list one hundred pairs of REAL values punched one pair per card. To make the output easier to read, print a blank line after each group of 5.

Shown below is a program to solve the problem. The MOD function (which gives the remainder in a division) is used to determine if the number of pairs just processed is a multiple of 5. Note that there is no ELSE group in the IF-THEN-ELSE construct (the ELSE statement is missing). This is perfectly permissible in WATFIV. The printing of a blank line is required only when the test condition is true.

```
C EXAMPLE 3.5 (MISSING ELSE GROUP)
      N = 1
      WHILE (N .LE. 100)
          READ,X,Y
          PRINT,X,Y
          IF(MOD(N,5) .EQ. 0) THEN
              PRINT,' '
          END IF
          N = N + 1
      END WHILE
      STOP
      END
```

The flowchart logic is below.

Flowchart showing null ELSE group

The logic defined by the IF-THEN-ELSE used in this example could also be coded in the following equivalent ways.

a) IF(MOD(N,5).EQ.0) THEN   b) IF(MOD(N,5).NE.0) THEN
       PRINT,' '   ELSE
   ELSE   PRINT,' '
   END IF   END IF

In (a) the ELSE has been included but since nothing appears between it and the END IF no actions will be taken when the condition is false. In (b) the relationship tested has been reversed and therefore the blank line will be printed only when the logical expression is false. The THEN group is null. That is, if N is not a multiple of 5 do nothing otherwise print a blank line. The style of programming in

(b)   is not recommended simply   because it is natural   to
expect somthing to follow the THEN.   If we immediately see
an ELSE our chain of thought is broken.   As we have seen in
this example it is always possible to write the   logical
expression so that the THEN group is non-null.

     The IF-THEN-ELSE construct is one of the   most powerful
logic tools in the entire language because it allows us to
do   different   things   depending   on   the   truth of   a
relationship.   When many IF-THEN-ELSE's are   nested within
each other, careful attention is necessary to insure that
the desired logic is described.   This task is made
relatively easy by vertically aligning the IF-THEN, the ELSE
and the END IF statements in each construct.   You should
always think of the construct as a single block of
statements with a single entry point (the IF-THEN statement)
and a single exit point (the END IF statement).

ELSEIF

     The problem of selecting which   of two groups of
statements to execute occurs in many programming problems.
The form of the IF construct that we have seen thus far
provides a two-way, either-or kind of choice. If the number
of choices is three or four or more as it was in the
interval selection problem, you can still find the right
group of statements to execute by nesting or imbedding IF
constructs one within the other as was done in example
programs 3.3 and 3.4. In many problems however, the most
natural way to select the desired group of statements is to
examine each possibility one after another.   In WATFIV this
can be done using ELSEIF statements within an IF-THEN-ELSE
construct.

     Consider the same interval selection problem, namely:
determine which of the four intervals x≤0, 0<x≤15, 15<x≤30,
x>30 contains a given value of X. The logic used to solve
this problem is defined by the algorithm below.

          1. Get a value for X
          2. If X ≤0 then
               .1 interval = 1
             otherwise if X ≤ 15 then
               .1 interval = 2
             otherwise if X ≤ 30 then
               .1 interval = 3
             otherwise
               .1 interval = 4
          3. Print X and the value of interval
          4. Stop

The program below is a translation of this logic. It contains only one IF construct.

```
C EXAMPLE 3.6 CASE SELECTION WITH ELSEIF
      READ,X
      IF(X.LE.0.) THEN
        INTVAL=1
      ELSEIF (X.LE.15.) THEN
        INTVAL=2
      ELSEIF (X.LE.30.) THEN
        INTVAL=3
      ELSE
        INTVAL=4
      END IF
      PRINT,X,' IS IN INTERVAL',INTVAL
      STOP
      END
```

In this program the truth of X.LE.0 is evaluated first. If true, then the statement "INTVAL=1" is executed before control is transferred to the statement following the END IF. If X.LE.0 is false, the THEN group is skipped and execution continues with the first ELSEIF statement. The expression X.LE.15 is tested and if true, the statement "INTVAL=2" is executed before control transfers out of the construct. If X.LE.15 is false, a third test is made using similar logic and actions. Should all three logical expressions be false for a given value of X, the ELSE group "INTVAL=4" is executed before leaving the construct.

A very important point is that the IF in an ELSEIF is _not_ the start of an IF construct or IF statement. The structures below are _not_ equivalent.

```
IF ... THEN               IF ... THEN
  .                         .
  .                         .
ELSEIF ... THEN           ELSE
  .                           IF ... THEN
  .                         .
END IF                    END IF
```

The ELSEIF statement on the left is a single statement even though the word ELSEIF could be written as two separate words. The ELSEIF statement is executable. On the right the ELSE and the following IF begin two different statements. (A new line begins an new statement unless it is made a continuation of the previous line.) Therefore the IF begins an inner IF construct and would have to have a matching END IF statement which is not shown.

3.11   The IF-THEN-ELSE Construct   75

A second example. Suppose each of 500 data records contains a single INTEGER value. These values fall into two ranges. Negative values are either -10, -5 or -2; non-negative values include 79, 84 and 93 although other positive values may occur. The problem is to count:

1) the total number of negative values
2) the number of occurrences of -10, -5 and -2
3) the total number of non-negative values
4) the number of occurrences of 79, 84, and 93
5) the number of occurences of non-negative values
   other than 79, 84 and 93

An algorithm for solving the problem is shown below.

1. Set all counts to zero
2. Repeat the following 500 times
   .1 Get a value for N
   .2 If the value is negative then
      .1 Add one to the negative count
      .2 Add one to the count for the
         particular value (-10, -5 or -2)
   Otherwise
      .1 Add one to the non-negative count
      .2 If the value is one of 79, 84 or 93
         .1 Add to the appropriate counter
      otherwise
         .1 Add one to 'other non-negative'
3. Print the results
4. Stop

In the program which follows, three IF constructs are used. The outermost one separates the negative values from the non-negative values. It contains a THEN and an ELSE but no ELSEIFs. Its THEN group contains an IF construct in which each ELSEIF statement tests for one of the negative values. Note the absence of an ELSE group. When a value is non-negative, the logic used consists of an IF construct containing two ELSEIFs and an ELSE. The ELSE group will be executed only if N is not equal to 79, 84 or 93. That is an ELSE group is executed only if the expression in the IF statement and those in all intervening ELSEIF statements are false.

What happens if a negative value other than -10, -5 and -2 is read? It would cause NUMNEG to increased by 1 but will not cause any of the individual negative counters to be increased. After the program has executed the difference between NUMNEG and NEG10+NEG5+NEG2 would indicate how many such values had been read.

```
C    EXAMPLE 3.7  NESTED IF'S WITH ELSEIF'S
     INTEGER OTHER
C    SET COUNTS TO 0
     NUMNEG=NUMPOS=0
     NEG10=NEG5=NEG2=0
     NUM79=NUM84=NUM93=OTHER=0
C    READ AND PROCESS 500 VALUES
     I=1
     WHILE (I.LE.500)
       READ,N
       IF (N.LT.0) THEN
         NUMNEG=NUMNEG+1
         IF (N.EQ.-10) THEN
           NEG10=NEG10+1
         ELSEIF (N.EQ.-5) THEN
           NEG5=NEG5+1
         ELSEIF (N.EQ.-2) THEN
           NEG2=NEG2+1
         END IF
       ELSE
         NUMPOS=NUMPOS+1
         IF (N.EQ.79) THEN
           NUM79=NUM79+1
         ELSEIF (N.EQ.84) THEN
           NUM84=NUM84+1
         ELSEIF (N.EQ.93) THEN
           NUM93=NUM93+1
         ELSE
           OTHER=OTHER+1
         END IF
       END IF
       I=I+1
     END WHILE
C    PRINT THE RESULTS
     PRINT, 'IN THE 500 VALUES READ, THERE ARE'
     PRINT,NUMNEG,' NEGATIVE VALUES CONSISTING OF'
     PRINT,NEG10,NEG5,NEG2,' VALUES OF -10,-5 AND -2'
     PRINT,NUMPOS,' NON-NEGATIVE VALUES CONSISTING OF'
     PRINT,NUM79,NUM84,NUM93,' VALUES OF 79,84 AND 93'
     PRINT,'AND',OTHER,' OTHER POSITIVE VALUES'
     STOP
     END
```

When writing IF constructs make sure the IF, ELSEIF, ELSE and END IF statements are aligned. This makes the program structure and logic much clearer.

```
---------------------------------------------------------------
|                   The IF-THEN-ELSE Construct                |
|                                                             |
|    Form:                                                    |
|                                                             |
|            IF ( logical expression) THEN                    |
|              .                                              |
|              .                                              |
|            ELSEIF (logical expression) THEN                 |
|              .                                              |
|              .                                              |
|            ELSEIF (logical expression) THEN                 |
|              .                                              |
|            etc.                                             |
|              .                                              |
|            ELSE                                             |
|              .                                              |
|              .                                              |
|            END IF                                           |
|                                                             |
|    Rules:                                                   |
|            1. The word DO may optionally follow THEN or     |
|               ELSE.                                         |
|                                                             |
|            2. ELSEIF   statements   are   optional.   If    |
|               present,  they  must  precede  the  ELSE      |
|               statement.   ELSEIF   is   an   executable    |
|               statement.                                    |
|                                                             |
|            3. The ELSE statement is optional and non-       |
|               executable.                                   |
|                                                             |
|            4. The END IF statement is required and non-     |
|               executable.                                   |
|                                                             |
|            5. Operation.  Beginning  with  the  logical     |
|               expression in  the  IF  statement, logical    |
|               expressions  are  evaluated  sequentially     |
|               until a  value of true  is found.   If and    |
|               when found,  the statements  in the  THEN     |
|               group  which  immediately  follows  are       |
|               executed before  control transfers  to the   |
|               statement following the END IF.  If all of    |
|               the  logical expressions are false,  the      |
|               statements following the ELSE (if present)    |
|               are executed.                                 |
|                                                             |
---------------------------------------------------------------
```

Exercise 3.1 (IF Constructs)

1. For each of the following program segments determine what value(s) will be printed.

a)   IF(2.NE.5/2) THEN
            PRINT,'NOPE'
        ELSE
            PRINT,'YEP'
        END IF

b)   IF(IFIX(SQRT(5.)).GE.2.236)THEN
            PRINT,'GREATER'
        ELSE
            PRINT,'LESSER'
        END IF

c)   IF(MAXO(4,-8/(-3)).LE.1+2**2) THEN
            PRINT,'ONE'
            IF(ISIGN(-1,4).NE.-1) THEN
                PRINT,'AND TWO'
            ELSE
                PRINT,'AND THREE'
            END IF
        ELSEIF(100.GE.100)THEN
            PRINT,'NOT TWO OR THREE'
        END IF
        PRINT,'AND FOUR'

2. For each of (a) thru (d) below write an IF-THEN-ELSE construct (perhaps containing others within it) to print the appropriate message depending on the value of N.   Assume the value of N has been read from a data card.

   For example suppose the requirement is:

        requirement   message
          N=2   'EQUALS 2'
          N≠2   'NOT 2'

   The solution would be

        IF(N.EQ.2) THEN
            PRINT,'EQUALS 2'
        ELSE
            PRINT,'NOT 2'
        END IF

		Message	
a)	N> MOD(7,N)	BIGGER	
	N≤ MOD(7,N)	SMALLER	
b)	5<N≤15	BETWEEN	
	otherwise	OUTSIDE	
c)	N>50 or N<(-20)	SPREAD	
	N≥-20 and N<0	RANGE 2	
	otherwise	RANGE 3	
d)	N=2	TWO	Do it two ways,
	N=4	FOUR	once without any
	N=6	SIX	ELSE's and once
	N=8	EIGHT	with ELSE's
	N=10	TEN	

3. Suppose three ranges of integer values are called
   A,B,C.   For each assume the statement "READ,N"
   has been previously executed.   You are to
   indicate in which range or ranges the value of N
   lies.   In each   case use as few IF-THEN-ELSE
   constructs as possible.   If the value does not
   lie in any of A, B or C, print 'NONE'.

	A	B	C
a)	0 to 15	16 to 25	26 to 50
b)	0 to 15	16 to 25	0 to 25
c)	0 to 15	5 to 20	10 to 25
d)	less than 0	≠4	≠2
e)	1 to 100	20 to 80	50 to 60

4. Consider Example 5   in   the   previous section
   (printing pairs   of numbers).   Change the
   position of   the IF   construct and/or   the
   relationship tested to solve the following two
   problems. Do not use any additional statements.
   Print the blank line before each group of five
   pairs:

   a) including the first pair
   b) excluding the first pair

5. In example programs 3.3, 3.4 and 3.6,   three
   methods for determining the interval in which a
   number lay were shown. Assuming that the chance
   of finding a number in   each of the four
   intervals is the same,   which is the more
   efficient method?   Hint: What is the average
   number of logical expressions which must be

evaluated in each method in order to locate the
correct interval?

3.3 Testing Multiple Conditions

Frequently one requires that more than one condition be
true before taking a particular action. For example suppose
you want to print the value of X if it lies in the interval
0.5 to 1.7.   This can be done using the following single
logical expression.

```
IF((X.GE.0.5) .AND. (X.LE.1.7)) THEN
   PRINT,X
END IF
```

In order for the entire condition to be true, both
relationships must be true. If either or both are false, the
THEN group will be skipped.   We say that the relationships
(X.GE.0.5) and (X.LE.1.7) have been "anded".   If R1, R2, R3
and R4 are relationships which are either true or false then
the logical expression

$$(R1.AND.R2.AND.R3.AND.R4)$$

will be true if and only if all of R1,   R2,   R3 and R4 are
individually true.   The test made in the previous example
could also   be made using   the following   nested IF
constructs.

```
IF(X.GE.0.5) THEN
   IF(X.LE.1.7) THEN
      PRINT,X
   END IF
END IF
```

Suppose the value of X is to be printed if X lies
outside the interval (.5,   1.7).   A sufficient condition is
that either X<.5 or X>1.7.   This test could be made using
the following IF construct.

```
IF(X.LT.0.5) THEN
   PRINT,X
ELSEIF(X.GT.1.7) THEN
   PRINT,X
END IF
```

The two conditions could also be tested using the following
single logical expression.

```
              IF((X.LT.0.5).OR.(X.GT.1.7)) THEN
                 PRINT,X
              END IF
```

When a pair of conditions are combined in this manner we say they have been "ored". In general, if R1, R2, R3 and R4, say, are relationships each of which is either true or false, then the logical expression

$$(R1.OR.R2.OR.R3.OR.R4)$$

will be true if <u>one</u> <u>or</u> <u>more</u> of R1, R2, R3, R4 is true.

Occasionally for the sake of clarity or convenience one wishes to test a condition to see if it is not true, that is, false. For example if the logical expression (X.LT.1.7) is true then necessarily the relation (X.GE.1.7) must be false. To test the falseness of a condition you can prefix the logical expression with the operator .NOT.. For example the pair of IF-THEN statements below are equivalent.

```
   IF (X.LT.1.7) THEN          IF (.NOT.(X.GE.1.7) ) THEN
```

To be precise, the use of the operator .NOT. changes the "truth value" of the logical expression which it precedes. Thus if R is a relationship which is true then .NOT.R is false. If R is false then .NOT.R is true.

Suppose R1, R2, R3 and R4 are four relationships each of which is true or false. How are we to evaluate the truth value of a logical expression such as:

$$(R1.AND.R2.OR..NOT.R3.AND.R4)$$

As well as rules for evaluating arithmetic expressions, there are rules or priorities for evaluating logical expressions which contain the operators .AND., .OR., and .NOT.. The operations are performed in the following order.

    .NOT.   has the highest priority

    .AND.   has the second highest priority

    .OR.   has the lowest priority

Processing proceeds left to right in each case and the order in which operations are performed may be modified by using brackets to indicate operations evaluated in the order shown below.

That is the expression is evaluated as if written as:

  ((R1.AND.R2).OR. ((.NOT.R3).AND.R4))

If 'T' denotes true and 'F' denotes false then the truth value of the expression below is evaluated as shown.

    T.AND.F.OR..NOT.F.AND.T = T.AND.F.OR.T.AND.T
                            = F .OR. T
                            = T

A summary of the priorities of the various operators used in WATFIV is shown in the following table.

```
Summary of Operator Priorities

  1. Evaluation of functions  (right to left)

  2. Brackets (innermost first)

  3. Arithmetic Operators
        Exponentiation (right to left)
        Multiplication and  Division  (left   to
        right)
        Addition and Subtraction (left to right)

  4. Relational operators (left to right)
        .LT. .LE. .EQ. .NE. .GT. .GE.

  5. Logical operators
        .NOT. (left to right)
        .AND. (left to right)
        .OR. (left to right)
```

Your decision to use or not to use the logical operators .AND., .OR. and .NOT. is a matter of personal preference. However complicated a relationship may look it can always be written using one or more IF constructs which do not involve the operators .AND., .OR., and .NOT.. For example,

```
    IF((A.LT.B).OR..NOT.(C.EQ.D).AND.(E.GE.F)) THEN
       STOP
    END IF
```

is equivalent to

```
        IF(A.LT.B) THEN
           STOP
        ELSEIF (C.NE.D) THEN
           IF(E.GE.F) THEN
              STOP
           END IF
        END IF
```

For a further discussion and more examples of logical
values and operators the reader is referred to Chapter 15.

3.4 The Logical IF Statement

There is a special form of the IF statement which allows
you to execute a single statement when the condition tested
is found to be true.   It is called a Logical IF statement.
The correspondence between a logical IF statement and an
equivalent IF construct is illustrated in the example below.

```
    Logical IF Statement              IF Construct

    IF (A.EQ.B) PRINT,A           IF (A.EQ.B) THEN
                                     PRINT,A
                                  END IF
```

There are three important points:

i) In the Logical IF statement the word "THEN" is not
used.(This is how the compiler can distinguish between a
Logical IF and an IF-THEN-ELSE).

ii) The action to be taken when the logical expression
is true is restricted to a single executable statement.
This means a Logical IF cannot be used to execute a WHILE or
an IF construct because each involves more than one
statement.

iii) The statement executed when the expression is true
cannot be another Logical IF statement.

The general form and rules of the logical IF statement
are summarized below.

```
┌──────────────────────────────────────────────────────────────┐
│                                                                │
│                    Logical IF Statement                        │
│                                                                │
│   Form:     IF (logical expression) trailer statement          │
│                                                                │
│   Rules:1. The trailer statement may be any executable         │
│            statement excluding another  Logical IF or          │
│            the first statement of a construct.                 │
│                                                                │
│         2. When  the logical  expression is true  the          │
│            trailer statement  is executed  and unless          │
│            it   causes   the   program  execution   to         │
│            terminate or control to  be transferred to          │
│            some other point in the program,  the next          │
│            statement following the Logical IF will be          │
│            executed  after execution  of the  trailer          │
│            statement.                                          │
│                                                                │
│         3. When the logical expression  is false,  the         │
│            trailer statement is ignored and execution          │
│            proceeds sequentially.                              │
│                                                                │
└──────────────────────────────────────────────────────────────┘
```

The Logical IF statement is primarily a convenience. It means that an if-then action can be put in a single program line rather than the three lines required by the equivalent IF construct.   In some versions of Fortran there is no IF-THEN-ELSE construct,   only the Logical IF statement. .In these cases the Logical IF is used in conjunction with a "GO TO" statement to define the program logic.   (GO TOs are described in Section 3.7 and in Appendix I).

*3.5 Executing One of Several Cases (DO CASE)

Quite often the data being processed falls into one of several distinct categories or cases.   The cases may be associated with days of the week,   employee department numbers, sales codes, intervals of numbers, etc. As we have seen, selection of the appropriate case can be made using a sequence of ELSEIFs to test each possibility one after the other. In general, this is the recommended approach. If the number of cases is relatively small (say 10 or less) and if it is meaningful to number and distinguish the cases as 1, 2, 3, etc. using an INTEGER variable, then you may want to use the DO CASE construct to define the program logic.

Suppose the cases are identified by the value of an

INTEGER variable called ICODE. The task is to read 50 values of ICODE and to count the number of values of ICODE equal to 1, 2 and 4. A value of 3 can be ignored. All other values are invalid and should be displayed with an appropriate error message. The program below solves the problem and illustrates all of the important features of the DO CASE construct.

```
C EXAMPLE 3.8 USING A DO CASE
C
      INTEGER COUNT1,COUNT2,COUNT4
      COUNT1=COUNT2=COUNT4=0
      N=1
      WHILE (N .LE. 50)
         READ,ICODE
         DO CASE ICODE
           CASE
              COUNT1=COUNT1+1
           CASE
              COUNT2=COUNT2+1
           CASE
           CASE
              COUNT4=COUNT4+1
           IF NONE
              PRINT,ICODE,' IS INVALID'
         END CASE
         N = N+1
      END WHILE
      PRINT,'COUNTS ARE',COUNT1,COUNT2,COUNT4
      STOP
      END
```

The DO CASE construct in the example involves one executable statement (the DO CASE) and three types of non-executable statements (4 CASE statements, 1 IF NONE statement and 1 END CASE statement). Note that the third CASE statement is immediately followed by the fourth. This simply means do nothing if ICODE is 3.

Here are the rules for the DO CASE construct.

```
┌─────────────────────────────────────────────────────────────┐
│                                                               │
│                      DO CASE Construct                        │
│                                                               │
│    Form:            DO CASE i                                 │
│                     CASE                                      │
│                        statements(s)                          │
│                     CASE                                      │
│                        statement(s)                           │
│                        .                                      │
│                        .                                      │
│                        .                                      │
│                     CASE                                      │
│                        statement(s)                           │
│                     IF NONE                                   │
│                        statements(s)                          │
│                     END CASE                                  │
│                                                               │
│    Rules:  1. i is a simple full-word integer variable        │
│                                                               │
│            2. The first CASE statement is optional            │
│                                                               │
│            3. The IF NONE block is  optional.  The word       │
│               DO may optionally follow the word NONE.         │
│                                                               │
│            4. Operation: If the value of i is between 1       │
│               and the number of  CASEs,  then the i'th        │
│               case block  is executed  and control  is        │
│               passed   to   the    statement   following      │
│               END CASE                                        │
│               If  i is  negative  or  greater than  the       │
│               number of  CASEs then the  IF NONE block        │
│               is  executed  (if  it  is  present)   and       │
│               control  is  passed   to  the  statement        │
│               following the END CASE.                         │
│                                                               │
└─────────────────────────────────────────────────────────────┘
```

   Although the naturalness of the words CASE, IF NONE and
END CASE may improve the readability of a program,   this
benefit is   generally outweighed   by the   restrictions
previously mentioned. Furthermore, many versions of Fortran
do not include the DO CASE construct as part of the language
which can be processed.

*3.6 GUESS-ADMIT-END GUESS

   The problem of selecting which of the four intervals
$x \leq 0$, $0 < x \leq 5$, $15 < x \leq 30$, $x > 30$ contained a given value of x was
solved using IF-THEN-ELSE constructs in Section 3.2. The
approach used there is the recommended one.   An alternative

method is the following:

      1. Get a value for x
      2. Guess correct answer using the following logic:
          .1 Select an interval
          .2 If x is not in the interval then
               .1 Quit further analysis and try
                   another interval
            else
               .1 Save the result
      3. Print the result
      4. Stop

    A program which translates this logic into WATFIV and
which uses the GUESS-ADMIT-END GUESS construct is shown
below.

```
C   EXAMPLE 3.9  INTERVAL SELECTION USING GUESS
    READ,X
    GUESS
      IF (X.GT.0.) QUIT
      INTVAL=1
    ADMIT
      IF (X.GT.15.) QUIT
      INTVAL=2
    ADMIT
      IF (X.GT.30.) QUIT
      INTVAL=3
    ADMIT
      INTVAL=4
    END GUESS
    PRINT,X,' IS IN INTERVAL',INTVAL
    STOP
    END
```

The idea is as follows. We begin by GUESSing an interval. If
the guess turns out to be wrong, then QUIT further analysis
of that guess and ADMIT the next possibility. The QUIT
statement (which has other more important uses described in
the next section) is used to transfer control out of one
group and into the next. If a QUIT statement is not
executed, control transfers to the end of the construct
following execution of statements in a group. ADMIT
statements are non-executable and simply partition the
statements within the construct into the various guesses,
possibilities or cases.

    You are likely asking yourself "What advantage does the
GUESS construct have over IF constructs which use ELSEIFs to
separate the cases?" In this example there are none. The

one advantage the GUESS construct has is that one or more
statements can be executed within a group before deciding
the guess was wrong and admitting the next possibility. When
ELSEIFs are used, all information necessary to select the
case must be available at the time the IF construct is
entered. In an IF construct this also means that once a
THEN group has been entered the only exit is to the end of
the construct. (You cannot go from one THEN group to another
without using one of the explicit control statements
described in the next section.)

    The GUESS construct is not part of standard Fortran and
is not used in examples in the remainder of the book.

3.7 Non-Sequential Execution (QUIT and GO TO)

    Computer programs   should be   executed sequentially
starting at the beginning and going straight thru to the
end. When analyzing a program the only time you should need
to "back-up" occurs when the end of a WHILE construct is
reached.   This section and the one which follows describe a
group of statements which allow you to execute statements in
a non-sequential fashion by explicitly pointing to the next
statement to be executed. Generally speaking, analyzing and
writing programs containing these explicit control
statements is more difficult because the resulting program
lacks the easy-to-follow top-to-bottom structure.   It has
also been proved that any programming task can be solved
without using any of these statements.   The action of
transferring control to a statement is sometimes called
branching. This section describes the two simplest explicit
control statements -- the QUIT statement and the
unconditional GO TO statement.   The other explicit control
statements are described in section 3.8 and are included
because these statements provide the only means of control
in some versions of Fortran.

The QUIT Statement

    The QUIT statement is used to exit from a construct.
The example structures below illustrate this idea when a
QUIT is used within WHILE and IF constructs.

```
WHILE (...)                      IF (...) THEN
   .                                .
   .                               QUIT
   .                                .
 QUIT                            ELSE
   .                                .
   .                               QUIT
   .                                .
END WHILE                        END IF
```

In the WHILE construct, execution of a QUIT causes control
to be immediately transferred to the statement following the
END WHILE. Similarly, when a QUIT is executed within either
a THEN group or an ELSE group, control is transferred to the
statement following the END IF. Note that QUIT always
causes a forward transfer of control.

When constructs are nested one within the other, QUIT
can be used to exit from more than one construct by
following QUIT with an INTEGER constant representing the
number of constructs to quit. For example, the statement
"QUIT 2" below means both the IF and WHILE constructs are
"quitted".

```
C   EXAMPLE 3.10   QUITTING MORE THAN ONE CONSTRUCT
      I=1
      WHILE (I.LE.10)
        PRINT,I
        IF (I.EQ.5) THEN
          QUIT 2
        END IF
        I=I+1
      END WHILE
      STOP
      END
```

When this program is executed, only the values 1 thru 4 are
printed. What would happen if "QUIT 1" or equivalently
"QUIT" had been used instead of "QUIT 2"? After a little
thought you will realize that the IF construct would serve
absolutely no purpose.

The general rules for QUIT are the following.

The QUIT Statement

Form: QUIT   or   QUIT n

Rules: 1. If present, n must be a non-negative
          INTEGER constant not greater than the
          nested level of the construct in which it
          appears.

       2. Operation.
          a) When used with the following constructs:
                 WHILE
                 IF-THEN-ELSE
                 DO CASE
                 LOOP (see Chapter 4)
                 AT END (see Chapter 5)
             control transfers to the statement
             following the END of the construct.
          b) When used within a REMOTE BLOCK (see
             Chapter 8) control is returned to the
             statement following the EXECUTE which
             invoked the BLOCK.
          c) When used within a GUESS-END GUESS
             construct (see Section 3.6) control is
             transferred to the statement following
             the next ADMIT statement if present or
             to the statement following the
             END GUESS if no further ADMIT
             statements are within the construct.
          d) When used within the range of a DO-loop
             (see Chapter 4) control is transferred
             to the statement following the object
             statement of the DO-loop.

       3. Execution of QUIT n causes the n innermost
          constructs (commencing with the one in
          which the QUIT n appears) to be exited.
          In the outermost of the n, control is
          transferred to the statement defined by
          Rule 2 above.

The Unconditional GO TO Statement

    The unconditional GO TO provides an even greater degree
of explicit control than QUIT.   It allows you to direct
control to a particular statement -- not just exit from a

construct.   This is done by using <u>statement numbers</u>.   A
statement number is an integer value in the range 1 thru
99999 which may be placed anywhere in columns 1 to 5 of an
executable statement.   A statement   number provides a
reference point for the statement so that control can be
explicitly transferred to that statement from some other
point in the program.   It has no relationship to the line
number which the compiler places beside each line in the
program on the program listing.

   We shall translate the following algorithm into Fortran
using unconditional GO TOs to override the normal sequential
execution of statements.

```
         1.      Read a value of x
         2.      If  x≤10 then
                    .1 Set  y = 3x
                    .2 Set  z = 4x
                 Otherwise  (x>10)
                    .1 Set  y = x
                    .2 Set  z = 2x
         3.      Print,x,y,z
         4.      Stop
```

The program is shown below.

```
         C EXAMPLE 3.11  UNCONDITIONAL GO TO
               READ,X
               IF(X.GT.10)  GO TO 27
                  Y = X
                  Z = 2*X
                  GO TO 3599
         C
              27   Y = 3*X
                   Z = 4*X
         C
           3599 PRINT,X,Y,Z
                STOP
                END
```

In this example the first unconditional GO TO statement is
the trailer statement in the Logical IF;   the second, the
stand-alone statement "GO TO 3599".   In each case the
meaning is clear -- the next statement to be executed is the
one having the statement number given.   The general form and
rules of the Unconditional GO TO are shown below.

```
┌──────────────────────────────────────────────────────┐
│                                                        │
│                  Unconditional GO TO                   │
│                                                        │
│   Form:             GO TO n                            │
│                                                        │
│   where n  is the  statement number  of an  executable│
│         statement                                      │
│                                                        │
│   Rules 1. n cannot be a variable                      │
│         2. GO TO can be written as one word GOTO       │
│         3. Control  transfers  to the   statement  with│
│            statement number n                          │
│         4. A GO TO cannot transfer control             │
│            - to a non-executable statement             │
│            - into the range of a DO-loop (Chapter 4)   │
│            - into or  out of  a REMOTE  BLOCK  (see     │
│            Chapter 8)                                   │
│         5. A GO TO can be used  to transfer control to │
│               executable statements within constructs. │
│               When this happens, execution proceeds as │
│               if executed in the normal manner.        │
│                                                        │
└──────────────────────────────────────────────────────┘
```

In the remainder of this book the unconditional GO TO is occasionally used in example programs.

*3.8 Other Explicit Control Statements

The statement "GO TO n" is unconditional in the sense that the transfer of control is not dependent on the truth of a relationship. There are however three explicit control statements in which the branching is conditional upon either the value of an integer or upon the value of a numeric expression. These are the:

                Computed GO TO
                Assigned GO TO and ASSIGN
                Arithmetic IF

Each will be described in turn.

The Computed GO TO

The Computed GO TO provides a method of "going to" one of several statements depending on the value of an INTEGER variable. It is the forerunner of the DO CASE construct described previously in this chapter. Here is an example.

GO TO (10,20,30,40), NUMBER

This Computed GO TO statement is equivalent to the following set of Logical IF statements.

IF(NUMBER.EQ.1) GO TO 10

IF(NUMBER.EQ.2) GO TO 20

IF(NUMBER.EQ.3) GO TO 30

IF(NUMBER.EQ.4) GO TO 40

...

The dots following the fourth IF statement indicate that if none of the four relationships tested is true, then the statement following the last IF is the next one executed.

The Computed GO TO is used to define conditional control based on the value of an INTEGER variable which lies in the range 1,2,3,...,K where K is a positive INTEGER constant. If the value of the INTEGER variable being tested is outside the range 1,2,3,...,K then the statement immediately following the Computed GO TO is the next one executed.

The general form and rules are shown below.

```
+----------------------------------------------------------------+
|                                                                |
|                      Computed GO TO                            |
|                                                                |
|    Form:         GO TO (s1,s2, ...,sk), i                      |
|                                                                |
|    where s1,s2, ...,sk are the statement numbers of            |
|             executable statements.  (Assume k denotes          |
|             some positive integer constant)                    |
|          i is an INTEGER variable                              |
|                                                                |
|    Rules:1. If the value of the INTEGER variable is n,         |
|             control transfers to the statement having          |
|             sn as a statement number.                          |
|          2. If the value of the variable lies outside          |
|             the range 1 thru k, the next statement             |
|             executed is the one following the Computed         |
|             GO TO.                                             |
|                                                                |
+----------------------------------------------------------------+
```

Two errors frequently made by programmers using Computed GO TOs for the first time are:

i) Forgetting to put the comma ahead of the INTEGER variable being tested.

ii) Forgetting that the Computed GO TO can only be used to test the value of an INTEGER variable and not an INTEGER expression.

The pair of statements below shows how a Computed GO TO could be used to transfer control to statements 17, 18, or 19 depending on whether the variable IYEAR has a value in the range 1700-1799, 1800-1899, or 1900-1999.

$$J = (IYEAR-1600)/100$$

$$GO\ TO\ (17,18,19),J$$

ASSIGN and Assigned GO TO

The ASSIGN statement allows you to ASSIGN a statement number to a variable and then either immediately or later go to the "value" of the variable.   It is therefore one method of controlling where you should go after executing a block of statements.   The program below illustrates its use.   The problem is to read and print groups of four REAL values and stop when the first of any four has a value of 0.

```
C EXAMPLE 3.12  ASSIGN AND ASSIGNED GO TO
C    USED FOR LOOP CONTROL
C    SET UP RETURN POINT FOR LOOP
        ASSIGN 53 TO LOOP
C
C      READ-PRINT LOOP
    53 READ,A,B,C,D
         IF(A.EQ.0.) ASSIGN 14 TO LOOP
         PRINT,A,B,C,D
       GO TO LOOP,(53,14)
C
    14 STOP
       END
```

In the Assigned GO TO, the value of LOOP is compared with each of the statement numbers in the list.   Control transfers to the matching number.   An error occurs if no match is found.

```
┌──────────────────────────────────────────────────────────────┐
│                                                                │
│                  ASSIGN and Assigned GO TO                     │
│                                                                │
│     Form:          ASSIGN s TO i                               │
│                                                                │
│                    GO TO i,(s1,s2, ...,sk)                     │
│                                                                │
│     where s is the number of an executable statement;          │
│           i is an INTEGER variable;                            │
│           s1,s2, ...,sk are statement numbers of               │
│             statements in the program.                         │
│                                                                │
│     Rules 1. The value  of "i" can  only be  assigned to       │
│              the  variable using  an ASSIGN  statement.        │
│              It    cannot    be    used    in   arithmetic     │
│              expressions.                                      │
│           2. The value of the variable must match one of       │
│              the numbers s1,s2, ...,sk.                        │
│                                                                │
└──────────────────────────────────────────────────────────────┘
```

There is no need to confuse the ASSIGN statement with
the Assignment (=) statement.   The ASSIGN statement is only
used in conjunction with the Assigned GO TO statement.   The
Assignment statement of course is used to assign the value
of expressions (not statement numbers) to variables.

Arithmetic IF

Occassionally we   may want to determine if a   value is
positive, negative or zero and take (usually)   different
actions depending on the result. The Arithmetic IF provides
this decision-making capability in a single statement.
Consider the following example.

                    IF (X-2) 10,20,30

The logic embedded in this statement is, if x-2 is negative
go to statement 10; if x-2 is zero go to statement 20; if
positive go to statement 30. In other words it contains the
same logic as the following sequence of Logical IF
statements

                IF (X-2.LT.0.) GO TO 10
                IF (X-2.EQ.0.) GO TO 20
                IF (X-2.GT.0.) GO TO 30

The general form and logic of the Arithmetic IF statement is
summarized below.

```
r------------------------------------------------------1
|                                                      |
|                  The Arithmetic IF                   |
|                                                      |
|    Form:          IF (expression) s1,s2,s3           |
|                                                      |
|    where expression is any numeric value;            |
|         s1,s2,s3 are  statement numbers  of executable |
|           statements in the program.                 |
|                                                      |
|    Control is transferred to                         |
|              s1 if the expression has a negative value |
|              s2 if the expression equals zero        |
|              s3 if the expression has a positive value |
|                                                      |
L------------------------------------------------------J
```

* **Exercise 3.2** (GO TO questions)

1. In each of the following determine which statement will
   be the next one executed after the statements shown have
   been executed.   State the values of all variables
   appearing in the sequence at that point in time.   Assume
   all variables are typed by the first-letter rule.

   a)   I=MOD(MOD(21,17),-3)
               IF(I*I-I) 5,6,7
            8 ....

   b)   A=2.6
               K=3+IFIX(A)
               IF(IDIM(3-K,8)) 2,18,4
           18 K=2
               GO TO 7
            4 A=2.*K
               STOP
            2 ......

   c)   Z=A=2.
               IF(Z**2.LE.A+3) IF(A-2.) 6,11,15
            6 ....

2. For each of the following Logical IF statements write
   an equivalent Arithmetic IF.

   a)   IF(A.LT.B) GO TO 10
            6 ....

b)   IF(A.GT.B) GO TO 8
               IF(R.GT.A) GO TO 7
         5 ......

3. Explain the error in each of the following.

    a)   IF(A=B) GO TO 7
    b)   IF(X),5,25,871
    c)   IF(A-2) GO TO 17
    d)   IF(B-C.GT.14.) 10,11,12
    e)   IF(10.LT.A) IF(B.GT.C/D) GO TO 5
    f)   IF((X.LT.Y)/2.) GO TO 4

4. For each of the following sequences of statements,
   determine which statement will be the next one
   executed.

    a)   I=2
               GO TO (25,7,4,82),I
          82 ......

    b)   JJ=2**3/3-4
               GO TO(6),JJ
          10 ......

    c)   A=-4.7
               K=INT(DIM(ABS(A),6.3))
               GO TO (5,8,12),K
          15 ......

    d)   R=17.
               L=IFIX(R)/5
               IF(R-8..LT.R/3) GO TO(3,6,9),L
          18 ......

    e)   ASSIGN 10 TO LVAR
               IF(2.NE.5/2) ASSIGN 5 TO LVAR
               GO TO LVAR,(10,5,11)
           1 ......

    f)   ASSIGN 4 TO J
               I=3*3/3*3
               IF(I.EQ.1) ASSIGN 16 TO J
               IF(I-2) 1,4,3
           3 GO TO J,(2,4,16)
           1 GO TO (5,12,17),I
          22 ......

5) Replace each of the following with an equivalent
    Computed GO TO.

   a)   Assume K is 1,2, or 3

          IF(K-2) 1,17,3

   b)   IF (LUMP.EQ.3) GO TO 7
          IF (LUMP.EQ.1) GO TO 7
          IF (LUMP.NE.2) GO TO 19
       7 ....

   c)   IF(I.GT.2) GO TO 12
          IF(I.LT.1) GO TO 12
          IF(I.NE.1) GO TO 8
       7 ......

6. Assume I has one of the values 1,2,3,97,98,99.   Write a
   sequence of WATFIV control statements which will cause
   control to be transferred to: statement 333 if I is
   either 1 or 99;   statement 444 if I is either 2 or 98;
   statement 555 if I is either 3 or 97.
   a) Using 1 Logical IF and 1 Arithmetic IF
   b) Using 1 Logical IF and 1 Computed GO TO
   c) Using 1 Assignment statement and 2 Logical IFs
   d) Using 1 Assignment statement and 1 Arithmetic IF
   e) Using 1 Assignment statement and 1 Computed GO TO

3.9 STOP, PAUSE and CONTINUE

The STOP Statement

    All the example programs used thus far have included a
STOP statement.   This instruction stops   any further
execution of instructions and causes the job statistics such
as compile time,   execution time and memory used to be
printed.   It is permissible to put a number after the word
STOP (eg: STOP 246).   This form of the STOP instruction
causes the number to be printed on the computer operator's
typewriter.   In most computer centers however, the presence
of a number following the word STOP is ignored by the WATFIV
compiler and hence no number is printed.   More than one STOP
instruction may be used in a program but the first one
encountered at execution time terminates the job.

* The PAUSE Statement

    A PAUSE statement causes a _temporary_ halt in the
execution of instructions. It is usually used to permit the
computer operator to perform some special task such as

putting special forms in the printer, or mounting a reel of tape on a tape drive. When the operator has completed the required task he presses a start button and processing resumes. In most installations a PAUSE statement is ignored by the compiler. In those cases where it is not ignored it may take one of the following three forms.

PAUSE   - no message or number is printed

PAUSE n   - where "n" is a number which is printed on the operator's typewriter

PAUSE 'message to operator' - the symbols between the quote signs are printed on the computer operator's typewriter

CONTINUE

A CONTINUE statement is, in one sense, an instruction which causes nothing to happen. Consider the following example.

```
X = 1
CONTINUE
PRINT,X
STOP
END
```

When used this way it simply means "carry on with the next instruction". It does have a very worthwhile purpose however when teamed up with the DO statement described in the next chapter.

3.10 Summary

1. Several means are available for programming algorithms in which different steps or substeps are to be executed depending on the value of an expression or the truth of a relationship. The IF-THEN-ELSE construct and the Logical IF statement are two of those most frequently used.

2. Program statements and constructs are executed in the order in which they are written unless the statement causes control to be transferred to some other statement in the program. QUIT and the simple GO TO are the most commonly used explicit control statements.

3.11 Programming Problems

3.1   Write a program which reads an INTEGER value and determines the number of non-zero digits in the number. Hint: Divide the number by 10, 100, 1000, etc. and add one to a counter if the quotient is non-zero.

3.2   Read a pair of INTEGER values M and N. Read a value of K. Determine if the last K digits in each number are the same. The output should appear as "LAST __ DIGITS OF ___ AND ___ ARE EQUAL (UNEQUAL)".

3.3   Read the lengths of the sides of a triangle. Print "0" if the lengths do not form a triangle; "1" if the sides are all unequal; "2" if the triangle is isosceles; "3" if the triangle is equilateral.

3.4   Temperatures in Fahrenheit (F) may be converted to Celcius (C) and vice-versa using the formulas:

$$F = \frac{9}{5} C + 32 \qquad\qquad C = \frac{5}{9} (F - 32)$$

Write a program which reads ten pairs of values punched one pair per card. The second value of each pair is a temperature in degrees. The first value is a "1" if conversion from Centigrade to Fahrenheit is required, a "2" if conversion from Fahrenheit to Centigrade is required. Print ten lines of the form "___ DEGREES F (C) EQUALS ___ DEGREES C (F)".

3.5   The value of the square root of a number may be calculated by starting with two estimates -- one high (H) and one low (L). A better estimate is then (H+L)/2. A check can be made of the new estimate to see if it is high or low. If high, it can be used as the new H value, if low, as the new L value. The process can then be repeated until any desired accuracy is obtained. Write a program which uses 3 and 4 as initial estimates of the square root of 12. Use the procedure above until the estimate differs from the true value (found using the SQRT function) by less than .01. Print the high and low estimates before each new estimate is calculated.

3.6   Read in any four non-negative INTEGER values. Call them I1, I2, I3, and I4. Replace them with the four values |I1-I2|, |I2-I3|, |I3-I4|, and |I4-I1|. If they are all equal, print the four values. If at least two of them are different, continue the process using the

replacement values as the starting values. Continue
until all four differences are equal. Print the values
of I1, I2, I3 and I4 at each stage of the calculations.

3.7   The day of the week for any date consisting of a year
      (Y), a month (M) and day (D) can be found using the
      following formula.

$$\text{weekday} = \text{MOD}(K, 7) + 1 \quad \text{where}$$

$$K = D + 2M + \frac{3M+3}{5} + Y + \frac{Y}{4} + \frac{Y}{100} + 1$$

All divisions in the formula are INTEGER divisions. To
use the formula, Jan. and Feb. of a year must be
considered as months 13 and 14 of the previous year. For
example, Jan. 26, 1980 should be considered as the 26th
day of the 13th month of 1979. In the formula, a value
of 1 for the weekday represents Monday, 2 a Tuesday,
etc.. Read several dates including your own birthday
and print the day of the week for each. Stop when the
year has a negative value.

3.8   Read the X-Y coordinates of three points. Determine if
      the third point and the origin lie on the same side of
      the line which goes thru the first two points. Print
      "YES" if they do and "NO" if they don't. Print the
      coordinates of the three points.

3.9   Modify programming problem 2.13 in the following way.
      Read values of X, n, i, and PER where: X is the amount
      of the loan; n is the number of payments; i is the
      annual interest rate; PER is the number of months
      between payments. Calculate the size of the payment made
      in each period using the given formula. Note that the
      interest rate for a period is related to the annual
      interest rate in the following way: (period rate + 1)**m
      = (annual rate +1) where "m" is the number of periods in
      a year.

3.10 For any twelve hour period, determine the times to the
      nearest minute when the minute hand is as far past six
      as the hour hand is away from six.

3.11 Consider any four digit number. Let K1, K2, K3 and K4
      be the values of the four digits in the number. Form a
      new number by adding the squares of the digit values.
      Repeat the process (find the digits, square and add)
      each time obtaining a new number. Write a program which

reads in a four digit number and generates new numbers
until either a value of one is found or until a value of
twenty is found for the second time. One of these events
will occur regardless of the number you start with!

3.12 Find the x which produces the largest value of y using
the formula $y=Ax+B$ when x is in the interval beween C
and D. Read the values of A, B, C and D from a card.

3.13 Find the value of x which produces the largest value
of y using the formula $y=Ax^2+Bx+C$ when x is in the
interval between D and E. Read the values of A, B, C, D
and E from a data card. Test your program using at least
the following three sets of values.

    a) A=-1, B=0, C=9, D=-4, E=4
    b) A=+1, B=-4, C=1, D=2, E=8
    c) A=-1, B=6, C=-2, D=-1, E=2

3.14 A rectangular room has a length, width and height of
L, W, and H respectively. The length of the room runs in
an East-West direction. An ant is located on the East
wall a distance AH above the floor and AN North of the
South wall.   The ant's food is stuck on the West wall a
distance FB below the ceiling and FS south of the North
wall. Write a program which reads values of L, W, H, AH,
AN, FB and FS and calculates the shortest distance the
ant must travel to reach its food.   Hints: The shortest
distance is a straight line which will include travel
along <u>one</u> of the ceiling, floor, South wall or North
wall. (Naturally parts of the East and West walls will
have to be covered as well.) To evaluate the lengths of
the four paths, pretend the room is made of cardboard
and "unfold" it in four different ways to see the four
paths. The length of each path can be calculated easily
using the Pythagorus Theorem.

3.15 A corridor three feet wide and seven feet high makes a
right-angled turn into another corridor having the same
dimensions (The corner is "L" shaped.). A plumber has a
long thin rigid pipe which he wants to take around the
corner.   a) What is the longest length of pipe which
will go around the corner? b) What is the narrowest
width of corridor which will permit an eight foot pipe
to go around? c) Do your answers to (a) and (b) change
if the corner is "T" shaped?   Write a program to answer
these questions.

3.16 Modify your program for question 3.15 so that it will
work if the corridors intersect at an angle of x

degrees.   Assume   x   is   the   acute   angle   at   the
intersection.   Answer questions   (a)   and   (b)   of   the
previous problem for values of x of 15, 30,   45,   60 and
75 degrees.

3.17 Brownsville, Jonesville and Smithville are located on
the   same   highway.   The distances   are   shown   in   the
following diagram.

Brownsville   Jonesville   Smithville

Assume   that   cars   travelling   from   Smithville   to
Brownsville leave Smithville at one minute intervals and
travel at a constant rate of 45 miles per hour. Suppose
you leave Jonesville heading for Smithville just as a
Ford is leaving Smithville heading for Brownsville. When
you reach Smithville, you immediately turn around and
head for Brownsville. a) At what constant rate must you
drive to reach Brownsville at the same time as the Ford?
b) How many cars do you pass on your trip? Include both
the cars you encounter on your trip to Smithville and
the cars you pass on you trip to Brownsville.

3.18 An airline operates planes which have first-class and
economy seats. If a customer approaches a ticket clerk,
the clerk asks which type of seat is wanted.   If that
type is available, a ticket is issued for that type.   If
not available, the customer is asked if the alternate
type of seat would be acceptable (provided one is
available).   If it is acceptable, a ticket of the
alternate type is issued. If it is not acceptable, no
ticket is issued.   Write a program which will print one
of the messages "ISSUE FIRST CLASS", "ISSUE ECONOMY", or
"DONT ISSUE TICKET" based on the rules above. Input to
the program consists of four INTEGER values punched on a
card. The variables to which these four values will be
assigned have (respectively) the following meanings.

        WANT =   1 if customer wants first-class
                 2 if customer wants economy

        ALTNAT = 1 if customer will take alternate type
                 0 if customer won't take alternate type

        FAVAIL = 1 if first-class seat is available
                 0 if first-class seat is not available

EAVAIL = 1 if economy seat is available
         0 if economy seat is not available

For example, a data card containing "2 1 0 1" means:
the customer wants an economy seat; he will take the
alternate type; no first class seat is available; an
economy seat is available. Therefore the message "ISSUE
ECONOMY TICKET" should be printed.

Test your program by reading sixteen different data
cards --   one for each of the sixteen possible
combinations of the four values. Print an appropriate
message after each card is read.

3.19 Write a program to print all integers in the range 100
   to 500 which have the property that the digits in the
   number are different.   Print the results 4 numbers per
   line.

3.20 A decision table is a method of describing rules for
   making decisions in a tabular form. Shown below is a
   simple decision table for deciding whether or not to get
   up in the morning.

| | | R U L E S | | | | |
		1	2	3	4	5
Conditions	Went to bed late	Y	Y	N	N	N
	Have a morning class			Y		N
	Test today	Y	N		Y	N
Actions	Get up	X		X	X	
	Stay in bed		X			X

The five decision rules in the   table show which of two
actions to take depending on three yes-no conditions.
The yes-no conditions are: Did you go to bed late?; Do
you have a morning class?; Do you have a test today?.
The five decision rules are defined by the entries in
the five columns of the table. Consider Rule (column) 1.
It says that if you went to bed late and if you have a
test today, then you should get up. In this rule, the
action you take is independent of whether or not you
have a morning class (There is no entry in Rule 1 for
the second condition).   Rule 5 says for example that if
all three conditions are negative, then sleep in.

   Suppose 5 data cards have been prepared each of
which contains three INTEGER values. The first value is

a 1 (meaning went to bed early) or a 0 (did not go to bed early); The second is a 1 (morning class) or a 0 (no morning class); the third is 1 (test today) or 0 (no test today). Write a program which reads the data and for each set prints messages describing the conditions which are represented and the action to be taken.

3.21 Write a program to reflect the logic described by the decsion table below. Choose a suitable form for representing the conditions as data values. After reading each data record and echoing the conditions, output a line of the form 'COMMISSION RATE IS __ PERCENT' or 'CASE SHOULD BE INVESTIGATED'.

			RULES		
Sales Commssion Table	1	2	3	4	5
Units sold < 100	Y		N	N	E
Units sold 100-199		Y	N	N	L
Units sold 200-299			Y	Y	S
With company more than 2 yrs			Y	N	E
Commision is 2% sales	X				
Commission is 3% of sales		X			
Commssion is 4% of sales			X		
Commssion is 5% of sales				X	
Investigate					X

CHAPTER 4   LOOPS AND LOOP CONTROL

Questions Answered In This Chapter

1. What is meant by loops and loop control?

2. What three methods are available for defining
   program-controlled loops easily?

4.1 Loops and Loop Control

In Chapter 1 it was suggested that many algorithms can
and should be written so that a single instruction or set of
instructions which must be repeated several times is written
only once. By doing this a great deal of flexibility is
usually added to the algorithm and the time to execute the
extra instructions associated with this approach is usually
insignificant compared to the saving in programming and
keypunching time realized.

A set of steps in an algorithm, (a set of statements in
a program), which is repeated several times in succession is
commonly called a processing loop.

If we are to use a computer to process more than one job
during its working life there must be a way to prevent a set
of instructions from being repeated an infinite number of
times. The means which is used to accomplish this is called
loop control. Loop control may be external to the program or
under program control.

External control refers to things such as: the operator
hits the "stop button"; the computer equipment breaks down;
or a timer reaches a certain limit. The study of this type
of loop control is not relevant to our purpose which is to
learn to use the WATFIV language.   Methods of internal loop
control, that is, methods in which the program decides it is
time to stop repeating a set of instructions are very
important to our purpose.

4.2 Program-Controlled Loops

In a program-controlled loop there exists a set of
instructions to be executed each time the loop is executed.
The decision to execute this set of instructions can be made
either before or after the execution of these instructions.
The two cases are shown below.

Case 1.   Decision Before   Case 2. Decision After

         (While ... do)   (DO until)

For many algorithms the program logic can be described
using either the decision first or the decision after logic.
In WATFIV the WHILE construct provides the decision first
logic and the DO-loop provides a form of the decision after
logic.   The WHILE construct is the more general because it
allows for the possibility that the loop instructions should
not be executed even once.   The WHILE construct which we
have used in all examples thus far is summarized in Section
4.3.   DO-loops are described in Sections 4.4 thru 4.5.

4.3 WHILE: A Summary

The WHILE construct involves four kinds of statements:

1. one or more statements to initialize the expression
   to be tested in the WHILE statement;

2. a WHILE statement containing the logical expression
   which is evaluated before each loop execution;

3. one or more statements to be executed when the
   logical expression is true (One of these must
   eventually cause the test expression to become
   false);

4. an END WHILE statement to define the end of the
   construct.

The simple example below contains one more than the minimum
possible number of statements.   Which one is unnecessary?

```
        N = 1
        WHILE(N .LE. 10)
           PRINT,N
           N = N + 1
        END WHILE
```

The form and rules of the WHILE construct are summarized below.

```
+-----------------------------------------------------------+
|                                                           |
|                      WHILE Construct                      |
|                                                           |
|                 WHILE (logical-expression)                |
|        range of     ( .                                   |
|          the        {  .    statement(s)                  |
|          block      ( .                                   |
|                 END WHILE                                 |
|                                                           |
|  Rules:                                                   |
|                                                           |
|    1.  If the logical-expression is  true,  statements    |
|        following the  WHILE statement  and preceding      |
|        the    END WHILE    statement    are    executed.  |
|        Control then returns to the WHILE statement.       |
|        If the   expression  is   false,   control   is    |
|        transferred  to the  statement following  the      |
|        END WHILE statement.                               |
|                                                           |
|    2.  The  WHILE  statement  cannot  be  the  trailer    |
|        statement in  a Logical  IF statement  or the      |
|        object statement in a DO-loop.                     |
|                                                           |
|    3.  The  END WHILE  statement is  a  non-executable    |
|        statement.                                         |
|                                                           |
|    4.  Transfers of control.                              |
|        Control  may  be transferred  to  a  statement     |
|            outside the range from  a statement inside     |
|            the range either by using  a QUIT statement    |
|            or a a GO TO statement.                        |
|        Control  may  be transferred  to  a  statement     |
|            inside the range from  a statement outside     |
|            the  range.    When  this  happens,   upon     |
|            reaching the END WHILE statement,  control     |
|            transfers to the WHILE statement.              |
|                                                           |
+-----------------------------------------------------------+
```

There is another type of WHILE statement called the WHILE-EXECUTE statement. Because it is only used in conjunction with REMOTE BLOCKs (described in Chapter 8) its use will be described at that time. A WHILE statement can also be terminated by an UNTIL statement. (The UNTIL statement is described in Section 4.7)

4.4 DO-Loops

Frequently one wishes to execute the instructions in a loop either a fixed number or a maximum number of times. Consider the following method for finding the square root of a number.

Suppose E is an estimate of the square root of a number X. (The number and the estimate can be any positive values.) Newton developed a formula which said, given X and E, an improved estimate of the square root can be obtained by calculating the value of:

$$E - \frac{E^2 - X}{2E}$$

Furthermore, if one repeats this calculation enough times, the sequence of improved estimates will converge to (become indefinitely close to) the value of the square root of X. If we let X be the number and let our initial estimate E be X/2., then the algorithm below could be used to find 10 improvements to our initial estimate.

```
1.    Get a value for X
2.    Set E=X/2.
3.    Repeat step 3.1 ten times
      .1  Get improved E using the formula
4.    Print the estimate
5.    Stop
```

To translate step 3 ("Repeat step 3.1 ten times") using a WHILE loop it is necessary to set up a counter which starts at 1 and goes up to 10 as is done below.

```
COUNT = 1
WHILE (COUNT .LE. 10)
   get improved estimate
   COUNT = COUNT + 1
END WHILE
```

The program below illustrates an alternative method which employs a DO-loop to control the loop repetitions.

```
C EXAMPLE 4.1  DO-LOOP EXAMPLE 1
      READ,X
      E = X/2.
C
      DO 88 I=1,10,1
         E = E - (E**2-X)/(2*E)
   88 CONTINUE
C
      PRINT,X,E
      STOP
      END
```

In the example the three statements

```
      DO 88 I=1,10,1
         E = E - (E**2-X)/(2*E)
   88 CONTINUE
```

constitute a <u>DO-loop</u>.   More specifically,   the   statement
"DO 88 I=1,10,1" says:

>   "Do all statements down to and including statement 88
>   as many times as would happen using a counter I
>   which starts at 1 and goes up to 10 in steps of 1."

Thus the Assignment and CONTINUE statements (the <u>range</u> of
the DO-loop in this example) are executed 10 times.

    The CONTINUE statement in this DO-loop serves a purpose
similar to an END WHILE statement.   However a CONTINUE
statement is an executable statement whereas an END WHILE
statement is not.   (A CONTINUE can be used on its own in
which case it simply means   "carry on with the next
instruction".)   Although   not   necessary,   it   is   good
programming practice to make the last statement in the range
of a DO-loop a CONTINUE statement.   (The statement whose
statement number appears in the DO statement should be a
CONTINUE statement.)

    What values are printed by executing the following DO-
loop?

```
      DO 756 N=4,24,5
         PRINT,N
  756 CONTINUE
```

The values 4,9,14,19 and 24 will be displayed.   The two
statements in the range of the DO-loop (PRINT,N and
CONTINUE) are executed for values of N starting at 4 and
going up to 24 in steps of 5.

Consider the statement:

DO 17 I=1,10,1

This DO statement contains the five items of information necessary to control the number of repetitions of a loop. These are:

i) The number of the last statement in the set of instructions to be repeated. This statement is called the <u>object</u> of the DO. In the example above the object of the DO is statement 17. The set of statements which are being repeated is called the <u>range</u> of the DO.

ii) The name of the counter -- called the <u>index</u> of the DO. In the example the DO index is the variable I.

iii) The three values which are used to initialize, increment and test the counter are called the <u>parameters</u> of the DO. The names given to these parameters are:

a) The <u>initial value</u>: the starting value of the counter

b) The <u>increment</u>: the value added to the counter <u>after</u> each repetition

c) The <u>test value</u>: the value to which the counter is compared after the addition of the increment

The general form of a DO-loop is shown below.

DO s index=initial,test,increment

range
of the   .
DO   .
            .
s ... (object statement)

A four-step algorithm is defined by every DO statement.

1. Set the index = initial value.
2. Execute the statements in the range of the loop.
3. Add the increment to the current value of the index.
4. If the index is less than or equal to the test value go to step 2.

Note that the decision to repeat the loop is made after the
loop instructions have been executed.

    Each of the three DO statements below has an   error.
Why?

```
        DO 99 I=10,1,-1
        DO 426 COUNT=5,15,2
        DO 81 J=1,2*K,3
```

The first is not permitted   because the increment is
negative.   All three DO-loop parameters (the initial value,
the test value and the increment) must have <u>positive</u> INTEGER
values (be positive-valued variables or constants).   The
second is unacceptable because the DO-loop index COUNT is a
REAL variable (unless of course it had been declared as an
INTEGER variable).   The DO-loop index -- the variable which
assumes the role of a counter -- can only be an INTEGER
variable.   The third DO statement is invalid because an
expression such as 2*K cannot be used to specify any of the
DO-loop parameters.   Parameters must be positive INTEGER
constants or INTEGER variables having positive values.

    There are still several unanswered questions about DO-
loops including: Can the DO-loop index and/or parameters be
used and changed within the loop?   How about outside the
loop?   Can you exit from a DO-loop before completing all
repetitions of the loop?   Can you jump into the middle of a
loop without executing the DO statement?   Answers to these
and other questions are found in the examples below.   A
complete summary of DO-loop rules is found at the end of the
chapter.

<u>Example 2 Using the DO-loop Index and Parameters</u>

    A problem.   Read a pair of INTEGER values called LOW and
HIGH (Assume both are positive).   Calculate HIGH*(V-LOW) for
each value V in the range LOW thru HIGH.   A suitable program
is the following.

```
        C EXAMPLE 4.2  DO-LOOP EXAMPLE 2
                INTEGER V,HIGH
                READ,LOW,HIGH
                DO 53 V=LOW,HIGH
                    PRINT,V,HIGH*(V-LOW)
            53 CONTINUE
                STOP
                END
```

Some comments.   It is necessary to declare V and HIGH as
being INTEGER variables because the DO-loop index and

parameters must be INTEGER-valued. Secondly, the third DO statement parameter, the increment, has been omitted and by default is assumed to be 1. Third, it is permissible to use the index and parameters in arithmetic expressions.

What if the value of HIGH was less than LOW? Because the statements in the loop are executed once before the increment is added and the test made, the PRINT instruction would be executed once with V having a value of LOW. There would be no further repetitions because V+1 would be greater than HIGH.

One further point. Although the index and parameter values can be used in expressions in the range of the loop they cannot be <u>changed</u> by any statement within the loop. An attempt to assign V a value for example, would produce an execution-time error.

Example 3 Transfers out of a DO-loop

Suppose you want to calculate the value of

$$1/(5x^3 - x^2 + 4x - 7)$$

for x = 1., ..5, 2., 2.5, ..., 10. If any of the values make the division undefined, exit form the loop and display the x-value. The program below solves the problem.

```
C EXAMPLE 4.3  DO-LOOP EXAMPLE 3
      DO 77 I=2,20
         X = I/2.
         Y = 5.*X**3 - X**2 + 4.*X - 7.
         IF (Y .EQ. 0) GO TO 88
         PRINT,X,1./Y
   77 CONTINUE
      STOP
   88 PRINT,'UNDEFINED FOR',I/2
      STOP
      END
```

Note that the x-values are obtained easily by using a DO-loop index which is double the x-value wanted at each iteration. This satisfies the requirement that the DO-loop index be an INTEGER variable. Exercise 4.1 #5 gives you practice in creating DO-loops to generate given sequences of numbers.

If the division is undefined, "GO TO 88" is executed. That is, control transfers to a statement outside the loop from one inside the range of the DO-loop. This is perfectly

permissible.   When this happens the value of the index
variable outside the loop is that at the time of exit.   Thus
I/2. in the second PRINT statement is the value causing the
division to be undefined. If, however, control transfers to
the   statement following   the object   statement because   all
repetitions of the loop have been completed, (that is, the
loop has been satisfied), the value of the index variable is
"uncertain" -- its value cannot be stated with certainty and
therefore should not be used in expressions.

Transfers into the range of DO-loop are   not permitted
except by executing the DO statement itself.   For example,
the following program structure is invalid.

```
        DO 47 I=1,10
                 .
     2    X = ...
                 .
    47 CONTINUE
           .
           .
        GO TO 2
           .
```

With the proper use of IF-THEN-ELSEs most transfers of
control into and out of DO-loops can be avoided.   For
example, a better program than the one used in Example 4.3
above is the following.

```
        C EXAMPLE 4.3B
              DO 77 I=2,20
                 X=I/2.
                 Y = 5.*X**2 - X**2 + 4.*X - 7.
                 IF (Y .EQ. 0) THEN
                     PRINT,'UNDEFINED FOR',X
                     STOP
                 ELSE
                     PRINT,X,1./Y
                 END IF
           77 CONTINUE
              STOP
              END
```

Number of Repetitions of a DO-loop

The maximum number of repetitions of a DO-loop is easy
to determine once the values of the parameters are known.
Shown below are several examples. Each reflects   the fact
that the loop is always executed once and that the test for
a $\leq$ condition is made after the increment has been added.

DO Statement	Maximum # of Repetitions
DO 22 I=14,1	1
DO 835 KJR=2,17,5	4
DO 835 KJR=2,18,5	4
DO 3 LEO=1,99,4	25

4.5 Summary Of DO-Loop Rules

1. General Form.

$$\text{range of} \atop \text{the DO} \left\{ \begin{array}{l} \text{DO s index = initial,test,increment} \\ . \\ . \\ . \\ \text{s object statement} \end{array} \right.$$

a) "s" must be the number of an executable statement which cannot be a DO, simple GO TO, Computed GO TO, Assigned GO TO, Arithmetic IF, STOP or PAUSE.

b) The index must be a simple INTEGER variable.

c) The parameters must have positive INTEGER values. They can be either constants or simple INTEGER variables.

d) If the increment is omitted it is assumed to be 1.

e) The index and the parameter values cannot be changed by any statement inside the range of the DO.

2. Transfers of Control.

a) Control cannot pass to a statement within the range of the DO from a statement outside the range of the DO except via the DO statement itself.

b) Control may pass from any statement inside the range of the DO to any statement outside the range of the DO using either a QUIT statement or a GO TO statement. When this happens:

i) If the transfer is from any statement other than the object statement, the value of the index is known outside the range and equals the value of the index at the time the transfer occurred.

ii) If the transfer occurs because the specified

number of repetitions have been completed,
the value of the index is uncertain.

3. Maximum number of Executions of the Object Statement.

a) If the test value is less than the initial value the
object statement will be executed once.

b) If the test value is equal or greater than than the
initial value the object statement will be executed

$$1 + \frac{test - initial}{increment}$$

times where the division above ignores any remainder.

Exercise 4.1

Assume all variables are typed by default.

1. What are the five items of information present in any DO
statement?

2. State in words what is meant by the statement:

DO 89 J=11,45,2

3. For loops defined by the following DO statements,
determine the maximum number of repetitions of the object
statement.

a) DO 5 I=2,5
b) DO 6 J=14,98,14
c) DO 7 K=9,7,2
d) DO 8 LOOP=1,1,1
e) DO 9 MAXO=100,203,50

4. Each of the following statements or sequences contains an
error. What is it?

a) DO 10, KK=1,10
b) DO 12 J=10,1,-1
c) DO MAX=3,30,2
d) DO 99999 MINIMUM=12,2
e) DO 44 N=2,N
f) DO 585 KLM=6,K*2-1,1
g) DO 871 X=1,80,90

```
h)        DO 36 I=1,12,2
             ....
             IF(...) I=I+1
             ...
     36 CONTINUE

i)        DO 583 MAT=12,143,12
     17      CONTINUE
             ....
    583 GO TO 17
```

5. In many programs, the requirement that the DO-loop parameters have positive INTEGER values means that it is necessary to employ a formula which transforms the index value to one of the desired values. For example to calculate the sum of the values 2.5,4.5,6.5,...,32.5, one could write:

```
   SUM=0.                          SUM=0.
   DO 10 I=2,32,2                   DO 10 I=1,16
      X=FLOAT(I)+.5     or             X=2.*FLOAT(I)+.5
      SUM=SUM+X                        SUM=SUM+X
10 CONTINUE                       10 CONTINUE
```

In each of the following, write one DO statement and an Assignment statement to convert the successive index values to those shown.

```
a) 10., 20., 30.,...,180.
b) .25, .50, .75,..., 2.75, 3.0
c) 10, 9, 8, ...,1
d) -5,-4,-3,...,3,4,5
e) 5,4,3,...,-3,-4,-5
f) 0,1,2,0,1,2,0,1,2,0,1,2  (Hint: use the MOD function)
g) 1,2,3,4,1,2,3,4,1,2,3,4,1,2,3,4
h) -5,-4,-3,-2,-1,-5,-4,-3,-2,-1
i) 10.,6.,2.,-2.,10.,6.,2.,-2.
j) 101,202,303,404,...,1010
```

6. In the program below, how many times will the value of K be printed?

```
               K=10
               DO 1 I=1,30,2
                  PRINT,K
                  IF(MOD(I,5).EQ.0) PRINT,K
                  IF(I/3*3-I) 4,1,1
          4       PRINT,K
          1 CONTINUE
               STOP
```

7. Can you think of any worthwhile purpose for including either of the following in a program?

    a) DO 1 J=1,1,1   b)   DO 17 LUMP=1,100
                                17 CONTINUE

8. What values are printed by the following statements?

```
            NUM=0
          2 DO 5 I=1,100
               NUM=NUM+1
               IF(NUM/20-2 .EQ. 0) GO TO 2
               IF(NUM/20-2 .GT. 0) GO TO 4
          5 CONTINUE
          4 PRINT,I
            STOP
```

4.6 Nested Loops

Here's a problem. Compute the value of the expression:

$$z = \frac{x^2 - 2xy + y^2}{(x + 4)(y + 20)}$$

for x = 1,2,3,4,5 and with each of these x values use y values of 30,28,26,...,4. A suitable algorithm follows.

    1. For x = 1,2,3,4,5 do
     .1   For y = 30,28,26,...4 do
              .1   calculate z
              .2   print z
    2. Stop

The program below is a translation of the algorithm.

```
   C EXAMPLE 4.4  NESTED DO-LOOPS
         DO 20 I=1,5
            X = I
            DO 10 J=4,30,2
               Y = 34. - J
               TOP=(X**2-2.*X*Y+Y**2)
               BOT=(X+4.)*(Y+20.)
               Z = TOP/BOT
               PRINT,X,Y,Z
      10      CONTINUE
      20 CONTINUE
         STOP
         END
```

This program contains a pair of <u>nested DO-loops</u>. The J-loop as defined by "DO 10 J=4,30,2" is called the <u>inner</u> loop and the loop which has I as an index is called the <u>outer</u> loop. The structure of a pair of nested loops is shown below. The purpose of using such an arrangement is to repeat a set of instructions as part of a larger set of instructions which are themselves being repeated under loop control.

```
                              DO 20 I=__,__,__
                                .
                                DO 10 J=__,__,__
   outer    inner               .
   loop     loop                .
                           10        CONTINUE
                                .
                           20 CONTINUE
```

The two DO-loops above end on different CONTINUE statements. It is acceptable however for outer and inner DO-loops to have the same object statement. Since this usually makes the program structure more difficult to see, the practice of using separate CONTINUE statements is recommended.

Now, suppose the denominator in the expression for z was changed to (x-4)(y-20) so that the division is undefined for x=4 and for y=20. If the message "Z UNDEFINED" is to be printed when either of these values occur the algorithm would have to be modified to check for x=4 in the outer loop and y=20 in the inner loop.

```
      C EXAMPLE 4.5  NESTED DO-LOOPS WITH EXITS
            DO 20 I=1,5
            X = I
            IF (X .EQ. 4.) THEN
               PRINT, 'Z UNDEFINED'
            ELSE
               DO 10 J=4,30,2
               Y = 34. - J
               IF (Y .EQ. 20) THEN
                  PRINT,'Z UNDEFINED'
               ELSE
                  TOP=(X**2-2.*X*Y+Y**2)
                  BOT=(X-4.)*(Y-20.)
                  PRINT,X,Y,TOP/BOT
               END IF
      10        CONTINUE
            END IF
      20 CONTINUE
            STOP
            END
```

In WATFIV there is no limit to the number of loops which can be nested one within the other except that no program may have more than 255 DO-loops in total.

The rule that transfers must not be made into the range of a DO-loop from outside the loop means that DO-loops cannot be overlapped in the manner shown below.

```
          DO 7 I=__,__,__
             .
          DO 12 J=__,__,__
             .
       7 CONTINUE
             .
       12   CONTINUE
```

Exercise 4.2

Assume all variables are typed by default.

1. For each of the following determine the values which are printed when the program is executed.

```
a)    X=5.7E-1                 b)   X=-.0023E04
      DO 6 I=1,10                   DO 7 J=10,100,10
        DO 5 J=4,8,2                  IF(J.EQ.50) PRINT,X
          PRINT,X                     DO 6 K=1,3
      5   CONTINUE                      PRINT,X
      6 CONTINUE                   6   CONTINUE
                                   7 CONTINUE
```

```
c)    YZ=AINT(SQRT(2.))         d)     DO 5 K=1,4
      PRINT,YZ                          N=K+1
      DO 11 M1234=1,5                   DO 3 L=K,10,N
        PRINT,YZ                          PRINT,L
        DO 2 N1234=1,4                    M=K*L+20
          PRINT,YZ              3      CONTINUE
      2   CONTINUE                     PRINT,M
        XZ=FLOAT(M1234)          5 CONTINUE
        PRINT,XZ
      11 CONTINUE
```

2. The sequence of statements below shows an infinite loop. What is the sequence of numbers which will be printed over and over again if the statements are executed?

```
      1 DO 88 I=1,7
          IF(MOD(I,2).EQ.0) GO TO 3
          PRINT,I
      3     DO 77 J=5,25,5
              IF(J.EQ.IFIX(SQRT(FLOAT(J)*I))) GO TO 1
              PRINT,J
     77     CONTINUE
     88 CONTINUE
```

3. In the program below suppose that the time between
   successive executions of statement 15 is .001 seconds.
   a) How long does it take to execute the program?
   b) Why should .001 be regarded as an <u>average</u> time
      between executions of statement 15?

```
             DO 15 I=1,1000
              DO 15 J=1,60
               DO 15 K=1,60
                DO 15 L=1,24
                 DO 15 M=1,365
                  N=1
          15 CONTINUE
```

4. Explain the error in each of the following.

   a)   DO 1 I=1,10
                 ...
                 DO 2 J=3,8
                 ...
              1 CONTINUE
              2 CONTINUE

   b)   DO 3 I=17,12,3
                   IF(I.EQ.17) GO TO 3
                   DO 3 J=6,24,6
                 ...
              3 CONTINUE

   c)   DO 12 K=1,5
                 ...
             10   CONTINUE
                 DO 2 J=1,4
                   IF(...) GO TO 10
             17   CONTINUE
                 ...
                   IF(A.NE.B) A=B
              2   CONTINUE
                 ...
                 GO TO 17
             12 CONTINUE
```
```

5. Suppose each of the sequences of values given are
   required in some program. Write a pair of DO statements
   and one or more Assignment statements to print the
   sequence of values indicated in each case. For example:
   To print the sequence 2.,4.,6.,8.,2.,4.,6.,8., one could
   write:

```
            DO 2 I=1,2
                DO 1 J=2,8,2
                    X=FLOAT(J)
                    PRINT,X
         1      CONTINUE
         2 CONTINUE
```

   a) 2,3,4,5,6, 4,5,6,7,8
   b) 1,2,3,4,10,20,30,40,100,200,300,400
   c) 35,34,33,32,31,15,14,13,12,11,-5,-6,-7,-8,-9
   d) 0,-1,-2,0,-1,-2,0,-1,-2,0,-1,-2
   e) 1.25,1.50,1.75,3.25,3.50,3.75,5.25,5.50,5.75
   f) -.125,-1.375,-2.625,-3.875
   g) 1001,101,11,2002,202,22,3003,303,33
   h) 1,1,1,0,0,3,3,3,0,0,5,5,5,0,0
   i) 1,-30,+500,-7000,+90000,-1100000
   j) 1,1,2,1,2,3,1,2,3,4,...,1,2,3,4,5,6,7,8,9,10
   k) 10;10,9;10,9,8;...;10,9,8,...3,2,1
   l) 1,2,3,4,5,6,7,1,3,5,7,1,4,7
   m) 90;81,80;72,71,70;63,62,61,60;...;9,8,7,...,2,1,0

*4.7 The LOOP Construct

   The WATFIV compiler recognizes a third construct for
loop control (the others being the WHILE construct and the
DO-loop). The LOOP-END LOOP construct is not part of
standard Fortran. It is used only in this section.

   The LOOP construct defines a sequence of one or more
statements which are to be executed over and over. For
example, to print the value 1234 an infinite number of times
(in theory at least), the LOOP construct below could be
used.

```
            LOOP
                PRINT, 1234
            END LOOP
```

   A QUIT or GO TO statement is used to exit from a LOOP
construct. Shown below are two equivalent programs, each of
which prints the values from 1 thru 10.

```
C   USING A WHILE                    C   USING LOOP-END LOOP
    I=1                                  I=1
    WHILE(I.LE.10)                       LOOP
      PRINT,I                              PRINT,I
      I=I+1                                IF(I.LE.10)  QUIT
    END WHILE                            END LOOP
    STOP                                 STOP
    END                                  END
```

Using the WHILE construct, the decision to continue repetitions is made at the beginning of the loop. With the LOOP construct, the decision to exit from the construct can be made anywhere within the loop. This is its most significant advantage. As with other constructs, LOOPs may include and/or be nested within other constructs.

*The UNTIL Statement

The end of the LOOP and WHILE constructs can be defined by an UNTIL statement rather than an END WHILE or END LOOP statement respectively. Each of the programs below prints the values from 1 thru 10.

```
C   USING WHILE-UNTIL              C   USING LOOP-UNTIL
    I=1                                I=1
    WHILE(I.LE.10)                     LOOP
      PRINT,I                            PRINT,I
      I=I+1                              I=I+1
    UNTIL(I.GT.10)                     UNTIL(I.GT.10)
    STOP                               STOP
    END                                END
```

In both examples the UNTIL statement specifies a condition for repeating the loop. If an UNTIL statement is used with a WHILE construct, two different logical expressions can be evaluated in making the repetition decision -- one in the WHILE statement and one in the UNTIL statement. That is, a sequence of statements could be executed " as long as condition ____ is true or until condition ___ is true". Whether or not this is an advantage is a debatable point.

The UNTIL statement has the general form

UNTIL (logical expression)

It is an executable statement which can only be used to define the end of a WHILE or LOOP construct. It is not part of standard Fortran and is not used in examples in the remainder of the book.

4.8 Summary

1. Many algorithms, and hence programs, contain sequences of instructions which must be executed more than once in order to solve the problem. The method used to control the number of repetitions can either be external to the program or under program control.

2. Three powerful methods of defining program controlled loops are available to the WATFIV programmer. The WHILE construct is very flexible. With it the decision to execute the loop is placed at the beginning of the loop. A DO-loop can also be used and is particularly convenient when an INTEGER-valued counter is associated with the loop repetitions. In the case of a DO-loop, the decision to repeat is made following each execution of the loop instructions. The LOOP construct allows the decision to exit from the construct to be made at any point in the construct.

4.9 Programming Problems

4.1 Tabulate values of the function $(X^2-X+7)/(X^2+2)$ for the values of x below. Use DO-loops to generate the x-values.

   a) 1, 2, 3, ..., 20
   b) 3, 6, 9, ..., 24
   c) 0, -1, -2, ..., -8
   d) 12, 10, 8, ..., -10

4.2 Tabulate values of the function

$$y = \frac{3\sin^3 x + 4\cos^3 x}{16x^2 + 8x - 3}$$

   for $x = -1, -3/4, -1/2, ... 3/4, 1$. Skip over values of x which make the division undefined.

4.3 If x_0 is an initial estimate of the value of $1/\sqrt{X}$, successively better estimates are given by x_1, x_2, etc. where $x_n = .5x_{n-1}(3-Xx^2_{n-1})$, n=1,2,... . Use this procedure in a program to calculate the fifth estimate of $1/\sqrt{2}$. Use .4 as your initial estimate. Print each estimate.

4.4 Suppose division could not be done on a computer. One method of obtaining increasingly accurate approximations to a value of $1/A$ is to calculate x_0, x_1, x_2, etc. where x is some initial estimate of the reciprocal and the value $x_n = x_{n-1} (2 - A x_{n-1})$, $n=1,2,3,\ldots$. Write a program which calculates the tenth approximation to a value of $1/3$ (i.e: A=3) using the method described above. Use .3 as your initial estimate.

4.5   The sum of cubes of the numbers one thru N is equal to the square of the sum of the numbers one thru N. For example, $1^3 + 2^3 + 3^3 = (1+2+3)^2$. Suppose you want to use this fact to find an approximate value of the square root of the number K. This could be done in the following way. Find M such that the sum of cubes of the numbers one thru M is less than K and the sum of cubes of the numbers 1 thru (M+1) is greater than K. (If by chance the sum of cubes equals K, the square root is exactly $1+2+3+\ldots+M$.) Conclude that the square root of K lies somewhere between the sum of the values 1 thru M and the sum of the values 1 thru M+1. Write a program which reads a value of K and computes an approximate square root using this method. Accuracy can be improved by multiplying K by an even power of ten and dividing the result by one-half the power of ten used. For example, to find the square root of 12.357, use 123570 as the value of K and divide the result by 100.

4.6   The sequence of numbers 1, 1, 2, 3, 5, 8, 13, ... is called the Fibonacci sequence. Each term in the sequence except the first two (which are each equal to one) is obtained by adding the previous two terms. Write a program which reads a value of N and prints the first N terms of the sequence on separate lines. Between each value printed, print the ratio of the current term to the previous term. What is apparently true about these ratios as the terms become larger?

4.7   The probability that no two people in a group of N people have the same birthday is given by the formula

$$P_n = P_{n-1} \left(1 - \frac{N-1}{365}\right) \qquad \text{where } P = 1$$

Use this formula in a program which determines the smallest number of people such that the probability of no matching birthdays is less than one-half. Assume the result occurs for N less than fifty. Use a DO statement in generating the values of P_2, P_3, ... Compare each value to one-half to determine if it is necessary to exit from the DO-loop.

4.8   At a party of N couples, the men pull a lady's name
      out of a hat to see who their partner will be for the
      next activity. The chance that no man draws his wife's
      name can be obtained from the following relationship.

$$P_n = \frac{n-1}{n} P_{n-1} + \frac{1}{n} P_{n-2} \qquad \text{where } P_1 = 0, \text{ and } P_2 = .5$$

      Read a value of N and calulate the probability that no
      man draws his wife's name for groups of people of 1, 2,
      3, ..., N.

4.9   A family of functions of x; $F_1(x)$, $F_2(x)$, $F_3(x)$, ...
      is defined by the following relationships.

$$F_1(x) = 1, \quad F_2(x) = x, \quad F_n(x) = \frac{2n-1}{n} F_{n-1}(x) - \frac{n-1}{n} F_{n-2}(x)$$

      where n = 2, 3, 4, ...

      Write a program which reads a value of x and calculates
      the first ten functions of x as defined above.

4.10 Read a value of N. Assume N is ten or less. Print out
      all triples of positive integer values which add up to
      N. Print out all triples of non-negative integer values
      which add up to N.

4.11 Tabulate values of the function

$$z = \frac{x^2 - 2xy + 3y^2}{xy + 3x + 2y + 4}$$

      using all pairs of x and y values in the ranges
      x=1,2,3,...,6; y=1,2,3,4,5. Use a pair of nested DO-
      loops to generate the x and y values.

4.12 Read a value of K. Assume K is six or less. Print the
      values of MOD(K,M+N), MOD(K,M*N) and MOD(K,M**N) where M
      and N can take any values in the set 1,2,3,...,(K-1).

4.13 Suppose computers could only multiply and divide by
      two. (In fact, this isn't far from the truth!) The
      product of any two numbers M and N can still be done
      using the "Russian" method of multiplication. It
      consists of successively dividing the smaller number by
      two (ignoring any remainder) and successively
      multiplying the larger value by two. As this process is

being carried out, add to a total only those multiples
of the larger value for which the division of the
smaller produced an odd quotient. For example, to
multiply 37 by 65 the following results would be
obtained.

```
      37              65
      18             130 (not added to total)
       9             260
       4             520 (not added to total)
       2            1040 (not added to total)
       1            2080
                    ----
                    2405 (the total)
```

If you don't believe it, what is 37 times 65? Write a
program which reads a pair of values and calculates
their product using the above technique.

Questions Answered In This Chapter

1. How does a program answer the three questions associated with any input operation? These are:

Where (on what device) are the values recorded?
What variables are to be assigned values?
How are the values recorded on the input medium?

2. What is meant by the terms "format-free input" and "formatted input"?

As we already know, there are two ways of assigning values to variables used in a WATFIV program -- by using an Assignment statement and by using a READ statement. This chapter describes a different form of the READ statement from the one previously discussed. It permits you, the programmer, to completely control the input values to be assigned to variables used in a program.

5.1 Input - The Three Questions

i) Where are the values recorded?

The most frequently used medium for recording values to be assigned to variables has been the punched card. A card reader is a device whose sole function is to send electrical signals to the memory of the computer describing the hole patterns punched in the card. Almost all computers have other devices which can also be used to input values to the computer memory. Typewriters, magnetic tape drives, magnetic disk drives, and "light pens" are examples of other input devices. More and more programs and data are being typed in directly or on-line using a cathode ray tube display device with an attached keyboard. In this chapter, however, we shall always assume the input device is a card reader and hence the answer to the question "Where are the values recorded?" is "On punched cards in the card reader.".

ii) How are the values recorded on the cards?

A card has eighty columns and one symbol can be punched in each column. Since values can be punched anywhere in a card, it is necessary to know which columns contain the value to be assigned to each variable. Furthermore, if the values contain decimal points and/or exponents as may be the case for REAL values, it is necessary to provide information as to the position of the decimal point and/or the value of the exponent. As will be seen, this "how" information can either be punched on the card or provided by the program.

iii) What variables are to be assigned values?

The answer to this question depends entirely on the requirements of the program. The READ statement will contain a list of variables to be assigned values.

The purpose of this section is to describe how these questions are answered when programming in the WATFIV language. There are two methods for reading values punched on cards. The methods are called <u>format-free</u> input and <u>formatted</u> input. The essential difference is that when using format-free input, the programmer leaves it up to the WATFIV processor to determine how the values have been punched on the cards. In examples used in the book thus far, the READ statement has been of the format-free type. The WATFIV routines have been responsible for deciding what columns were used to punch the values. Under formatted input, the programmer provides this information by using an extra statement called a FORMAT statement to describe how the values have been punched in the cards.

Regardless of which type of method is used, there is the option of:

a) Explicitly naming the input device to be the card reader.

b) Providing the number of a statement in the program to which control will be transferred if you attempt to read a card and there aren't any more.

The available alternatives are as follows.

Forms Of The READ Statement

	Format-Free Input	Formatted Input
Input device assumed to be card reader	READ,input list	READ #,input list # FORMAT (how info)

Input device named as being card reader	READ(5,*) list	READ (5,#) list # FORMAT(how infor)
"Out of cards" action specified	a) READ(5,*,END=n) list	a) READ(5,#,END=n)list # FORMAT(how info)

	b)
	READ,input list
	  AT END
	   .
	   .
	  END AT END
		b)
		READ #,input list
		  AT END
		   .
		   .
		  END AT END
		# FORMAT(how info)

	c)
	READ(5,*) list
	  AT END
	   .
	   .
	  END AT END
		c)
		READ(5,#) list
		  AT END
		   .
		   .
		  END AT END
		# FORMAT(how info)

The statement in the upper left hand corner of the table is the only type of READ statement which has been discussed until now. Before looking at some examples, observe that the thing that is common to all ten cases is the input list. An input list is simply a list of variables, separated by commas, which defines the variables to be assigned values by executing the READ statement. Expressions such as I+J are not permitted in an input list since it would not be known how much of the input value is to be assigned to I and how much to J.

5.2 Format-Free Input

(a) READ,input_list

The discussion of this form of the READ statement is essentially a review of the ideas presented in Chapter 2, Section 6. When using this form of the READ statement, the values to be assigned to the variables in the list are punched one or more per card. The values can be separated by commas and/or one or more blank columns. The WATFIV program scans each card looking for numbers punched in the card. As each value is located, it is assigned to the next variable in the input list. The WATFIV program reads as many data

cards as is necessary to "satisfy" the input list. Once a
data value has been assigned to each variable in the input
list, any excess values punched on the last data card read
are ignored. The examples below illustrate this and other
ideas. Assume all variables are typed by the first-letter
rule.

    i)   READ,I,JOHN,KRUMB
   $ENTRY
      2,   2345
    -17

   Result: I=2, JOHN=2345, KRUMB=-17

  ii)   READ,X,Y,LAUGH,Z
  $ENTRY
  245E+04
      -000325.-7
  123456 -81

 Result: X=2450000, Y=-.0000325, LAUGH=123456, Z=-81.

    Observe that when punching REAL values, it is not
necessary to punch a decimal point or an "E" (if an
exponent is used). The decimal point is assumed to
follow the last digit of the number. The exponent value
is taken from the digits following the "+" or "-" sign.
If you should happen to punch more than seven digits for
a REAL value, the number is rounded as well as possible
to seven significant digits. If an INTEGER value exceeds
the allowed limit or if an exponent is outside the
permitted range, an error occurs.

iii)   READ,I,A,B
  $ENTRY
  -17 , -2.0E4
      +6.5,3.1

Result: I=-17, A=-20000., B=6.5, the value 3.1 is unused

   One feature of format-free READ statements which is
infrequently used permits you to put a repetition factor in
front of a data value. The following example illustrates
how.

       READ,I,J,A,B,C
  $ENTRY
  2*0, 3*4.96

  Result: I=0,J=0, A=4.96, B=4.96, C=4.96

If an INTEGER constant and a "*" appear in front of a data
value when it is read in using a format-free READ statement,
the effect is to repeat the data value the number of times
specified   by   the   constant   appearing   in   front   of   the
asterisk.   If a large number of variables in an input list
are to be assigned the same value, this feature can save
some keypunching time.

(b) READ(5,*) list

In this type of format-free READ statement, the number 5
is used to specify the card reader as the input device.   The
asterisk indicates format-free.   In WATFIV, all input-output
devices attached to the computer are given a number. In many
computer centers the   number 5 is used to   identify the card
reader.   If it is different from 5, you simply change the
number in the READ statement to its appropriate value.   The
device number can also be assigned to an INTEGER variable.
For example, the pair of statements:

        INPUT=5
        READ(INPUT,*) input list

is equivalent to the single statement:

        READ(5,*) input list

Note that when using this form of the format-free READ
statement, there is no comma preceding the first element of
the input list.   The symbols "(5,*)" replace the comma.

It is only natural to ask why one would want to use this
type of READ statement. There are two situations when it may
be appropriate. First, you may be testing a program which
will eventually use some input device other than the card
reader. Once the program has been tested using the card
reader for input, the device number can be changed to its
appropriate value. Secondly, perhaps the READ statement will
be converted to a formatted READ after the testing phase. To
make this change it is simply a matter of replacing the "*"
with the   number of an appropriate   FORMAT statement.
(Formatted input is discussed in the next section.)

(c) Reading an unknown number of data cards

In many programs the number of data values to be read is
not known in advance. Under these circumstances, there are
two common ways of providing this information.

i) The first data card contains a value indicating how many data cards or values are to be read.

ii) The last data value is some special number such as 999999. Each value read is compared to this value and when an equal condition is found, no more values are read.

An alternate way of reading an unknown number of values is simply to keep on reading values until there are no more cards to be read.

In WATFIV there are two methods of specifying an out-of-cards action. The first and recommended method uses the AT END statement or the AT END construct; the second uses the optional "END=" parameter in a READ statement.

AT END Statement and Construct

Suppose we want to read and print the values of an unknown number of REAL values punched one value per card. Program 5.1 below uses the AT END statement to turn on a switch indicating that no more data values are present.

```
C EXAMPLE 5.1 USE OF AT END
      INTEGER DATA
      DATA=1
      READ, X
        AT END, DATA=0
      WHILE ( DATA.EQ.1)
        PRINT, X
        READ, X
          AT END, DATA=0
      END WHILE
      STOP
      END
```

In this program the value of the INTEGER variable DATA is used to indicate the presence or absence of data. Each time an attempt is made to execute the READ statement, the statement "AT END, DATA=0" is ignored unless there is no data. If the input file is empty (no data exists), the trailer statement DATA=0 is executed. Because this trailer statement does not cause a transfer of control elsewhere in the program, execution continues with the statement following the trailer. This is why the first READ is put immediately ahead of the WHILE statement and why the READ is the last step in the loop; it means the value of DATA is tested immediately after each attempted READ.

An AT END <u>construct</u> can be used instead of an AT END <u>statement.</u> The AT END construct allows more than one statement to be executed when the out-of-data condition is true. The AT END statement in the example above could have been replaced by the AT END construct below.

```
           AT END
             DATA=0
           END AT END
```

Note that no comma follows the AT END. This is how the compiler distinguishes between the AT END statement and the AT END construct.

```
AT END Statement and Construct

    Statement                      Construct

    READ ...                       READ ...
    AT END, trailer statement      AT END
                                      .
                                      .   statement(s)
                                      .
                                   END AT END

1.  The AT END statement must immediately follow
    the READ statement to which it applies. The
    word DO is optional after AT END.

2.  AT END Statement
    .1  If an end-of-data condition is not detected
        during the READ operation, control transfers
        to the statement following the trailer.
    .2  If the end-of-data condition exists, the
        statement following the trailer is executed
        and unless this causes control to be
        transferred elsewhere, execution continues
        sequentially.

3.  AT END Construct
    .1  If an end-of-data condition is not detected
        during the READ operation, the AT END
        construct is ignored.
    .2  If the end-of-data condition exists,
        statements following the AT END are executed
        sequentially and execution continues with
        the statement following the END AT END.
```

4. The READ statement associated with an AT END
   block cannot be:
   a) the trailer in a Logical IF statement.
   b) the object statement in a DO-loop.
   c) used with direct access files or core-to-
      core READ operations (Chapters 20 and 21)
   d) used when the "END=" parameter (see below)
      is used in the READ preceding the AT END
      statement.

5. Control may be transferred to a statement
   inside the range from a statement outside the
   range. When this happens, the END AT END
   statement is ignored.

*The 'END=' Parameter

The same read and print problem could have been
programmed using an 'END=' parameter to specify a GO TO
action when the end of data condition is found.

```
C EXAMPLE 5.2 USE OF THE END=N IN A READ STATEMENT
C       READ LOOP (GO TO 14 WHEN OUT OF DATA)
     1 READ(5,*,END=14) X
          PRINT,X
       GO TO 1
    14 STOP
       END
```

In this program the statement "GO TO 1" causes the READ
statement to be executed over and over. When the attempted
READ encounters an out of data condition, control is
transferred to the statement whose number appears in the
"END=" parameter of the READ statement. Note that this
transfer of control does not take place until an attempt is
made to read a non-existent card.

5.3 Formatted Input -The Concepts

When using any one of the three types of format-free
READ statements discussed in the previous section, the
WATFIV program is responsible for scanning the data cards
and trying to make some sense out of the values punched in
them. If however, you, the programmer, know which card
columns are used to store the values to be assigned to the
variables in the input list, you can make the job of the
WATFIV program somewhat easier by describing how the values

have been punched in the card.   Since you describe usage of
the card columns, it is not necessary to separate the data
values by   commas or   blank columns.   This means more data
values can be   recorded   on a   card.   Furthermore, it is
possible to omit the decimal point and/or exponent when
punching REAL values by including this information in the
program.

    When the "how" information is   contained in the program,
a FORMAT statement is used to describe the usage of the card
columns.   The READ statement is   still used to   answer the
questions "where" and   "what".   In   addition,   the READ
statement contains   a   pointer   to a   FORMAT statement
containing the "how" information.

    The first type of formatted READ statement has the
general form:

                    READ fmt#, input list
            fmt# FORMAT(how information)

    In this first type of formatted READ statement,   the
input device is assumed to be the card reader. The "fmt#" is
any valid   statement number and is a pointer to   the FORMAT
statement describing how the values have been punched in the
card(s).   FORMAT statements are non-executable statements
and may be placed anywhere in the program. Some programmers
prefer to put them all together at the beginning or the end
of the program. Different READ statements can point to the
same FORMAT statement.

    The purpose of a FORMAT statement is to describe where
on the card the value for each of the variables in the input
list can be found. This is accomplished by providing two
items of information for each variable in the list.   These
two items are represented by the blanks in the following
sentence.   "Beginning in card column ___, the value for the
next variable in the input list is found in the next ___
columns of the card."   Let's look at an example.

5.4 Formatted Input of INTEGERS

    A simple example is shown below.

            READ 800,JOHN,LOOP

        800 FORMAT(T1,I4,T8,I3)

    In this example, the FORMAT statement says: "The value
for the first variable in the input list can be found

starting in column 1 (T1);   it is an INTEGER value and
occupies the next four columns of the card (I4).   The value
for the second variable in the input list can be found
beginning in column 8 (T8);   it is an INTEGER value, and
occupies the next 3 columns of the card (I3)." Thus if the
symbols punched in the card columns were:

then the value assigned to JOHN would be -27, and that
assigned to LOOP would be 196.   The symbol "b" is used to
denote a blank column.

      In this example, the "T1" and "T8" are pointers to card
columns 1 and 8 respectively.   A code of the form "Tp"
appearing in a FORMAT statement means: "beginning in column
p ...".   Since there are 80 columns in a card, the value of
"p" must be an INTEGER constant in the range 1 thru 80.   Any
attempt to reference a column beyond eighty causes an error.

      The symbols "I4" and "I3" are examples of "Integer
masks".   A mask must be provided for each variable in the
input list.   The word "mask" is appropriate in that the
value assigned to a variable is that which is "seen thru the
mask". By changing the mask used with a variable, different
values may be assigned to the variable.   Masks appearing in
a FORMAT   statement are matched one-for-one   with the
variables in the input list, beginning from the left.   The
general form of the Integer mask (I-mask for short) is "Iw"
where "w" denotes the number of columns reserved for
punching the INTEGER value.   The value of w is often called
the field width. An I-mask must be provided for each INTEGER
variable in the input list.

Operation of the I-mask

      For each of the following examples,   assume that the
symbols punched in the card are those which appear in the
card columns covered by the I-mask.   The symbol "b" denotes
a blank column.

Symbols Appearing In The Card Columns	I-mask	Value Assigned To The Variable
b123	I4	123
b-b99	I5	-99
b-99	I4	-99
+1bbb	I5	1000
-b2b7b	I6	-2070
b1b3b5b7	I8	1030507
9999999999	I10	error (too many digits)
123.	I4	error (invalid symbol)
12,3456	I7	error (invalid symbol)

(handwritten note to the left of table: "data deck")

These examples show that when using an I-mask:

i) The minus sign can appear anywhere to the left of the first digit.

ii) Blank columns at the beginning, the middle, or the end of the number are treated as zeros.

iii) Error messages result if the data value is outside the permitted range for an INTEGER or if the number is not an INTEGER constant.

iv) The value of "w" must be a positive INTEGER constant.

The link-up between variables in the input list, masks in the FORMAT statement, and values punched on the card is summarized in the following diagram.

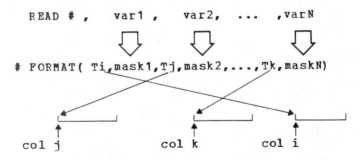

In words, the value which is assigned to the mth variable in the input list is found in the columns covered by the mth mask in the FORMAT statement.

Exercise 5.1

1. For each of the following determine the value assigned to an INTEGER variable if the I-mask shown is used with the data symbols on its left.

Symbols In Columns	Mask	Value
a) b123	I4	_____
b) +bb45	I5	_____
c) b-3bb	I5	_____
d) -b2b4b	I6	_____
e) +-3456	I6	_____
f) 24.7b	I5	_____

2. Suppose the READ statement

          READ 20,M,N,LUCKY

   appears in a program and the data card which is read in by executing the statement contains the values:

   card   ⌠0   1   2
   columns   ⌡1234567890 1234567890

                -b147b2589.24b399bbb

   What values would be assigned to the variables M,N,and LUCKY using each of the FORMAT statements which follow?

   a)   20 FORMAT(T1,I4,T12,I3,T15,I1)
   b)   20 FORMAT(T1,I2,T12,I6,T4,I4)
   c)   20 FORMAT(T9,I2,T14,I1,T1,I7)
   d)   20 FORMAT(T1,I3,T1,I4,T1,I5)

3. Given the READ statement:

          READ 15,MAX,J12,NO

   and a data card containing the values:

   card   ⌠0   1   2
   columns   ⌡1234567890 1234567890123

                123-5b4321-2.+6789bbbbb

   Write FORMAT statements which would cause the variables MAX,J12, and NO to have the following values when the READ statement is executed.

    a) MAX=23, J12=432, NO=6789
    b) MAX=-2, J12=89000, NO=-5
    c) MAX=504, J12=78,   NO=-504
    d) MAX=12, J12=50,   NO =-504321
    e) An error message

4. What is the error in each of the following?

    a)   800 FORMAT(T12,I0)
    b)   801 FORMAT(T1,I28,T75,I7)

5.5 Formatted Input of REAL Values (The F-Mask)

    When defining card columns containing values .to be
assigned to REAL variables, an F-mask can be used. Consider
the following example.

            READ 825,X,Y
        825 FORMAT(T1,F5.2,T6,F8.3)

    There are two variables in the input list and two masks
in the FORMAT statement,   an F-mask of "F5.2" for the
variable X,   and an F-mask of "F8.3" for the variable Y.
Furthermore, these masks are positioned to start in columns
1 and 6 respectively.   If the first 13 columns of the data
card contain the symbols:

            one   ten   twenty
             ↓   ↓   ↓
    card   ⎧0   1   2
    columns ⎨ 1234567890 1234567890

        -b345bbbb2529
        ‿‿‿‿‿ ‿‿‿‿‿‿‿‿
        F5.2   F8.3

the value assigned to X would be -3.45,   and the value
assigned to Y would be 2.529. As you might have guessed, the
numbers "w" and "d" in the mask "Fw.d" are such that "w"
specifies the number of card columns covered by the mask and
"d" specifies the number of digits to the right of the
decimal.

Operation of an F-mask

    The general form of an F-mask is Fw.d where w is the
field width (number of card columns reserved for the value),
and d is the number of digits to the right of the decimal
point.   The examples in the following table show the effect
of using different F-masks with various data values.

	Symbols Covered By Mask	Mask	Value Assigned To The Variable
i)	12345	F5.2	123.45
ii)	-b603	F5.4	-.0603
iii)	-b603b	F6.0	-6030.
iv)	987.65	F6.2	987.65
v)	987.65	F6.4	987.65
vi)	bb+2b.b	F7.3	20.0
vii)	12345678	F8.1	1234568.

These examples show that when using an F-mask:

i) Blank columns are treated as being zeros.

ii) If no decimal point is punched in the card, the value of d in the mask is used to insert a decimal point such that d digits appear to the right of the decimal point in the number.

iii) If a decimal point is punched in the card, the value of d in the mask is ignored. (examples (v) and (vi)).

iv) If the value punched contains more than 7 significant digits, only 7 significant digits are stored. The number may or may not be rounded properly to 7 digits.

v) The only symbols which may appear in card columns covered by an F-mask are the digits 0 thru 9 and the symbols + - and . .

5.6 Formatted Input of REAL Values (The E-mask)

REAL values can also be read using an E-mask. The E-mask has the general form "Ew.d" where "w" denotes the number of card columns covered by the mask, and "d" denotes the number of digits to the right of the decimal point. The E-mask must be used if a number has been punched with an exponent. This occurs primarily when the absolute value of the number being read is either very large, eg: 1.25×10^{25}, or very small, eg: $.2479 \times 10^{-60}$. When indicating the value of the exponent, we can be very sloppy in the way it is punched. For example, to indicate that a number is to be multiplied by ten-to-the-eighth, the exponent can be written in any of the following ways: E+08, E08, E8, E+8, +08, +8. An exponent of -7 can be written as: E-07, E-7, -7, or -07. If the E does not appear in the number, then the sign of the exponent must appear. Some examples follow.

	Symbols Covered By Mask	Mask	Value Assigned To The Variable
i)	+b2.5E+01	E9.1	2.5×10^1
ii)	-bbb3.41-60	E11.2	-3.41×10^{-60}
iii)	bb.0045E2b	E10.3	$.0045 \times 10^{20}$
iv)	123	E3.2	1.23
v)	-7766E-3	E8.4	$-.7766 \times 10^{-03}$
vi)	-7766+30	E8.4	$-.7766 \times 10^{30}$
vii)	123456789	E9.2	1234568.
viii)	50.0E2bb	E8.1	error (exponent too large)

These examples illustrate the following points:

i) Blanks are treated as zeros.

ii) If an exponent is not punched, an exponent of zero is assumed (example(iv)).

iii) If a decimal point is punched, the "d" is ignored.

iv) If an "E", "+" or "-" appears and no "." is present, the decimal point is positioned "d" positions to the left of the "E", "+" or "-" before multiplication by the specified power (examples(v) and (vi)).

v) If more than 7 significant digits are punched, the number is rounded to 7 digits. Note: the 7th digit may or may not be correctly rounded.

vi) If the exponent is outside the permitted range (roughly plus or minus 75) an error occurs.

Example (iv) could of course have been read using an F-mask of F3.2 as well as the E-mask E3.2 and in this sense, E-masks can be used anywhere F-masks can be used. The converse is not true however. If a value of .123E+02 was read under an F-mask, an error would occur since the "E" is considered an invalid character in columns covered by an F-mask.

5.7 Input Containing REAL and INTEGER Values

In the examples of formatted READ statements used thus far, the variables in the input lists have been of the same type. The following examples illustrate formatted input in which the input list contains a mixture of variable types.

    i)   READ 50,JACK,EXTRA,FILE,MINMUM
                50 FORMAT(T2,I3,T6,F4.1,T10,F5.3,T16,I1)

        If the data card contains the symbols:

card   ⎰0   1   2
columns   ⎱12345678901234567890

        5-36b.0097.388bbbbbb

the values assigned to the variables would be: JACK=-36, EXTRA=.009, FILE=7.388, MINMUM=0.

    ii)   READ 87,JKL,EEK
                87 FORMAT(T5,I2,T5,F4.1)
            $ENTRY
            bbbb-6.2b

The execution of the READ statement results in JKL having a value of -6 and EEK having a value of -6.2. This illustrates that card columns can be "used twice" by positioning two or more masks so that they overlap.

    iii)   READ 555,X,LOST,AA,Z9888
                555 FORMAT(T4,F7.3,T80,I1,T19,I8,T46,F10.5)

Without even knowing what is punched in the card, we can state with certainty that an error message will be produced. To see why, it is simply a matter of matching up the variables in the input list with the masks in the FORMAT statement.

        X   LOST   AA   Z9888

        F7.3   I1   I8   F10.5

Since AA is a REAL variable and its mask is I8, the message "FORMAT CODE AND DATA TYPE DO NOT MATCH" will be printed. In other words, an I-mask must be used with INTEGER variables and cannot be used with REAL variables. Similarly, F-masks and E-masks can only be used with REAL variables.

5.8 A Second Method Of Positioning Masks

Suppose we wish to assign values to the variables DO, N57, and BBB. Assume the values for these three variables are found in columns 1&2, 3 thru 6, and 7&8 respectively. Suppose the appropriate masks are F2.0, I4, and F2.1. We could explicitly position the masks using the FORMAT statement

FORMAT(T1,F2.0,T3,I4,T7,F2.1) .

We could also implicitly position the masks using

FORMAT(F2.0,I4,F2.1) .

The idea here is that if a T-code is not used to position a mask, the mask position is obtained by starting the first mask in column 1 and each successive mask in the column following the last column covered by the previous mask. Thus the mask F2.0 covers the columns 1&2, the mask I4 covers columns 3 thru 6, and the mask F2.1 covers columns 7&8. Implicit positioning of masks can be combined with explicit positioning of masks as the following example shows.

READ 75,K1,K2,K3,K4,K5
75 FORMAT(I6,I3,T80,I1,T14,I2,I2)

This results in the following assignment of variables, masks and card columns.

Variable	Mask	Card Columns Covered	Type Of Positioning
K1	I6	1-6	implicit
K2	I3	7-9	implicit
K3	I1	80	explicit
K4	I2	14-15	explicit
K5	I2	16-17	implicit

5.9 The X-Code

Another technique for positioning masks to cover the correct card columns is to use an X-code to skip over unused columns. Suppose the value for ICOUNT is punched in columns 3 thru 5 and the value for JHIGH is punched in columns 9 thru 13. When used with the statement

READ 1000, ICOUNT, JHIGH

the following FORMAT statements are equivalent.

```
  i)    1000 FORMAT(2X,I3,3X,I5)
 ii)    1000 FORMAT(2X,I3,T9,I5)
iii)    1000 FORMAT(T3,I3,3X,I5)
 iv)    1000 FORMAT(T3,I3,T9,I5)
```

Each of these four FORMAT statements causes the masks to be positioned as shown below.

```
card       ⎧0         1         2
columns    ⎨12345678901234567890
           ⎩
              I3    I5
```

A code of "nX" appearing in a FORMAT statement causes the next n columns of the card to be skipped over. The value of n must be a positive INTEGER constant.   In the first FORMAT statement for example,   the sequence "2X,I3,3X,I5" causes the first two columns to be skipped over,   the next 3 are used for the mask I3,   then 3 more columns are skipped and the mask I5 covers the next 5 columns.

Is the FORMAT statement

        1000 FORMAT(T9,I5,T3,I3)

equivalent to the four others? The answer is "no". It does position a mask of I5 to cover columns 9 thru 13 and a mask of I3 to cover columns 3 thru 6. However, when used with the READ statement

        READ 1000, ICOUNT, JHIGH

the value assigned to ICOUNT would be taken from columns 9 thru 13 and that for JHIGH, from columns 3 thru 6. This is not what was wanted.   This example emphasizes the very important point that the mask for each variable, and hence the card columns in which the value is found depend only on the order in which the masks appear in the FORMAT statement.

The following pair of statements show how an X-code could be used to skip all 80 columns of a card.

        READ 1
      1 FORMAT(80X)

Notice that the input list is empty, it does not contain any variable names. This is quite permissible since our objective was simply to read a card and ignore anything punched in the card. Note that any masks following "80X" would cause an error since they would be positioned beyond the last column available. An easier way of skipping over data cards which aren't needed is described in the following section.

5.10 The Slash "/" Code

The appearance of a slash symbol in a FORMAT statement causes a new card to be read. Format codes following the "/" apply to the card read in as a result of the slash. The example below illustrates its effect.

                READ 50,L,M,N,X

            50 FORMAT(I6,/,I3,I7,//,T40,F11.6,///)

When this READ statement is executed, a total of seven data cards will be read. The locations in which the value of each variable in the input list will be found is described in the following table.

Variable	Mask	In Card #	Columns
L	I6	1	1-6
M	I3	2	1-3
N	I7	2	4-10
X	F11.6	4	40-50
		5,6,7	1-80 ignored

Understanding the effect of a slash is simple. There are two points to keep in mind.

i) The left bracket following the word FORMAT causes the first card to be read.

ii) As the FORMAT statement is scanned left to right, each slash encountered causes another card to be read. Masks and other format codes apply to the last card read.

By applying these two ideas to the example given, the results shown in the table should become apparent.

Exercise 5.2

*Assume all variables have default typing.

1. For each of the following, fill in the missing item of information.

Symbols In Card	Mask	Value Assigned
a) bb.0123	F7.4	_____
b) b-1.bbb	_____	-1.000
c) -2345	F5.2	_____
d) -2377	_____	-237.7
e) .000002	F7.__	.000002
f) b1b2b3b	_____	1020.30

2. Given the pair of statements:

        READ 1,IP,ALPHA,L9,BETA
      1 FORMAT(T5,I6,2X,F7.1,I1,T21,F3.0)

  and a data card containing:

    card   {0   1   2   3
    columns   {1234567890123456789012345 67890

        bbb-2473bb77399.568b452.bbbbbb

  Fill in the missing information in the table below.

Variable	Mask	Mask Positions	Value Assigned
a) IP	____	_____	_____
b) _____	____	13-19	_____
c) _____	____	_____	0
d) BETA	____	_____	_____

3. Write three or more FORMAT statements which are equivalent to:

        FORMAT(F17.6,T25,2X,I3,T18,F5.0)

4. Suppose a data card contains the symbols:

    card   {0   1   2
    columns   {1234567890 123456789012345

        b-2.46bbb32581.97b43.b2bb

  Suppose the READ statement which causes the data card to be read is:

        READ27,A,J,C,M,D

  Write FORMAT statements which will cause the variables in the input list to be assigned the values indicated.

(handwritten: No code) *(handwritten: Least possible formatting codes)*

	A	J	C	M	D
a)	-2.4	6	32581.	97	43.02
b)	-2.	600	81.97	43	2.0
c)	4.6	-2	1.97	600	3.0
d)	6000.3	581	43.02	0	-2.46
e)	.460	20	.000325	8	70.43
f)	.003	32	32.581	32581	2581.970

5.11 Two Handy Short Cuts

a) Repeat Factors For A Single Mask

Suppose the answers to a true-false test containing fifty questions are punched in the first 50 columns of a card and a "1" is used to indicate "true", a "0" to indicate "false". To read the answers would mean the input list would contain fifty variable names and its associated FORMAT statement would look like: "FORMAT(I1,I1,I1,...,I1)" where the I1 mask was repeated fifty times. In situations where the same mask is repeated more than once, a repeat factor can be put in front of the mask to indicate the number of times the mask is to be repeated. For the example referred to above, the FORMAT statement could be written as FORMAT(50I1), or FORMAT(31I1,7I1,12I1) or some other combination which would produce the desired 50 repetitions of the mask I1.

A repeat factor can be placed in front of any valid mask. The value of the factor must be a positive INTEGER constant. Thus "2.I1" and "NI1" are invalid. A FORMAT statement such as "FORMAT(F12.3,F12.3,I6)" could be shortened to "FORMAT(2F12.3,I6).

b) Group Factors For A Set of Codes

Suppose that in the true-false data referred to above, we were only interested in the answers to questions 5,10,15,...,50. This would mean the READ statement would have ten variables in the input list, and the FORMAT statement could be written as:

FORMAT(4X,I1,4X,I1,4X,I1,...,4X,I1)

where the pair of codes "4X,I1" appears ten times. This can be written in the shorter form:

FORMAT(10(4X,I1))

The inner brackets and their contents are called a group, and the "10" preceding the group is called the group count. Groups and group counts are handy tools for repeating a set of format codes. Groups can be nested just like DO-loops except the maximum depth of nesting is two. That is, we can have a group within a group, but not a group within a group within a group. The following three FORMAT statements are equivalent. Each contains nine masks.

    FORMAT(F7.3,I1,2X,I1,2X,F7.3,I1,2X,I1,2X,F7.3,I1,2X,I1,2X)

    FORMAT(3(F7.3,I1,2X,I1,2X))

    FORMAT(3(F7.3,2(I1,2X)))

In the third case, "(F7.3,2(I1,2X))" is called the outer group and (I1,2X) is called the inner group. As always, when interpreting expressions involving brackets, proceed from the innermost brackets outwards. One further point. Are the FORMAT statements below equivalent?

    FORMAT(10F6.3)   FORMAT((10F6.3))   FORMAT(10(F6.3))

Technically, the answer is "No, they are all different.". In the first and second cases, the 10 is a repeat factor. In the third, it is a group count. Furthermore, the second contains a group with an assumed group count of one. The first does not contain a group. In this example, it doesn't matter which one is used. In more complex FORMAT statements, it may matter. This point will be clarified in the following section.

5.12 Two Unanswered Questions

In each of the examples discussed thus far, the number of masks in the FORMAT statement has been the same as the number of variables in the input list. It is only natural to ask the following two questions.

   i) What happens if there are more masks than variables?

   ii) What happens if there are fewer masks than variables?

Question 1 (More Masks Than Variables)

The first question is easy to answer. If there are more masks than variables, only those format codes preceding the first unnecessary mask are processed. One example should suffice. Consider the statements:

```
          READ 27,J,K,A
      27 FORMAT(2(I3,1X),F7.2,10X,I8)
```

The variables J and K each have a mask of I3. The variable A
has a mask of F7.2. The code 10X is processed and the mask
I8 is ignored. The reason for pointing out that the 10X is
processed is to emphasize that codes up to the first
unnecessary mask are processed. In this example, the 10X
has no effect but had slash codes preceded the mask I8, they
would have been processed.

Question 2 (Fewer Masks Than Variables)

    When there are fewer masks than variables in the input
list,   the question "What happens?" is easy to answer
provided there are no groups. Consider the following
example.
```
          READ 14, X, Y, Z
      14 FORMAT(F6.0)
```

The execution of the READ statement causes a card to be read
and the value of X is found in columns 1-6 of the first
card.   Since there are no more masks and since there are no
groups, the FORMAT statement is repeated. The left bracket
following the word FORMAT can be viewed as causing the next
card to be read.   Thus the value for Y is found in columns
1-6 of the second card. Since no mask has yet been found for
Z, the process is repeated again and hence the value for Z
is found in columns 1-6 of the third data card.   Thus the
pair of statements above is equivalent to the following set
of four statements.

```
          READ 14,X
          READ 14,Y
          READ 14,Z
      14 FORMAT(F6.0)
```

    Provided that there are no   groups in the FORMAT
statement, the rule is that if there are fewer masks than
variables,   the format codes are used once and then the
FORMAT statement is repeated. During this recycling process,
the left bracket following the word FORMAT causes the next
data card to be read. The recycling process is repeated
until a mask has been found for each variable in the input
list.

    A word of caution. The statements

```
          READ 10,N,X,Y
      10 FORMAT(I6,F11.3)
```

will cause an error.   The reason is that the mask for Y is
found by recycling the FORMAT statement.   This means an
attempt is made to   associate the I-mask   I6 with the REAL
variable Y, hence the message "FORMAT CODE AND DATA TYPE DO
NOT MATCH".

    When there are groups present in the FORMAT statement,
the part of the FORMAT statement that is recycled over and
over until a mask has been found for each variable in the
input list can be described as "beginning with the group
count of the group whose right bracket is nearest the right
hand end of the FORMAT statement".   This probably sounds
complicated but the three examples below should make the
idea clear.   The arrow in each case shows the portion of the
set of format codes which are recycled.

              FORMAT(...10(...)...)
                      ↑

              FORMAT(...2(...)...(...)...)
                             ↑

              FORMAT(...3(...4(...)...6(...)...)...)
                      ↑

5.13 Other Forms of the Formatted READ Statement

    For each type of format-free READ statement, there is an
equivalent formatted READ statement. The three types are:

    READ fmt#, input list

    READ(5,fmt#) input list

    READ(5,fmt#,END=n) input list

    READ fmt#, input list   or   READ fmt#,input list
      AT END   AT END, statement
       .
       .
       .
      END AT END

    READ(5,fmt#) input list   or   READ fmt#,input list
      AT END   AT END, statement
       .
       .
       .
      END AT END

All examples so far have used the first type in which the input device is assumed to be the card reader and in which no statement number was provided to which control would be transferred if an attempt was made to read a non-existent data card.

Recall that the "5" is used to specify the card reader as the input device and that the device number of the card reader can be stored in an INTEGER variable.

If an AT END statement or construct or the "END=" parameter is used, the rules are the same as described in Section 5.3 for format-free input. The rule that the AT END must immediately follow the READ to which it applies means that the FORMAT statement cannot come between the READ and the AT END.

Exercise 5.3

Assume all variables are typed by default.

1. Given a data card with the symbols "01234567" in columns 1 to 8, what values are assigned to G,H, I and J by the following statements?
   ```
        READ 100,G,H,I,J
   100 FORMAT(2X,2F3.2,T2,2(1X,I2))
   ```

2. For each of the FORMAT statements below:
   a) How many masks are there in the statement?
   b) What part of the FORMAT statement would be recycled if there were more variables than masks?
   c) How many cards would be read if the input list contained twenty variables?
   d) On what card, and in what columns of that card is the value assigned to the 12th variable in the list?
   e) If the eighth variable is REAL, would an error occur?

   ```
     i) FORMAT(2I6,3X,F7.2)
    ii) FORMAT(T5,8F1.0,2X,I5)
   iii) FORMAT(2I12,3I3,F6.1)
    iv) FORMAT(1X,2(I18,3F2.2),2X,3(I4))
     v) FORMAT(2I1,2(2X,F7.4,2(3X,I2)))
   ```

3. Suppose two data cards are such that the first contains the symbols "1234567890" in columns one thru ten and the second contains the symbols "0987654321" in columns one thru ten. Assume both cards have blanks in columns eleven thru eighty. Given the statement,

   ```
        READ 44,X,M,Y,N
   ```

write a single FORMAT statement containing no slashes
which will result in the assignment of values to variables indicated in the table below.

	X	M	Y	N
a)	12.34	5	678.	900
b)	12345.6	89	9876.5	32
c)	678.90	12	543.21	9
d)	4.5	78	90.	76
e)	34.56	78	9.87	65
f)	67.8	90	9.8	21

5.14 A Word About Commas

Each format code used in the examples has been separated
from those preceding or following it by a comma. It is not
necessary to use commas if their omission would not cause
any ambiguity in the meaning of the FORMAT statement. As an
example, the pair of codes "3X,F6.3" could be written as
"3XF6.3" without an error message being produced.   On the
other hand, we could not write "T5,2I1" as "T52I1" since
this could also mean "T52,I1". As a general rule, use commas
to separate format codes.   It can't hurt and it makes the
FORMAT statement more readable.

*5.15 Literals In Input FORMAT Statements

This section describes a type of format code which is
almost never used in input operations.   A "literal" is
simply a string of symbols. Literals can be defined in two
ways.   Depending on which method is used to define the
literal, it is called a "Quote-type" literal or an "H-type"
literal. Examples of each appear in the following table.

Symbol String	As A Quote-Type Literal	As An H-Type Literal
ABCDE	'ABCDE'	5HABCDE
PAYROLL REPORT	'PAYROLL REPORT'	14HPAYROLL REPORT
JAN. 1,1980	'JAN. 1,1980'	11HJAN. 1,1980

As can be seen from the foregoing examples, Quote-type
literals are defined by enclosing a string of symbols in
single quotes. H-type literals (sometimes called Hollerith
strings or Hollerith constants) are defined by prefixing the
symbol string with "nH" where n represents the number of
symbols in the string, including blanks.   H-type literals

are the only literals recognized by some Fortran compilers.
Either type is acceptable in WATFIV.

If a literal is present in a FORMAT statement used in a
READ operation,   the symbols punched in the card columns
covered by the literal replace the symbols of the literal in
the FORMAT statement when the READ statement is executed.
Literals are positioned in precisely the same way as masks
are positioned (implicitly or explicitly).

Consider the following two examples.

a)   READ 900,K
          900 FORMAT('WIPED OUT',I4)
              ...
      $ENTRY
      WITH THIS1234

          Result: K has a value of 1234 and the FORMAT
                  statement has become "FORMAT('WITH THIS',I4)"

b)   READ 900
          900 FORMAT(T2,5HXXXXX)
              ...
      $ENTRY
       HELLO

          Result: The FORMAT statement is changed to
              FORMAT(T2,5HHELLO)

In both of these examples, the symbols of the literal in
the FORMAT statement are changed to the symbols appearing in
the card columns covered by the literal.

What is the purpose of having literals in FORMAT
statements? There are two reasons.   First, it provides a
means of   changing a FORMAT statement.   Much better
techniques exist however and are described in Chapters 16
and 21.   Second, literals do serve a valuable function in
FORMAT statements used for output.   Use of this technique
may mean the same FORMAT statement can be used for both
input and output (formatted output is discussed in the next
chapter).   In spite of these reasons,   the inclusion of
literals in FORMAT statements used for input is of very
little practical value.

*5.16 The G-Mask

The G-mask is a general purpose mask which can be used
to read both REAL and INTEGER values under control of a
FORMAT statement. Its general form is "Gw.d" where "w"
denotes the number of card columns covered by the mask and
"d" denotes the number of digits to the right of the decimal
point. The value of d is ignored (and in fact ".d" may be
omitted) when a G-mask is used with an INTEGER variable.
The examples which follow show that the effect of the mask
Gw.d is the same as that of the mask Iw, if used for an
INTEGER variable; and the same as the mask Ew.d, if used for
a REAL variable. The G-mask is used primarily to save time
writing FORMAT statements. Its use may also mean that input
lists can be altered with no change required in the
associated FORMAT statement.

Type Of Variable	Symbols In Cols. Covered by Mask	G-Mask	Value Assigned To Variable
INTEGER	12345	G5	12345
INTEGER	-1234b	G6.3	-12340
REAL	12345	G5.2	123.45
REAL	12.345	G6.2	12.345
REAL	.024E-2	G7.3	.00024
REAL	24E-2	G5.1	.024

*5.17 F-Mask Modification - The P-Code

Numbers punched in card columns covered by an F-mask can
be multiplied by a power of ten before the value is assigned
to a variable. This operation, often called decimal scaling,
is done by prefixing an F-mask with a P-code. A prefix of
the form "sP" causes the value to be divided by 10**s.

The table below shows the effect produced for several
combinations of data values and modified F-masks.

Symbols In Columns Covered by Mask(s)	Mask(s)	Value(s) Assigned To Variable(s)
12345	F5.2	123.45
12345	2PF5.2	1.2345
12345	0PF5.2	123.45
12345	-3PF5.2	123450.
876.5	2PF5.3	8.765
8.765	-1PF5.3	87.65
12345678	-1P2F4.0	12340. & 56780.
12345678	-1PF4.0,F4.0	12340. & 56780.
12345678	-1PF4.0,0PF4.0	12340. & 5678.

The general form of the P-code is "sP" where "s" is an INTEGER constant. The rules of usage as illustrated by the foregoing examples are:

a)   Using only the F-mask, determine the value in the card columns covered by the mask. Assign 10**(-s) times this value to the input variable.

b)   If a repeat factor is used, the format code is "sPrFw.d" where "r" is the repeat factor. See the third last example.

c)   Any P-code encounted applies to all subsequent F-masks used in the FORMAT statement <u>unless</u> its effect is negated by another P-code. (See the last two examples.)

Most people have difficulty remembering whether a positive "s" in a code "sP" means multiply by ten to the s or ten to the minus s.   Well, the German word for "one" is "eins" and eins way to remember the rule is:

$$\underline{Ex}ternal\ value = \underline{IN}ternal\ value\ \times\ 10^{\underline{s}}$$

on the card   in the computer   in the code
                                        "sP"

Note that the underlined letters spell "EINS".

Why use P-codes?   Their most important use is in converting REAL numbers with fractional values to whole numbers. Recall that many exact decimal values (5.21 for example) are stored with a small error in a computer because their representation in the base two number system has a non-terminating fractional value. Whole numbers are stored exactly. Therefore, to improve accuracy in critical computations such as payroll calculations, it may be desirable to convert a REAL input value such as a wage rate to a whole number prior to performing any arithmetic with the value. After calculations have been completed, division by an appropriate power of ten can be done to obtain the final result.

Another use of decimal scaling is simply to drop or add zeros to a value. For example, values in the range zero thru nine could be made into millions using the code -6PF1.0.

A final question. Why do the two sets of statements below cause X to have slightly different values? If you know why, you know why P-codes are sometimes used.

```
        READ 900,X                       READ 901,X
   900  FORMAT(-2PF4.2)             901  FORMAT(F4.2)
        ...                              X=X*100.
        ...                              ...
   $ENTRY                           $ENTRY
   5.21                             5.21
```

*5.18 The ERR=m Parameter

The READ statement in WATFIV can include the sequence of symbols "ERR=m" as a parameter. If present, "m" is the number of an executable statement in the program to which control will be transferred if a machine or hardware error occurs during the transmission of the data from the input device to the computer memory. It may appear with or without the END=n parameter in both formatted and format-free READ statements as shown in the following table.

Format-Free   { READ(device,*,ERR=m) list

                        or

                  READ(device,*,END=n,ERR=m) list

Formatted   { READ(device,fmt,ERR=m) list

                        or

                  READ(device,fmt,END=n,ERR=m) list

In the foregoing table, the order of the "END=" and "ERR=" parameters doesn't matter.

When should the "ERR=" parameter be used? When using WATFIV, a portion of the WATFIV processor remains in memory during the execution of a program and acts somewhat like a "mother hen". If a transmission error occurs, the mother hen feature intercepts the error and prints an appropriate error message before the job is terminated. For this reason it is not necessary to use the ERR=m parameter when running under WATFIV. If, however, you wish to attempt further execution of the program or print your own error message, the ERR=m parameter could be included in a READ statement.

A second reason for its inclusion would be that you intend to compile your source program using one of the many Fortran compilers available. In some of these, the mother hen feature is not present and hence you are responsible for handling transmission errors to your satisfaction.

5.19 Summary

1. There are three questions which must be answered in any input operation. These are:
   a) What variables are to be assigned values?
   b) On what device are the values recorded?
   c) How are the values recorded on the input medium?

2. The programmer answers question (a) by defining an input list of variables.

   The programmer answers question (b) by writing the READ statement either as:

   READ,list   or READ(5,...) list .

   The programmer may or not answer question (c). If he does not, the input operation is said to be format-free. With format-free input, WATFIV is resposible for determining how the values have been recorded on the input medium. If the programmer provides the "how" information, the operation is said to be formatted. In this case, a FORMAT statement is used to describe the usage of the card columns.

3. When using formatted input, a mask must be provided for each variable in the input list. The following points are significant.
   i) Masks are assigned to variables in the input

list in a left to right fashion.
ii) An I-mask is used for INTEGER variables.
iii) An F-mask or E-mask is used for REAL
     variables.

4. Masks may be positioned:
   i) Explicitly (using a T-code)
   ii) Implicity (card columns are used sequentially)
   iii) A combination of (i) and (ii)

5. An X-code may be used to skip over unused columns.

6. A slash code may be used to read in another card.

7. Repeat factors and group counts can be used to reduce
   the effort of writing long strings of format codes.

8. Repeat factors, group counts, and values of p, n, w,
   and d in the codes Tp, nX, Iw, Fw.d, Ew.d must be
   positive INTEGER constants.

5.20 Programming Problems

In each of the following problems use formatted input
statements unless specifically requested to use format-
free input.

5.1   The input to the program consists of payroll data.
Each of ten different employee's data is punched on a
single card according to the following rules.

card cols.	mask	item
1-3	I3	employee number
4-6	F3.2	regular wage rate
7-9	F3.1	regular hours worked
10-12	F3.2	overtime wage rate
13-15	F3.1	overtime hours worked

Read the cards one at a time and calculate the gross pay
for each employee. Print the total number of regular
hours, overtime hours, regular pay, overtime pay and
total pay for the ten employees. For each of the ten
employees print a line of the form "GROSS PAY FOR
EMPLOYEE ___ IS $ 0.ddddddddEee".

5.2   If an equation can be written in the form x-F(x)=0,
then, subject to certain conditions, a root of the
equation can be found by obtaining increasingly accurate

approximations of the root. If x_n is some initial
estimate of the root, then x_1, x_2, ... will be better
estimates where $x_n = F(x_{n-1})$. Suppose $F(x)$ has the form
$A/(x+B)$ and the initial estimate is called C. Write a
program which reads values of A, B and C each of which
is punched using a mask of F4.2. Calculate increasingly
accurate estimates of the root until the change in two
estimates is less than .0001. Print every tenth estimate
as well as the final estimate. Test your program using
first: A=12.3, B=5.4, C=2.0; secondly, A=3.90, B=-4.
C=2.0.

5.3   Write a program to solve two equations in two unknowns
of the form

$$Ax + By = C$$
$$Dx + Ey = F$$

Read values of A, B and C from one data card and the
values of D, E and F from a second data card. Use the
"END=" parameter in the first read statement and test
your program on an unknown number of pairs of equations.

5.4   Read an unknown number of INTEGER values punched one
value per card. Print the largest and smallest value of
those that are read as well as each value which is read.
Use the AT END construct.

5.5   A fraction of the form

```
         a
      --------
  b  +   a
        --------
     b  +   a
          --------
         b  +  ...
```

is called a continued fraction. Its value may be
approximated to any desired accuracy by evaluating

A_0/B_0 , A_1/B_1 , A_2/B_2 , etc. where

$A_0 = 0$, $A_1 = a$, and $A_n = aA_{n-2} + bA_{n-1}$ for $n=2, 3, ...$

$B_0 = 1$, $B_1 = b$, and $B_n = aB_{n-2} + bB_{n-1}$ for $n=2, 3, ...$

Write a program which reads several pairs of values of

values of "a" and "b" and for each, calculates A_{10}/B_{10} .
Test your program on at least the following two cases.
(i) a=1, b=1; (ii) a=1, b=2.

5.6   Write a program to make change for the purchase of
      items under one dollar.   Input to the program consists
      of pairs of REAL numbers, the first being the cost of
      the purchase and the second the amount of money given to
      the cashier.   Use the minimum number of coins chosen
      from pennies, nickels, dimes and quarters to make up the
      change.   Print the amount of the purchase,   the money
      given, and the number of coins of each type in the
      change.   Test your program using the values below.
      Punch the data so it can be read with the FORMAT
      statement

                 99 FORMAT (3X,F3.0,1X,F5.2)

              Cost(¢)   Paid($)

                 50   1.00
                 47   .50
                 25   .25
                 17   1.00
                 71   .75

Questions Answered In This Chapter

1. How do we answer the three questions associated with any output operation, namely:

   - Where (on what device) are the values to be displayed?
   - What values are to be displayed?
   - How are the values to be displayed?

2. What do the terms "format-free" and "formatted" mean when applied to output operations?

In the examples used thus far, the results of computations have been printed using a PRINT statement. The values appearing on the page were spaced out across successive lines according to rules which are incorporated into the WATFIV processor. The purpose of this chapter is to describe how you, the programmer, can control the appearance and placement of printed values.

6.1 Output - The Three Questions

i) Where are the values recorded?

The most frequently used medium for displaying the results of calculations done during the execution of a program is the printed page. Most large computer systems have one or more high speed printers, one or more typewriters, and possibly several TV-type display devices. A typewriter prints characters at a typical rate of thirty characters per second. A high speed printer can print at a rate of a thousand or more lines per minute. Video display devices are even faster but do not produce a permanent record which can be kept for later reference. In this chapter we shall assume the answer to the question "Where are the values recorded?" is "On a high speed printer.".

In WATFIV there are two verbs which cause information stored in the computer memory to be transmitted to a printer. These are the verbs "PRINT" and "WRITE". When using the PRINT statement it is not necessary to identify the printer as being the output device. When using the WRITE statement, it is. The differences between PRINT and WRITE statements are discussed at the end of this section.

ii) What values are to be printed?

    Output statements normally contain an output list.
The elements of the list are the variables, constants or
expressions whose values are to be printed. The elements
of the list must be separated by commas. Examples of
valid output lists are:

        i) X,I
       ii) 333,ABC,-6.0E+24/BB
      iii) +(X+Y)/(X-Y)

These output lists contain two, three, and one element
respectively.   An important point which is sometimes
forgotten is illustrated in example (iii). That is that
expressions appearing in output lists cannot start with
a left bracket. If a bracket is necessary, as in this
example, a plus or minus sign must appear in front of
the left bracket. The reason is to avoid having the
expression interpreted as a special kind of element
which will be discussed in the next chapter.

iii) How are the values to be printed?

    When sending values to the printer by using either
a PRINT statement or a WRITE statement, you have a
choice. You can either let WATFIV decide where the
values will appear on the page or you can control the
placement of values. When WATFIV assumes the
responsibility of positioning the output, the term
format-free is used. When you are in control, the term
formatted is used to describe the operation. When using
formatted output, a FORMAT statement is used in
conjunction with either the PRINT or WRITE statement.
The FORMAT statement supplies the "how" information.
The four types of output statements are shown in the
following table.

Forms Of Output Statements

	Format-Free Output	Formatted Output
Output device assumed to be the printer	PRINT,output list	PRINT #,output list # FORMAT(how info)
Printer named as the output device	WRITE(6,*) list	WRITE(6,*) list # FORMAT(how info)

The statement "PRINT,output list" is the only type of output statement considered previously.

6.2 Three Facts About Printed Output

The following facts are true for both format-free output and formatted output.

1. a) A line of printing contains 10 symbols per inch. Note: A blank is considered to be a symbol.

   b) There are either six or eight lines of printing in each vertical inch. (Control depends on a manual adjustment of the printer.) This means that 66 or 88 lines can be printed on the normal page of eleven inches.

2. Each line of printing has 133 print positions. One symbol can be stored in each position. Only the symbols stored in positions 2 thru 133 are printed. The symbol stored in position 1 is used to control the vertical spacing and is not printed. The number 133 applies to the most commonly used printer. You should check with your computing center to find out the "width" of the print line.

3. After each line is printed, blanks are put in all 133 print positions. This means you automatically start with a clean slate before sending any symbols you want printed to the printer.

For reasons which will become apparent in Section 6.17, the topic of formatted output will be discussed first.

6.3 Formatted Output - The Concepts

The two types of formatted output statements are:

                PRINT #, output list
            # FORMAT(format codes)

                        and

                WRITE(6,#) output list
            # FORMAT(format codes)

The only difference in the two forms of output statements is that when using the WRITE statement, the printer is named as being the output device. In most computing centers, the number 6 is used to identify the

high-speed printer.   If it is different,   the appropriate
value should be   used in the WRITE statement.   For
convenience, the PRINT command will be used in the examples
of this chapter.   The WRITE statement may be preferable if
the output which is being sent to the printer will
eventually be sent to some other output device such as a
card punch or magnetic tape drive.   In such cases, it is a
simple matter to change the device number to the desired
value.   In addition, some of the programming languages in
the Fortran family of languages do not accept the PRINT
statement.   The number of the output device can be stored in
an INTEGER variable. Thus the statement pair

                IPRINT=6
                WRITE(IPRINT,#) output list

is equivalent to the statement "WRITE(6,#) output list".

    When using formatted ouput, the programmer must control:

    a) The horizontal position of the symbols being printed.
       i.e: the position of the item along the print line.

    b) The vertical position of the symbols being printed.
       That is, how many lines below the last line printed.

    c) The appearance of REAL values including:
        i) whether or not an exponent is to be printed,
       ii) how many digits are to appear to the right of
           decimal point.

    These three types of information are included in a
FORMAT statement which is linked to a PRINT or   WRITE
statement by its statement number.   FORMAT statements can
appear anywhere in a program. Some programmers prefer to put
them all   together at the beginning or end of the program.
Several PRINT or WRITE statements can refer to the same
FORMAT statement.

    The principles of horizontal control, vertical control,
and appearance of printed items can be illustrated by
considering the output of INTEGER values.   Once these
techniques are understood,   they can be easily extended to
the printing of REAL values and literals.

6.4 Formatted INTEGER Output

    INTEGER values in WATFIV range from -2147483648 to
+2147483647. This means that, including a possible negative
sign, an INTEGER value could occupy as many as eleven print

positions (one position per symbol). Most INTEGER values
used in a program do not contain ten digits and therefore
fewer than eleven print positons are necessary to display
the value.

    To print an INTEGER value in WATFIV you must specify
which print positions are to be reserved for displaying the
value. This is done by telling the compiler two things .--
the first (leftmost) print position reserved and secondly,
how many print positions to reserve. Consider the following
example.

                PRINT 900, -85
            900 FORMAT(T2,I3)

The PRINT statement indicates that a value of negative
eighty-five is to be printed and that the positions in which
it is to be printed are described in the FORMAT statement
having the statement number 900. In the FORMAT statement
the code "T2" points to print position two. The "I" in the
code "I3" says that an INTEGER value is to be printed and
the "3" means three print positions are to be reserved for
displaying the value. Therefore the effect of the sequence
"T2,I3" is to reserve print positions two, three and four
for displaying an INTEGER value. This means that when the
PRINT statement is executed, the symbols "-85" appear in the
second, third and fourth print positions.

    Consider the following pair of statements.

                PRINT 901, 7294, -38
            901 FORMAT(T3,I4,T8,I3)

Result: A line is printed in which the following symbols
        appear in the print positions shown.

                one   ten
                 ↓   ↓
    print   ⎧0   1
    positions ⎨123456789012

    symbols   7294 -38

In this example the "T3" and "T8" are examples of "T-codes".
A code of the form "Tp" where "p" is some integer value in
the range 1 thru 133 means "beginning in print position p
...". The "I4" and "I3" are examples of "Integer masks" (I-
masks). An I-mask is used for each INTEGER value in an
output list. The word "mask" is appropriate because the
appearance of the value printed is that which is "seen" thru

the mask. By changing the mask, the appearance of the printed line can be changed. The general form of an I-mask is "Iw" where "w" specifies how many print positions are to be reserved.

You are no doubt wondering what will happen if more (or fewer) print positions are reserved than are necessary to display a value. The following table contains several examples which illustrate how an INTEGER value appears within the positions reserved by its I-mask. In the table the symbol "b" denotes a blank.

	Value Being Printed	Mask	Symbols Stored In Reserved Positions
i)	12345	I5	12345
ii)	12345	I6	b12345
iii)	12345	I3	***
iv)	0	I2	b0
v)	-0	I3	b-0
vi)	-12345	I6	-12345
vii)	-12345	I8	bb-12345
viii)	-12345	I5	*****

These examples illustrate the following points regarding the use of an I-mask.

   i) If the number is positive, the plus sign is not printed. See examples (i) thru (iv).

  ii) If the number is negative, the negative sign appears to the left of the leftmost digit. See examples (v) thru (viii).

 iii) If more print positions are reserved than are necessary to print the value, blanks are added to the left of the value to fill out the excess print positions. To be precise, the surplus positions to the left of the value are unchanged by the insertion of the value in the rightmost positions. Since the print positions are all initially blank before processing of the format codes begins, this normally means that the excess positions contain blanks.

  iv) If fewer positions are reserved than are necessary to store the value, the print positions reserved by the mask are filled with asterisks. It is not necessary to reserve a position for the sign of a positive or zero value.

To summarize: INTEGER values (constants, variables and expressions) appearing in an output list can be positioned anywhere across a print line. This is done by providing an I-mask for each INTEGER value in the output list. The first position covered by the mask is determined by the T-code which preceeds the mask. At execution time, the codes in the FORMAT statement are scanned left to right. As each T-code - I-mask combination is encountered, the next item in the output list is picked up and its value is stored in the print positions covered by the mask.

Two additional points. In the codes "Tp" and "Iw", the "p" and "w" must be unsigned positive integer values. Any position referred to by a T-code or covered by an I-mask must be in the range 1 thru 133. For example, the FORMAT statement "FORMAT(T130,I6)" causes the message "FORMATTED LINE EXCEEDS BUFFER LENGTH" to be printed. The reason is that the mask "I6" extends beyond position 133.

Exercise 6.1

1. What T-code must preceed a mask so that it will start in position 100?

2. If the T-code "T75" preceeds the mask I8, what is the last position reserved by the mask?

3. Write a sequence of T-codes and I-masks to reserve the print positions 16-24, 25, and 80-90 for three INTEGER items appearing in an output list.

4. a) Write a FORMAT statement which, when used with the statement "PRINT 82,-123,4567,89" will put the symbols -123456789 in print positions 8 thru 17.

   b) For the same PRINT statement as used in (a), write a FORMAT statement which will cause the symbols 4567b89bb-123b to appear in print positions 2 thru 15. Check the correctness of your FORMAT statements by using the computer to print the results.

5. Predict the output obtained by executing the statements below. Check your prediction using the computer.

```
       PRINT 99,333,22,1
    99 FORMAT(T10,I3,T10,I2,T10,I1)
```

6. Explain the difference between:

   PRINT,100,200   and PRINT 100,200

6.5 Vertical Control

The preceding section described one method of
positioning values along a print line. In order to control
the vertical positioning of printed items, we make use of
print position number 1. The symbol stored in position 1 is
called the Vertical Control Character, or VCC for short. The
VCC is not printed but all symbols stored in the remaining
132 positions are. The different symbols and the effect of
using each is shown in the following table.

Vertical Control Character	Action	Meaning: "The line is printed ...."
1	new page	at the top of the next page
+	no space	on the same line as the last line
blank	single space	on the line below the last line
0	double space	on the line two lines below the last line printed
-	triple space	on the line three lines below the last line printed

Any Vertical Control Character other than one of the
five in the table has the same effect as a blank.

To cause the desired VCC to be put in print position one
is simply a matter of enclosing the VCC in a pair of single
quotes and putting the code T1 ahead of it. For example, the
sequence "T1,'0'" causes a zero to be stored in position one
and therefore the line will be printed on the second line
following the last line printed. The program below prints
the number 1 at the top of a page; the number 2 underneath
it; and the number 3 after two blank lines have been left.

```
      C EXAMPLE 6.3 EXAMPLE OF VERTICAL SPACING CONTROL
            PRINT 100,1
            PRINT 200,2
            PRINT 300,3
            STOP
      100 FORMAT(T1,'1',T2,I5)
      200 FORMAT(T1,' ',T2,I5)
      300 FORMAT(T1,'-',T2,I5)
            END
```

The output produced is:

```
print        {
positions    {1234567890

                1    (at the top of a page)
                2
                b }  two blank
                b }      lines
                3
```

6.6 A Second Method Of Horizontal Control

When the VCC or a mask is positioned along the print line by putting a T-code in front of the element, the format element is said to have been positioned explicitly. If a T-code does not preceed a format element, the VCC or mask is said to be positioned implicitly. When implicit positioning is used, print positions are assigned consecutively to the format elements beginning with print position one. Some examples will illustrate this second method of horizontal control. The seven FORMAT statements which follow each put: a "0" in position one; the mask I6 in positions 2-7; and the mask I5 in positions 8-12.

     i)   FORMAT('0',I6,I5)

    ii)   FORMAT('0',T2,I6,I5)

   iii)   FORMAT('0',I6,T8,I5)

    iv)   FORMAT(T1,'0',I6,T8,I5)

     v)   FORMAT(T1,'0',T2,I6,I5)

    vi)   FORMAT(T1,'0',T2,I6,T8,I5)

   vii)   FORMAT(T2,I6,T8,I5,T1,'0')

In example (i), there is no T-code preceding the VCC and therefore the zero is stored in the first available print position, namely, position 1. Since no T-code preceeds the mask I6, the next 6 print positions are used for the mask I6. Similarly, since no T-code preceeds the mask I5, it is positioned implicitly in positions 8-12. In example (ii), the T-code "T2" is unnecessary since the mask I6 would be positioned in positions 2 thru 7 anyway. Examples (ii) thru (v) and (vii) show that a combination of implicit and explicit positioning of format elements may be used. Note that in these seven examples, the mask I6 always preceeds

the mask I5 in the list of format elements. This is
necessary if we are to claim that the seven examples are
equivalent. Keep in mind that regardless of where a mask is
positioned on the print line, the first mask in the format
codes is used with the first item in the output list; the
second with the second, etc. Thus the FORMAT statement

FORMAT('0',T8,I5,T2,I6)

is not equivalent to any of the seven since the order in
which the masks I6 and I5 appear is different.

6.7 The X-Code

When positioning masks along a print line, an X-code can
be used to skip over consecutive print positions. The X-
code has the form "nX" where "n" is the number of positions
to be skipped. The value of "n" must be an unsigned positive
INTEGER constant. The output produced by the pair of
statements below illustrates the effect of an X-code.

PRINT 3,-1234567
3 FORMAT(' ',4X,I10)

Since there are no T-codes, all items in the FORMAT
statement are positioned implicitly. Thus the VCC is stored
in position 1, the next four print positions are skipped
because of the code 4X, and the next ten positions are used
for printing the value of -1234567 according to the mask
I10. If a T-code preceeds an X-code, it specifies the first
print position to be skipped. The sequence "T91,5X" for
example, causes positions 91 thru 95 to be skipped.

The following example emphasizes the facts that: the
print positions are initially all blank; the elements in a
FORMAT statement are processed left to right; only those
positions which contain symbols after the operation of an I-
mask are changed by the operation of the mask. The output
produced by the statements:

PRINT 900, 111111, 2222, 33
900 FORMAT(T2,I6,T2,2X,I4,T2,I6)

is
    print   ⎰
    positions ⎱1234567

        112233

The sequence of events leading to this result is

```
print       {
positions   {1234567

            bbbbbbb     (initially all blank)
            b111111     (after the codes "T2,I6")
            b112222     (after the codes "T2,2X,I4")
            b112233     (after the codes "T2,I6")
```

6.8 "Hiding" The VCC

In previous examples, the vertical control character was stored in print position one either implicitly or explicitly. Since an X-code of "1X" also leaves a print position unchanged, the FORMAT statement FORMAT(1X,...) is equivalent to FORMAT(' ',...). Another way of putting a VCC in position one is to let the first position reserved by a mask do the job. The FORMAT statements below are equivalent.

```
     i) FORMAT(' ',I14,...)
    ii) FORMAT(1X,I14,...)
   iii) FORMAT(I15,...)
```

Each causes position one to have a blank. We must be a little careful however in permitting the first position of a mask to be used as the VCC. What is the output of the following pair of statements?

```
          PRINT 300,1475
      300 FORMAT(I4)
```

The result is that a value of 475 will be printed at the top of a page! This happens because the mask I4 is positioned implicitly in positions 1 thru 4. When the value in the output list is used with the mask I4, a 1 is stored in the first print position. A VCC of 1 of course, causes a skip to the top of a page and since the VCC is never printed, only the digits 475 appear.

Exercise 6.2

1. For each of the following FORMAT statements, write at least two other FORMAT statements which are equivalent.

```
    a)   FORMAT('+',T5,I12)
    b)   FORMAT(I14,T20,I3)
    c)   FORMAT(I12,T1,'0',20X,I3)
```

2. Predict the output of the following sets of statements.

Check your predictions using the computer.

a)   PRINT 2,1,2,3
      2 FORMAT('1',I2,2X,I4,2X,I3)

b)   PRINT 5,1,2,3
      5 FORMAT('0',I2,T14,I1,T6,I4)

c)   PRINT 8, -1,-2
      8 FORMAT(I2,T1,I2)

d)   N=17
        PRINT 14, N,MOD(18,N),MOD(N,18),N/3
     14 FORMAT(I10,2X,I3,T1,'0',20X,I4,1X,I2)

e)   PRINT 16,1234567,IFIX(SQRT(10000.))
     16 FORMAT(' ',I6,T4,I3)

6.9 Printing REAL Values

In order to print the values of expressions and variables appearing in the output list which are REAL values, it is simply a matter of using an F-mask or E-mask instead of an I-mask. The E-mask is used when the number is to be printed with an exponent. The E-mask should be used for printing values which are either very large, for example $5. \times 10^{20}$, or very small, for example $5. \times 10^{-20}$. It is also a good idea to use an E-mask if you are uncertain as to the value being printed. The F-mask is usually used for values which are somewhere in the range between .0000001 and one million. When using either of these masks, you must specify the number of print positions reserved for displaying the value and the number of digits to be printed to the right of the decimal point. The effect of using F-masks and E-masks is shown in the examples which follow.

Operation of the F-mask

General form: Fw.d where w is the number of print reserved, and d is the number of digits to the right of the decimal.

	Value of Number	F-mask	Symbols Stored In The Print Positions
i)	123.45	F7.2	b123.45
ii)	123.45	F10.4	bb123.4500
iii)	123.45	F6.0	bb123.
iv)	123.45	F6.1	b123.4
v)	123.45	F4.3	****

vi)	-123.45	F7.2	-123.45
vii)	-123.45	F9.3	b-123.450
viii)	-123.45	F5.0	-123.
ix)	-123.45	F4.0	****
x)	0.0	F2.0	0.
xi)	10.**20	F8.0	********
xii)	10.**(-9)	F8.6	0.000000
xiii)	.5	F3.1	0.5
xiv)	.5	F2.1	**
xv)	-.5	F4.1	-0.5

These examples illustrate the following points when using F-masks to display REAL values.

i) The sign is not printed unless the value is negative. In this case the sign appears immediately to the left of the value.

ii) If more positions are reserved than are necessary to display the value, the print positions not used for the negative sign, digits or decimal point are left unchanged. The value occupies the rightmost positions reserved by the mask. If the absolute value of the number being printed is less than 1.0 a zero is printed to the left of the decimal point. This means that when using the mask Fw.d, that w must be at least two larger than d for positive values and at least three larger than d for displaying negative values.

iii) If fewer positions are reserved than are necessary to display the value, asterisks are stored in the positions reserved by the mask.

iv) The value printed never contains an exponent. This means that numbers less than .0000001 in absolute value will be shown as a zero since only seven significant digits are stored for REAL values. Numbers which have a large absolute value will appear correctly (to seven significant digits), provided a sufficient number of positions are reserved for displaying the value.

v) If significant digits are dropped because of the value of d in the mask, the number is rounded to d decimal places. Rounding in the sixth decimal place or the digit in the seventh place may be inaccurate because of the internal representation of the number.

Operation of the E-mask

General form: Ew.d where w is the number of positions
reserved, and d is the number of
digits appearing to the right of the
decimal point.

Numbers printed using an E-mask have the general form:

$$s0.dddddddEsee$$

where: the first "s" denotes the sign of the number; the
second "s" denotes the sign of the exponent; and each "d"
represents a digit in the number. The number of digits
appearing between the decimal point and the "E" is
determined by the value of "d" in the mask Ew.d. The
following examples illustrate the effect of an E-mask.

	Value of Number	E-mask	Symbols Stored In The Print Positions
i)	123.45	E12.5	b0.12345Eb03
ii)	123.45	E15.7	bb0.1234500Eb03
iii)	123.45	E13.7	0.1234500Eb03
iv)	123.45	E12.7	************
v)	-123.45	E14.5	bb-0.12345Eb03
vi)	-123.45	E13.7	************
vii)	0.0	E10.3	b0.000Eb00
viii)	9876.543	E12.4	bb0.9877Eb04
ix)	-.00067890	E10.2	b-0.68E-03

These examples illustrate the following points
regarding the use of E-masks.

i)   The sign of the number and the exponent are not
     printed unless these values are negative.

ii) If more positions are reserved than are required to
     display the number, the print positions not used
     for a negative sign (if the number is negative),
     the leading zero, the decimal point, the digits in
     the number, the E, the sign of the exponent, the
     value of the exponent, are unchanged when the
     number is stored in the reserved positions. The
     number is stored in the rightmost positions
     reserved by the mask.

iii) If fewer positions are reserved than are necessary
     to display the value, asterisks are stored in the
     positions reserved by the mask. Note that there are

seven positions of overhead if a number is negative
and six positions of overhead if the number is
positive or zero. This means that the value of w in
the mask Ew.d must be at least seven larger than d
when printing negative values, and at least six
larger than d when printing positive values. The
overhead positions are for the sign of the number,
the leading zero and decimal point, and the four
positions required by the exponent.

iv) If significant digits are dropped because of the
value of d in the mask, the number is rounded to d
digits. Rounding in the sixth decimal place or in
fact, the digit appearing in the seventh decimal
place may be inaccurate because the internal
representation of REAL values does not use the
decimal number system.

The program sequence below shows that E-masks and F-
masks are positioned in precisely the same way as I-masks.

```
C EXAMPLE 6.4 POSITIONING REAL MASKS
      A=-.0064
      B=5.273E2
      C=-0.
      PRINT 50,A,B,C
   50 FORMAT('0',T13,F8.4,2X,F7.1,T2,E11.3)
```

Result:

```
           one        ten        twenty
            ↓          ↓           ↓
print     (0          1           2
positions { 1234567890 1234567890 123456789
```

```
            0bb0.000Eb00b-0.0064bbbb527.3
```

```
           '0'   E11.3     F8.4  2X   F7.1
                 (C)       (A)        (B)
```

When the print list contains a mixture of INTEGER and
REAL items, the FORMAT statement must contain a set of I-
masks and E or F masks so that INTEGER items are used with
I-masks and REAL items are used with either an E or F mask.
For example, without knowing any other details of the FORMAT
statement, we can state with certainty that an error occurs
when the following pair of statements is executed.

```
      PRINT 75,-(17/3+4),SIN(X),3.6E2,1
   75 FORMAT(...I12,...E16.3,...F7.2,...F8.4,...)
```

The reason that the message "FORMAT CODE AND DATA TYPE DO NOT MATCH" will be printed is that the fourth item in the output list is INTEGER valued and the fourth mask in the FORMAT statement is an F-mask which can only be used with REAL values.

*6.10 The General Mask - The G-Mask

A G-mask can be used in place of any mask. Because of this, it can sometimes make the writing of FORMAT statements easy for a beginning programmer. Its general form is "Gw.d" where "w" denotes the number of print positions to be reserved and "d" denotes (for REAL values) the number of significant digits to be printed.

When used with INTEGER values, the mask "Gw.d" is equivalent to the mask "Iw". The symbols ".d" can be omitted.

When used with REAL values, the mask "Gw.d" is equivalent to either

$$Ew.d \qquad or \qquad F(w-4).c \; , \; 4X$$
$$Where \; c = d - \text{"order of magnitude"}$$
(number of digits to the left of the decimal point).

Which one of the above is used depends on the value being printed. If X<.1 or d < "order of magnitude" then the E-form is used: Otherwise, the F-form is used. The following examples illustrate the various cases of G-mask output.

Value To Be Printed	G-Mask	Symbols In The Mask Positions	Equivalent Code(s)
12345	G5	12345	I5
12345	G5.3	12345	I5
.01	G9.2	b0.10E-01	E9.2
.1	G9.2	b0.10bbbb	F5.2,4X
9.9	G9.2	bb9.9bbbb	F5.1,4X
99.	G9.2	bb99.bbbb	F5.0,4X
100.	G9.2	b0.10Eb03	E9.2

If the magnitude of REAL values which are printed with G-masks are not known at the time the program is written, it is wise to make "w" at least seven larger than "d" so that sufficient positions are available should the F-form be used.

*6.11 Mask Modification - The P-Code

A P-code can be used to change the <u>appearance</u> of REAL values printed using an E-mask and to change the <u>value</u> of REAL values printed using an F-mask. In either case the P-code has the form "sP" where "s" is called the scale factor.

Use With E-Masks

When used with an E-mask, the P-code controls the position of the first significant digit relative to the decimal point. For example, a value of .2345E+03 can be displayed as 23.45E+01 by putting the code "2P" in front of the mask E9.2. In general, the format code "sPEw.d" causes:
"w" print positions to be reserved for displaying a value;
"s" digits to be printed to the left of the decimal point;
"d" digits to be printed to the right of the decimal point.
The value of "s" can be positive, negative or zero. Other examples are shown in the following table.

Value Of Number	Mask	Symbols In Reserved Positions
7.123	E12.4	bb0.7123Eb01
7.123	0PE12.4	bb0.7123Eb01
7.123	2PF12.4	b71.2300E-01
7.123	-3PF12.4	bb0.0007Eb04

These examples illustrate the following points.

    i)   A scale factor of zero is ignored.

    ii)   The "d" in the code "sPEw.d" determines the number of digits appearing to the right of the decimal point and <u>not</u> the number of significant digits printed.

   iii)   If "s" is positive, the decimal point appears s positions to the right relative to the output produced with no scale factor. The exponent value is modified to reflect the change.

    iv)   When "s" is negative, s zeros are placed ahead of the the first significant digit and the exponent value is adjusted to reflect the change.

Use With F-Mask

When a scale factor of "sP" is placed in front of an F-mask, the value of the number is multiplied by 10**s <u>before</u> the number is printed according to the F-mask. Some examples follow.

Value Of Number	Mask	Symbols In Reserved Positions
123.	0PF8.1	bbb123.0
123.	2PF8.1	b 12300.0
123.	-2PF8.1	bbbbb1.2

Why would one want to change the value of a REAL number before printing it? The reason is primarily to obtain increased accuracy when working with fractional values. Recall that many fractional values are stored as good approximations to the actual value. The following two sequences show how P-codes can be used to improve accuracy. Each sequence finds the sum of five values of one-fifth.

```
     X=.2                        X=2.
     Z=X+X+X+X+X                 Z=X+X+X+X+X
     PRINT 8,Z                   PRINT 8,Z
   8 FORMAT(E15.7)             8 FORMAT(-1PF4.1)
```

Result: the symbols printed   Result: b1.0 is printed
       are bb0.9999999E 00

In the left hand sequence, X has a value of .2. The tiny error associated with the internal representation of this value when compounded five times in an addition operation results in a value very close to 1 but not exactly 1. In the right hand sequence however, X is given an integer value. And, since integer values are stored accurately, the value of Z is ten. Then when the scale factor of -1 is applied when printing the value of Z, the result is the correct value of one. If writing programs in which extreme accuracy is important, it may be necessary to convert fractional values to integer values. Then, at output time, division by an appropriate power of ten can be performed using P-codes.

There are three additional points concerning the use of P-codes. First, a P-code appears in front of any repetition factor which might be used with a mask. For example, to modify the four masks defined by "4E15.3" using a scale

factor of three, the code should be written as "3P4E15.3".
Second, any scale factor present in a FORMAT statement
applies to all masks which follow it unless subsequently
modified by another P-code. This may mean a zero scale
factor may be required to erase the effect of an earlier P-
code. For example, the two FORMAT statements below <u>are</u>
equivalent.

> FORMAT(-1PE16.5, F7.2)

> FORMAT(-1PE16.5, -1PF7.2)

Third, if a P-code is used as a scale factor for a G-mask
(G-masks are discussed in the previous section.) the effect
of the P-code depends on whether or not the G-mask takes on
the E-form or the F-form (assuming REAL output items). This
means that you should be extremely careful when using scale
factors with G-masks because, depending on the value of the
output item, the scale factor may only cause a change in
appearance or it may cause a change in value.

6.12 Literals

A literal is a string of symbols. Literals are used to
explain the output, print report headings or as we have
already seen, define the VCC. Examples of literals are:
'1','DAILY REPORT', 'X=', etc.. A literal then, is simply a
string of characters enclosed by a pair of single quotes.
The number of print positions occupied by a literal is
simply the number of symbols between the quotes. Literals
can be included in FORMAT statements and are positioned in
the same way that masks are positioned. Thus a T-code can
be used to specify the print position to be occupied by the
first symbol in the literal. A literal can also be
positioned implicitly in which case the first position
reserved for the literal is the one immediately following
the last position reserved by the preceding element in the
the FORMAT statement. The effect of executing the
statements:

> Y=-2.6573
> PPINT 1,Y
> 1 FORMAT('1','THE VALUE OF Y=',F8.4)

is to print the line

> THE VALUE OF Y= -2.6573

at the top of the page. Since no T-code preceeds the
literal "THE VALUE OF Y=", its symbols will occupy positions

2 thru 16 of the print line. This FORMAT statement contains two literals. The VCC can be the first symbol in a longer literal. For example, the two literals in the foregoing example could have been combined in the following equivalent way.

                1 FORMAT('1THE VALUE OF Y=',F8.4)

What is the effect of the following pair of statements?

                PRINT 2
                2 FORMAT('0PROGRAMMING IS DIFFICULT',T17,'EASY')

The symbols printed are,

                PROGRAMMING IS EASYICULT

Since the FORMAT statement is processed left to right, the sequence "T17,'EASY'" causes print positions 17-20 to contain the symbols "EASY". Since the positions 17 thru 25 previously contained the word DIFFICULT, only the first four letters of DIFFICULT are affected by the symbols in the literal 'EASY'. This explains the output produced.

     One further point. Suppose you would like to print the word "IT'S". If it is necessary to have a quote as one of the symbols in the literal, then two consecutive quotes must be used. The literal "IT'S" for example is defined as 'IT''S' but still would occupy four print positions which would contain the symbols IT'S. Similarly, a literal containing six consecutive apostrophes (''''''), defines a literal consisting of the symbols ''.

* H-type Literals

     An H-code is an alternate means of defining a literal. Its general form is "nHsss...s" where each "s" denotes a symbol and "n" is the number of symbols in the literal. Examples of H-type literals are "7HTUESDAY", "1H*", and "10HTIME TABLE". H-type literals are positioned in precisely the same way as quote-type literals. For example, the statements below are equivalent.

                FORMAT('0',T20,'ONE',T10,'TWO')

                FORMAT(1H0,T20,3HONE,T10,3HTWO)

     Most programmers prefer using quote-type literals to H-type literals. The reason is simply that the number of symbols in an H-type literal must be counted if an H-type literal is used. Some Fortran compliers do not permit quote-type literals and therefore H-type literals must be used.

6.13 The Slash "/" Code

As has been described previously, the symbol stored in the first print position controls the vertical spacing of printed output. A second method of causing the paper to move forward one or more lines is to use a slash code in the FORMAT statement. When the "/" symbol is encountered in a FORMAT statement, three things happen.

i)   A line is printed made up of the symbols stored in the print positions by the action of the format elements processed before the slash was encountered.

ii) All print positions are set to blanks.

iii) The format codes following the slash are processed as if they were the first codes in another FORMAT statement.

Note that the slash symbol itself is not stored in any print position. It merely triggers the printing of a line which displays the current contents of the print positions.

The following pair of examples illustrates the effect of the slash code.

```
Example (i)     JKL=4000
                YY=-2.34E-06
                PRINT 8,JKL,YY
              8 FORMAT('1JKL=',I5,/,' YY=',E10.3)
```

Result: Two lines are printed at the top of a page and
        appear as:
```
                JKL= 4000
                YY= -0.234E-07
```

In this example, note that the VCC for the second line printed is hidden in the literal ' YY='. This blank which begins the literal causes the line to appear on the line immediately following the first line printed.

```
Example (ii)    JKL=4000
                YY=-2.34E-06
                PRINT 2,JKL/1000,YY*10.E+4
              2 FORMAT(///,' JKL/1000=',I3//,'0YY*10000=',
               *F9.5,//)
```

When executed, the output consists of:

```
a blank line    (due to first slash)
a blank line    (due to second slash)
a blank line    (due to third slash)
JKL/1000=   4   (due to slash following the mask I3)
a blank line    (due to second slash after the mask I3)
a blank line    (due to VCC of 0 in the literal 'OYY...'
YY*10000=  -0.02340 (due to first slash after F9.5)
a blank line    (due to second slash after F9.5)
a blank line    (due to  reaching the end of format codes)
```

This second example illustrates the following points.

> i) It is not necessary to use commas to separate slash codes from each other or from other elements in the FORMAT statement. eg: "I3//'OYY*10000='".

> ii) Frequently when using slashes, the list of format elements is lengthy and it is necessary to use a continuation card to continue the set of format elements. Recall that this is done by punching a non-zero, non-blank character in column six of the continuation card and viewing columns 7 thru 72 of this card as being appended to the right of column 72 of the previous card.

> iii) Regardless of whether or not there are slash codes in the FORMAT statement, a line is printed when the right bracket at the end of the FORMAT statement is encountered.

Although a slash code can be used to produce blank lines, its actual function is to cause a line to be printed before the end of the FORMAT statement is reached.

6.14 Two Short Cuts

(a) Repetition Factors

If there are five INTEGER elements in an output list and each is to be displayed using a mask I8, the five masks can either be written as "I8,I8,I8,I8,I8" or more conveniently as "5I8". In other words, a positive INTEGER constant put in front of any mask has the effect of repeating the mask the number of times defined by the constant.   The FORMAT statement below contains five masks.

FORMAT ('0',2F5.1,2X,3I6)

It is equivalent to the statement,

                    FORMAT('0',F5.1,F5.1,2X,I6,I6,I6) .

    Repetition factors must be positive INTEGER constants.
Examples of invalid repetition factors are NI17 and 3.F12.1.

   (b) Groups and Group Counts

    If you wish to repeat a set of format codes instead of
just a single mask, it is simply a matter of enclosing the
group of codes to be repeated within brackets and putting a
group count in front of the left bracket. For example, the
two FORMAT statements below are equivalent.

                    FORMAT('0',2(I3,1X,E17.5))
                    FORMAT('0',I3,1X,E17.5,I3,1X,E17.5)

In the first FORMAT statement, the number 2 is a group count
which causes the group (I3,1X,E17.5) to be repeated twice.
If a group count is omitted, it is assumed to be 1.

    It is permissible to have groups within a group but one
cannot have a group within a group within a group. That is,
groups can only be nested to a depth of two. A FORMAT
statement containing nested groups is:

                    FORMAT('1',2(2X,3(I3,F7.2),I5))

In this FORMAT statement, there are 14 masks. The order in
which they appear is: I3,F7.2, I3,F7.2, I3,F7.2, I5,
I3,F7.2, I3,F7.2 I3,F7.2,I5. Sometimes when using groups,
one forgets how many print positions are being "chewed up"
by the format codes. For example, the FORMAT statement above
reserves a total of 75 print positions. Suppose the mask I3
had been changed to I15. In this case, the set of format
elements would span 147 print positions. Since there are
only 133 available, an error would result and the job would
be terminated.

    Are the following statements equivalent?

            i)   FORMAT(2I5)
           ii)   FORMAT((2I5))
          iii)   FORMAT(2(I5))

The answer is "That depends.". Technically, the "2" in (i)
and (ii) is a repetition factor whereas in (iii), it is a
group count. Furthermore, (ii) contains a group and (i) does

not. If the PRINT or WRITE statement which used one of these
FORMAT statements contained either one or two elements in
its output list, they would all produce the same result. If
not, the output produced by (iii) would be different. The
reasons for this difference are explained in the next
section.

Exercise 6.3

1. Fill in the third column of the table below indicating
   the symbols stored in the positions reserved by the mask.

Item In Output List	Mask	Symbols In Mask Positions
a) -12345	I7	
b) -12345	I5	
c) 12345.	F8.2	
d) - 123.45	F7.1	
e) .00024E-02	F9.4	
f) -.00025	E10.2	
g) 2.0006	E12.5	
h) 10.E5	F8.0	
i) 10.E-10	F9.7	
j) 2.64	I4	
k) 3	F4.0	

2. For each of the following, state the positions reserved
   by each mask and/or literal in the FORMAT statement.

   a) FORMAT('0',T5,I8,T2,I3)
   b) FORMAT(F12.7,3X,T20,F8.0,T17,'X=')
   c) FORMAT('1X(I)= '/E20.6,F17.4)
   d) FORMAT(T5,I8,2X,E15.6,T1,'12345')

3. Consider the FORMAT statement:

   FORMAT('0',2(3I2,3X),3F6.2,3(2X,F8.0))

   With respect to this statement,

   a) How many groups are there?
   b) How many masks are there?
   c) What is the 5th mask?
   d) What positions are reserved by the first F8.0 mask?
   e) Which mask reserves positions 13 and 14?
   f) What positions are reserved by the third F6.2 mask?
   g) If the fifth item in the output list was REAL, would
      an error occur?

h) If the eighth item in the output list had a value of
    12345.67, what symbols would be printed in the print
    positions reserved by its mask?

4. Predict the output of the following PRINT statements.
   Check your predictions using the computer.

a)   X=+49.
     I=-25
     PRINT 3,X**(1./2.),I
   3 FORMAT('1',F3.0,T1,I4)

b)   PRINT 1,2.,3.,4,5,6,7.,8.,9,10,11
    1 FORMAT('1',2(3X,2F4.1,I4,2I5))

6.15 Two Unanswered Questions

    In all the examples of formatted output appearing
previously, the number of masks in the FORMAT statement has
been the same as the number of items in the output list. It
is only natural to ask:

    i) What happens if there are fewer items in the output
       list than there are masks in the FORMAT statement?

    ii) What happens if there are more items in the output
        list than there are masks in the FORMAT statement?

Question 1. (Fewer items than masks)

    The set of format elements is processed left to right.
When a mask is detected, the next item in the output list
is picked up and put in the print positions reserved by the
mask. This means that if there is a surplus of masks in a
FORMAT statement, sooner or later a mask will be found for
which there is no element in the output list. When this
happens, the first excess mask and all format codes which
follow it are ignored and the line is printed using the
symbols stored in the print positions up to that point. One
example should suffice. When the statements:

            X=2.34
            Y=5.
            PRINT 999,X
        999 FORMAT('1 X=',F5.2,/,'   Y=',F5.2)

are executed, the symbols:

            X= 2.34
            Y=

appear on two lines at the top of the next page. Note that the slash and the second literal are processed since they preceed the first unnecessary mask. Had there been other format elements after the second F5.2 mask, they would have been ignored.

Question 2. (More items than masks)

When there are more items in the output list than there are masks in the FORMAT statement, the answer to the question "What happens?" is "That depends.". It depends on whether or not there is a group in the FORMAT statement. However, regardless of whether or not there are groups, we can state with certainty that more than one line will be printed. The reason for this fact is that each time the end of the FORMAT statement is reached, a line is printed which displays the contents of the print positions. Furthermore, a mask must be found for each item in the output list. Thus the lack of sufficient masks can be viewed as a third method of vertical control. Let's look at a simple example.

```
      PRINT 10,1,2,3
10 FORMAT(' ',I3)
```

When executed, three lines will be printed. Clearly the first element in the output list will be used with the mask I3. Then the end of the FORMAT statement is encounted and so a line is printed with a 1 appearing in print position four. Then all print positions are set to blanks. However, there are two more elements in the output list. In order to find a mask for the second element in the output list, the FORMAT statement is recycled beginning from the left bracket which defines the set of format codes. This means that the value 2 is stored in print position four. Again we reach the end of the FORMAT statement and so a second line is printed with the value 2 appearing directly below the value 1. Since a mask has not yet been found for the third item in the output list, this recycling process is repeated and the value 3 is printed below the value 2.

The rule illustrated by this example is:

"Provided there are no groups in the FORMAT statement, a line is printed each time the end of the FORMAT statement is reached. The set of format codes are repeated over and over again until a mask has been found for each item in the output list."

Naturally, during this recycling process, an I-mask must be the first one encountered for each INTEGER item, and an

E-mask or F-mask must be the first one encountered for each REAL item.

When there are one or more groups present in the FORMAT statement, the groups determine the part of the FORMAT statement which is recycled. Consider the following example.

```
        PRINT 777,1,2,3
    777 FORMAT(' ',(I3))
```

The only difference between this example and the previous one is that the FORMAT statement now contains the group "(I3)" with an assumed group count of 1. When the PRINT statement is executed, the output appears as:

```
print       ⎰
positions   ⎱1234567

       bbb1
       bb2
       bb3
```

This result is obtained in the following way. The VCC for the first line is a blank and the item 1 is therefore stored in position four using the mask I3. A line is printed because the end of the FORMAT statement has been reached. The mask for the second item is found by recycling to the group count of the group appearing in the FORMAT statement. Since, in this example, the group count is one by default, the value 2 is stored using the mask I3 which spans the first three print positions. The VCC for this second line then, is the symbol in the first position reserved by the mask I3. Again the end of the FORMAT statement is reached causing a line to be printed and the 2 appears in position three. This process is repeated in order to find a mask for the third item and so the 3 appears underneath the 2.

If it was desired to have the three values appear underneath each other, then either the group could be left out as was done previously, or the FORMAT statement below could have been used.

```
        FORMAT(' ',(T2,I3))
```

If there is more than one group in a FORMAT statement, the format elements which are recycled may be stated as:

"Beginning with the group count of the group whose rightmost bracket is nearest the end of the FORMAT statement".

The arrows in the following three cases indicate the point at which the set of format elements are recycled.

FORMAT (...3 (...)...)

FORMAT (...2 (...)...5 (...)...)

FORMAT (...(...)...4 (...3 (...)...)...)

One further example is:

```
            X1=19.7
            X2=179.3
            X3=-6.
            X4=8.2E-1
            PRINT 666,1,X1,2,X2,3,X3,4,X4
     666 FORMAT('1',2(' X',I1,'=',F7.2,2X))
```

The output produced appears as:

```
print        ⌠0          1          2
positions    ⌡1234567890 1234567890 12345

            1bX1=bb19.70bbbX2=b179.30
            bX3=bb-6.00bbbX4=bbb0.82
```

In this example there are eight items in the output list and four masks in the FORMAT statement, all of which are part of the group. When the format codes are recycled beginning with the group count the VCC for the second line is obtained from the first character of the literal ' X'. This is the reason the symbols on the second line are shifted one position to the left.

Exercise 6.4

1. How many lines of output are produced in each of the following if the PRINT statement is PRINT 1,100,200,300 ?

a)   1 FORMAT(' ',I4)
b)   1 FORMAT(3I5)
c)   1 FORMAT(' ',2I5)
d)   1 FORMAT(' ',2(3X,I4))

2. Predict the output of each of the following. Check your predictions by using the computer.

```
a)        PRINT 70, -(3.**4),-2**5,0.
      70  FORMAT(' 1THREE**4=',E11.2,T21,I4)

b)        PRINT 80
      80  FORMAT(' ',6('OVER AND OVER '))

c)        PRINT 90,11,2
      90  FORMAT(I2)

d)        PRINT 100,3.5,4.5
     100  FORMAT(' ',T10,'ITEM1=',F4.1,T2,'ITEM2=')

e)        PRINT 110,123,123,123
     110  FORMAT(' ',3X,2('123',I3))
```

3. With respect to the FORMAT statement,

```
        FORMAT(' LINE',5I1,3(1X,2I3,2X,3I2))
```

a) How many masks are there? (Don't forget repetition factors and group counts.)
b) How many positions are reserved by the X-codes?
c) If the output list contains 16 INTEGER items, how many times is the word "LINE" printed?
d) If the output list contains the values 0,1,2,...,98,99, then,
    i) How many lines are printed?
    ii) What values are printed on the 2nd line, the 6th line, the last line?
    iii) In what print positions do the values 2, 16, 48 and 99 appear?
    iv) On how many lines does print position 11 contain a blank?

6.16 A Word About Commas

In each of the example FORMAT statements, commas have been used to separate adjacent format elements. This practice is recommended since it improves the readability of the FORMAT statement. Commas can be omitted if their omission does not cause any ambiguity. The pair of FORMAT statements below are equivalent.

```
        FORMAT(T5,'LITERAL',2I1,T15,'END')
        FORMAT(T5'LITERAL'2I1T15'END')
```

If a sequence such as "T11,I11,1X" appears in a FORMAT statement, both commas are necessary since their omission would permit the codes to be interpreted as "T1,1I1,11X". As a general rule, use commas to separate format codes.

*6.17 Format-Free Output

When a programmer chooses to use one of the two statements available for producing format-free output of printed values, he is primarily interested in seeing the results of computations performed in the program and is not particularly concerned with the precise positioning of values on the page. The two forms of the format-free output statement are:

PRINT,output list

WRITE(6,*) output list

The "6" in the WRITE statement is the device number usually associated with the high speed printer. It may be different which means you would change it to its appropriate value. The device number can also be assigned to an INTEGER variable and the variable name used in place of the "6" in the WRITE statement. The reasons for using the WRITE instead of the PRINT are similar to those suggested in the case of formatted output.

When a format-free output statement is used,

    i) The pair of codes 1X,I12 is used for each
       INTEGER item in the output list.

    ii) The pair of codes 1X,F20.7 is used for each
        REAL item in the output list.

This means the outputs produced by the following are identical.

    i)   PRINT,1234567,.1234567

    ii)   WRITE(6,*) 1234567,.1234567

    iv)   PRINT 99,1234567,.1234567
        99 FORMAT(1X,I12,1X,F20.7)

    iv)   WRITE(6,99) 1234567,.1234567
        99 FORMAT(1X,I12,1X,F20.7)

One further point. When using format-free output, if the total number of print positions reserved by the default format codes exceeds the number of available print positions, then extra lines are printed using the same technique until all output items have been printed.

6.18 Summary

1. When printing items which are stored in the computer memory, the following three questions must be answered.

    i) Where (on what device) are the items to be printed?

    ii) What values or symbols are to be displayed?

    iii) How are the values to appear on the output device?

    In WATFIV, the programmer answers the "What" question by defining an output list of items to be displayed. He answers the "Where" question by either using the word PRINT or by using the WRITE statement with a pointer to the high speed printer. If the appearance of items on the page is controlled by the programmer, the output is formatted. If WATFIV looks after the placement of the items, the output is format-free.

2. Formatted Output.

    With formatted output, the appearance of the printed output is controlled by a set of codes which are included in a FORMAT statement. The FORMAT statement is linked to the PRINT or WRITE statement by its statement number.

    The position along the print line at which an item is printed depends on the positions spanned by the mask associated with the output item. Masks are matched one for one, beginning from the left, with items in the output list. An I-mask must be used for each INTEGER item and an E-mask or F-mask must be used for each REAL item. Masks may be positioned either explicitly or implicitly.

    There are three techniques for controlling the line on which an item is printed. These are:

    i) By the vertical control character stored in print position one.

    ii) By the use of one or more slash codes.

    iii) By having fewer masks in the FORMAT statement than there are items in the output list.

    Literals can be included in the FORMAT statement and they are positioned in the same way as masks.

The format codes discussed in this chapter are:

Iw - the mask for INTEGER items

Fw.d - a mask for REAL items

Ew.d - a mask for REAL items

Tp - a code to explicitly position an item

nX - a code to skip over print positions

/ - a code to cause a line to be printed

' ' - used to define literals

r - used to repeat a mask r times

g - used to repeat a set of codes g times

g(...) - used to repeat a group of format elements

In the above, the lower case letters must be positive INTEGER constants.

3. After any line is printed, blanks are stored in all print positions.

6.19 Programming Problems

6.1   Punch ten data cards, each containing a different person's height H (in inches) and weight W (in pounds). Write a program which reads the cards one at a time and prints a table of the form shown below.

```
HEIGHT          WEIGHT          CHARACTERISTIC

 XXX             XXX             XXXXX
 XXX             XXX             XXXXX
 etc.            etc.            etc.
```

Use a mask of I3 to print the height and weight. For the characteristic print: "SKINNY" if W<3.8H-118; "FAT" if W>4.2H-132;   "NORMAL"   otherwise.   Note   that   three different FORMAT statements, each containing a different literal, will be required.

6.2   Add   to   the   program   for   the   previous   question calculations to determine the average height and average weight of the ten people. In addition, print a count of the number of skinny, fat and normal people. Print the three additional items of information as shown below.

```
AVERAGE HEIGHT IS XXX.X INCHES
AVERAGE WEIGHT IS XXX.X POUNDS
NUMBER OF SKINNY PEOPLE IS XX
NUMBER OF FAT PEOPLE IS XX
NUMBER OF NORMAL PEOPLE IS XX
```

6.3   Two ladders of lengths twenty feet and thirty feet respectively are positioned across a laneway between two buildings as shown in the following diagram. They cross at a point eight feet above the ground. How wide is the laneway?

Print your   answer as   "THE LANE   IS XX.XXX FEET WIDE". Obtain your answer by starting with two estimates -- one high say 21, and one low, say 3. Use the average of the high and low estimates as a better estimate. Calculate where the ladders would cross if the lane had a width equal to the new estimate. Based on this result, use the new estimate to replace either the previous high estimate or the previous low estimate. Repeat the procedure. Continue repetitions until the difference in two successive estimates is less than .001.   Can you find an equation which, when solved, would give the exact value of the width? (This is not an easy equation to find.)

6.4   Check balancing. A deck of cards contains a deposit-withdrawal code in column one and a dollar amount of the form XXX.XX in columns three thru eight. A "1" in column one   indicates   a   deposit   and   a   "2"   indicates   a withdrawal. The dollar amount indicates the size of the deposit or withdrawal.   Write a program which reads an unknown number of cards and for each prints either

```
$XXX.XX DEPOSIT, BALANCE IS NOW $XXXX.XX
                    or
$XXX.XX WITHDRAWAL, BALANCE IS NOW $XXX.XX
```

Assume the starting balance is zero. If the attempted withdrawal is larger than the balance, print the line "WITHDRAWAL   OF $XXX.XX   WOULD   EXCEDE   BALANCE,   NOT PROCESSED".

6.5   The product of (x-a)(x-b)(x-c)(x-d) is a fourth degree
       polynomial of the form $px^4+qx^3+rx^2+sx+t$. Write a program
       which reads values of "a",   "b",   "c",   and "d"   and
       calculates the values of p, q, r, s, t.   Print a line of
       the following form.

       (___) X**4+ (___) X**3+ (___) X**2+ (___) X+ (___)

       where the dashes represent the values calculated.

6.6   Read an unknown number of data cards each of which
       contains two INTEGER values. Each of the values is
       either a 1, a 2, or a 3. Count the total number of ones,
       twos and threes and print a line of the form "MORE 2'S
       THAN 1'S OR 3'S" based on the counts obtained.   Use only
       one FORMAT statement in your program.

Questions Answered In This Chapter

1. Why are some seemingly easy problems awkward to program using our present knowledge?

2. How can we define and use sets of variables which will make the programming of these problems easy?

3. What is compile time initialization?

7.1 It Looks Easy But ...

Suppose we are to write a program to solve the following simple problem.

1. Read a value of N. (assume N is 5 or less)
2. Read N more values.
3. Print the N values read during step 2 in the reverse order to which they were read. Print only one value per line.

Before looking at the program below, spend a couple of minutes trying to set up a program which will solve the problem.

One method which could be used to solve the problem is the following.

```
C EXAMPLE 7.1 PRINT N VALUES IN REVERSE ORDER
C ASSUME N IS 5 OR LESS
      READ,N
      IF(N.GE.1)  READ,X1
      IF(N.GE.2)  READ,X2
      IF(N.GE.3)  READ,X3
      IF(N.GE.4)  READ,X4
      IF(N.GE.5)  READ,X5
      IF(N.GE.5)  PRINT,X5
      IF(N.GE.4)  PRINT,X4
      IF(N.GE.3)  PRINT,X3
      IF(N.GE.2)  PRINT,X2
      IF(N.GE.1)  PRINT,X1
      STOP
      END
```

There are three important observations we should make.

i) Since the values must be printed in reverse order, we must read all N values before any lines can be printed.

ii) Since there may be as many as five values to be read, there must be five variables in the program to store the five possible values. Furthermore, a separate READ statement containing a single variable in the input list must be used to assign values to the variables since it is not known at the time the program is written how many variables are to be assigned a value.

iii) If the value of N was permitted to be very large, the program would be ridiculously long since we cannot use a looping technique. In order to use a looping technique, we would have to be able to change the name of the variable in the READ statement.

To summarize, the awkwardness arises from the facts that we don't know how many values are to be read until the program is executed and we have no way of changing the name of a variable in a WATFIV statement and thus cannot use a looping technique.

What we would like to do would be to set up a program of the following type. The program contains several errors but we are simply trying to develop the idea.

```
        READ,N
        DO 29 i=1,N
            READ, Xi
     29 CONTINUE
        i=N
        WHILE(i≥1)
            PRINT,Xi
            i=i-1
        END WHILE
        STOP
```

Observe that the name of the variable in the READ list and PRINT list is dynamic. The variable name changes as the value of i changes. In all programs thus far, the name of any variable appearing in a WATFIV statement has been fixed. The primary purpose of this chapter is to describe how we can change the name of a variable which is used in a statement.

In WATFIV, the REAL and INTEGER statements are used to specify the type of value to be taken on by a variable. In particular, they have been used to override the first letter rule. The REAL and INTEGER statements can also be used to <u>define sets of variables.</u> For example, a set of variables could be defined for use in the foregoing problem using the statement:

REAL X(5)

This declaration statement:

    i) Defines a set of variables called X. There are five elements in the set, and

    ii) The names of the variables in the set X are: X(1), X(2), X(3), X(4) and X(5). Each of these five variables takes on REAL values.

The set X is called a one-dimensional array of variables. The variables X(1),X(2),X(3),X(4) and X(5) are called singly-subscripted variables. For each of these variables, the number inside the brackets is called the subscript. Thus the subscript of the variable X(3) is 3. The program below shows how we could use the set X to make the programming of our original problem much easier.

```
C EXAMPLE 7.2 USING SUBSCRIPTED VARIABLES
      REAL X(5)
      READ,N
      DO 49 I=1,N
         READ,X(I)
   49 CONTINUE
      I=N
      WHILE(I.GE.1)
         PRINT,X(I)
         I=I-1
      END WHILE
      STOP
      END
```

In this program, the statement "READ,X(I)" will be executed N times. Each time it is executed, the value of I changes and so the name of the variable in the input list, namely X(I), changes. Similarly, the name of the variable in the output list of the PRINT statement changes as the value of I changes. In this case a WHILE loop is more convenient to use than a DO loop for the printing step because the parameters of a DO loop must be positive. That is, we could not use a statement like DO 17 I=N,1,-1.

When using a REAL or INTEGER statement to define sets of variables, an INTEGER constant is put in brackets following the set name. The value of this constant defines the dimension of (number of elements in) the set. Both of the statements below violate the rule that the number of elements in a set must be defined by a positive INTEGER.

                    INTEGER ABC(M)
                    REAL S1923(6.0)

If it is not known at the time the program is written how many variables might be needed, the set should be defined to have the maximum number of variables that might possibly be required.

The statement

                    REAL LUCKY(20),JACK,BOOK(1000)

defines a total of 1021 REAL variables for use in a program. Twenty of these belong to the set LUCKY and their names are LUCKY(1),LUCKY(2),LUCKY(3),...,LUCKY(20). JACK is called a simple (or scalar or non-subscripted) REAL variable and is included in the declaration statement simply to override the first-letter rule. BOOK is the name of a set of 1000 REAL variables whose elements are BOOK(1), BOOK(2), BOOK(3), ... ,BOOK(1000).

Any valid WATFIV name can be used as a set name. For example, DADDY9, GOTO, J12345 are valid set names whereas OHNO+, 9POT, and ABCDEFG are invalid.

In this book, the words "set" and "array" are synonyms. Each refers to a collection of variables. Variables in the same set or array differ only by the value of their subscripts.

7.2 A Second Example Using Subscripted Variables

One of the more famous sequences of numbers is called the Fibonacci sequence. The first few numbers in the sequence are 1,1,2,3,5,8,13,21,... . Each number in the sequence, except for the first two, is obtained by adding the previous two values. Suppose we wish to write a program to print the first twenty numbers in the sequence all on the same line. We will require 20 variables in the output list of the PRINT statement and if we wish to calculate the values of these twenty variables using a looping technique, we will need variable names which can be changed "on the go". A suitable program is shown below.

```
C EXAMPLE 7.3 FIBONACCI NUMBERS
      INTEGER F(20)
      F(1)=1
      F(2)=1
      DO 6 I=3,20
         F(I)=F(I-1)+F(I-2)
    6 CONTINUE
      PRINT 900,F
  900 FORMAT('1',20I6)
      STOP
      END
```

There are two new ideas in this program. The first is that the statement "PRINT 900,F" is used to print the values. The output list of this statement contains the name of a set of variables which is used to create an output list consisting of the variables in the set. Using a set name in an output list is a short form way of putting all the variables in the set in the output list. We should consider this output list as having twenty items. Secondly, the variables F(I-1) and F(I-2) are used in the statement which calculates the successive values in the sequence. This is perfectly permissible in WATFIV and in fact, any arithmetic expression can be used to specify a subscript value. With reference to the set F used in the program, it would be permissible to include variables such as the following in the program.

   i)   F(20-I**J/K)

  ii)   F(1.5)

 iii)   F(ABS(SIN(3.*ALOG(6.))-.0001))

  iv)   F(32*3)

   v)   F(-2)

  vi)   F(F(4))

 vii)   F(F(F(6)-2)-3))

Since the names of the variables in the set are F(1), F(2), F(3),...,F(20), each of the above must reduce to one of these variable names or an error will result since we would be attempting to reference a variable which was not an element of the set F. In each of the seven examples given, the subscript value is either a REAL or INTEGER expression.

7.5   A Second Example Using Subscripted Variables   201

In example (i), the expression "20-I**J/K" must have a value in the range 1 to 20. If not, an error would occur.

In example (ii), the subscript has the REAL value 1.5 . If a subscript is REAL valued, the fractional part of the REAL number is truncated and thus the variable F(1.5) is equivalent to the variable F(1).

In example (iii) we know the value of the SIN function will be between +1 and -1, and so the value of the subscript will be a fraction in the range 0 to something less than 1. When the fraction is truncated, the variable being named is F(0) and since this variable is not an element of the set F, an error will occur.

Examples (iv) and (v) also produce errors since the variables F(96) and F(-2) are not in the set F.

Example (vi) is interesting in that the subscript expression is the name of a variable in the same set. F(4) has the value of the fourth number in the sequence, namely 3. This means that F(F(4)) is the same as F(3) and hence the value of F(F(4)) is 2. Note that F(F(9)) would cause an error since F(9) has a value 34 and F(34) is not in the set.

Example (vii) is an extension of the idea presented in example (vi). Thus the evaluation of example (vii) proceeds as follows: F(F(F(6)-2)-3)=F(F(8-2)-3)= F(8-3)=F(5)=5.

7.3 Valid and Invalid Uses

Suppose you and I have calculated the values of the first twenty Fibonacci numbers independently of one another and have stored the results in the sets YOUFF and MYF respectively. The sets have been defined by the statement:

INTEGER MYF(20),YOURF(20)

If we wanted to compare the two sets of results, we might write a statement such as:

IF (MYF.NE.YOURF) GO TO 999

Unfortunately, this type of statement is not permitted. All arithmetic expressions, logical expressions, and Assignment statements which reference values in a set must refer to a specific element of the set. This means that a statement such as "MYF=YOURF", or an expression such as "MYF-YOURF" is invalid. Thus in order to compare the two sets of values, we should set up a DO-loop such as the following.

```
           DO 3 I=1,20
              IF(MYF(I).NE.YOURF(I)) GO TO 999
        3 CONTINUE
```

Errors will result for each of the statements shown
below because a subscripted variable is used.

    i)   DO CASE F(I)   - in DO CASE statements

    ii)   GO TO(2,76,843,1),F(I)   - in Computed GO TOs

    iii) a) ASSIGN 6 TO F(I)   } - in ASSIGN statements and
        b) GO TO F(I),(4,8,6,23)}   Assigned GO TOs

    iv) a) DO 10 JJ=F(I),100
       b) DO 10 JJ=1,F(I)   } _ in any DO
       c) DO 10 JJ= 1,100,F(I)   statement
       d) DO 10 F(I)=1, 10

Exercise 7.1

1. Consider the program below.

```
           REAL A(4)
           DO 8 I=1,4
              A(I)=FLOAT(I)*2.+3.
              PRINT,A(I)
        8 CONTINUE
           STOP
```

a) Is each variable in the set assigned a value? Why?
b) How many values printed are prime numbers?
c) Why doesn't an error message result since the values
   assigned to variables in the set A are outside the range
   one to four?

2. Consider the statements:

```
           INTEGER BAC(5)
           DO 1 JKL=1,5
              BAC(6-JKL) = JKL
        1 CONTINUE
```

a) What is the value assigned to BAC(4)?
b) What variable has the value 4?

c) What is the value of:
    i)   BAC(2)*3/BAC(3)
    ii) MOD(BAC(4),3)+MOD(3,BAC(4))
   iii) BAC(4)**BAC(3)**BAC(4)
    iv) (BAC(3)-BAC(2).LT.BAC(1)/4)   (true or false?)
    v) BAC(BAC(BAC(BAC(1))))

3. What is the error in each of the following. Assume the sets A and HAPPY have been defined by:

       INTEGER A(2)
       REAL HAPPY(3)

a)   A(2)=HAPPY(4)
b)   X=HAPPY

c)   I=3
     A(1)=I
     HAPPY(1)=IDIM(I,A(I))

d)   J=IFIX(A(1))
e)   A=AMOD(3.,2.5)

4. Define a set of INTEGER variables called SET. Write a DO statement and one other statement to assign the values below to successive elements of SET.

   a)   2,5,8,11,14,17
   b)   -5,-4,-3,-2,-1
   c)   -5,-7,-9,-11,-13
   d)   1,3,7,15,31,63
   e)   1,0,1,0,1
   f)   1,0,-1,1,0,-1

7.4 Input-Output of Subscripted Variables

Input

Suppose an array X has been defined using the statement "REAL X(6)". Values are to be assigned to the six variables in the set X by reading the values from data cards. Four different ways of doing this are:

    i)   READ,X(1),X(2),X(3),X(4),X(5),X(6)

    ii)   READ,X

   iii)   DO 99 I=1,6
            READ,X(I)
       99 CONTINUE

iv)   READ,(X(I),I=1,6)

In (i), the input list contains six elements. In (ii), only the set name appears following the comma. This is equivalent to defining an input list which contains all the variables in the set and hence is equivalent in every way to method (i). Thus in method (ii), there are really six elements in the input list and using the set name is just a short form way of creating the desired list.

In method (iii), the READ statement contains only one element and is executed six times.

Method (iv) is completely equivalent to methods (i) and (ii). The symbols "(X(I),I=1,6)" are called an implied DO-loop. The purpose of an implied DO-loop is to create a list of variables using a DO-loop. In this example, the implied DO defines a set of six variable names which are the elements X(I) as I goes from 1 to 6 in steps of 1. In other words, the input list defined by the implied DO is X(1), X(2), X(3), X(4), X(5), X(6). The rules for writing implied DO-loops are similar to those for the DO statement except that the word "DO" does not appear and the loop is defined by enclosing the information in brackets. Implied DOs are handy tools for creating input or output lists as later examples will show.

The general form of an implied DO-loop is

(list, index = initial, test, increment)

The "list" contains one or more variables, expressions and/or array names. (Expressions such as "I+J" are not allowed if the implied DO-loop belongs to the input list of a READ statement.) The terms "index", "initial", "test" and "increment" serve the same purposes as when present in a DO statement. The list is repeated once for each value of the index specified by the parameters.

Are the four methods equivalent? The answer is a qualified "yes". Methods (i), (ii) and (iv) are definitely equivalent in that each of these uses only one READ statement and the input lists in each case are identical even though they are created in different ways. Method (iii) on the other hand, requires that the READ statement be executed six times, and therefore a minimum of six data cards will be read using method (iii). This means that if the data values were punched on separate cards, the four methods would be equivalent. If more than one value appeared on any card, method (iii) could not be used.

Output Of Subscripted Variables

Suppose a set of 400 INTEGER variables has been defined by the statement "INTEGER N(400)" and suppose that values have been assigned to each of the variables in the set.   We are required to print the 400 values so that eight are printed on each line.   The mask I10 is to be used for each value printed. Four methods of achieving this result are:

```
i)      PRINT 900, N
    900 FORMAT(' ',8I10)

ii)     PRINT 900,(N(J),J=1,400)
    900 FORMAT(' ',8I10)

iii)    DO 6 I=1,393,8
            PRINT 900,(N(I+J-1),J=1,8)
      6 CONTINUE
    900 FORMAT(' ',8I10)

iv)     DO 7 I=1,50
            PRINT 900,(N((I-1)*8+J),J=1,8)
      7 CONTINUE
    900 FORMAT(' ',8I10)
```

In example (i), the set name is used to create an output list of 400 items. The order of the elements in the set is of course N(1),N(2),N(3),...,N(400).   Since the FORMAT statement contains only eight masks: the values of N(1) thru N(8) will be printed on the first line. The FORMAT statement will be recycled and the next 8 values will appear on line 2. This process will be repeated until 50 lines have been printed.

In (ii), an implied DO-loop is used to create the same ouput list as in method (i). Method (ii) is therefore equivalent in every way to method (i).

In method (iii),   the PRINT statement will be executed for values of I of 1,9,17,25,...,393. The output list of the PRINT statement contains 8 variables   created by the implied DO. When I is 1, the variables are N(1),N(2),...,N(8). When I is 9, the variables are I(9) thru I(17), and so on until when I is 393, the output list is I(393),I(394),...,I(400). Thus the required fifty lines will be printed.   In this example, the value of I specifies the value of the subscript of the first variable printed in each line.

In example (iv), the value of I is the line number. If we know the line number, we can determine the eight variables whose values are to be printed on that line. An implied DO is used to create a list of the eight variables which are to appear on line I. For example, when I is two, the eight variables in the list are N(9),N(10),...,N(16).

Suppose that we wanted to print the 400 values in the set N in four columns so that the values of N(1) thru N(100) appeared in column 1, those of N(101) thru N(200) in column 2, etc. That is, the values are to be positioned as shown below.

N(1)	N(101)	N(201)	N(301)
N(2)	N(102)	N(202)	N(302)
N(3)	N(103)	N(203)	N(303)
.	.	.	.
.	.	.	.
.	.	.	.
N(100)	N(200)	N(300)	N(400)

Four different methods of achieving this result are:

```
i)      DO 4 I=1,100
            PRINT 54,N(I),N(I+100),N(I+200),N(I+300)
        4 CONTINUE
       54 FORMAT(' ',4I8)
```

```
ii)     DO 5 I=1,100
            PRINT 54,(N(I+J-100),J=100,400,100)
        5 CONTINUE
       54 FORMAT(' ',4I8)
```

```
iii)    PRINT 54,(N(I),N(I+100),N(I+200),N(I+300),
        * I=1,100)
       54 FORMAT(' ',4I8)
```

```
iv)     PRINT 54,((N(I+J-100),J=100,400,100),I=1,100)
       54 FORMAT(' ',4I8)
```

In examples (i) and (ii), the PRINT statement is executed 100 times, once for each value of I. In both of these cases the ouput list contains four elements, the only difference being that an implied DO-loop is used to create the output list in example (ii).

In examples (iii) and (iv), the output list contains 400 elements but of course only 100 lines will be printed since the FORMAT statement contains four masks. In example (iii), there are four items preceding the definition of the implied DO-loop. This means that the output list is created by repeating this set of four variables, once for each value of I. In other words, the first few variables in the output list of example (iii) are: N(1),N(101),N(201),N(301), N(2),N(102),N(202),N(302),... . Since four values are printed on each line, the required output will be produced.

In example (iv), an inner implied DO is used to create the same four variable names which appeared in the implied DO of example (iii). This inner implied DO consisting of:

(N(I+J-100),J=100,400,100)

defines the variables N(I),N(I+100),N(I+200),N(I+300) and this list is repeated for each value of I. Thus (iii) and (iv) are equivalent. This fourth example shows that implied DOs can be nested in the same way that ordinary DO-loops are nested. In this example, the J-loop is the innermost and therefore the value of J will range over its permitted set of values before the value of I is changed.

A word of caution. The commas shown in these examples of implied DO-loops are necessary and cannot be omitted. Note that a comma must precede the index of each loop and that if implied DOs are nested, a comma follows the right bracket of each inner loop.

With respect to the foregoing example, how could you cause the first printed line to appear at the top of a page and the remaining 99 lines to be single spaced? To do this using the technique of examples (i) and (ii) would require two PRINT statements each using a different FORMAT statement. The first would be used to print the first line and the second would be used for the other 99 lines. Using the method of example (iii) or (iv) however, the following FORMAT statement could be used.

54 FORMAT('1',1(T1,4I8))

It works because the masks for elements printed on the second and subsequent lines are positioned explicitly beginning with the group count instead of the beginning of the FORMAT statement. This example assumes of course, that the values assigned to elements of the set require seven or fewer print positions including a negative sign.

One could use an implied DO to print a line of 132 zeros across the top of a page as follows:

```
        PRINT 21,(0,K=1,132)
     21 FORMAT('1',132I1)
```

What would be printed using the following pair of statements?

```
        PRINT 571,((J-1,J=1,10),I=1,12)
    571 FORMAT('1',120I1)
```

The output list contains 120 INTEGER constants. They are generated by calculating values of J-1 as J goes from 1 to 10 for each value of I as I goes from 1 to 12. Thus the digits 0 thru 9 are repeated 12 times across the first line on a page.

Exercise 7.2

1. Suppose a set of 12 variables has been defined by:

```
        INTEGER S(12)
```

Suppose the first four data cards contain the symbols, beginning in column 1,

```
        -27bb30bbb4
        bb5b627bbb3
        b89bbb1b109
        b15637bb88b1
```

What values are assigned to variables in S using the following READ statements?

a)
```
            READ 6,S
          6 FORMAT(3I4)
```

b)
```
            DO 2 J=1,10,3
                READ 8,S(J),S(J+1),S(J+2)
          2 CONTINUE
          8 FORMAT(3I4)
```

c)
```
            DO 3 K=1,4
                L=(5-K)*3
                READ 5,S(L),S(L-1),S(L-2)
          3 CONTINUE
          5 FORMAT(I2,I5,I3)
```

d)   READ 7, (S(M) ,S(M+1) ,M=1,11,2)
          7 FORMAT (2I2,1X,I2)

e)   READ,S

2. Suppose the sets D and T are defined by:

          REAL D(16) ,T(16)

For each of the following, state the number and order
of the variables appearing in the output list.

a)   PRINT,T,D
b)   PRINT,(T(I) ,D(I) ,I=1,16)
c)   PRINT,(T(I-1),T(I),I=2,16,2)
d)   PRINT,((D(I+J-1) ,J=1,4) ,I=1,13,4)
e)   PRINT,((T(I+J-1) ,J=1,13,4) ,I=1,4)

3. Consider the statements:

          INTEGER WEE(5)
          WEE(3) =1
          DO 7 N=1,2
              WEE (N+3) =3-N
              WEE (3-N) =3+N
          7 CONTINUE

a) What are the values assigned to the elements of WEE?

b) For each of the following, describe the output.

    i)   PRINT 1,WEE
          1 FORMAT(' ',I3)

    ii)   PRINT 2, (J,WEE(J) ,J=1,5)
          2 FORMAT(' WEE(',I1,') =',I2)

    iii)   PRINT 3,WEE(5)
            PRINT3, (WEE(6-K) ,K=2,5,1)
          3 FORMAT(' ',2(I3,2X,I2))

4.   Write a pair of statements to cause a line containing
100 symbols to be printed across the top of a page. The
required symbols are ten zeros followed by ten ones
followed by ten twos etc.. Use a pair of implied DOs to
create the output list. How could this be done using
only one implied DO?   How could it be done using no
implied DOs?

7.5 Tables Of Variables

Frequently our understanding of a problem is made easier if we picture a set of numbers as being stored in a table. For example, suppose we made a door-to-door survey of six houses on a street with the idea of finding for each house, the number of pre-school children, public school children, high school children, and adults. We might record the results as shown below.

	PRE-SCHOOL	PUBLIC	HIGH SCHOOL	ADULTS
House 1	0	1	2	2
House 2	2	0	0	2
House 3	0	0	0	1
House 4	1	2	0	2
House 5	1	0	1	2
House 6	0	2	3	2

In this table of numbers there are six horizontal rows, one for each house, and four vertical columns, one for each type of information collected. A rectangular array of numbers such as this is often called a <u>matrix.</u> We can refer to any position in a matrix by specifying a row number and column number. For example, the number in position (5,2) of the table above refers to the number in row 5 and column 2, that is, the number of public school children in the fifth house. Similarly, the sum of the numbers in positions (2,1), (2,2), (2,3) and (2,4) represents the total of the numbers in row 2 of the table, that is, the total number of people in the second house. The sum of the numbers in positions (3,3), (4,3), (5,3) and (6,3) represents the total number of high school children in houses three thru six.

If we want to use the information in the table to answer questions such as: "Which houses have no pre-school children?"; "How many adults are there in the six houses?"; or, "Which house has the fewest children?", then we must be able to give a name to each of the 24 items of information in the table. In order to write programs to answer questions such as those above, a set of twenty-four variables must be defined. Furthermore, it would be very helpful if the name given to each of the variables referred to one of the positions in the table.

In WATFIV, an appropriate set of variables could be defined using the statement

        INTEGER S(6,4)

This statement defines a set of 24 INTEGER variables. The
names of these variables are:

$$S(1,1) \quad S(1,2) \quad S(1,3) \quad S(1,4)$$

$$S(2,1) \quad S(2,2) \quad S(2,3) \quad S(2,4)$$

$$S(3,1) \quad S(3,2) \quad S(3,3) \quad S(3,4)$$

$$S(4,1) \quad S(4,2) \quad S(4,3) \quad S(4,4)$$

$$S(5,1) \quad S(5,2) \quad S(5,3) \quad S(5,4)$$

$$S(6,1) \quad S(6,2) \quad S(6,3) \quad S(6,4)$$

The set S is called a two-dimensional array (or matrix
or table) of variables. Any variable in the set S such as
S(3,2) is called a doubly-subscripted variable. When using
doubly-subscripted variables, the first subscript always
refers to the row number and the second subscript will
always refer to the column number. The two subscripts are
always separated by a comma.

The general structure of a table of values is shown in
the following diagram.

In the diagram above, the shaded box is the (i,j) th
element of the table since it is in row i and column j.

The following program reads the twenty-four values to be
assigned to the elements of S.   Four numbers are punched on
each of six cards. The four numbers correspond to the four
items of information obtained about each house.   The output
of the program is the total number of public school children
in the six houses.

```
C EXAMPLE 7.4 SURVEY ANALYSIS 1
      INTEGER S(6,4),PUBSUM
C
C      READ IN 24 ITEMS OF DATA, ONE ROW AT A TIME
       DO 8 I=1,6
          READ, (S(I,J),J=1,4)
    8 CONTINUE
C
C      TOTAL UP THE PUBLIC SCHOOL CHILDREN
       PUBSUM=0
       DO 11 I=1,6
          PUBSUM=PUBSUM+S(I,2)
   11 CONTINUE
C
       PRINT 80, PUBSUM
   80 FORMAT('0','TOTAL IN PUBLIC SCHOOL IS',I3)
       STOP
       END
```

In this program, the READ statement is executed once for
each value of I as I goes from 1 to 6 in steps of 1.   The
implied DO in the READ statement is used to create an input
list of the four variables $S(I,1),S(I,2),S(I,3)$ and $S(I,4)$.
This means that the four values punched on the Ith data card
are assigned to the variables in row I of the table.

The statement "PUBSUM=PUBSUM+S(I,2)" is executed once
for each value of I in the range 1 thru 6.   This means that
the six values added to PUBSUM are those in column 2 of the
matrix.

The same set of rules which apply to singly-subscripted
variables also apply to doubly-subscripted variables.

The program below could be used to find out which house
has the most people.   To do this we must find the total
number of people in each house.   As each total is obtained,
the total is compared to the highest total found previously.
In this program the variable BIGHSE is used to identify the
house with the most people.

```
      C EXAMPLE 7.5 SURVEY ANALYSIS 2
            INTEGER S(6,4),HOUSE,BIGHSE
            READ,((S(I,J),J=1,4),I=1,6)
            MOST=0
            DO 12 HOUSE=1,6
      C          FIND THE NUMBER OF PEOPLE IN HOUSE
                 NPEEPL =0
                 DO 4 J=1,4
                    NPEEPL=NPEEPL+S(HOUSE,J)
         4       CONTINUE
      C          CHECK FOR LARGEST SO FAR
                 IF(NPEEPL.GT.MOST) THEN
                    MOST=NPEEPL
                    BIGHSE=HOUSE
                 END IF
        12 CONTINUE
            PRINT 777,BIGHSE,MOST
       777 FORMAT('1HOUSE ',I2,' CONTAINS',I2,' PEOPLE')
            STOP
            END
```

In this example, a pair of nested implied DOs was used
in the READ statement to create an input list of 24
variables. J, being the second subscript, refers to the
column and since the J-loop is inside the I-loop, the 24
variables are named row-by-row, that is: row 1 followed by
row 2 followed by row 3 etc.. Note also the statement "DO
12 HOUSE=1,6". It is permissible to use HOUSE as a DO-loop
index since it was declared as being an INTEGER variable in
the declaration statement which was also used to define the
set S.

Suppose we wanted to print the twenty-four values in the
table so that the six numbers in column 1 of the table were
printed on the first line, the six in column 2 on the second
line, those in columns three and four on the third and
fourth lines respectively. Three equivalent methods of
doing this are shown below.

```
      i)        DO 15 J=1,4
                   PRINT 27,(S(I,J),I=1,6)
             15 CONTINUE
             27 FORMAT(' ',6I3)

     ii)        PRINT 27,((S(I,J),I=1,6),J=1,4)
             27 FORMAT(' ',6I3)

    iii)        PRINT 27,S
             27 FORMAT(' ',6I3)
```

In method (i), the output list contains six elements which are the six variables in column 1 of the table. The PRINT statement is executed once for each column in the table.

In method (ii), the pair of nested implied DOs create an output list of twenty-four variables such that the set of six variables in columns 1,2,3 and 4 follow each other.

In method (iii), only the set name appears in the PRINT list. It is important to remember that this creates a list in which the variables are named <u>column-by-column.</u> This same idea applies in creating an input list for a READ statement.   For example, suppose we had written the statement:

                    READ,S

in programs 7.4 or 7.5. Since this would create an input list in which the variables appeared column-by-column, it would mean the four values which should be stored in row 1 would actually be assigned to the first four variables in column 1. The next four would be assigned to the last two variables in column 1 and the first two variables in column 2. This process of filling up the columns one after the other would continue until the entire table was filled.   In fact, the only variables which would necessarily have the correct values would be S(1,1) and S(6,4) since they are the first and last elements in the list regardless of whether or not the variables are named row-by-row or column-by-column. Further examples are provided in the exercises.

The reason why a set name creates an output list in which variables appear in column-by-column order is discussed in detail in Chapter 10.   Until then, this is one fact which you must remember.

<u>Exercise 7.3</u>

1) Consider the following table of numbers.

         2   5   -7   3
         4   8   22   7
         5   9   -8   3

a) How many rows and columns are there?
b) What is the element in position (3,2)?
c) What are the positions of the prime numbers?
d) What is the sum of the elements in the second row?, the third column?

2. Suppose A and B are two sets of 6 INTEGER variables each. The variables in A are arranged into two rows and three columns. B has three rows and two columns.

   a) Define the sets.
   b) What subscript values appear in A but not in B?
   c) Suppose the value assigned to A(I,J) is I+J for all elements in A and the value of B(I,J) is I-J for all elements in B. Then:
       i) What pairs of I and J values are such that
          B(I,J)+A(I,J)=2*I ?
      ii) What pairs of I and J values are such that
          B(I,J)-A(I,J)=-2*J ?
     iii) What is the value of,
          A(1,1)*B(1,1)+A(1,2)*B(2,1)+A(1,3)*B(3,1) ?

      iv) What is the output of:

          1.   PRINT 5,((A(I,J),J=1,3),I=1,1)
                5 FORMAT(3I2)

          2.   J=2
                PRINT 4,(A(J,K)*B(K,J),K=3,5,4)
                4 FORMAT(I6)

          3.   DO 6 I=1,3
                   PRINT 8,MOD(A(2,I),A(1,I))
                6 CONTINUE
                8 FORMAT(3I3)

       v) What is the value of:

          1. A(B(2,1),A(1,2)) ?
          2. B(A(2,B(3,1))-1,B(A(1,B(3,1)),1)) ?

3. In what order do the variables appear in the output lists in the PRINT statements below? Assume Q has been defined by:
          REAL Q(4,2)

   a) PRINT,Q
   b) PRINT,(Q(J,1),Q(J,2),J=1,4)
   c) PRINT,((Q(K,NUM),Q(K+2,NUM),K=1,2),NUM=1,2)
   d) PRINT,(Q(5-J,2),Q(5-J,1),J=1,4)

4. What is the output of the following:

          PRINT 10,(((I+J+K-2,K=1,3),J=1,6,5),I=1,4,3)
          10 FORMAT(' ',6I3)

5. Suppose the sets X and Y have been defined by:

                REAL X(5,2),Y(2,5)

Write three statements (2 DOs and an Assignment statement) which will transfer the values in X to those in Y such that Y(I,J) is given the value of X(J,I).

7.6 Higher Dimensioned Arrays

Suppose the house survey referred to in the preceding section was taken in two different years for the same six houses. This would mean we would have two tables of data, each of which contained 24 data items organized into six rows and four columns. A set of 48 variables could be defined by the statement:

                INTEGER S(6,4,2)

In this case, the set S is called a three-dimensional array and variables in the set S are triply-subscripted variables. Our interpretation of the variable S(I,J,K) is that I denotes the house number, J the type of information, and K, the year in which the survey was done. In WATFIV, it is permissible to define sets of variables having as many as seven dimensions.

When working with sets having three or more dimensions, the appearance of the set name in an input or output list defines a list of variables such that the rightmost subscript is varied the least rapidly, and the leftmost subscript is varied the most rapidly. This is the same rule which applies to two dimensional sets except that it is much easier to state the rule in the two-dimensional case as "the variables are ordered column-by-column". As an example, in order to print the 48 items of information obtained in the two surveys so that one number is printed on each line, then the following five methods are equivalent. In each case the FORMAT statement is "20 FORMAT(I3)".

    i)   PRINT 20,S

    ii)   PRINT 20,(((S(I,J,K),I=1,6),J=1,4),K=1,2)

    iii)   DO 9 K=1,2
              PRINT 20,((S(I,J,K),I=1,6),J=1,4)
          9 CONTINUE

```
iv)      DO 18 K=1,2
            DO 17 J=1,4
               PRINT 20,(S(I,J,K),I=1,6)
   17       CONTINUE
   18 CONTINUE

v)       PRINT 20,((S(I,J,1),I=1,6),J=1,4),((S(I,J,2),
      *  I=1,6),J=1,4)
```

The reason they are all equivalent is simply that the order in which the variables are named is the same in all cases. Although there are different numbers of elements in the output lists, the fact that there is but a single mask in the FORMAT statement will cause the results to be the same.

7.7 Assignment of Values at Compile Time

In Chapter 2 it was stated that there are two ways to give a value to a variable. The first is to use an Assignment statement such as "A=3.2". The second is to use a READ statement such as "READ,A". There is a third way which differs from these two methods in that the assignment of the value to the variable is made at compile time rather than execution time. (The Assignment statement and the READ statement are executable statements which mean that the action specified by them occurs during the execution of the program and not during the translation of the program into machine language.) Sometimes it is convenient to give a value to a variable during the compilation of a program so that when the program starts executing, the variable will already have an appropriate value. How to do this is the topic of this section. Keep in mind that compile time assignment of values is a matter of convenience and not of necessity.

To calculate the sum of the first fifty natural numbers, we might write the program:

```
C EXAMPLE 7.6 ASSIGNMENT AT EXECUTION TIME
      INTEGER SUM
      SUM=0
      DO 4 I=1,50
         SUM=SUM+I
    4 CONTINUE
      PRINT,SUM
      STOP
      END
```

In this program, the variable SUM must be set to zero before the total can be calculated and this has been done using the Assignment statement "SUM=0". To assign a value of zero to SUM at compile time, the program would look like:

```
C EXAMPLE 7.7 ASSIGNMENT AT COMPILE TIME
      INTEGER SUM/0/
      DO 4 I=1,50
         SUM=SUM+I
    4 CONTINUE
      PRINT,SUM
      STOP
      END
```

The statement "INTEGER SUM/0/" declares SUM as being an INTEGER variable and also causes the compiler to assign SUM an initial value of zero. Some other examples of compile time initialization of variables are:

   i)   REAL X/3.2E04/,JACK/2./,LOOP

   ii) INTEGER A,B/5000/,C/0/

   iii) INTEGER F(3)/1,2,3/

   iv) REAL ZZ(4)/4*0./,B(2)/0.,0./

   v)   INTEGER COUNT(10)/2,5*0,4*1/

   vi) REAL T(3,4)/12*0./

   vii) REAL A(3,2)/3*0.,3*8./

In example (i), the variable X is given an initial value of 32000., the value of JACK is initialized to 2., and LOOP is simply declared as being a REAL variable.

In (ii), the variables A,B, and C are declared as INTEGER variables and B and C are initialized to 5000 and 0 respectively.

In example (iii), the three variables in the set F are given values such that F(1) is 1, F(2) is 2 and F(3) is 3.

In (iv), the four variables in the one-dimensional array ZZ are all initialized to zero. The "4*" indicates that the constant which follows is to be used 4 times. The two elements of B are both set equal to zero and this pair of initializing values could also have been written as "/2*0./" instead of as shown.

In example (v) the variable COUNT(1) is initialized to 2; the variables COUNT(2) thru COUNT(6) are each set equal to zero; and the remaining four variables in the set are given an initial value of 1.

In example (vi), the matrix of twelve variables in the set T are all initialized to zero.

In example (vii), the variables A(1,1),A(2,1) and A(3,1) are set to zero, and those in column 2 namely, A(1,2), A(2,2), and A(3,2) are given a value of 8. In other words the order in which the constants appearing between the slashes are assigned to elements in a matrix is column-by-column. This of course is the same order in which variables appear in an input or output list created by the use of the set name.

Five common errors occur when using REAL or INTEGER statements to initialize variables. Statements (i), (ii) and (iv) below will produce error messages. Statements (iii) and (v) will produce warning messages.

   i)   REAL A/2/ Reason: The constant must be of the same
              type as the variable being initialized.

   ii) REAL X(2)/ALOG(10.),SIN(.3)/ ,Reason: The initial-
              izing value(s) must be constants.

   iii) INTEGER OK(2)/0,0,0/ ,Reason: There are fewer var-
              iables than initializing constants.

   iv) REAL NOP(3)/2*0./ Reason: There are more variables
              than initializing constants.

   v)   REAL X/1./ Y/2./ Reason: Comma missing before Y.

*7.8 The DATA Statement

In some non-WATFIV versions of Fortran, initial values cannot be specified using a type declaration statement. Instead, they must be specified by a DATA statement. The pair of statements below is equivalent to the single statement "REAL M/1./".

                REAL M
                DATA M/1./

The rules for DATA statement usage are similar to those discussed in the previous section. A summary can be found at the end of this section.

The DATA statement has three advantages. First,
variables of different types can be initialized in the same
DATA statement. For example, the single statement

        DATA I/4/, A/3./

is equivalent to the pair of statements

                INTEGER I/4/
                REAL A/3./

Secondly, the variables to be given initial values can be
defined by an implied DO-loop. For example, the statements
below define X to be a table of REAL variables having two
rows and seven columns. Variables in row one are given a
value of ten and those in row two a value of twenty.

                REAL X(2,7)
                DATA (X(1,I),I=1,7)/7*10./, (X(2,I),I=1,7)/7*20./

A pair of nested DO-loops could have been used instead of
the two single loops shown. Note that to achieve the same
effect without using implied DO-loops would require a
statement such as the following.

        REAL X(2,7)/10.,20.,10.,20.,10.,20.,10.,20.,10.,20.,
      * 10.,20.,10.,20./

The reason for the long string of initializing constants is
that the initial values are assigned column-by-column. This
means "/7*10.,7*20./" would not produce the correct result.

Third, in a very few exceptional cases the DATA statement
must be used. These cases concern restrictions on the
ordering of statements within a program and are discussed in
Chapter 17.

    The rules of the DATA statement are as follows.

    i) Any variable whose type is not specified by the
       first-letter rule must have the type declared by a
       statement which precedes the DATA statement in
       which the variable appears. Shown below are valid
       and invalid ordering of statements.

        Valid   Invalid
            INTEGER X   DATA X/2/
            DATA X/2/   INTEGER X

ii) Specification of an array must precede any DATA statement used to initialize variables in the array. For example,

<u>Valid</u>   <u>Invalid</u>
    REAL A(3)   DATA A/3*0./
    DATA A/3*0./   REAL A(3)

iii) Specific variables in an array can be initialized. The variables can, if desired, be defined by an implied DO-loop. The DO parameters must be constants. For example,

    INTEGER S(100)
    DATA S(74)/463/, (S(I),I=1,99,2)/50*1/

Nested loops may be used.

iv) The initializing values do not need to immediately follow the variable being initialized. That is, a list of variables can be followed by a list of initial values as illustrated in the following example.

    REAL X(2)
    DATA X(1),K,A,X(2)/0.,999,-8.,0./

v) The number of initial values in a list must be the same as the number of variables preceding the list. A constant must have the same type of value as the variable which it initializes.

*7.9 The DIMENSION Statement

A DIMENSION statement can be used to define sets or arrays of variables. However, elements in arrays which are defined by a DIMENSION statement are typed by the first-letter rule unless the set name appears in a type declaration statement. Furthermore, the DIMENSION statement cannot be used to specify initial values for elements in an array.

The statement which follows defines X to be a set of ten REAL variables and KSET to be a set of six INTEGER variables.

    DIMENSION X(10), KSET(6)

To override the first-letter rule, the set name should
appear in a type declaration statement. For example, either
pair of the following statements define P to be an array of
twelve INTEGER variables having four rows and three columns.

```
          INTEGER P              DIMENSION P(4,3)
          DIMENSION P(4,3)       INTEGER P
```

Two methods are available for performing compile time
initialization of elements of arrays defined by a DIMENSION
statement. First, a REAL or INTEGER statement can be used as
shown in the following example.

```
          DIMENSION A(3),K(4,5)
          REAL A/2.,17.,-5./
          INTEGER K/20*0/
```

Second, a DATA statement can be used. For example, the three
statements above could be replaced by the following pair.

```
          DIMENSION A(3), K(4,5)
          DATA A/2.,17., -5./, K/20*0/
```

Note that when using either method, only the set name
appears in a statement used to specify initial values.

The primary advantage of a DIMENSION statement is that
it permits arrays having different types of variables to be
defined in the same statement. Furthermore, in some versions
of Fortran, it is the only statement which can be used to
define sets of variables. In WATFIV, its use is only a
necessity in very special cases. These cases are discussed
in Chapter 17 (See "Ordering of Statements".).

7.10 Summary

1. Frequently we must write programs in which we do not know
   at the time the program is written:

       a) How many variables are required,
       b) Which variables will have values needed for some
          special purpose.

2. This problem can be overcome in WATFIV by defining a set
   of variables using a REAL or INTEGER declaration
   statement which specifies not only the set name but also
   the number of variables which might be needed. Variables
   which are elements of sets have dynamic variable names.
   That is, the name of the variable can be changed by

changing the value of the subscript(s). This introduces a great deal of flexibility into programs because it permits the use of an iterative approach which otherwise could not be used.

3. For convenience, sets of variables may be thought of as being in a simple list (a vector), or organized in a rectangular array (a matrix).

4. Implied DO-loops are handy tools for creating input and output lists.

5. It is permissible and sometimes convenient to initialize variables at compile time. The REAL and INTEGER statements can be used for this purpose.

7.11 Programming Problems

7.1   Read five INTEGER values from a single card and store them in a set of variables called K. On four successive lines print the values; the subscripts of the variables which have positive values, negative values, and zero values.

7.2   Read a set of ten INTEGER values punched on a single card.   Print all pairs of values from the set which add up to twelve.

7.3   Read a set of ten INTEGER values each of which represents some person's age. Determine which two persons are: closest in age; farthest apart in age.

7.4   Suppose A and B are sets of eight INTEGER values each. Read the two sets of values using implied DO-loops. Print those values which are in: both A and B; either A or B or both; A but not B; B but not A; either A or B but not both.   Test your program using the following sets of values.

              A = (2, 5, 8, 4, 7, 1, 6, 10)
              B = (9, 8, 4, 10, 3, 5, 12, 11)

7.5   Read four cards each of which contains seven REAL values representing daily temperatures (one card per week). For each week, calculate the average temperature and the maximum and minimum temperatures. Calculate the average, high and low temperatures for the four week period. Display your results as shown below.

```
                   TEMPERATURES
             M    T    W    TH   F    S    S    AVG    HI   LO
WEEK 1      XX.  XX.  XX.  XX.  XX.  XX.  XX.   XX.X  XX.  XX.
WEEK 2      XX.  XX.  XX.  XX.  XX.  XX.  XX.   XX.X  XX.  XX.
WEEK 3      XX.  XX,  XX.  XX.  XX.  XX.  XX.   XX.X  XX.  XX.
WEEK 4      XX.  XX.  XX.  XX.  XX.  XX.  XX.   XX.X  XX.  XX.
                                                ----   --   --
            FOUR WEEK STATISTICS               XX.X  XX.  XX.
```

7.6 Add additional statements to the program for the
previous problem so that the average, high and low
temperatures for each day of the week are calculated.
Display the additional information using appropriate
FORMAT statements.

7.7 Most credit cards have an account number in which the
last digit is called the "check digit". Its value
depends on the values of the other digits. When the
account number is read from a card, the last digit is
compared with what it should be based on the other
digits in the number. Suppose an account number has ten
digits (including the check digit). One method of
calculating the check digit is as follows. Find the sum
of the 2nd, 4th, 6th and 8th digits (beginning from the
left). Call this total SUM1. Form a number consisting of
the first, 3rd, 5th, 7th and 9th digits. Multiply this
value by two and add the digits in the result. Call this
total SUM2. Add SUM1 and SUM2 and subtract the last
digit from ten to obtain the check digit. For example,
to see if the number 2520764263 is valid: we have
SUM1=5+0+6+2=13; now 2*22746 = 45492 and therefore
SUM2=4+5+4+9+2 = 24; thus SUM1 + SUM2 = 37 and so the
check digit should be 10-7=3. Thus the account number is
valid. Write a program which reads an unknown number of
ten digit account numbers and determines which are valid
(the check digit agrees with that calculated according
to the rules above). When testing your program use at
least two valid account numbers. Note that to obtain
SUM2 you will need to extract the individual digits in a
number. This can be done by repeatedly dividing the
number by ten and using the remainder as the value of
the next digit.

7.8 Start with any four digit INTEGER value in which at
least two of the digits have different values. Form the
largest and smallest possible numbers from the digits.
Subtract them to give a new number. Compare the number
to 6174. If equal, stop. If not, repeat the entire
process until the number 6174 is obtained. (It will show

up in at most seven steps regardless of the number you start with!) For example, if you start with 1998 you get successively: 8082 (from 9981 - 1899); 8532 (from 8820 - 0288); 6174 (from 8532 - 2358). Print your starting value and each number obtained during the procedure.

7.9   Write a program which reads an INTEGER value and finds all of its divisors. For example, the divisors of 6 are 1, 2, 3, and 6.   Store the divisors in a vector called VEC.   For each element of VEC, determine how many divisors it has. (For the example, these would be 1, 2, 2, and 4. Store these values in a vector called NDIVS. Find the sum of cubes of the elements of NDIVS and compare this with the square of the sum of the elements of NDIVS.   They will be equal!   This is a general procedure for finding sets of numbers having this property. Write a program which reads several values and generates the set of values associated with each input number according to the rules above.

7.10 Read an unknown number (less than fifty) of INTEGER values one at a time. Stop when any value occurs for the second time. Print the message "THE VALUE XX WAS THE XX AND XX VALUE IN THE SEQUENCE".

7.11 Write a program which reads in three pairs of X-Y values representing the coordinates of the vertices of a triangle.   Read the coordinates of a fourth point. Determine if the fourth point lies inside, on the edge of, or outside the triangle defined by the first three points. Print the coordinates of all four points along with an appropriate message.

7.12 Suppose values of the function $(x^2-2x+3)/(3x^3-2x^2+5)$ are to be calculated for various values of x.   The values of x to be used are obtained in the following way.   On the first data card a value of N is punched which indicates the number of ranges of values of x to be used. Assume N is twenty-five or less. Beginning on the same card which contained the value of N, N pairs of numbers are punched.   The first number in each pair denotes the lowest value in the range of integer values to be used.   The second number in the pair denotes the highest value in the range. For example, if there were two pairs of numbers say 2,5 and 11,15, the values of x to be used would be 2,3,4,5 and 11,12,13,14,15.   Print out "UNDEFINED" if the denominator has a value of zero. Use a table called DOLIM having 25 rows and 2 columns to store the pairs of numbers defining the ranges of x-values to be used.

7.13 Write a program which reads in the house survey data shown in the table at the begining of section 7.5. Punch the data for each house on a separate card. Answer the following questions. Which house has the most children? Which houses have more than one child in high school? What is the ratio of children to adults in each house? In the houses containing no children in public school or at least one pre-school child, what is the average number of high-school children?

7.14 A data card contains twenty INTEGER values each of which is zero or some positive value. Read the values and store them in a vector called DATA. Print the values in DATA. Create a new set of values called DENSE from the elements of DATA as follows. If there are N consecutive zero values in DATA, store a value of -N in the next element of DENSE. If an element of DATA is positive, store its value in the next element of DENSE. (See example below.) Print the values in DENSE. Finally use the elements of DENSE to generate the original set of values by reversing the logic used to create DENSE. Store the re-created set of values in COPY and print its values. For example,

```
DATA   2 3 0 0 0 0 1 5 7 0 0 8 4 0 9 6 0 0 3 0

DENSE  2 3 -4 1 5 7 -2 8 4 0 9 6 -2 3 0

COPY   2 3 0 0 0 0 1 5 7 0 0 8 4 0 9 6 0 0 3 0
```

7.15 Read ten INTEGER values and store them in the first row of a table having two rows and ten columns. Find the smallest value and store its column number in a variable called BEGIN. Find the second smallest value and store its column number in row two of the column containing the smallest value. Continue to find successively larger values and store their column numbers in row two of the column containing the previously found value. Finally, in row two of the column containing the largest value, store a zero. (See the example below.) Having done this use the value of BEGIN and the row two values to print the original set of values in order of smallest to largest. For example,

column	1	2	3	4	5	6	7	8	9	10
Row 1	15	-10	12	-19	8	45	-11	66	30	-2
Row 2	9	10	1	7	3	8	2	0	6	5

and

BEGIN = 4 (points to column 4)

Write the program in such a way that it will work for
any ten INTEGER values.

7.16 The Ackermann function ACK(i,j) is defined as follows.
ACK(0,j)=j+1;   ACK(i,0)=ACK(i-1,1);   ACK(i,j) = ACK(i-1,
ACK(i,j-1)). Write a program which stores the values of
ACK(0,0)   thru ACK(9,9)   in a ten-by-ten table.   The
element in the ith row and jth column should be the
value of ACK(i-1,j-1) .

7.17 Here is a game you can try with a friend. Each player
writes down three non-negative integer numbers which add
up to five.   Examples are (0 0 5),   (1 3 1),   (2 2 1),
etc.. Compare your numbers with those of your opponent.
The person who has the higher first number gets seven
points (no points if a tie). The higher second number is
worth five points and the higher third number is worth
four points. Play ten times.   The winner is the one with
the highest total number of points.   Write a program
which generates all possible triples of numbers which
can be used in the game. Use these to identify the rows
and columns of a matrix. In the (i,j)th element of the
matrix, store the point value which would be obtained by
someone who chose the triple associated with row i if
his opponent chose the triple associated with column j.
Print the values in the matrix with appropriate row and
column headings.

CHAPTER 8   REMOTE BLOCKS

Questions Answered in This Chapter

1. How can the statements corresponding to a particular
   step or substep in an algorithm be grouped together
   and referred to by name? What are the advantages of
   forming these blocks of statements?

2. How can a block of statements which is required at
   several points in a program be written only once and
   yet executed at the appropriate times?

This chapter and the two which follow describe methods
for breaking a program up into blocks or segments. When
partitioned, each program section typically defines a step
in an algorithm or a particular computational routine.
There are important advantages associated with writing a
program in modules. Each results in better control of the
programming process.

A REMOTE BLOCK (described in this chapter) is usually
associated with a single step or substep in an algorithm. A
subprogram (described in Chapters 9 and 10) is more
frequently associated with a special computational routine
such as sorting a set of numbers, solving a system of
equations or computing the value of a function. Both
REMOTE BLOCKs and subprograms provide a means of
partitioning the logic of a program into small, well-
defined, single-purpose modules. This modularity means
programming design, coding and testing can be done in a more
organized and rigorous manner.

8.1 A Simple Payroll Problem

Suppose you are required to calculate the weekly net pay
of each of 100 employees in a firm. For each employee the
following information is available:

            item   variable name

   1. employee number   EMPNO
   2. regular hours worked   REGHRS
   3. regular hourly pay rate   REGRAT
   4. overtime hours worked   OVTHRS
   5. overtime hourly pay rate   OVTRAT

Assume that the data for each employee is punched on a
single card and can be read using a format-free READ

statement.   The   employees net pay   is to be   calculated as
follows

             NETPAY = GRSPAY - TAX

where   GRSPAY = REGHRS * REGRAT + OVTHRS * OVTRAT

and   TAX is 10 percent of grosspay (GRSPAY)   on earnings
                up to $200 and 20 percent on earnings over $200.

You already have the knowledge to solve this problem.   The
purpose of the   following   discussion is   to   show how   the
structure of the program can be made more evident by the use
of REMOTE BLOCKs to isolate and   name blocks   of statements
that have a single purpose.   First however, an algorithm is
needed.

             1. For each employee
                 .1 get the employee data
                 .2 calculate net pay
                 .3 print the net pay
             2. Stop

In this algorithm the logic to calculate the net pay is well
defined.   In the   program below,   this logic has been made
into a REMOTE BLOCK with the name PAY.   Study the example
carefully.

```
C EXAMPLE 8.1 PAYROLL CALCULATION
      REAL NETPAY
      DO 99 I=1,100
          READ,EMPNO,REGHRS,REGRAT,OVTHRS,OVTRAT
          EXECUTE PAY
          PRINT,EMPNO,NETPAY
   99 CONTINUE
      STOP
C
      REMOTE BLOCK PAY
          GRSPAY = REGHRS*REGRAT + OVTHRS*OVTRAT
          IF(GRSPAY .LE. 200) THEN
              TAX = .1 * GRSPAY
          ELSE
              TAX = 20. + .2*(GRSPAY-200)
          END IF
          NETPAY = GRSPAY - TAX
      END BLOCK
      END
```

In this program there are three new types of statements.   An
EXECUTE statement is used to execute a REMOTE BLOCK.   It has

the general form

        EXECUTE name

where name is the name of the REMOTE BLOCK to be EXECUTEd. After the REMOTE BLOCK has been EXECUTEd, control returns to the statement following the EXECUTE statement. (In the example control returns to the "PRINT,EMPNO,NETPAY" statement.) All REMOTE BLOCKs have the following structure:

        REMOTE BLOCK name
               .
range of   .   statements in
the block   .   the block
        END BLOCK

Both the REMOTE BLOCK and END BLOCK statements are non-executable. The statements in the block must be followed by an END BLOCK statement. A complete list of rules appears at the end of the chapter.

In the example we used a single REMOTE BLOCK to code the step "Calculate net pay". Consider now the three substeps associated with this step.

       .1   calculate gross pay
       .2   calculate tax
       .3   netpay = grosspay - tax

The statements below define three REMOTE BLOCKs which could be used to replace the single REMOTE BLOCK called PAY in Example 8.1. As well as the REMOTE BLOCK for the entire step, separate REMOTE BLOCKs have been used for calculating the gross pay and the tax. The TAX is calculated with the assistance of the built-in functions AMIN1 and AMAX1.

```
          REMOTE BLOCK PAY
             EXECUTE GRSPAY
             EXECUTE TAX
             NETPAY = GRSPAY - TAX
          END BLOCK

          REMOTE BLOCK GRSPAY
             GRSPAY = REGHRS*REGRAT + OVTHRS*OVTRAT
          END BLOCK

          REMOTE BLOCK TAX
             TAX = AMIN1(20.,.1*GRSPAY) +
        *         AMAX1(0.,.2*(GRSPAY-200.))
          END BLOCK
```

Some comments.   Note that the REMOTE BLOCKs GRSPAY and TAX
have names which are also names of variables.   This is
permissible in WATFIV.   This example also shows that the
execution of REMOTE BLOCKs may be nested one inside the
other.   REMOTE BLOCKs however cannot be defined one within
the other.   That is, REMOTE BLOCK definitions cannot overlap
in any way and all must precede the END statement.

    Why use REMOTE BLOCKs?   Most algorithms involve several
steps and substeps. A REMOTE BLOCK is a convenient means of
isolating a block of statements in a step or substep and
giving it a name.   The block can then be executed using a
single statement.   For example, a three-step algorithm
involving input, calculation and output could be coded using
the program structure below.

```
                    EXECUTE INPUT
                    EXECUTE CALCS
                    EXECUTE OUTPUT
                    STOP

                    REMOTE BLOCK INPUT
                       .
                       .
                    END BLOCK
                    REMOTE BLOCK CALCS
                       .
                       .
                    END BLOCK
                    REMOTE BLOCK OUTPUT
                       .
                       .
                    END BLOCK
                    END
```

There are some people who believe that the mainline logic of
all programs should consist of a sequence of EXECUTE
statements.

8.2 Logic for a General READ loop

    In many problems an unknown number of data cards must be
processed.   As described in Chapter 5 there are several
methods of handling the problem. This section describes one
procedure that has several advantages.   An algorithm for a
general read loop is the following.

```
         1. get the first record
         2. while records exist do
             .1  process the record
             .2  get the next record
         3. stop
```

To control the while-loop suppose we give the INTEGER variable NODATA an initial value of 0 and change it to 1 when no further input records are available. Therefore the while-loop should be executed as long as NODATA equals zero. A refinement of our algorithm is therefore:

```
         1. Set NODATA = 0
         2. Get input data
               if none, set NODATA = 1
         3. While NODATA = 0 do
              .1 process data
              .2 get input data
                   if none, set NODATA = 1
         4. Stop
```

In the program structure below, the statements to read the input data and update the value of NODATA have been converted to the REMOTE BLOCK "INPUT".

```
  C PROGRAM STRUCTURE FOR GENERAL READ LOOP
  C
        NODATA = 0
        EXECUTE INPUT
        WHILE (NODATA .EQ. 0)
            .
            .            process the data
            .
           EXECUTE INPUT
        END WHILE
        STOP
  C
        REMOTE BLOCK INPUT
           READ, input list
               AT END, NODATA=1
        END BLOCK
```

This structure illustrates a further reason for using REMOTE BLOCKs. If the same logic is required at two or more points in an algorithm, then by defining the logic as a REMOTE BLOCK, it need only be written once and EXECUTEd wherever needed.

8.3 The WHILE-EXECUTE Statement

Suppose the REMOTE BLOCK below is used to read data cards containing a single INTEGER value. The variable NODATA is set equal to 1 when there are no further cards to process.

```
REMOTE BLOCK INPUT
    READ,N
    AT END, NODATA=1
END BLOCK
```

If an error is found in the data, we simply want to "flush" the input stream (read all the remaining data cards without processing them). The error routine can be programmed using the single WHILE-EXECUTE statement

```
WHILE (NODATA .EQ. 0) EXECUTE INPUT
```

This statement says execute the REMOTE BLOCK called INPUT repeatedly until NODATA does not equal 0. That is, read cards one after another until the end of data is reached.

The WHILE-EXECUTE is a convenience, not a necessity. The preceding example statement is equivalent to the three statement WHILE-loop below.

```
WHILE (NODATA .EQ. 0)
    EXECUTE INPUT
END WHILE
```

The general form of the WHILE-EXECUTE statement is:

```
WHILE (logical expression) EXECUTE name
```

The WHILE-EXECUTE statement cannot be used as the trailer statement of a Logical IF statement or as the object statement in a DO-loop.

8.4 Rules for REMOTE BLOCK and END BLOCK

General Form

```
                REMOTE BLOCK name
range of            .
  the               .     statement(s)
  block             .
                END BLOCK
```

Rules

1. The name of the REMOTE BLOCK may be any valid WATFIV
   name. Each REMOTE BLOCK must have a unique name.
   The name may be the same as the name of a
   variable or subprogram used in the segment. No
   ambiguity results from this duplication of names.

2. A maximum of 255 REMOTE BLOCKS may be defined in a
   program segment.

3. The statements in the range of the block may be any
   valid WATFIV or WATFIV-S statements or block
   structures   subject   to   the   following   two
   restrictions:
   a) Another REMOTE BLOCK may not be <u>defined</u> within
      the range of a REMOTE BLOCK.
   b) No statement may transfer control to a point
      outside the block except as noted in Rule 5
      below. An attempt to do this will result in
      a compile-time error.

4. A block may only be entered by means of an EXECUTE
   statement. Block execution is terminated by
   executing either the statement preceding the
   END BLOCK statement or a QUIT statement.
   Attempts to transfer control to a statement
   within the block from a statement outside the
   block will result in an execution-time error.

5. Subprograms may be called from within a block. A
   block may contain an EXECUTE statement causing
   another REMOTE BLOCK to be executed. Any chain of
   blocks executed in this way must not form a loop.
   (A block may not EXECUTE itself either directly
   or indirectly.)

6. Blocks may be defined anywhere in a program segment.
   Any executable statement preceding a REMOTE BLOCK
   statement should cause a transfer of control.
   Similarly, the first executable statement not
   belonging to another REMOTE BLOCK which follows
   an END BLOCK statement should have a statement
   number. Otherwise it can never be executed.

7. The REMOTE BLOCK and END BLOCK statements are non-
   executable statements. Comments may follow the
   words "END BLOCK". Warning! If the comment
   contains an "=" symbol, the statement may be
   compiled as an Assignment statement.

Exercise 8.1

1. What is the output from each of the following?

```
a)  X=1.               REMOTE BLOCK A       REMOTE BLOCK B
    EXECUTE A              X = X*2             X = 2*X
    EXECUTE B          END BLOCK            END BLOCK
    PRINT,X                                 END
    STOP
```

```
b)      N = 2
        EXECUTE TOMMY
        IF(N*2 .GT. 2) EXECUTE TOMMY
        PRINT,N
        STOP
        REMOTE BLOCK TOMMY
          N = N/2*N**2
        END BLOCK
        END
```

```
c)      X = Y = 3.
        EXECUTE JOAN
        WHILE(X .LT. 10.) EXECUTE JOAN
        STOP
        REMOTE BLOCK JOAN
          IF(X .NE. Y)   QUIT
          EXECUTE BARB
        END BLOCK
        REMOTE BLOCK BARB
          Y = Y + 1.
          X = X - 1.
          PRINT,X
        END BLOCK
        END
```

2. What is the error in each of the following?

```
a)      EXECUTE JOHN
        STOP
        REMOTE BLOCK JOHN
            PRINT,5
        END BLOCK
```

```
b)      REMOTE BLOCK A
            PRINT,1
        END BLOCK
        REMOTE BLOCK B
          PRINT,2
        END BLOCK
```

c)   X = 1.
        WHILE(X .LE. 10.) EXECUTE TIGER
        STOP
        REMOTE BLOCK TIGER
          X = X + 1.
          EXECUTE LION
        END BLOCK
        REMOTE BLOCK LION
          X = X + 2.
          EXECUTE TIGER
        END BLOCK
        END

d)   I = 4
        EXECUTE MARY
        STOP
        REMOTE BLOCK MARY
          J = I + J
        END BLOCK
        END

3. Suppose there were no IF statements available in the language. Could you use WHILEs as a substitute? Discuss.

8.5 Summary

1. REMOTE BLOCKs provide a means of grouping together statements associated with a particular task such as a step or sub-step in an algorithm and referring to them by name.

2. The modularity resulting from the use of REMOTE BLOCKs results in a more clearly-defined program structure and assists in organizing program writing and testing.

8.6 Programming Problems

8.1 One method of generating INTEGER "random" numbers is as follows. Pick a large integer value, say 1792534165. Square it and extract the middle 5 digits (those in the thousands thru the ten millions postions). Call this number N1. Square N1 and take the middle 5 digits calling the result N2. Continue the process of squaring and extracting. The sequence of numbers N1,N2,N3,... is usually one which has no detectable or predictable pattern. Such a random sequence of numbers -- N1,N2, etc. -- can be converted to numbers which lie in the interval (I,J) by calculating I+MOD(N,J-I+1) for

each number in the sequence. Write a program to
generate 30 random numbers in the range 7 thru 15. On
each line print the value of N1 and the derived number
in the (7,15) range. Use a REMOTE BLOCK for the step
in the algorithm which squares and extracts the 5 digit
number.

8.2 Suppose the equations of two straight lines are

$$A1x + B1y = C1$$
$$A2x + B2y = C2$$

For any given values of A1,B1,C1 and A2,B2,C2 the lines
may be parallel, coincident, perpendicular or oblique
depending on the values of the A's, B's and C's. The
mathematical relationships are as follows.

Orientation	Mathematical Relationship
parallel	A1*B2 = B1*A2
coincident	parallel and A1*C2 = C1*A2
perpendicular	A1*A2 = B1*B2
oblique	not parallel and not perpendicular

Write a program which reads an unspecified number of
A,B,C triples. For each pair of triples read, print
the two equations and one of "PARALLEL", "COINCIDENT",
"PERPENDICULAR" or "OBLIQUE". Stop when an out-of-data
condition is detected. Note that there will be an even
number of data cards. Test the program on at least the
following four pairs of lines.

$$2x + 3y = 4 \qquad 2x - 3y = 4$$
$$8x + 12y = 16 \qquad 6x + 4y = 12$$

$$5x + 13y = 0 \qquad 4x - y = 8$$
$$13x + 5y = -65 \qquad 64x - 16y = 1$$

In the program, use a REMOTE BLOCK to READ each pair of
data cards describing the two lines; a REMOTE BLOCK to
check parallelism and one to process non-parallel
lines.

8.3 Binary Search. Suppose you have a vector X of 100 real
values ordered such that $X(I) \leq X(I+1)$ for I=1,99. A
value of Y is read and you want to determine if the

value of Y is already stored in X.   Naturally you could
use the brute force method method of comparing Y with
X(1), Y with X(2),   etc. looking for a match.   A more
efficient way is to compare Y with the middle element
of X, X(50) and if Y<X(50) search X(1) thru X(50);   if
equal the search is over; if Y>X(50) search X(51) thru
X(100). If not equal, continue with the same technique
(compare Y to the middle element of the elements
remaining).   By repeatedly dividing any remaining
interval in two, either a match will be found or all
possibilities will have been exhausted.   This search
method is known as a binary search.

     Write a program which reads a value of N,   then N
more values and stores them in a vector X. Assume N is
25 or less. Read 10 more values and for each determine
if it matches one of the N values previously read. Use
a binary search.   Use a REMOTE BLOCK called BSERCH to
perform this search.   The program should include the
following statements.

```
     REAL X(25)
     READ,N
     DO 1 I=1,N
         READ,X(I)
   1 CONTINUE
     DO 2 I=1,10
         READ,Y
         EXECUTE BSERCH
   2 CONTINUE
     STOP
```

8.4 In ten-pin bowling the game   is divided into ten
    "frames".   In each frame, the player has at most two
    chances to knock down all ten pins.   The score in any
    frame is determined as follows.

name	# of balls thrown	pins knocked down	score
strike	1	10	10 + pins knocked down on next 2 throws
spare	2	10	10 + pins knocked down on next throw
open frame	2	<10	# of pins knocked down

Should a bowler get a spare or strike in the 10th frame he throws one or two additional balls respectively in order to obtain his score for the tenth frame. The largest number of balls a player can throw in one game is therefore 9*2+3=21.

Write a program which reads the number of pins knocked down on each throw and prints the frame-by-frame score. Use at least one non-trivial REMOTE BLOCK in the program. Test your program on the following three cases. The data for each game can be read using the format codes 21I3.

```
 8  1  7  3  9  1  9  0  9  1 10 10  7  1  7  3  9  1  9
 9  1  9  0  8  2  8  2  7  2 10  6  0 10  9  0  9  0
10 10  7  2  9  1 10 10 10  7  0  8  2 10 10  4
```

Questions Answered In This Chapter

1. Remote Blocks (described in the previous chapter) are very useful when we wish to execute the same sequence of instructions at several points in a program. What are the disadvantages of this approach?

2. What are subrograms and how do they overcome these disadvantages and limitations?

In this chapter, the concept of writing a program in pieces or segments is reviewed and extended. There are many reasons for writing a program in segments. Some are:

- The same segment can be used in different programs with no changes required in the statements of the segment.

- The segments can be tested independently of one another to make sure each segment works before linking them together.

- A library of segments can be built up which can be linked together in different ways to solve a wide range of problems.

- Different programmers can write and test segments which will be linked together to solve a problem and the programmers needn't be concerned about the variable names or statement numbers used by other programmers.

In this chapter we shall begin by writing a routine to calculate factorial N. Next we shall incorporate the routine into a REMOTE BLOCK. After discussing the awkwardness of this approach, it will be shown that by making the routine a "subprogram", the awkwardness is removed. The routine will be converted to two different types of subprograms, a SUBROUTINE subprogram and a FUNCTION subprogram. Subprograms are one of the most powerful tools available to WATFIV programmers. Knowledge of their purpose and rules of use will greatly increase your programming competence.

9.1 A Problem Requiring Factorials

For any non-negative integer N, factorial N (often written as N!) is defined by

$$N! = N(N-1)(N-2) \ldots 3 \times 2 \times 1$$

and 0! is defined equal to 1. Suppose we are to read values for K, L and M and compute the value of

$$\frac{K!}{L!M!}$$

The algorithm is straightforward.

```
1. Get values for K, L and M
2. Set   FACTK = K!
3. Set   FACTL = L!
4. Set   FACTM = M!
5. Print   FACTK/(FACTL*FACTM)
6. Stop
```

When writing the program for this algorithm the only real challenge is in calculating the value of the factorials. Clearly we could set up three WHILE-loops, one for each of K, L and M and perhaps this brute-force approach isn't too bad. But what if we had to calculate 20 or 50 or hundreds of separate factorial values? We would like to code the factorial algorithm once and the execute it wherever it is needed in the program.

We shall do this first using a REMOTE BLOCK to calculate the factorial. After discussing the disadvantages of this approach we will see how some of these disadvantages can be eliminated by using a SUBROUTINE subprogram to calculate a factorial value. Following a discussion of SUBROUTINEs the factorial routine will be converted into a FUNCTION subprogram.

First we need an algorithm for obtaining the factorial of an INTEGER variable such as N. Let's call the result FACTN.

```
1.  FACTN = 1
2.  If N > 1 then do
         For i=2,3, ...,N do
              Set FACTN = I times FACTN
3.  Stop
```

In the program which follows, this algorithm has been converted into a REMOTE BLOCK called NFACT and EXECUTEd three times to calculate the values of K!, L! and M! needed to compute K!/(L!M!).

```
C EXAMPLE 9.1   FACTORIAL PROBLEM
      READ,K,L,M
C COMPUTE FACTORIAL K
      N = K
      EXECUTE NFACT
      FACTK = FACTN
C COMPUTE FACTORIAL L
      N = L
      EXECUTE NFACT
      FACTL = FACTN
C COMPUTE FACTORIAL M
      N = M
      EXECUTE NFACT
      FACTM = FACTN
C PRINT RESULT
      PRINT,K,L,M,FACTK/(FACTL*FACTM)
      STOP
C
      REMOTE BLOCK NFACT
         FACTN = 1.
         IF(N .GT. 1) THEN
            DO 17 I=2,N
               FACTN = FACTN*I
17          CONTINUE
         END IF
      END BLOCK
      END
```

What has been achieved using this approach? One obvious advantage is that the factorial routine has been written only once instead of three times. This results in a:

- saving of programming time
- saving of compile time
- saving of memory required to
      store the program

Are there any disadvantages? Consider what must be done to use the REMOTE BLOCK called NFACT.

1. assign a value to N
2. EXECUTE the block
3. assign the value of FACTN to the
      appropriate variable

That is, three statements must be executed for each use of the factorial routine. If many such uses were required, coding and entering these triples of statements would be somewhat tedious. Wouldn't it be nice if all three actions could be coded in a single statement?

To understand a second potential cause for concern suppose that several programs must be written each of which requires us to calculate one or more factorials. If we were to take the NFACT routine and "drop it" into another program, what difficulties, if any, might there be?

For one thing, since our factorial routine uses statement number 17, no program which made use of the routine could use this statement number elsewhere in the program. Also, since the factorial routine uses the variable names N, FACTN, and I, errors could result if these variables were used indiscriminately for other purposes elsewhere in the program.

If this weren't bad enough, suppose we had several pre-written routines which we planned to use in different programs. For example, one might write a routine to find the roots of a quadratic equation, find the largest or smallest value in a set, calculate the average of a set of numbers, etc.. If each of these had to have their own set of variable names and statement numbers, it would soon be a messy business to make profitable use of these pre-written routines.

Fortunately in FORTRAN all of these disadvantages are overcome by making the routine a subprogram. In other words, when a subprogram is used:

    i) The variable names and statement numbers used in the subprogram can also be used in the mainline program or in other subprograms and no confusion or ambiguity is introduced.

    ii) The assignment of "mainline" values to variables used in the subprogram before it is executed and the "return" of values calculated or changed by executing the subprogram is automatic (taken care of by machine language instructions generated by WATFIV at compile time).

There are two commonly used types of subprograms. They are called FUNCTION subprograms and SUBROUTINE subprograms.

The similarities of the two types far outweigh the differences. Each type is easy to use. We shall begin with SUBROUTINE subprograms.

9.2 SUBROUTINE Subprograms

A First Example

The first task is to see how the factorial routine can be converted to a SUBROUTINE subprogram. After completing this description, we will show how the SUBROUTINE is used in the solution of our original problem.

When the factorial routine is written as a SUBROUTINE called CALFAC it appears as:

```
          SUBROUTINE CALFAC(N,FACTN)
          FACTN=1.
          IF(N.GT.1) THEN
              DO 2 I=2,N
                  FACTN=FACTN*I
    2         CONTINUE
          END IF
          RETURN
          END
```

Remarks:

1. The first statement of the SUBROUTINE contains three types of information. These are:

```
   type of the      name of the       parameters of
   subprogram       subprogram        the subprogram



   SUBROUTINE        CALFAC          ( N , FACTN )
```

2. A "RETURN" statement is used to return control back to the program which requested execution of the subroutine.

3. An "END" statement is used to define the end of the statements in the subprogram.

It remains to see how to use the SUBROUTINE CALFAC in solving our original problem which was to calculate the value of K!/(L!M!). A suitable mainline program is the following.

```
C EXAMPLE MAINLINE USING CALFAC SUBROUTINE
      READ,K,L,M
      CALL CALFAC(K,FACTK)
      CALL CALFAC(L,FACTL)
      CALL CALFAC(M,FACTM)
      ANSWER=FACTK/(FACTL*FACTM)
      PRINT,ANSWER
      STOP
      END
```

Remarks:

1. The statement which calls the SUBROUTINE into action is a "CALL" statement.

   A CALL statement contains:

                     name of the SUBROUTINE
                         being called   arguments

            CALL   CALFAC (K , FACTK)

2. The name of the SUBROUTINE is CALFAC. Any valid WATFIV name can be used.

3. The arguments are simply values or variables which are used by the SUBROUTINE or which are to be assigned a value by the execution of the SUBROUTINE subprogram.

4. When the CALL statement is executed, the values of K and FACTK are assigned to the corresponding parameters N and FACTN. Control then passes to the SUBROUTINE. When the RETURN statement in the SUBROUTINE is executed, the reverse process occurs. That is, the values of the parameters N and FACTN are assigned to the variables K and FACTK. Control then transfers to the statement immediately following the CALL statement. It doesn't matter that FACTK did not have a value assigned to it before the CALL statement is executed. After all, that was the purpose of calling the SUBROUTINE -- to obtain a value for FACTK. Similarly, it doesn't matter when returning from the SUBROUTINE that the value of N is assigned to K since the SUBROUTINE did not change this value during its execution. If the value of N had been changed in the SUBROUTINE however, the values of K before and after the execution of the SUBROUTINE would be different.

The mainline and the subprogram are placed between the $JOB and $ENTRY cards in any order.   Most programmers prefer to put the mainline segment ahead of any subprograms used but this is not necessary. The organization of the card deck for a job containing a single SUBROUTINE subprogram is shown below.

```
          $JOB
          C MAINLINE PROGRAM
                  ...
                  ...
                  ...
                  END
          C
                  SUBROUTINE name (parameter list)
                  ...
                  ...
                  END
          $ENTRY
```

    In all the programs considered thus far, there has only been a mainline segment. Regardless of how many subprograms are included in a job, there must be one and only one mainline segment. The compiler can tell which segment is the mainline since all subprograms have a unique statement as the first one of the subprogram. The first statement executed in any job is always the first executable statement in the mainline. What happens after that depends on the program. Subprograms can use any of the executable statements available in the language. This means that subprograms can have READ, PRINT or STOP statements if they are appropriate to the purpose of the subprogram.

    One further point.   Each program segment must have an END statement. This lets the compiler know that this is the end of the segment. The $ENTRY statement follows the last segment and is used as a signal to stop compilation and begin execution.

    Before looking at a second example, it would be wise to summarize the ideas developed this far. These can be illustrated by examining the program structure below.

```
  C MAINLINE PROGRAM          SUBROUTINE name(p1,p2,...,pN)
      .                            .
      .                            .
      CALL name(a1,a2,...aN)       .
      .                         RETURN
      .                            .
      END                       END
```

When the CALL statement is executed, the sequence of events is as follows:

1. The values of the <u>arguments</u> a1,a2,...,aN are assigned to the <u>parameters</u> p1,p2,...,pN.

2. Control is passed to the first executable statement in the SUBROUTINE.

When a RETURN statement is executed (there may be several),

1. The values of the   parameters p1,p2,...pN,   are assigned to the arguments a1,a2,...,aN.

2. Control is passed to the statement following the CALL statement. (If a CALL statement is the object of a DO, the effect is the same as if a CONTINUE statement had followed the CALL.)

Naturally there must be the same number of elements in the argument and parameter lists and furthermore the corresponding elements in each list must be of the same type (either REAL or INTEGER).

A Second Example

Suppose we need to solve a series of equations of the form,

$$ax^2 + bx + c = 0.$$

The values of x which satisfy this equation can be calculated from the values of the coefficients "a", "b", and "c" using the well-known formulae:

$$\text{root } 1 = \frac{-b + \sqrt{b^2-4ac}}{2a}$$

$$\text{root } 2 = \frac{-b - \sqrt{b^2-4ac}}{2a}$$

A program which reads values of the coefficients and prints the roots of the equation is shown below.   In this program, it is assumed that (b^2-4ac) is non-negative.   If "a" has a value of zero, the job is terminated.

```
      C EXAMPLE 9.2 ROOTS OF EQUATION
            READ,A,B,C
            WHILE(A .NE. 0)
               CALL QUAD(A,B,C,ROOT1,ROOT2)
               PRINT 70,ROOT1,ROOT2
         70    FORMAT(' ROOT1=',E20.6,',ROOT2=',E20.6)
               READ,A,B,C
            END WHILE
            STOP
            END
      C
            SUBROUTINE QUAD(X,Y,Z,ONE,TWO)
            PRINT 70,X,Y,Z
         70 FORMAT('0EQUATION (',F9.4,')X**2+(',F9.4,
           *')*X+(',F9.4,')=0.')
            D=SQRT(Y*Y-4.*X*Z)
            ONE=(-Y+D)/(2.*X)
            TWO=(-Y-D)/(2.*X)
            RETURN
            END
      $ENTRY
      2., 5., 3.
      0., 0., 0.
```

When the program is executed with the data cards shown, the
output appears as:

```
      EQUATION (    2.0000)X**2+(    5.0000)X+(    3.0000)=0.

      ROOT1=        -0.1000000E 01,ROOT2=       -0.1500000E 01
```

In this example, the argument and parameter lists each
contain five variables. When the CALL statement is executed,
the SUBROUTINE parameters X, Y, Z, ONE, TWO are assigned the
values of A, B, C, ROOT1, ROOT2 respectively.   It doesn't
matter that ROOT1 and ROOT2 have not been assigned a value
in the mainline since they will be assigned the values of
the parameters ONE and TWO when the RETURN is executed.   The
execution of the RETURN statement also causes A, B and C to
be assigned the values of X,Y, and Z.   Since these latter
three variables were not assigned new values in the
SUBROUTINE, the values of A, B and C will be unchanged by
executing the SUBROUTINE.

To further illustrate this point, consider the following
example.

```
C EXAMPLE 9.3
      X=Y=1.
      DO 10 I=1,5            SUBROUTINE SUB(A,B)
         CALL SUB(X,Y)       A=A+B
         PRINT,X             RETURN
   10 CONTINUE               END
      STOP
      END
```

In the SUBROUTINE, the value of the parameter A is changed.
This means that each time the RETURN is executed, the value
of the argument X will be different from the value preceding
the execution of the SUBROUTINE. The parameter B, on the
other hand, is not changed by executing "SUB" and so the
five lines printed will display the values 2., 3., 4., 5.,
and 6.

A Third Example

Suppose we are required to write a SUBROUTINE which
scans an array of ten INTEGER values and determines the
position of the element in the set having the smallest
value. The "input" to the SUBROUTINE will be the set of ten
values and the "output" will be the value of the subscript
of the element having the smallest magnitude. The algorithm
used in the subprogram which follows assumes initially that
the first element of the set is the smallest and then
examines each of the remaining nine values in the set to see
if any are smaller than the smallest found so far.

```
      SUBROUTINE FIND(SET,LOC)
C A SUBROUTINE TO DETERMINE THE POSITION OF THE
C SMALLEST VALUE IN A SET OF 10 INTEGER VALUES
      INTEGER SET(10),SMALL
      LOC=1
      SMALL=SET(1)
      DO 6 I=2,10
         IF(SET(I).LT.SMALL) THEN
            SMALL=SET(I)
            LOC=I
         END IF
    6 CONTINUE
      RETURN
      END
```

This SUBROUTINE could be used in the following way.
Suppose a set of 10 INTEGER values is read and the values
are to be printed in order of increasing magnitude. A
brute-force algorithm for solving this problem is:

1. Read in the set of 10 values.
2. Find the position of the smallest and
     print the value in that position.
3. Find the position of the smallest, excluding
     that found in step 2, and print the value in
     that position.
4. Find the position of the smallest, excluding
     those found in steps 2 and 3, and print the
     value in that position.
5. ...
6. ...
   .
   .
11. Find the position of the smallest, excluding
      those found in steps 2 thru 10, and print the value
      in that position.
12. Stop

In order to use an iterative approach, a method of
"excluding those found in steps 2 thru ..." must be found.
An easy way of accomplishing this is to replace the smallest
value found each time by some very large number. By doing
this, the position of the smallest value will change each
time because the very large value, say, 999999, will not be
the smallest in the set. Thus an algorithm for the mainline
would be.

      1. Read in the set of 10 values
      2. Repeat steps 2.1 and 2.2 ten times.
         .1 Find the position of the smallest
             element and print the value in
             that position.
         .2 Replace the value by 999999.
      3. Stop.

A translation of this algorithm is:

```
C EXAMPLE 9.4 SORTING 10 INTEGERS
      INTEGER NUM(10),POS
      READ,NUM
      DO 6 I=1,10
         CALL FIND(NUM,POS)
         PRINT,NUM(POS)
         NUM(POS)=999999
    6 CONTINUE
      STOP
      END
```

In this mainline segment, the set name "NUM" has been used
to create a set of ten arguments. These ten, plus the

variable "POS", correspond one-to-one with the parameters defined by "(SET,LOC)" in the SUBROUTINE FIND. Note that when a set is passed back and forth between program segments, that

  i) Only the set name appears in the argument and
     parameter lists.

 ii) The array must be defined in each segment.

iii) The arrays defined in the two segments must be of
     the same type and have the same number of elements.

Before summarizing the rules of SUBROUTINE usage, it should be pointed out that SUBROUTINES can call other SUBROUTINES. This idea is illustrated in the program structure below.

```
C MAINLINE                      SUBROUTINE SUBA(...)
     .                               .
     .                          CALL SUBB(...)
  CALL SUBA(...)                     .
     .                          CALL SUBC(...)
     .                               .
  END                           END
```

In this program structure, SUBB could not contain a CALL to SUBA since this amounts to a subprogram calling itself. If this was permitted, it would mean the values assigned to the parameters of SUBA as a result of the mainline CALL would be wiped out and it would also wipe out the means of returning to the mainline. For these reasons, an error results if a subprogram attempts to call itself either directly or indirectly.

9.3 Basic Rules of SUBROUTINE Usage

1. The general form of a CALL statement is:

        CALL name (a1,a2,a3,...,aN)

    where,

        a) "name" is the name of a SUBROUTINE subprogram.
           The name can be any valid WATFIV name.
        b) "(a1,a2,a3,...,aN)" is the argument list. An
           argument can be: a variable name, a set name, or
           an arithmetic expression or constant.

2.   A SUBROUTINE statement must be the first statement in
any SUBROUTINE subprogram. Its general form is:

    SUBROUTINE name(p1,p2,p3,...,pN), where

    a) "name" is the name of the SUBROUTINE.
    b) "(p1,p2,p3,...pN)" is the parameter list.   A
       parameter can   be either a non-subscripted
       variable or a set name.

3. a) The number of arguments must equal the number of
       parameters.

    b) The type (REAL or INTEGER) of each argument must be
       the same as the type of the corresponding parameter.

    c) If an argument is a set name, the corresponding
       parameter must be a set having the same dimensions.

4.   The execution of a RETURN statement (there can be any
number in a subprogram) causes control to be transferred
to the first statement following the CALL.

5.   The value of   each argument is assigned   to the
corresponding parameter before control passes to the
SUBROUTINE.   The value of each parameter is assigned to
the corresponding argument before control returns to the
calling segment.

6.   Initialization of subprogram parameters at compile time
is not allowed.

7.   A SUBROUTINE may transfer control to another subprogram
provided that any chain of subprogram transfers does
not form a loop.

8.   If an argument is a constant, an expression, a DO-loop
index,   or a DO-loop parameter,   the value of the
corresponding parameter in the subprogram cannot be
changed.   If the value of   the parameter is changed
during the execution of the subprogram, an error message
will be printed and the job terminated after control
returns to the calling segment.

9.   If the same element appears more than once in an
argument list, no change should be made in the value of
any of the corresponding parameters during the execution
of the subprogram since this would mean the argument
would not have a unique value when control returned to
the mainline.

Exercise 9.1

1. For each of the following, describe the output.

a)
```
        I=2                        SUBROUTINE FCN(K,L)
        CALL FCN(I,J)              L=K**2-3*K+5
        PRINT,I,J                  RETURN
        STOP                       END
        END
```

b)
```
        REAL AB(10)/10*1./         SUBROUTINE ADD(TAB)
        DO 3 N=1,4                 REAL TAB(10)
          CALL ADD(AB)             DO 6 I=2,10,2
      3 CONTINUE                     TAB(I-1)=TAB(I-1)-1
        PRINT 14,AB                  TAB(I)=TAB(I)+1
     14 FORMAT(' ',5F4.0)        6 CONTINUE
        STOP                       RETURN
        END                        END
```

c)
```
        M=0                        SUBROUTINE R(J,N)
        DO 1 J=1,4                 DO 2 K=1,J
          CALL R(J,M)                N=N+K
      1 CONTINUE                  2 CONTINUE
        PRINT,M                    RETURN
        STOP                       END
        END
```

d)
```
        READ,X                     SUBROUTINE IN(Z)
        CALL IN(Y)                 READ,Z
        PRINT,X,Y                  RETURN
        READ,P                     END
        CALL IN(Q)         $ENTRY
        PRINT,P,Q            -2.
        STOP                 -3.,      -4.
        END                  5.,       6
                             7.
```

e) Take your time on this one.

```
        INTEGER L/1/,K/2/          SUBROUTINE HELP(K,L)
        CALL HELP(L,K)             INTEGER KL/5/
        CALL HELP(K,L)             KL=KL*K/L
        PRINT,L,K                  K=KL*L
        STOP                       RETURN
        END                        END
```

Hint: The second time HELP is called, the value of KL will not be 5. It will be the value it had after the SUBROUTINE finished executing the first time.

```
    f)    KA=1                      SUBROUTINE SUB
          3 CALL SUB                INTEGER N/1/
            PRINT,KA                IF(N.GT.10) STOP
            KA=KA+1                 N=N+1
            GO TO 3                 RETURN
            END                     END
```

2. Determine the error in each of the following.

```
    a)  CALL SUB(X,Y)              SUBROUTINE SUB(Z)

    b)  CALL AB(I,3.**2-5)         SUBROUTINE AB(J,NA$)

    c)  INTEGER MAX(1)             SUBROUTINE T6666(J,R)
        CALL T6666(MAX,R)

    d)  REAL A(10),JO              SUBROUTINE ADD(B,ZY)
        CALL ADD(JO,A)             REAL B(100)

    e)  CALL EVERY(3)              SUBROUTINE EVERY(OH)

    f)  CALL (A,B,C,D,E)           SUBROUTINE (W,X,Y,Z,E)

    g)  CALL TROOP(MAT(10),F)      SUBROUTINE TROOP(MAT(10),F)

    h)  CALL OOPS(5.3)             SUBROUTINE OOPS(S)
                                   REAL S(1)

    i)  X=SUB(Y)                   SUBROUTINE SUB(Y)

    j)  CALL WRONG(A)              SUBROUTINE WRONG(1.375)

    k)    ABC=5.                   SUBROUTINE OOPS(RST,XYZ)
          CALL OOPS(ABC,DEF)       RST=RST+XYZ
          STOP                     RETURN
          END                      END

    l)    X=Y=2.                   SUBROUTINE POWER(X,Y,Z)
          CALL POWER(X,Y,X)        Z=X**Y
          STOP                     RETURN
          END                      END
```

9.4 FUNCTION Subprograms

The other type of frequently used subprogram is called a
FUNCTION subprogram. The differences between FUNCTION
subprograms and SUBROUTINE subprograms are few. The choice
of which type to use in a given situation is largely a
matter of personal preference.

To illustrate some aspects of FUNCTION subprograms, the routine to calculate factorial N will be converted to a FUNCTION subprogram called FACTN.

```
C FUNCTION SUBPROGRAM TO CALCULATE FACTORIAL N
      FUNCTION FACTN(N)
      FACTN=1.
      IF(N.GT.1) THEN
          DO 2 I=2,N
              FACTN=FACTN*I
    2     CONTINUE
      END IF
      RETURN
      END
```

Some remarks.

1. The first statement of the FUNCTION subprogram contains three types of information.

2. Within the subprogram, the FUNCTION name is used as a simple variable. It appears on both the left and right sides of an Assignment statement. Since there is no information to the contrary, the value of FACTN is REAL.

   This illustrates one of the important differences between FUNCTION subprograms and SUBROUTINE subprograms. The FUNCTION name is assigned a value in a FUNCTION subprogram. A SUBROUTINE name is simply used to identify the routine.

3. As with SUBROUTINES, a RETURN statement is used to transfer control back to the segment which activated the subprogram.

The FUNCTION subprogram FACTN could be used to help solve the original problem which was to calculate K!/(L!M!). A mainline segment which "calls" the FUNCTION subprogram to obtain the factorial values is shown below.

```
      C MAINLINE SEGMENT USING THE FUNCTION FACTN
            READ,K,L,M
            FACTK=FACTN(K)
            FACTL=FACTN(L)
            FACTM=FACTN(M)
            ANSWER=FACTK/(FACTL*FACTM)
            PRINT,ANSWER
            STOP
            END
```

Notice that the FUNCTION subprogram is "called" by using the FUNCTION name with an argument list in an expression. In other words, precisely in the same way that built-in functions are called. This is the second major difference between the two types of subprograms. That is, a CALL statement is used to activate a SUBROUTINE whereas the appearance of the FUNCTION name with an argument list "calls" a FUNCTION subprogram.

The word "calls" will be used for both SUBROUTINE and FUNCTION subprograms. The terms "calling segment" and "called segment" refer, respectively, to the segment from which and to which control passes regardless of the type of subprogram.

The general form of a program containing a mainline segment and a single FUNCTION subprogram is:

```
C MAINLINE SEGMENT                 FUNCTION name(p1,p2,...pN)
      .                                  .
      .                            name=.......
      =...name(a1,a2,...aN)              .
      .                                  .
      .                            RETURN
      END                          END
```

Some remarks.

1. A FUNCTION subprogram is called when the FUNCTION name followed by an argument list appears on the right hand side of an Assignment statement or as part of an expression.

2. When a FUNCTION subprogram is called,

   a) The values of the arguments are assigned to the corresponding parameters.
   b) Control is transferred to the first executable statement of the FUNCTION subprogram.

3. During the execution of the subprogram a value must be
    assigned to the FUNCTION name. The type of value taken
    on is based on the first-letter rule. (An example will
    be given shortly which shows how to explicitly type the
    FUNCTION value.)

4. When a RETURN statement is executed,

    a) The values of the parameters are assigned to
       the corresponding arguments.

    b) The value assigned to the FUNCTION name in
       the subprogram is assigned to the element in
       the expression which activated the FUNCTION.

    c) Execution continues from the point immediately
       following the appearance of the FUNCTION in
       the calling expression.

Three important differences between FUNCTION subprograms
and SUBROUTINE subprograms are:

    i) A CALL statement is used to call a
        SUBROUTINE. The appearance of the FUNCTION
        name and argument list invokes a FUNCTION
        subprogram.

    ii) With a SUBROUTINE, control returns to the
        statement following the CALL. In the case of
        a FUNCTION subprogram, execution continues
        from a point following the appearance of the
        FUNCTION name.

    iii) The assignment of argument values to
         parameter values and parameter values to
         argument values occurs for both SUBROUTINE
         and FUNCTION subprograms. However, with
         FUNCTION subprograms, an additional
         assignment is made when the RETURN statement
         is executed, namely, the value assigned to
         the FUNCTION name in the subprogram is taken
         on by the element in the expression which
         called the subprogram.

This third point indicates the kind of situation when
one would normally use a FUNCTION subprogram instead of a
SUBROUTINE subprogram. That is, when the purpose of the
subprogram is to calculate a single value. Since the purpose
of the factorial routine used as an example was just that,
to calculate a single value, most programmmers would choose

to make the routine a FUNCTION subprogram and not a
SUBROUTINE subprogram.

Because of the point to which control returns, a
FUNCTION subprogram can be activated several times within
the same statement. For example, the mainline to solve the
original problem could be shortened to the following four
statements.

```
            READ,K,L,M
            PRINT,FACTN(K)/(FACTN(L)*FACTN(M))
            STOP
            END
```

If a SUBROUTINE were used, a minimum of three additional
statements would have to be written. These would be required
for the three CALLs to obtain the values of the factorials.

Before summarizing the rules of subprogram usage, a
second example of a FUNCTION subprogram will be discussed.
The program could be used to sort a set of ten INTEGER
values. The purpose of the subprogram POINT is to produce a
pointer to the element in the set having the smallest value.
You will recall this same problem was solved previously
using a SUBROUTINE subprogram. (See Example Program 9.4.)

```
C EXAMPLE 9.5
    INTEGER NUM(10),POINT        INTEGER FUNCTION POINT(S)
    READ,NUM                     INTEGER S(10)
    DO 6 J=1,10                  POINT=1
      K=POINT(NUM)               DO 6 I=1,10
      PRINT,NUM(K)                 IF(S(I).LT.S(POINT))POINT=I
      NUM(K)=999999            6 CONTINUE
  6 CONTINUE                     RETURN
    STOP                         END
    END
```

This example shows how to override the first-letter rule
applied to a FUNCTION name. In the example, the name of the
FUNCTION is POINT which, by the first-letter rule, would
normally be REAL-valued. Since POINT is used as a subscript
in the mainline, it should be INTEGER valued. This means
POINT must be declared as having INTEGER values in both the
mainline and the FUNCTION subprogram. In the mainline, this
is done by using an INTEGER statement to inform the compiler
that POINT is to take on INTEGER values.   In the FUNCTION
subprogram, this is accomplished by preceding the word
"FUNCTION" with the word "INTEGER".

Thus to cause a FUNCTION to have a type of value different from that assigned by the first-letter rule the FUNCTION name must appear in a declaration statement in the calling segment, and the word REAL or INTEGER must precede the word FUNCTION in the first statement of the FUNCTION subprogram. With SUBROUTINES this is never necessary since the SUBROUTINE name is only the name of the routine and no value is assigned to the name.

Note that when using the built-in functions in the WATFIV library, it is not necessary to put the FUNCTION name in a declaration statement since the name of each built-in function is appropriate to the type of value taken on by the function.

9.5 Subprograms -- Rule Summary

The chart on the following page summarizes the basic rules of SUBROUTINE and FUNCTION subprogram usage. See Chapter 10 for further information on subprograms.

Exercise 9.2

Assume all variables are typed by default unless declared otherwise.

1. For each of the following, describe the output produced.

```
a)  I=4                         FUNCTION MN(K)
    J=MN(I)                     MN=1
    PRINT,J**2                  L=K*2*K
    STOP                        IF(L.EQ.K)  MN=2
    END                         RETURN
                                END

b)  REAL JAY,A/5./,B/3./        REAL FUNCTION JAY(I)
    C=AMOD(A,B)*JAY(A-B)        REAL I
    PRINT,A,B,C                 JAY=I+SIGN(I,-I)
    STOP                        RETURN
    END                         END

c)  INTEGER I/1/,J/2/,K/3/      FUNCTION F1(L)
    PRINT,F1(I)*F2(J,K)         F1=F2(L,L/2)
    STOP                        RETURN
    END                         END
                   FUNCTION F2(M,N)
                   F2=M*(M+N)*(M-N)
                   RETURN
                   END
```

```
***********************************************************************
*              *          SUBROUTINES          *          FUNCTIONS          *
***********************************************************************
*              *                                *  FUNCTION name(p1,p2,...,pN) *
* Definition   * SUBROUTINE name(p1,p2,...,pN)   *            or                *
*              *                                *  REAL FUNCTION name(p1,p2,...,pN) *
*              *                                *            or                *
*              *                                *  INTEGER FUNCTION name(p1,p2,...,pN) *
***********************************************************************
*              *                                *  Appearance of "name(a1,a2,...,aN)" *
* Activated by * CALL name(a1,a2,...,aN)         *  in an expression in the calling    *
*              *                                *  segment.                           *
***********************************************************************
* Return point * statement following the CALL   *  point in the statement following   *
*              * statement.                      *  the appearance of the function      *
***********************************************************************
* Permitted type of *      set names, simple or subscripted variables, constants,  *
* arguments for *                    and expressions                              *
***********************************************************************
* Permitted type of *             set names, simple variables                      *
* parameters   *                                                                   *
***********************************************************************
* Agreement of * There must be the same number of elements in each list. Sets must *
* arguments and * be defined as having the same number of elements in both segments. *
* parameters   * Corresponding elements must be of the same type.                   *
***********************************************************************
*              * 1. If an argument is a constant, expression, DO-loop index, or     *
*              *    DO-loop parameter, the corresponding parameter cannot be        *
*              *    changed while executing the subprogram.                         *
* Four Errors  * 2. Subprogram parameters cannot be given values at compile time.   *
*              * 3. If the same item appears more than once in an argument list,    *
*              *    the value of each of the corresponding parameters must not be   *
*              *    changed during the execution of the subprogram.                 *
*              * 4. A chain of subprogram linkages cannot form a loop.              *
***********************************************************************
```

```
d)   REAL X/1./                FUNCTION KELLY(Z)
     DO 3 I=1,4                KELLY=Z*Z/Z*Z
       X=KELLY(X)              RETURN
       PRINT,X                 END
   3 CONTINUE
     STOP
     END


e)   INTEGER BETA/10/,GREG,F   SUBROUTINE NEXT(A,B)
     CALL NEXT(GREG(BETA),F)   INTEGER A,B,C/2/
     CALL NEXT(GREG(BETA),F)   C=C+2
     PRINT,GREG(BETA),F        B=A+C
     STOP                      RETURN
     END                       END

              INTEGER FUNCTION GREG(MINI)
              INTEGER ALPHA/1/
              GREG=MINI-2*ALPHA
              RETURN
              END


f)   REAL LUMP,HUMP(4)/4*2./   REAL FUNCTION LUMP(BUMP,A)
     Z=LUMP(HUMP,HUMP(3))      REAL BUMP(4)
     PRINT,Z,HUMP(3)           BUMP(IFIX(A-1.))=DIM(-A,A)
     STOP                      LUMP=BUMP(1)
     END                       RETURN
                               END
```

2. Determine the error in each of the following.

```
    a)   Y=FUNCTION ADD(3.)        FUNCTION ADD(X)

    b)   PRINT,ZZ(5)               INTEGER FUNCTION ZZ(J)

    c)   T=INTO(FLOAT(3))          FUNCTION INTO(LUCKY)

    d)   REAL A(3)/3*0./           REAL FUNCTION AA(B(1),B)
         M=AA(A(1),A)              REAL B(3)

    e)   M=2.5                     FUNCTION AFTER(JASPER)
         CALL AFTER(2*M)

    f)   TITLE=6*FACT(3)           FUNCTION FACT(K)
                                   FACT=1
                                   IF(K.GT.1)FACT=FACT(K-1)
                                   RETURN
                                   END
```

g) (three errors)

```
A=B=5.5E-01                 SUBROUTINE LOCATE(X,Y)
CALL LOCATE(A,B)            Y=FIND(X,Y)
STOP                        RETURN
END                         END
        FUNTION FIND(A,B)
        B=A/B
        CALL LOCATE(B,A)
        RETURN
        END
```

h) MAX=MAX(2)   FUNCTION MAX(I)
                              MAX=I*FLOAT(I)
                              RETURN
                              END

i)   GAMMA=FCN(2,4,6)   FUNCTION (K,L,M)

j)   TEST=ARAN(6.0,B)   FUNCTION ARAN(A,B)
                              REAL B/5./,ARAN/1./
                              ARAN=A+B+ARAN
                              RETURN
                              END

9.6 Statement Functions

Occasionally the same formula is required at several points within a single program segment. Provided the formula value can be calculated in a single expression, the formula may be defined as a Statement Function. Once a Statement Function has been defined, it is used in the same way as any FUNCTION subprogram or built-in function. Using Statement Functions may make a program easier to understand and may also reduce the programming and keypunching time required to solve a problem.

Suppose the formula

$$\text{distance} = \text{velocity} \times \text{time} + \frac{1}{2} \text{ accel.} \times \text{time}^2$$

is required in a problem. A program which makes the formula into a Statement Function and subsequently uses it, is the following.

```
$JOB WATFIV
C EXAMPLE 9.6 STATEMENT FUNCTIONS
C STATEMENT FUNCTION DEFINITION
      DIST(VEL,TIME,ACC)=VEL*TIME+.5*ACC*TIME**2
C       START OF EXECUTABLE STATEMENTS
      READ,A,B,C
C       STATEMENT FUNCTION USAGE
      D=DIST(A,B,C)
      PRINT 900,A,B,C,D
  900 FORMAT(' VEL=',F6.2,' TIME=',F6.2,' ACC=',
     * F6.2,' DISTANCE=',F6.2)
      STOP
      END
```

   Note that the formula definition appears before the
first executable statement of the program. The formula is
used by including the name and an argument list in an
expression. That is, a Statement Function is called in
precisely the same way that a built-in function is called.

   The general structure of a segment containing a
Statement Function is shown below. Rules of usage follow.

```
$JOB    WATFIV
      .
      name(parameter list)=expression
      .
      .
C BEGINNING OF EXECUTABLE STATEMENTS
      .
      .
      ...=...name(argument list)...
      .
      .
      END
```

Rules For Statement Functions

1. The name of a Statement Function can be any valid
   WATFIV name. The parameter list contains one or
   more non-subscripted variables separated by commas.
   Elements in the parameter list are typed by the
   first-letter rule unless they have been typed by a
   previous statement. The expression can be any valid
   WATFIV expression involving the parameters and
   (optionally) other non-parameter variables,
   constants, built-in functions and other previously
   defined Statement Functions.

2. The function is activated by the appearance of

    name (argument list)

in an expression.   The arguments may be constants, variables or expressions. Arguments should agree in number and type with the corresponding parameters.

3. All Statement Function definitions   must be   placed ahead of   the   first   executable   statement   in   a segment.

4. Statement Functions can   only   be   used within   the program segment in which they are defined.

5. Variable   names   used   as   parameters   in   Statement Function definitions can be used as names of simple variables for other purposes in the segment.

Exercise 9.3 (Statement Functions)

1. For each of the following, state the values printed.

a)   F(X)=X*X-1.
            PRINT,F(3.)

b)   INTEGER A,B,MAT(2)/-3,4/
            A(B,C)=IABS(B*IFIX(C))
            G=7.94
            PRINT,A(MAT(1),G),A(MAT(2),G)

c)   REAL B(2)/1.,2.5/
            OOPS(I,J)=3-B(I)+I/J
            AHA(K,L)=3-OOPS(K,L)*I/J
            I=J=3
            PRINT,OOPS(2,I),AHA(IFIX(B(2)),J)

2. What is the error in each of the following?

a)   I=2
            B(K)=SQRT(K*100.)
            PRINT,B(I)

b) Two errors
            INTEGER Y/3/,Z,K(2)
            X(Y,M)=M*FLOAT(Y)+K(1)
            Z=X(3,17)
            PRINT,Z,SQRT(Y)

3. a) Can a Statement Function have no parameters? Why?

   b) How can the compiler tell whether a statement which begins "FUN(I)=..." is a Statement Function definition or an Assignment statement?

9.7 Summary

1. Routines which solve a set of equations, multiply matrices, sort a set of numbers, etc., are often required at different points in the same program, or in several different programs. The programmer has the choice of making the routine part of the mainline, into a REMOTE BLOCK or making the routine a SUBROUTINE or FUNCTION subprogram. A comparison of the approaches is shown below.

	Routine Is Part of the Mainline or REMOTE BLOCK	Routine Is A Subprogram
Variable names used in the routine can be used indiscriminently outside the routine.	no	yes
Statement numbers used in the routine can be used indiscriminently outside the routine.	no	yes
Routine can be accessed from inside a DO-loop.	no (yes if REMOTE BLOCK)	yes
Assignment of values to variables used in the routine is done by ...	statements written by the programmer	WATFIV
Assignment of values calculated in the routine to variables used in the mainline is taken care of by ...	statements written by the programmer	WATFIV
Can the routine be used easily in different programs?	no	yes

It is apparent from the above chart that subprograms are much more "portable" than REMOTE BLOCKs. None-the-less REMOTE BLOCKs are valuable aids in structuring large programs and may also be defined and used within subprograms.

2.   The use of Statement Functions may reduce programming time in cases where the same formula is required at several points within a segment.

9.8 Programming Problems

If a problem requests that only a subprogram be written, write a simple mainline to test the subprogram.

9.1   Write a SUBROUTINE subprogram called TRIAIR to calculate the area of a triangle from the length of the base and the altitude. The subprogram will have three parameters -- BASE, ALTUDE and AREA. The first two values are supplied by the calling segment. The value of AREA is calculated in the subprogram. Write a mainline segment which reads in five pairs of REAL values punched one pair per card. The values in each pair are the lengths of the base and altitude respectively. The mainline should print the input values and the area for each of the five triangles using appropriate FORMAT statements.

9.2   Make the subprogram TRIAIR in problem 1 a FUNCTION subprogram. Note that it will then have only two parameters, BASE and ALTUDE.

9.3   Write a SUBROUTINE subprogram in which the parameter is a vector of ten INTEGER values. The subprogram should reverse the order of the ten values before returning control to the calling segment.

9.4   Write a FUNCTION subprogram called DET which calculates the value of the determinant of a two-by-two matrix. The subprogram will have a single parameter, the name of the two-by-two matrix of REAL values.

9.5   Write a SUBROUTINE subprogram to solve a system of two equations in two unknowns. The SUBROUTINE should have the parameters COEFF, RS, ROOTS and IFLAG where: COEFF is a 2-by-2 matrix of the coefficients in the equations; RS is a vector of the right hand side values of the equations; ROOTS is a vector of the pair of values which solve the equations; IFLAG is calculated by the subprogram and has a value of zero if the equations have no solution, 1 if there is one solution, and 2 if there are an infinite number of solutions. For example, to solve

$$2x + 3y = 12$$
$$-4x + 8y = 4$$

The values passed to the SUBROUTINE would be

$$COEFF = \begin{pmatrix} 2. & 3. \\ -4. & 8. \end{pmatrix} \qquad RS = \begin{pmatrix} 12. \\ 4. \end{pmatrix}$$

The values calculated by the SUBROUTINE would be

$$ROOTS = (3., 2.) \qquad IFLAG = 1$$

9.6   Write a SUBROUTINE called RANDI to generate a set of 100 "random" INTEGER numbers R(1), R(2), R(3),... in the range J thru K. Use the following method. Set R(1) equal to any positive INTEGER value. For N=2, 3, ..., 100, set R(N)=MOD(25173*R(N-1),65536). This will generate 100 random numbers in the range 1 thru 65535. To reduce the range to that of J thru K, replace R(I) by

$$R(I) - R(I)/65535.*(K-J+1) + J$$

The parameters of the SUBROUTINE will be R, J, and K. Test your subprogram by writing a mainline segment which prints out the one hundred numbers generated by RANDI on ten lines of ten values each.

9.7   Use the SUBROUTINE RANDI written for the previous problem in this problem. Generate two hundred random INTEGER values in the range one thru six. Use these numbers to represent the outcome on one hundred throws of a pair of dice. That is, if the values of R(1) and R(2) were 3 and 6 respectively, this would mean the dice on the first throw showed 3 and 6. Write a program which answers the following questions about the hundred thows of the dice. How many times did each of the 36 possible results occur? Print the data in a table having six rows and six columns where the row indicates the value on the first die. The column indicates the value on the second die. What percentage of the time did each of the eleven possible totals 2, 3, 4, ..., 12 occur in the hundred throws? Print suitable headings followed by eleven lines of statistics.

9.8   Write a SUBROUTINE which has two parameters -- K, a set of twenty INTEGER values, and INSERT. Values in K

and the value of INSERT are passed to the subprogram.
The SUBROUTINE should insert the value of INSERT into
the set K so that values in K are non-decreasing
(increasing order of magnitude except for ties) and then
return control to the calling segment. Write a mainline
segment which initializes a set of twenty INTEGER values
called NSET to zero and then reads one INTEGER value
from each of twenty cards. After each value is read, use
the SUBROUTINE to insert the value in the proper
position in NSET. After the twenty values have been
read, print the values in NSET and verify that they have
been stored in order of increasing magnitude.

9.9   Write a FUNCTION subprogram called ANG which, for the
triangle shown below, calculates the size of angle A in
degrees.

$$\text{Note: } \cos A = \frac{b^2 + c^2 - a^2}{2bc}$$

The lengths of the sides "a", "b" and "c" are passed to
the subprogram. Test your subprogram by writing a
mainline segment which reads in the lengths of the sides
and uses ANG to calculate the sizes of the three angles
in the triangle.

9.10   The area of a regular polygon of N sides in which each
side has a length "s" is equal to $Ns^2\cot(180/N)/4$. Write
a FUNCTION subprogram called POLAIR having parameters N
and s to calculate the area. Test POLAIR by writing a
mainline segment which uses the subprogram to calculate
the areas of regular polygons of <u>perimeter</u> one having 3,
4, 5, ..., 20 sides.

9.11   Write three Statement Functions called SIND, COSD and
TAND to produce the sine, cosine and tangent values of
an angle in degrees. Use the Statement Functions in a
program which prints the cosecant, secant and cotangents
of angles of 10, 20, 30, ..., 80 degrees.

9.12   Write a Statement Function which will round off any
REAL value greater than 0.1 correct to N decimal places.
Assume N is positive. Note that this can be done by:
adding 5.*10.**(-N) to the value; multiplying by 10**N;
using the function AINT; dividing by 10**N. All of this
can be done in one statement. Test your function by

rounding the value of 12.73469 correct to 1, 2, 3, and 4 decimal places.

9.13 Write a Statement Function called LOGB having two parameters X and B. The value of the Function is the logarithm of X using base B. Note that

$$\log X = \log X / \log B$$

Use the Statement Function to print a table of the logs of the values one thru ten using bases 2, 4, 6, 8, and 10.

9.14 Write a Statement Function called KRON which has two INTEGER parameters M and N. The value of KRON should be zero if M and N are unequal and one if M equals N. You may find the IDIM built-in function useful in your function definition. Make up your own program to test the Statement Function.

CHAPTER 10   SUBPROGRAMS -- THE DETAILS

Questions Answered In This Chapter

1. How are numbers stored and organized in the computer?

2. When subprogram parameters take on values of the corresponding arguments, they can be "called by value" or "called by location". What is meant by these terms?

3. Variables used in a subprogram can automatically be given the values of variables used in other program segments by putting all such variables in a "common" area of memory. How is this done?

4. What is meant by execution time dimensioning of arrays? Why and how is this feature used?

5. If a subprogram must be written which requires the use of some other unknown subprogram, how is the compiler informed of this fact?

6. How can a subprogram be entered at some statement other than the first executable statement in the subprogram?

7. How can a SUBROUTINE return to a statement other than the one immediately following the "CALL" statment?

In the last chapter, the basic features of SUBROUTINE and FUNCTION subprograms were described. This knowledge may be sufficient to write and use all subprograms you will ever need. This chapter describes other "advanced" features of subprograms which, when used properly, may: (i) reduce the programming effort required; (ii) reduce the amount of memory used for instructions and data.

In order to use the features of the WATFIV language described in this chapter to best advantage, it is necessary to understand some of the basic concepts of how the memory is used by the compiler in translating a WATFIV program into machine language. Keep in mind that these topics are presented as concepts. The details of how these concepts have been implemented may be found in the WATFOR/WATFIV Implementation Guide available from the Computing Center at the University of Waterloo.

10.1 "Memory" Concepts

The memory (sometimes called storage) of a computer has thousands and often millions of memory cells or "bits". Each bit of the memory has a value of one or zero. In many computers, a memory cell is a little iron donut about an eighth of an inch in diameter, with several wires going thru the hole. By changing the quantity and direction of the current in the wires, the iron ring can be magnetized in either a clockwise or counter-clockwise direction. These two directions of magnetization represent the values of one and zero. One and zero are the two symbols used in the binary (base two) number system and the word "bit" is a contraction of the words "Binary digIT".

Bits are grouped together in sets of eight. A group of eight consecutive bits is called a byte. In order to be able to reference the contents (the bit pattern) of each byte, a unique number is associated with each byte of the computer memory. The number is called the address of the byte. Byte addresses start at zero and go up by one to the total number of bytes in the computer memory. These byte addresses are used in the machine language instructions generated by the compiler.

A group of thirty-two consecutive bits is called a word. The terms half-word and double word mean groups of sixteen and sixty-four consecutive bits respectively. The address of a half-word, full word, or double word is the address of its leftmost byte. The symbol "K" means 1024 bytes. For example, a computer having a 32K memory is one in which there are 32,768 bytes of memory. The diagram below shows the relationship between the sizes of the different quantities of memory. In the case of half-words, full words and double words, the asterisk denotes the byte used for addressing the storage locations.

Units Of Memory

```
                 .----.----.----.----.----.----.----.----.
Bytes            | *  | *  | *  | *  | *  | *  | *  | *  |
                 +----.----.----.----.----.----.----.----+
Half-Words       | *     | *     | *     | *     |
                 +----------.----------.----------.----------+
Words            | *             | *             |
                 +---------------------.---------------------+
Double Word      | *                                         |
                 '-------------------------------------------'
```

Each program segment is compiled separately. Recall that program segments each have an END card to separate the segment from any which may follow. After the last segment

has been compiled, and before execution begins, the segments
are linked together and the memory used by the program is
organized as shown on the following page.

Execution-Time Layout Of Memory

```
,--------------------------------------------------,
|                                                  |
|   Instructions for mainline segment              |
|                                                  |
|   Constants and simple variables used            |
|            in the mainline                       |
|--------------------------------------------------|
|   Instructions for subprogram 1                  |
|                                                  |
|   Constants and simple variables used            |
|            in subprogram 1                       |
|--------------------------------------------------|
|   Instructions for subprogram 2                  |
|                                                  |
|   Constants and simple variables used            |
|            in subprogram 2                       |
'--------------------------------------------------'


,--------------------------------------------------,
|        Array area for entire program             |
'--------------------------------------------------'
```

Remarks.

1. One full word of memory is reserved for each REAL
   or INTEGER constant. One full word of memory is
   reserved for each REAL or INTEGER variable.

2. The compiler creates one or more machine language
   instructions for each executable WATFIV statement
   in a program. Machine language instructions have
   the general form:

```
   ,-----------T-----------T-----------,
   |operation  |address 1  | address 2 |
   '-----------'-----------'-----------'
```

   For example,   when the statement "A=2.5" appears in a
program, the compiler:

   i) Creates a bit string of 32 ones and zeros
      which represents the REAL constant 2.5;
      reserves a word of memory for this bit
      pattern and remembers its address.

ii) Reserves a word of memory for storing the value of A and remembers its address.

iii) Creates a machine language instruction which essentially says, "Replace the bit pattern of the word at the address of 'A' with the bit pattern of the word at the address of '2.5'".

3. In the array area, a word of memory is reserved for each element in a REAL or INTEGER set of variables. For example, the statement:

INTEGER DATA(10)/10*0/

would cause ten consecutive words of memory to be reserved and the compiler would also store the bit pattern for the INTEGER value zero in each of the ten words. Similarly, an array defined by:

REAL X(3,2)

causes six words of memory to be reserved. The correspondence between the elements of the set and the six reserved words is shown below.

Note that elements in the set are assigned to words of memory "column-by-column". This is one reason why the use of a set name in an input or output list creates a list of variables which are such that the rightmost subscript varies least rapidly. (In the case of a matrix, this is the same as saying that the variables are named column-by-column.) By knowing the address of the word of memory reserved for the first element in a set and the number of rows and columns (or more precisely, the maximum value of each subscript), it is a simple matter to calculate the address of the word used to store any particular element of the set. This calculation is always done at execution time.

Note that the storage reserved for arrays follows the memory used by the constants and simple variables of the

last program segment.   The reason for putting the arrays in
a common area is discussed in the next section.

If you look at the statistics printed following the
execution of a WATFIV program,   you will observe that the
second line contains the information:

OBJECT CODE=xxxxx BYTES,ARRAY AREA=yyyyy BYTES,

TOTAL AREA AVAILABLE=zzzzz BYTES

The number of bytes of object code is the number of
bytes of memory used by the machine language instructions,
constants and simple variables used by all the program
segments. The array area is the number of bytes reserved for
the arrays.   Since there are four bytes to a word, this
value is four times the number of words, and hence four
times the total number of subscripted variables, used in the
program.   The total area available is simply the number of
bytes made available to your program.   This number will vary
from one computing center to another and is decided upon by
the computing center administration.   Knowing the total
number of bytes available means that you can determine the
maximum size of an array or arrays which could be used in a
particular program.

Exercise 10.1

1. What two values can a "bit" of memory have?

2. How many bits in a byte?, bytes in a word?,   bits in a
   double word?, half-words in 8K?

3. How many unique bit patterns can a byte have?

4. Since a REAL or INTEGER value occupies a word of memory,
   how many different REAL or INTEGER values can be
   represented?

5. For each of the following, determine the number of bytes
   of memory used by the elements in each statement.

        a) REAL JASPER,N
        b) INTEGER T67(5),GAMMA
        c) INTEGER ALPHIE(2,7),AGGIE(10,10,10)
        d) REAL B(1)/2./,A(15,3)

6. Suppose a set has been defined by "REAL G(6)" and that
   the address of the first word of memory reserved for G
   is 2036.   What is the address of G(2)?   What   is the

address of the last word of memory used by the the set G?

7. Suppose a set has been defined by "INTEGER S(4,6)". If the element S(2,3) is stored in a word whose address is 5048, what are the addresses of the following elements: S(1,1),S(4,6),S(3,3),S(2,5).

10.2 Value Assignments at CALL and RETURN Times

The FUNCTION subprogram below illustrates three different methods of assigning a value to a simple variable used in a subprogram.

```
FUNCTION FUNC(A)
REAL B/0.6/
READ,C
FUNC=A*B*C
RETURN
END
```

As you would expect, the compiler reserves a word of memory to store the value of FUNC as well as reserving a word for each of A, B, and C. When the FUNCTION is activated, the value for A is obtained by copying the bit pattern stored in the word reserved by the argument of the subprogram into the word reserved for the parameter A. The question we would like to answer is, "Since the value we want to use for A in the subprogram is already stored in some word of the computer's memory, why not have the subprogram instructions which reference A, refer to the word of memory in which the value is stored instead of working with a copy of the value? After all, wouldn't this save an extra word of memory and also mean that it would be unnecessary to execute a copy instruction?". The answer is, "Sure, Why not?". To do this, it is simply a matter of enclosing the parameter A in slashes. The label given to this method of assigning a value to a parameter is "call by location". The normal method is labelled "call by value". The difference in the two approaches is indicated in the program structures below.

Call By Value   Call By Location

```
FUNCTION FUNC(A)                 FUNCTION FUNC( /A/ )
  .                                .
  .                                .
FUNC=A*B*C                       FUNC=A*B*C
  .                                .
END                              END
```

The differences are:

i) If a parameter is called by location, no storage is
   reserved for the parameter in the area of memory
   occupied by the subprogram. Instead, those
   instructions in the subprogram which reference the
   parameter, refer to the memory locations occupied
   by the corresponding argument. This means that no
   copying operation is necessary either preceding or
   following execution of the subprogram.

ii) If a parameter is called by value, storage _is_
    reserved for the variable in the subprogram. The
    subprogram actually works with a copy of the
    argument value during the execution of the
    subprogram. When the RETURN is executed, the final
    value of the parameter is copied into the storage
    locations reserved for the argument.

Two other examples of parameter lists in which one or
more of the parameters are called by location are:

INTEGER FUNCTION SOME(/IJK/,ART,/NETPAY/)

SUBROUTINE BYEACH(A,B,/CYEAR/,/DYEAR/)

Note that parameters of SUBROUTINE subprograms can also be
called by location. The examples below, however, will
produce error messages.

FUNCTION AHA(/R,S/)   SUBROUTINE MID(/T/)
                                    REAL T(4,10)
Reason: Slashes must enclose
each parameter.   Reason: Only simple variables
                                    can be called by location.

Sets cannot be called by location because this process is
automatic in WATFIV. To further illustrate this idea,
consider the following program.

```
C EXAMPLE 10.1              SUBROUTINE VECSUM(X,TOTAL)
   REAL VEC(1000)           REAL X(1000)
   READ,VEC                 TOTAL=0.
   CALL VECSUM(VEC,SUM)     DO 1 I=1,1000
   PRINT,SUM              1 TOTAL=TOTAL+X(I)
   STOP                     RETURN
   END                      END
```

In this example, the parameter X is a set having 1000
elements. If X were called by value, it would mean that

1000 words of storage would be reserved for each of the sets VEC and X. It would also mean that a thousand copy operations would be necessary at the beginning and end of executing the subprogram. To avoid this waste of memory and execution time, arrays are automatically called by location. You can easily verify this fact by running the above program and observing that the array area is 4000 bytes, that is, a total of 1000 words.

When a parameter is a set of variables, the two items of information necessary to have the machine language instructions of the subprogram reference the correct word of memory for any variable in the set are the address of the word reserved for the first element in the set and secondly, the dimensions of the set. The first item of information (the address) is passed to the subprogram when it is called. The second, the dimensions of the set, are obtained from the statement which defines the set in the subprogram.

10.3 Execution-Time Dimensioning of Arrays

In examples used previously, all parameter arrays were defined as having precisely the same dimensions as the corresponding argument array. If this requirement had to be followed without execption, it would mean that the statement defining the parameter array would have to be changed each time the subprogram was used with argument arrays having different dimensions. It also might mean that a program would require several versions of the same subprogram in order to work with sets of different sizes.

In WATFIV, the dimensions of a parameter array can be supplied at execution time. In other words, at execution time, the calling segment can pass the dimensions of an array to the called segment. The two factors which make this feature possible are: One, parameter arrays are called by location and hence no storage is reserved for the array in the subprogram; Two, the calculation of the address of the memory locations reserved for any element in an array occurs at execution time and not at compile time. Consider the following example.

```
C MAINLINE                          SUBROUTINE SUB(A,N)
      REAL X(20)                     REAL A(N)
      .                              .
      .                              .
      .                              .
      CALL SUB(X,20)                 DO ___ I=1,N
      .                              .
      .                              .
      END                            END
```

In the program structure above, the number of elements in the set X is passed to the subprogram as an argument. At execution time, the subprogram parameter N will have a value of 20 before execution of the subprogram begins. More precisely, the value of N is used to determine the number of words in the set X which can be used by the subprogram SUB.

In the program structure below, the subprogram is used to read the values to be stored a set VALUE. At the time the program is written, it is not known how many values are to be read.

```
C MAINLINE                          SUBROUTINE READ(SET,SIZ)
      INTEGER VALUE(1000)           INTEGER SIZ, SET(SIZ)
      READ,NVALS                    READ,SET
      CALL READ(VALUE,NVALS)        RETURN
      .                             END
      .
      .
      END
```

There are several points illustrated by this example.

i) Since storage must be provided for the maximum number of values which might be read, the set VALUE has been defined in the mainline to reserve a thousand words of memory. The number of words actually used will, of course, depend on the value of NVALS.

ii) The number of elements in the parameter SET is passed to the subprogram via the parameter SIZ. Since the dimension of any set of variables must be an INTEGER constant or an INTEGER variable, the first-letter rule has been overridden by declaring the variable SIZ to be INTEGER.

iii) The set name is used in the READ statement of the subprogram to create the input list. The list will have SIZ items. Incidentally, this is the most efficient way to read in a variable number of elements. That is, use a subprogram in which the set dimensions are supplied at execution time and in which the set name is used to create the input list in the READ statement. A further discussion of this point can be found in Appendix G.

The following example should be studied closely. The FUNCTION subprogram NTOT is used to calculate the sum of the elements of an M by N matrix. The mainline program reads in the values of M and N and then reads in MN more values

before calling the subprogram. It is assumed that M and N
are both four or less and so the set A in the mainline has
been defined as having four rows and four columns.   The
question is, "What value is printed, and why?".

```
C EXAMPLE 10.2                          FUNCTION NTOT(X,M,N)
      INTEGER A(4,4)/16*0/              INTEGER X(M,N)
      READ,M,N                          NTOT=0
      READ,((A(I,J),J=1,N),I=1,M)       DO 8 I=1,M
      NSUM=NTOT(A,M,N)                     DO 7 J=1,N
      PRINT,NSUM                               NTOT=NTOT+X(I,J)
      STOP                         7     CONTINUE
      END                          8 CONTINUE
$ENTRY                                  RETURN
   3,3                                  END
      1,1,1,1,1,1,1,1,1
```

     When the program is executed, the value printed is 7 and
not 9! Here's why.

   i) When the mainline is compiled, sixteen words of
      memory are reserved for the set A since it has four
      rows and four columns. The first four are reserved
      for column 1,   the next four for column 2, etc..
      Initially, all sixteen words contain a value of
      zero.

  ii) When the program is executed, the values of M and N
      are both 3.   This means that the nine data values
      read by the mainline are stored in words 1 to 3, 5
      to 7, and 9 to 11 of the sixteen reserved for A.
      (See the diagram below.)

 iii) When the function NTOT is called, the address of
      the first word of A is passed to the subprogram.
      Since the parameters M and N are both equal to
      three, the subprogram assumes the array X(M,N)
      requires nine words of memory. (It has no reason to
      assume anything else.) Thus, when the elements of
      the parameter set X are summed, the total is
      obtained by adding the contents of the first nine
      words of memory reserved for A.   The diagram below
      should make these ideas clear.

          col.1 of A   col.2 of A   col.3 of A   col.4 of A

          col. 1   col. 2   col. 3
           of X   of X   of X

In order to obtain the desired answer of 9, the instructions in the subprogram must reference the correct words of memory. To do this we pass the overall dimensions of the array A, as well the part of A actually used, to the subprogram. The revised version is:

```
C EXAMPLE 10.3                        FUNCTION NTOT(X,K,L,M,N)
      INTEGER A(4,4)/16*0/            INTEGER X(K,L)
      READ,M,N                        NTOT=0
      READ,((A(I,J),J=1,N),I=1,M)     DO 8 I=1,M
      NSUM=NTOT(A,4,4,M,N)               DO 7 J=1,N
      PRINT,NSUM                            NTOT=NTOT+X(I,J)
      STOP                          7     CONTINUE
      END                           8 CONTINUE
                                      RETURN
                                      END
```

The foregoing program will cause proper correspondences between the elements of the argument array A and the parameter array X. In general, the rule is that if a parameter array is dimensioned at execution time and if the parameter array is a subset of the corresponding argument array, then the subprogram must be provided with the overall dimensions of the argument array as well as the portion of the array actually being processed if proper correspondence of elements is to be obtained. This extra information is not required in the case of one dimensional arrays because storage locations are assigned to variables in order of increasing subcript values.

The following example illustrates a somewhat different use of execution time dimensioning of arrays. In the program, the mainline segment reads in 100 REAL values and stores them in a set called VAL. The SUBROUTINE AVG is used to obtain one hundred different averages of elements in VAL. These are the averages of: all the values, all values except the first, all values except the first two, all values except the first three, etc.. This algorithm is by no means the most efficient but our purpose is to illustrate another use of execution-time dimensioning of sets.

```
C EXAMPLE 10.4 MOVING AVERAGES        SUBROUTINE AVG(RESLT,Z,N)
      REAL VAL(100)                   REAL Z(N)
      READ,VAL                        RESLT=0.
      DO 1 I=1,100                    DO 2 J=1,N
      CALL AVG(R,VAL(I),101-I)           RESLT=RESLT+Z(J)
      PRINT,R                       2 CONTINUE
    1 CONTINUE                         RESLT=RESLT/FLOAT(N)
      STOP                            RETURN
      END                             END
```

In the example, note that the second argument is the Ith element of the set VAL. The corresponding parameter is a set having a number of elements equal to the value of the third argument. At execution time, the address of VAL(I) is passed to the subprogram and this address is used as the address of the first element in the parameter set Z. As the value of I increases by one each time the subprogram is called, the number of elements in the set Z decreases by one. Furthermore, since the first element in the set Z is the Ith element in the set VAL, the SUBROUTINE will process the desired set of values.

This example illustrates a case where an argument is an element of a set and the corresponding parameter is a set. This situation is permissible provided the storage occupied by the parameter set does not extend beyond the storage reserved by the argument set. In the example, an error would occur for instance, if the third argument had a value of 102-I because the last element of Z would correspond to the 101rst element of VAL. Since the compiler only reserves a hundred words of memory for VAL, the error results.

A slightly different use of the principle described in the foregoing example is illustrated by the program below. In this program, the FUNCTION subprogram COLSUM is used to obtain the sum of values in a column of a matrix.

```
C EXAMPLE 10.5 COLUMN SUMS
      REAL MATRIX(100,100)
      READ,NROWS,NCOLS
      READ,((MATRIX(I,J),J=1,NCOLS),I=1,NROWS)
      DO 1 J=1,NCOLS
         PRINT 50, J ,COLSUM(MATRIX(1,J),NROWS)
    1 CONTINUE
   50 FORMAT(' COLUMN',I3,' SUM=',F10.4)
      STOP
      END

      FUNCTION COLSUM(X,NROWS)
      REAL X(NROWS)
      COLSUM=0.
      DO 2 I=1,NROWS
         COLSUM=COLSUM+X(I)
    2 CONTINUE
      RETURN
      END
```

In this example, the mainline defines a matrix of 100 rows and 100 columns. Data values are read into the first NROWS and NCOLS as shown below.

Only two arguments are passed to the subprogram. The
address of the first word of storage reserved for the Jth
column of MATRIX, and the number of elements in the column
which contain values. Since storage is reserved column by
column, the words of memory referenced in the parameter set
X correspond to the the first NROWS of memory reserved for
column J of the mainline set MATRIX. This example also
illustrates that corresponding sets in the argument and
parameter list need not have the same number of subscripts.
One further point. If a parameter is a set, no check is
made to see that the argument and parameter are of the same
type. The allowed correspondences between arguments and
parameters are summarized by the following three rules.

Rules of Argument/Parameter Correspondence

1. If a parameter is a simple variable, its type must be
    the same as the corresponding argument value(s). The
    argument can be a constant, expression, simple variable,
    subscripted variable or set. If the argument is a set,
    the value taken on by the parameter variable is that
    found in the first storage location used by the set.

2. If a parameter is a set, there is no restriction on
    the type of value of the corresponding argument.
    Furthermore, the argument may be a constant, expression,
    simple variable, subscripted variable, or set. The one
    requirement is that the storage locations required by
    the parameter set must not exceed those used to store
    the argument value(s). (Recall that when a parameter is
    a set, it is always called by location.) If the
    argument is a subscripted variable, the parameter set
    must not require more storage locations than used to
    store all variables in the argument set beginning with
    those used to store the subscripted variable which is
    the argument. (Example 10.4 illustrates this idea.)

3. Under no circustances can a parameter be a constant,
    expression or subscripted variable.

* Pseudo-Variable Dimensioning (PVD)

A technique known as pseudo-variable dimensioning may be used to define parameter array dimensions. Pseudo-variable dimensioning (PVD) means that if a parameter array is defined with a rightmost dimension of 1, then at execution-time it is assigned a value which will cause the parameter array to occupy as much of the memory reserved for the argument array as is possible.

Consider the following example;

```
$JOB    WATFIV   NOSUB
C EXAMPLE 10.6 PSEUDO-VARIABLE DIMENSIONING
C
        INTEGER N(5)/1,2,3,4,5/
        REAL X(10)/1.,0.,2.,0.,3.,0.,4.,0.,5.,0./
        CALL LEO(N,X)
        STOP
        END
C
        SUBROUTINE LEO(M,Y)
        INTEGER M(1)
        REAL*8 Y(2,1)
        PRINT,M(3)
        PRINT,Y(1,3)
        RETURN
        END
```

The values printed are 3 and 5.   PVD is in effect for both parameter arrays M and Y because each has been defined with a rightmost dimension of 1.   Therefore the dimension of the parameter array M is set to 5 and the rightmost dimension of the parameter array Y is set   to 2 at execution time.   This means Y occupies 8 of the 10 words used to store the argument array X.

Two job control options are related to PVD.   With the NOSUB option in effect (as in the example) no error message is generated by "PRINT,Y(1,3)" because Y(1,3)   occupies the 9th and 10th words of array X which contain the REAL*8 value 5.D00.   With the SUB job control option however the attempt to 'PRINT,Y(1,3)' causes a message 'SUBSCRIPT NUMBER 2 OF Y HAS THE VALUE 3' to be printed.   This results from the fact that subscript value 3 exceeds its execution-time bound of 2.   That is, the SUB option -- usually the default -- means subscript values are constrained by their defined maxima. With NOSUB the constraint is the   storage assigned to the argument array.

PVD is useful primarily when calling some commercially available subprograms. It permits the parameter arrays in these subprograms to "expand" to the size of the argument arrays.

10.4 Communication Via A Common Block

Communication between program segments can be achieved using argument and parameter lists. This two-way communication results from either having the parameter variable occupy the same storage locations as the argument (call by location), or by putting a copy of the argument value in the location reserved for the parameter (call by value). Another method is available to the WATFIV programmer. This second technique consists of:

i) Asking the compiler to reserve a block of storage which will be accessible from all program segments. (If desired, a shared block of memory can be accessed only from specific program segments.)

ii) Assigning variables used in a program segment to storage locations within the block in such a way that communicating variables share the same storage locations.

Consider the program structure below.

```
C MAINLINE                    SUBROUTINE NEW(....)
      COMMON X,Y              COMMON A,B
      .                           .
      CALL NEW(...)               .
      .                           .
      END                    END
```

In the foregoing program structure, the programmer has asked the compiler to reserve a block of memory which is to be common to (shared by) the program segments. A COMMON statement is used to make the request. The variables in the Common list are assigned sequentially to the storage locations of the "Common Block" of memory. Because of the statement "COMMON X,Y" in the mainline, the Common Block consists of two words of memory. The first word is used to store the value of X, and the second, the value of Y. In the subprogram, the compiler is told that values of A and B are located in the Common Block. Instructions in which A and B appear will reference the first two words of memory in the Block. Put another way, the addresses of X and A are the same and those of Y and B are the same. This of course means that changes in X are changes in A and that changes in Y

are changes in B. The following diagram illustrates these
ideas.

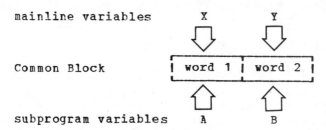

mainline variables   X   Y

Common Block

subprogram variables   A   B

    The following program computes the average of N REAL
values and also determines the largest and smallest values
in the set. The important features of COMMON statements are
illustrated by this example.

```
      C EXAMPLE 10.7 USING A COMMON BLOCK
            COMMON N,SMALL
            COMMON BIG
            REAL X(1000),SMALL/10.E70/,BIG/-10.E70/
            READ,N,(X(I),I=1,N)
            PRINT,AVG(X),SMALL,BIG
            STOP
            END

            FUNCTION AVG(X)
            COMMON M,HILOW(2)
            REAL X(M),SUM/0./
            DO 1 I=1,M
               SUM=SUM+X(I)
               IF(X(I).LT.HILOW(1))HILOW(1)=X(I)
               IF(X(I).GT.HILOW(2))HILOW(2)=X(I)
          1 CONTINUE
            AVG=SUM/FLOAT(M)
            RETURN
            END
```

Remarks

   i) Variables appearing in COMMON statements which
      follow the first COMMON statement of a segment are
      appended to the end of the Common list and thus
      increase the length of the Common Block. For
      example, the pair of statements

          COMMON A,B,C
          COMMON I,J,K

is equivalent to the single statement

        COMMON A,B,C,I,J,K

ii) If a variable in a Common Block is initialized at
    compile time, the COMMON statement in which the
    variable appears must precede the statement which
    defines the initializing value. For example,

        REAL BIG/-10.E70/
        COMMON BIG

    is invalid, whereas

        COMMON BIG
        REAL BIG/-10.E70/

    is acceptable.

    The reason is that the compiler must know the
    address of the variable being initialized in order
    to store the initial value.

iii) Sets of variables can be put in a Common Block. A
     COMMON statement can be used to define the set or,
     the set can be defined in a REAL or INTEGER
     statement and the set name put in the Common list.
     The set dimensions however, cannot be defined in
     both a COMMON statement and a type declaration
     statement. In the foregoing example, the statement
     "COMMON M,HILOW(2)" is used to define the set
     HILOW. The statement pair:

        REAL HILOW(2)
        COMMON M,HILOW

achieves the same result. The pair:

        REAL HILOW(2)
        COMMON M,HILOW(2)

would produce an error message since the set
dimensions are defined in two different statements.
When a COMMON statement is used to define a set of
variables, the first-letter rule determines the
type of variables in the set unless the set name
appears in a type declaration statement. For
example, the sequence

```
      INTEGER HILOW
      COMMON HILOW(2)
```

specifies that HILOW is a set of two INTEGER variables.

iv) A set of variables which is dimensioned at execution time cannot be in a Common Block. The set must be included in the parameter list. The values specifying the dimensions, however, may be stored in a Common Block. (In the example, the subprogram set X is dimensioned at execution time and the dimension of the set, namely M, was stored in the Common Block.) The following program structure would produce an error message because the array SET whose dimensions are supplied at execution time is in a Common Block.

```
C MAINLINE                        SUBROUTINE INSET
      REAL X(1000)                REAL SET(N)
      COMMON N,X                  COMMON N,SET
      READ,M                          .
                                      .
      .                               .
      CALL INSET                      .
      ..                              .
      END                         END
```

v) The elements in the Common lists of different program segments need not agree in number, type or length. In the example program, for instance, the Common list in the mainline has the items "N,SMALL, and BIG". The Common list in the subprogram is "M,HILOW". The correspondence between variables and storage locations is shown below.

No error message would result if a third segment included a statement such as "COMMON K(3)" even though K(1), K(2) and K(3) are INTEGER variables. It should be noted, however, that there are _very_ few circumstances where a programmer wants to use the same storage locations for variables of different types.

The length of Common Block is the total number of bytes of memory reserved by elements in the Common list. Since REAL and INTEGER variables occupy four bytes of memory, the length of the Common Blocks defined in the mainline and the subprogram of the example are twelve bytes. If the length of the Common Block defined in two different segments is not the same, a warning message is printed at compile time.

There are two other rules which are included here for the sake of completeness. The two error conditions described below result from attempting to store a value in two different storage locations. First, a subprogram variable or set cannot appear in both a parameter list and a Common list. The statement pair below, for example, is invalid.

```
SUBROUTINE SOLVE(X,A)
COMMON X
```

Second, an element of a Common list may also be an argument provided a subprogram does not assign a value to the corresponding parameter. The example structure below illustrates this type of error.

```
C MAINLINE                      SUBROUTINE NAME(Y)
      COMMON X                   COMMON Z
      .                          Z=...
      .                          .
      CALL NAME(Y)               Y=....
      .                          .
      END                        END
```

The use of a Common Block should be viewed as one method of providing communication between program segments. All subprogram variables stored in a Common Block are, in effect, called by location. Since elements of different Common lists need not agree in number, type, or length, added flexibility is achieved.

10.5 Multiple Common Blocks

If a program contains a large number of segments, some of which share a great deal of data in common and others very little, it may be desirable to define several Common Blocks -- each with a unique name, to make the programming task easier. In addition, the use of several Common Blocks

permits a certain degree of privacy in programs of a
confidential nature such as payroll. Even if there is more
than one Common Block, one block may be unlabelled. This
no-name or unlabelled block is the type discussed in the
previous section.

There are really only two differences between labelled
(named) Common Blocks and the unlabelled ("blank") Common
Block. These are:

   i) The labelled blocks have a name.

   ii) A special program segment called a BLOCK DATA
      subprogram must be used to perform compile-time
      initialization of variables located in a labelled
      Common Block.

Definition of Labelled Blocks

A COMMON statement is used to define a labelled block.
Several blocks may be defined in the same statement.
Previously defined blocks may be "added to" by other COMMON
statements.

Example (i)

```
COMMON /AREA1/ A,B,C
```

This statement defines a Common Block called AREA1.
Assuming A,B and C are simple REAL variables, the length
of the block is twelve bytes (three words). When
defining labelled blocks, the block name is enclosed in
slashes.

Example (ii)

```
COMMON P,Q,R/NAME1/I,Z(20)/NAME2/R,S,T,U
```

This single statement defines three Common Blocks.
Since no name precedes the elements P, Q and R, the
storage locations for these variables are in the
unlabelled Common Block. The items I and Z are in a
block called "NAME1". R,S,T,U are in a "NAME2" block.
The single statment above is equivalent to the following
three statements.

```
COMMON P,Q,R
COMMON /NAME1/I,Z(20)
COMMON /NAME2/R,S,T,U
```

Example (iii)

```
COMMON /BLK1/X,P//A,S,T/BLK2/M
COMMON U,V/BLK1/R/BLK2/Z
```

In this example, three Common Blocks are defined in the first COMMON statement. They are: BLK1 with elements X and P; the no-name (unlabelled) block (indicated by a pair of consecutive slashes with no name between them). The elements A, S and T are in the unlabelled block; BLK2 has the single element M. The second COMMON statement specifies that additional variables are to be stored in each of the three blocks. Since no block name precedes the elements U and V, they are added to the end of the unlabelled block. The elements R and Z are added to the end of BLK1 and BLK2 respectively. The pair of COMMON statements in this example has the same effect as the single statement

```
COMMON A,S,T,U,V /BLK1/X,P,R /BLK2/M,Z
```

COMMON Statement Rules

The general form of a COMMON statement is:

```
COMMON x1,x2,x3,...
```

i) Each x item consists of a list of variables, array names or array names followed by dimension information. Optionally, each list may be preceded by a name enclosed in slashes or by two consecutive slashes. Note that no commas precede or follow a slash. The double slash indicates that elements of the list are to be put in the unlabelled Common Block. If no slash follows the word COMMON, list elements preceding the first slash belong to the unlabelled Common Block. Those which follow a "/name/" belong to a block of the indicated name.

ii) If dimension information for an array is present in a COMMON statement, no other statement can contain the dimension information. The array type, however, may be specified by an explicit type declaration statement.

iii) Variables or arrays cannot be put in more than one Common Block.

iv) Sets which are dimensioned at execution time cannot be put in a Common Block.

v) Storage locations in a labelled block may only be
   initilized by means of a BLOCK DATA subprogram.
   Unlabelled Common Block storage locations can be
   initialized by a type declaration statement or DATA
   statement which follows the COMMON statement.

vi) Blocks need not have the same length in different
    program segments. A warning message is printed at
    compile time.

10.6 BLOCK DATA Subprograms

   A BLOCK DATA subprogram has one purpose -- to assign
initial values to storage locations in Common Blocks. It is
the only method available for initializing storage locations
in labelled Common Blocks but may also be used, at the
programmer's discretion, to specify initial values for
storage locations in the unlabelled Common Block. The
general form of a BLOCK DATA subprogram is as follows.

```
BLOCK DATA
  .
  .
  .
END
```

   The statements between the BLOCK DATA statement (which
must be the first statement) and the END statement (which
must be the last statement) are used to:

a) Define the structure of the Common Blocks containing
   storage locations to be given initial values.

b) Specify the initial values.

Example (i)

```
BLOCK DATA
COMMON /BLK1/I,A,S(12)
INTEGER I/2/
REAL S/12*0./
END
```

   In this example, values are assigned at compile time to
storage locations in the Common Block called BLK1. An
INTEGER value of 2 is stored in the first word of memory
of the block. The second word (used to store the value
of the variable A) is left unchanged and the remaining
twelve words in the block are given a bit pattern
representing the REAL value zero.

Example (ii)

```
            BLOCK DATA
            IMPLICIT INTEGER(A-D),REAL(I,N)
            REAL E(4)
            COMMON B,C /BBLK/E,F
            COMMON /ABLK/INS(3,2)//R
            REAL B,E/4*10./
            DATA B,C/2.,3/,((INS(I,J),J=1,2),I=1,3)
          * /2*1.,2*2.,2*3./
            INTEGER R/999/,F/0/
            END
```

The effect of the BLOCK DATA subprogram is to initialize
storage locations as shown below.

Unlabelled Block
```
┌──────┬─────┬──────┐
│  2.  │  3  │ 999  │
└──────┴─────┴──────┘
```

ABLK Block
```
┌──────┬──────┬──────┬──────┬──────┬──────┐
│  1.  │  2.  │  3.  │  1.  │  2.  │  3.  │
└──────┴──────┴──────┴──────┴──────┴──────┘
```

BBLK Block
```
┌──────┬──────┬──────┬──────┬──────┬──────┐
│ 10.  │ 10.  │ 10.  │ 10.  │ 10.  │  0   │
└──────┴──────┴──────┴──────┴──────┴──────┘
```

Rules For BLOCK DATA Subprograms

    i) A BLOCK DATA statement must be the first statement.
An END statement must be the last statement.

   ii) A BLOCK   DATA   subprogram   cannot   contain   any
executable statements. (Its purpose is strictly to
define initial   values.)   The   only   types   of
statements   permitted   are: IMPLICIT,   type
declaration statements, COMMON, DIMENSION and DATA.

 iii) An IMPLICIT statement, if used, must immediately
follow the BLOCK DATA statement.

   iv) All initializing values of a Common Block must be
located in the same BLOCK DATA subprogram.

    v) The standard rules for ordering statements must be
followed. These are as follows.

        a) DATA statements must follow any DIMENSION,
COMMON or type declaration statement which
references the variable or array.

b) If a type declaration statement is used to provide initial values for a simple variable, it must follow any COMMON statement which references the variable.

c) If a type declaration statement is used to define initial values for an array, it must follow the COMMON or DIMENSION statement which defines the dimensions of the array.

*10.7 EQUIVALENCE (Shared Storage Within A Segment)

The topic of this section does not rightfully belong in this chapter -- it has nothing to do with subprograms! However, the concepts necessary to understand the material of this section were not presented until the beginning of this chapter. This is the reason for its inclusion here.

Recall that COMMON statements are used as means of causing variables in different program segments to share the same storage locations. The EQUIVALENCE statement on the other hand is used to cause variables in the same program segment to share the same storage locations. For example, if the variables I and J are Equivalenced using the statement

                 EQUIVALENCE (I,J)

then any change in the value of I is automatically a change in the value of J and vice-versa.

The two programs below illustrate the effect of Equivalencing a pair of variables. In the program on the left, two INTEGER variables are Equivalenced and in the one on the right, an INTEGER and a REAL variable are Equivalenced.

```
EQUIVALENCE (I,J)              EQUIVALENCE(I,A)
INTEGER I/1/                   INTEGER I/1/
PRINT,J                        PRINT,A
STOP                           STOP
END                            END
```

Result: A value of 1 is   Result: A value of
        printed.   0.0000051E-79 is printed.

The reason for having different values printed in the two cases is not difficult to understand. In the program on the left, the variables I and J (both INTEGER) are Equivalenced. This means they are synonyms and are stored in the same word

of memory.   That is,   the bit pattern for I and the bit
pattern for J is the same.   When the statement "PRINT,J" is
encountered, the bit pattern stored in the word of memory is
treated as that of an INTEGER value and therefore has a
value of one.   In the program on the right, the same bit
pattern is present in the word of memory whose contents will
be printed.   This time, however, the print statement is
"PRINT,A" and therefore the bit pattern is interpreted as
being that of a REAL value. Put another way, the bit
patterns for an INTEGER value of one and a REAL value of
.0000051E-79 are identical.

     Why use the EQUIVALENCE statement?   The first and
perhaps most important reason for Equivalencing variables is
to save memory.   Suppose X and NUM are two arrays having 300
and 450 variables respectively. Provided the values of X and
NUM are used at different times in the same program, memory
could be saved by Equivalencing the two sets. The program
structure would be of the following type.

```
              REAL X(300)
              INTEGER NUM(450)
              EQUIVALENCE (X(1),NUM(1))
              READ,X
statements to      .
process the X      .
  values           .
              READ,NUM
statements to      .
process the        .
NUM values         .
                   .
```

Without the EQUIVALENCE statement in the foregoing example,
the array area for the program would be 300 words larger. In
situations where memory space is at a premium, this
technique may be valuable. In the foregoing example, either
or both of the set names "X" and "NUM" could have been used
instead of "X(1)" and "NUM(1)".   Use of a set name in an
EQUIVALENCE statement is effectively the same as using the
name of the subscripted variable which occupies the first
storage locations used to store the values in the set.

     The second reason is to permit different programmers who
are writing parts of the same program to use variable names
which are meaningful to them.   When the parts are put
together to form the program segment, EQUIVALENCE statements
are added to tell the compiler that different variable names
are really synonyms for each other and are to refer to the
same storage locations. Even if a program is written by one

person, he may inadvertently mispell a variable name in one or more program segments. By using an EQUIVALENCE statement, all spellings can be made equivalent.

A third reason involves Equivalencing a simple variable with an element of a set in order to use a simple variable name in a statement where a subcripted variable is not permitted. By doing so, a number of Assignment statements may be eliminated.

Rules For EQUIVALENCE

The EQUIVALENCE statement is used to inform the compiler that two or more variables within a segment are to share the same storage locations. This means that Equivalenced variables have the same address in the computer memory and also that they have the same bit pattern.

1. The EQUIVALENCE statement has the general form

    EQUIVALENCE (list1), (list2), (list3), ...

    where each list is a sequence of variable names and/or array names separated by commas. If a list element is an array name, it implies that the first variable in the array shares the same storage locations as other variables in the list. Regardless of the number of dimensions of an array, an array name may (optionally) be followed by a single subscript value. If the subscript has a value of "K", it means the variable in the Kth word of memory used to store the variables in the array is to be Equivalenced. In the following example, the variable MAT(3,2) is Equivalenced to the variable A. Recall that variables are stored column-by-column.

        REAL MAT(4,2)
        EQUIVALENCE (MAT(7),A)

    This is the one exception to the rule that a subscripted variable must have the same number of subscripts as there are dimensions in the array.

2. Any assignment of initial values to Equivalenced variables must be done by a statement which follows the EQUIVALENCE statement. The sequence

        REAL X/2./
        EQUIVALENCE (X,B)

is invalid whereas

        EQUIVALENCE (X,B)
        REAL X/2./

is valid.

3. Subprogram parameters and variables used in ASSIGN statements cannot be Equivalenced. Each of the following pairs of statements would cause an error.

        SUBROUTINE WR(X)   EQUIVALENCE (J,K)
        EQUIVALENCE (X,Z)   ASSIGN 12 TO J

4. An EQUIVALENCE statement cannot imply that a variable is stored in two different locations. Consider the following example.

        INTEGER A(10),B(10)
        EQUIVALENCE (A(1),B(1)), (A(2),B(5))

The error occurs since if A(1) and B(1) are made Equivalent then A(2) and B(2) must of necessity also be equivalent. The list "(A(2),B(5))" attempts to contradict this fact.

5. There are three rules with respect to Equivalencing variables in a Common Block.

a) In any list in an EQUIVALENCE statement, at most one element of the list can be in a Common Block.

b) If an array is Equivalenced to a variable in a Common Block, it may cause the Block to be "extended to the right". This is not an error but may cause unexpected results since other variables in the Common Block may unintentionally be Equivalenced to elements of the array. Consider the following example.

        REAL X(4)
        COMMON A
        EQUIVALENCE (A,X)
        COMMON B

The preceding four statements result in a Common Block having a length of 16 bytes. The variable B occupies the same storage locations as the variable X(2).

c) An EQUIVALENCE statement cannot be used to extend a Common Block to the left. That is, an EQUIVALENCE statement cannot cause the first variable in a Common Block to be Equivalenced to any array variable other than the first one in the array. The statement sequence below illustrates this type of error.

```
REAL X(5)
COMMON A
EQUIVALENCE (A,X(3))
```

The foregoing statements are attempting to force the alignment indicated in the following diagram.

boundary of Common Block

Exercise 10.2

1. For each of the following, state the values printed and the last value assigned to each variable.

a)
```
COMMON A(3)              SUBROUTINE ZIP
REAL A/1.,2*2./          COMMON X,Y,Z
CALL ZIP                 Z=AMAX1(X/Y,Y/Z)
STOP                     RETURN
END                      END
```

b)
```
COMMON J,K,L             FUNCTION KNOTS(M)
INTEGER J/2/,K/10/,L/3/  COMMON N,NN,NNN
M=0                      KNOTS=M+N*NN/NNN
DO 1 I=J,K,L             IF(KNOTS.GT.30) STOP
  M=M+I*J/K              RETURN
  PRINT,KNOTS(M)         END
1 CONTINUE
END
```

c)
```
COMMON X/TWO/Y           SUBROUTINE NUTS
COMMON /TWO/Z//W         COMMON /TWO/A,B//C,D
REAL X/2./,W/3./         B=AMIN1(C,D)
CALL NUTS                A=AMAX1(B,C,D)
PRINT,W,X,Y,Z            RETURN
STOP                     END
END
```

```
d)      EQUIVALENCE(X,Y)
        REAL X(2,3)/3*1.,3*2./
        REAL Y(6)
        PRINT,(Y(J),J=2,6,2)
        STOP
        END
e)      EQUIVALENCE (A,X,I,J)
        REAL A/2./,B/3./
        IF(X.NE.B) I=6
        PRINT,J
        STOP
        END
```

2. Describe the error in each of the following.

```
a)    REAL X(3)/3*0./          b)    COMMON /ONE/A//B
      COMMON A(3)/3*0./              REAL A/2./,B/4./

c)    REAL B(5,2),C(10)        d)    REAL B(5,2),C(10)
      COMMON B,C                     COMMON B
      EQUIVALENCE (B(4),C(1))        EQUIVALENCE(B(1),C(3))

e)    SUBROUTINE ANDON(X,Y,Z)
      REAL X(10)
      COMMON Y
      RETURN
      END

f)    COMMON A                 SUBROUTINE NEXT(X,Y)
      REAL A/40./              COMMON Z
      CALL NEXT(A,B)           X=Z+Y
      PRINT,B                  RETURN
      STOP                     END
      END
```

3. Consider the following sequence of statements.

```
           INTEGER ARRAY(3,4,5),MAT1(6,5)
           INTEGER MAT2(6,5),VEC(20,3),STRING(60)
           EQUIVALENCE (ARRAY,MAT1,VEC)
           EQUIVALENCE (ARRAY(31),MAT2,STRING(31))
           DO 1 I=1,60
              STRING(I)=I
         1 CONTINUE
```

a) What is the value of each of the following variables?
   STRING(4), VEC(8,1), MAT1(3,4), ARRAY(2,2,2)

b) For each of the following, name three other variables which share the same storage locations.
STRING(2), VEC(13,2), ARRAY(2,4,1), MAT2(3,4)

c) Describe the output produced by the formatted PRINT statements which follow.

```
        PRINT 900,MAT1
    900 FORMAT('0',6I5)

        PRINT 901, (VEC(K,2),K=1,20)
    901 FORMAT('0',2I10)

        PRINT 902, ((MAT2(K,L),L=1,5),K=1,6)
    902 FORMAT('0',5I6)

        PRINT 903,(((ARRAY(I,J,K),J=1,4),K=1,5),I=1,3)
    903 FORMAT('0',1(T2,5(4I3,2X)))
```

*10.8 Multiple Entries To Subprograms

When a subprogram is called, control normally passes to the first executable statement in the subprogram. This section describes a means of entering a subprogram at a statement other than the first executable statement in the subprogram. The method involves the use of ENTRY statements at those points in the subprogram where entry is permitted. The general form of the ENTRY statement is shown below.

ENTRY   name (parameter list)

Note that an ENTRY statement does not contain either the word FUNCTION or the word SUBROUTINE. The name which follows the word ENTRY in an ENTRY statement can be any valid WATFIV name. The parameter list has the same purpose as it does when used in a FUNCTION or SUBROUTINE statement.

To illustrate the use of an ENTRY statement, recall that whenever a part of a matrix is used in a subprogram, the overall dimensions of the matrix (as defined in the calling segment), as well as the dimensions of the part to be used in the subprogram, are passed to the subprogram. Now suppose a program is required to read ten different matrices and calculate the row sums of each. The following program could be used. Study it carefully as it illustrates most of the important features of ENTRY statement usage.

```
C EXAMPLE 10.8 MAINLINE
      REAL MATRIX(100,100),SUM(100)
      CALL DIMENS(MATRIX,100,100,SUM)
      DO 1 I=1,10
          READ,MROWS,NCOLS
          CALL READ(MROWS,NCOLS)
          CALL SUMALL(SUM)
          PRINT,(SUM(J),J=1,MROWS)
    1 CONTINUE
      STOP
      END

      SUBROUTINE DIMENS(X,KROWS,LCOLS,TOTAL)
      REAL X(KROWS,LCOLS),TOTAL(KROWS)
      RETURN
C
      ENTRY READ(M,N)
      DO 1 I=1,M
          READ,(X(I,J),J=1,N)
    1 CONTINUE
      RETURN
C
      ENTRY SUMALL(TOTAL)
      DO 3 I=1,M
          TOTAL(I)=0.
          DO 2 J=1,N
              TOTAL(I)=TOTAL(I)+X(I,J)
    2     CONTINUE
    3 CONTINUE
      RETURN
      END
```

In the example subprogram, there are, in effect, three different SUBROUTINES. DIMENS is simply used to obtain the overall dimensions of the matrix X and the array TOTAL. DIMENS is only called once by the mainline.

The statement "ENTRY READ(M,N)" defines the beginning of a sequence of statements which read and store data values in the first M rows and N columns of X. Note that is not necessary to include either X or the overall dimensions of X in the parameter list of the ENTRY point called READ. This information had been previously passed to the subprogram with the call to DIMENS.

The routine with the ENTRY point SUMALL needs only one parameter. The other information has been previously passed to the subprogram using calls to DIMENS and READ.

The rules of ENTRY statement usage are as follows:

i)   Any number of ENTRY statements may be used in a
subprogram. Each has the general form:

ENTRY name (parameter list)

where "name" is any valid WATFIV name and the
parameters must   agree with the   arguments as
described previously at the end of Section 10.3.

ii)   Within a SUBROUTINE, each ENTRY statement defines
an ENTRY point of a SUBROUTINE.   In a FUNCTION
subprogram,   each must be the ENTRY point of a
FUNCTION.

iii)   All declaration statements, Statement Functions,
etc. which are required in any part of the
subprogram must be placed at the beginning of the
entire subprogram.

iv)   Variables appearing in a parameter list need not
agree in number type or order with those of other
parameter lists used in the subprogram. However, if
the same   variable appears in more   than one
parameter list it must always be called the same
way (by location or by value).   For example, the
following structure is not permitted.

FUNCTION name1(X)
. . .
. . .
ENTRY name2(/X/)
. . .
. . .
END

v)   An ENTRY statement cannot be placed within the
range of a DO-loop.

vi)   ENTRY statements are not executed. At execution
time,   their existence is ignored if they fall
within the range of a sequence of statements which
is being executed.

vii)   When control passes to an ENTRY point, the value
of any non-parameter variable used in the
subprogram is the value most recently assigned to
it.

The use of ENTRY points is often a convenience when: two subprograms are very similar; only a part of a subprogram is required; initial values must be passed to a subprogram. Note that multiple entries to subprograms are almost never a necessity, simply a convenience.

*10.9 Multiple Returns From SUBROUTINES

The first RETURN encountered in a SUBROUTINE normally causes control to be transferred to the first statement following the CALL. In some circumstances, it may be that the processing done in the SUBROUTINE requires that control should be returned to some other statement. For example, an error condition detected in the SUBROUTINE may require that control be passed to an error routine in the mainline. To provide alternate return points from a SUBROUTINE (It makes little sense in the case of FUNCTION subprograms since they are typically used to calculate a single value.) the calling segment supplies the SUBROUTINE with a list of the statement numbers to which control can be returned.

In the following program, a normal RETURN is executed if all elements of a set X are positive; to statement 74 if all elements have negative values and to statement 12 otherwise.

```
C EXAMPLE 10.9                    SUBROUTINE TESTX(X,*,*)
      REAL X(10)                   REAL X(10)
      READ,X                       IF(X(1).EQ.0.)RETURN 2
      CALL TESTX(X,&74,&12)        DO 1 I=2,10
      PRINT,'X POSITIVE'             IF(X(I)*X(1).LE.0)RETURN 2
      STOP                       1 CONTINUE
   74 PRINT,'X NEGATIVE'          IF(X(1).LT.0)RETURN 1
      STOP                         RETURN
   12 PRINT,'X MIXED'             END
      STOP
      END
```

The foregoing program illustrates the important points concerning the use of the multiple RETURN feature. These are:

i)   In the calling segment, the argument list has the general form

           (...,&s1,...,&s2,...,&s3,...)

       where "s1", "s2", etc. are statement numbers of executable statements to which control is permitted to return . Each such statement number is preceded by an "&" symbol.

ii)   In the SUBROUTINE, an asterisk appears in the parameter list in those positions which correspond to the return points defined in the argument list. To return to the statement following the CALL, a simple RETURN statement is used. To return to the statement whose number is the nth return point in the argument list, the statement "RETURN n" is used in the subprogram. The value of "n" in "RETURN n" is usually an INTEGER constant but its value can also be assigned to an INTEGER variable. For example,

```
NEXT=4
RETURN NEXT
```

is permissible provided at least four return points have been specified in the argument list.

*10.10 EXTERNAL Subprograms

Suppose a subprogram is required which will find the maximum and minimum values of <u>any</u> function f(x). Suppose f(x) is defined for values of x of 1,2,3,...,100. O.K., so what's the problem? Well, if our routine is called MAXMIN, say, then we require some means of telling MAXMIN the name of the function "f" to be used in any particular instance. In other words, one of the arguments in any call to MAXMIN must be the name of the desired function. The corresponding parameter will "take on" this name at execution time. An EXTERNAL statement is used in the calling segment to specify that a particular argument represents the name of a built-in function or subprogram and not a numeric value. Suppose the largest and smallest values of the following two functions are required.

$$FA(i) = (50-i)^2/i^2 \quad \text{for } i=1,2,\ldots,100$$
$$FB(i) = 120 - (i-60)^2 \quad \text{for } i=1,2,\ldots,100$$

The following program could be used.

```
C MAINLINE                          FUNCTION FA(J)
      EXTERNAL FA,FB                 FA=(50.-J)**2/J**2
      CALL MAXMIN(BIG,SMALL,FA)      RETURN
      PRINT,'FA MAX AND MIN',        END
    * BIG,SMALL
      CALL MAXMIN(BIG,SMALL,FB)      FUNCTION FB(K)
      PRINT,'FB MAX AND MIN',        FB=120-(K-60)**2
    * BIG,SMALL                      RETURN
      STOP                           END
      END
```

```
            SUBROUTINE MAXMIN(BIG,SMALL,FUN)
            BIG=SMALL=FUN(1)
            DO 1 I=1,100
               X=FUN(I)
               IF(X.GT.BIG) BIG=X
               IF(X.LT.SMALL) SMALL=X
          1 CONTINUE
            RETURN
            END
```

In this program, the SUBROUTINE MAXMIN is called twice. Each time it is called, the last element in the argument list is the name of the function to be used by MAXMIN during its execution. In the mainline, the statement

            EXTERNAL FA , FB

informs the compiler that FA and FB are the names of two subprograms. It means that if either or both of FA and FB appear in an argument list then the name of the subprogram is to be passed to the called segment. (In actual fact, the address of the first executable instruction in the argument subprogram is passed to the called segment.)

In a subprogram, those parameters which correspond to arguments which appear in EXTERNAL statements are "dummy" subprogram names. In the example, for instance, the name FUN took the place of the subprogram name which was passed to MAXMIN at execution time. Note that the called subprogram (MAXMIN in the example) must know the number and type of arguments required to call an unknown subprogram.

The rules of usage of an EXTERNAL statement are few. The general structure of a segment containing one or more EXTERNAL statements is the following.

            EXTERNAL name1, name2, ...
            .
            .
            ... name(..name1,...,name2,...)
            .
            END

where: "name1", "name2", etc. are names of subprograms or
       built-in functions which, in the case of FUNCTIONs,
       may require their type to be specified.
       "name" is the name of a subprogram to which any
       element of the EXTERNAL list can be passed as an
       argument.

An EXTERNAL statement appears only in a calling segment. In the called segment, parameters corresponding to arguments which appear in an EXTERNAL list are "dummy" subprogram names. The called segment is written knowing that the dummy name will be replaced at execution time. The argument list used with the dummy name is not changed at execution time and therefore it must be appropriate for the external subprogram.

Exercise 10.3 (Multiple Entries, Returns and EXTERNAL)

1. For each of the following, state the last value assigned to each variable used in the program.

a)
```
      A=B=2                 SUBROUTINE X(P,Q,R)
      CALL X(A,B,C)         R=P/Q*Q
      CALL Y(A,B,C)         RETURN
      STOP                  ENTRY Y(A,B,C)
      END                   Z=AMAX1(R,C,P)
                            RETURN
                            END
```

b)
```
      REAL I                REAL FUNCTION I(J)
      INTEGER J/3/          I=J*2/8
      K=I(J)                RETURN
      K=L(K)                ENTRY L(M)
      STOP                  L=J+M
      END                   RETURN
                            END
```

c)
```
      INTEGER A/2/          SUBROUTINE B(/C/)
      CALL B(A)             INTEGER C
      A=A/3                 C=C*2
      CALL D(A)             RETURN
      STOP                  ENTRY D(J)
      END                   J=J**3/C
                            RETURN
                            END
```

d) In (c), let "C" be called by value.

e)
```
      INTEGER I/2/,J/3/     SUBROUTINE X(L,M,N,*)
      CALL X(I,J,K,&2)      N=MAX0(L/M,M/L,M,L)
      K=MAX0(K,J)           IF(N.GT.L) RETURN 1
    2 STOP                  RETURN
      END                   END
```

```
f)      REAL A(3)/3.,2.,1./    SUBROUTINE T(*,X)
      1 CALL T(&2,A)           REAL X(3)
        STOP                   IF(X(1)*X(3).LT.X(2))X(2)=3
      2 A(3)=3                 IF(-X(2)+X(3).GE.0)RETURN
        CALL T(&1,A)           N=X(3)
        STOP                   RETURN N
        END                    END


g)      INTEGER F,J/5/,A       INTEGER FUNCTION A(K,L)
        EXTERNAL F             A=K(L)/2
        J=A(F,J)/2             RETURN
        STOP                   END
        END                    INTEGER FUNCTION F(M)
                               F=2*M/3
                               RETURN
                               END
```

2. Identify the error(s) in each of the following.

```
a)      CALL A(2.,3.,Z)        SUBROUTINE A(X,Y,Z)
        CALL B                 Z=X+Y
        STOP                   ENTRY B
        END                    B=2*Z
                               RETURN
                               END


b)      J=ISQ(2)               FUNCTION ISQ(M)
      1 PRINT,J                IF(M.EQ.0) RETURN
        STOP                   RETURN 1
        END                    END


c)      B=ZIP(10.,SQRT)        FUNCTION ZIP(A,F)
        PRINT,B                EXTERNAL F
        STOP                   ZIP=F(A)
        END                    RETURN
                               END
```

10.11 Summary

1. The basic unit of memory is called a byte. It consists of
   eight bits (ones ond zeros) and has an address.   Other
   units of memory are a half-word (two bytes), full word
   (four bytes),   and double word (eight bytes).   A REAL
   value and an INTEGER value each occupy one word of
   memory.

2. For each program segment,   the compiler   uses a set of
   consecutive memory locations to store the instructions,
   simple variables, constants and expressions used in the
   segment. All arrays, Common Blocks and Equivalenced

variables are stored in a common area of memory.

3. A subprogram parameter can be called by value or called by location. If called by value, the value of the subprogram parameter is stored in memory locations which are part of those reserved by the compiler for that segment. If called by location, references to the parameter variable are references to the storage locations in which the calling segment value (argument) is stored.

4. The assignment of storage locations to variables in two-dimensional arrays (matrices) is done column-by-column. For higher dimensioned arrays, the rightmost subscript varies least rapidly when making the assignment of variables to storage locations.

5. Since parameter arrays are called by location, it is possible to specify the dimensions of a parameter array at execution time. If the parameter array is a subset of the argument array, the overall dimensions of the argument array as well as the dimensions of the subset should be passed to the subprogram. This will insure proper correspondences between variables and storage locations. A technique known as pseudo-variable dimensioning can also be used to provide dimension information for parameter arrays.

6. Program segments can communicate with one another by causing variables in different segments to share the same storage locations. This is done by defining one or more Common Blocks of memory. Variables in blocks which are labelled (have a name) can only be given initial values by using a BLOCK DATA subprogram.

7. Variables in the same segment of a program can be made to share the same storage locations by using an EQUIVALENCE statement.

8. Control may pass to a statement in a SUBROUTINE or FUNCTION subprogram to other than the first executable statement. This is done by specifying that certain statements are valid ENTRY points of the subprogram.

9. A SUBROUTINE subprogram may return control to a statement other than one following the CALL statement. This is done by making the statement numbers of the return points arguments in the call to the subprogram.

10. The name of a subprogram may be passed to a called

segment.   An   EXTERNAL   statement   specifies   those
subprogram names which may be used as arguments.

10.12 Programming Problems

In the following problems, make up a suitable mainline
segment to test the subprogram whenever a specific
mainline is not requested.

10.1   Write   a   SUBROUTINE   subprogram   which   has   two
parameters: N, a positive INTEGER value; K a set of N
INTEGER values. The subprogram should replace the value
of K(I) with K(I+1) - K(I) for I equal one thru N-1. The
value of K(N) should be set equal to K(1)-K(N). Write a
mainline segment which reads a value of N (no larger
than 20) and N more values which are stored in a
mainline vector.   Use the subprogram to replace the
values read with the differences described above. Print
the contents of the mainline vector before and after the
call to the subprogram.

10.2   Write a SUBROUTINE subprogram to assign a set of M*N
REAL values stored in a vector to the first M rows and N
columns of a matrix. Assume M and N are less than ten.
The mainline segment should read values of M and N, then
MN more values. The subprogram should assign the first N
values to row one of the parameter matrix,   the next N
values to row two, etc..   The subprogram will have six
elements in the parameter list: the overall dimensions
of the matrix;   the values of M and N; the vector
containing the MN values; the matrix in which the values
are to be stored.

10.3   Write a SUBROUTINE subprogram called MERGE to "merge"
two sets of ordered INTEGER values. The number of values
in each set should be passed to the subprogram. If the
names of the two sets of values are "S1" and "S2" and
have M and N elements respectively, the SUBROUTINE
should create a third set of M+N values made up of the
union of the values in S1 and S2. The values in the
third set should also be in order of increasing
magnitude. For example, suppose M=5 and S1=(2, 3, 7, 8,
9); N=4 and S2=(3, 5, 7, 10). The merged set is then (2,
3, 3, 5, 7, 7, 8, 9, 10).   The merging process can be
done efficiently by processing elements in S1 and S2 in
order and selecting the lower value of the two being
considered as the next value to be put in the merged
set. In the mainline, assume M and N are less than ten.

10.4 Use the subprogram written to solve the previous

problem to merge K sets of values. Assume K is five or
less. This can be done by having the mainline segment:
read the value of K; read the first two sets of values;
merge them using the subprogram; read the next set of
values; merge it with the previous merged sets; read the
next set; etc. The second, third, etc. data cards should
each contain the number of values in the set followed by
the actual values in the set. (The first data card
contains the number of sets.)

10.5   Write a FUNCTION subprogram called CENTIL having
parameters X, N and K where X is a set of N REAL values
in order of increasing magnitude and K is one of 10, 20,
30, ..., 90. The value of CENTIL calculated in the
subprogram should be the Kth percentile of the values in
X. The Kth percentile is a value such that K percent of
the values are less than it and 100-K percent of the
values are greater. Use CENTIL to calulate the tenth
thru ninetieth percentiles of a set of fifteen typical
marks out of one-hundred.

10.6   The Arithmetic Mean (AM), Geometric Mean (GM) and
Harmonic Mean (HM) of a set of N values X1, X2, X3, ...,
Xn are defined as follows.

$$AM = \frac{X1 + X2 + X3 + ... + Xn}{N}$$

$$GM = \sqrt[n]{X1\ X2\ X3\ ...\ Xn}$$

$$HM = \frac{N}{\frac{1}{X1} + \frac{1}{X2} + \frac{1}{X3} + ... + \frac{1}{Xn}}$$

Write a single program segment called AM in which GM and
HM are ENTRY points in the segment. Each of AM, GM, and
HM is to be a FUNCTION subprogram to calculate the
corresponding mean of a set of N REAL values.

10.7   The N coefficients of an (N-1)th degree polynomial
f(x) can be chosen so that the curve will pass thru any
N points in the XY plane. Suppose (X1,Y1), (X2,Y2), ...,
(Xn,Yn) are N points in the XY plane. The value of f(x)
which passes thru all N points is given by

$$f(x) = \frac{\sum_{i=1}^{n} (A_i Y_i) / (x - x_i)}{\sum_{i=1}^{n} \frac{A_i}{x - x_i}}$$

where $A_i = \dfrac{1}{\prod_{j \neq i} (x_i - x_j)}$

Write a REAL valued FUNCTION subprogram called INTERP which has two elements in the parameter list -- the value of N and the value of X for which the function value is to be calculated. In the subprogram and in the calling segment, define a Common Block containing a table of two rows and fifty columns. The row one values are the values of the X coordinates, those in row two, the corresponding Y coordinates. To test the subprogram, use eight data points generated in the following way. In row one store values of 0, 45, 90, 135, ..., 315. In row two store values of the sine of the corresponding angle in row one. Assume the row one values are in degrees. Use the subprogram INTERP to calculate estimates of the sine of angles of 15, 60, 105, 150, 195, 240. 285 and 330 degrees. For each of these print the estimated sine value, the true sine value, and the percent error resulting from using the approximating function.

10.8 A programming project. In physics, there are five commonly used equations which describe the relationships between distance (s), acceleration (a), final velocity (v), time (t) and initial velocity (u) of a moving body. Each of the five equations can be identified by the variable which does not appear in the equation. For this reason, they are sometimes known as the "SAVTU" equations. The equations are as follows.

"S" equation: $a = (v-u)/t$

"A" equation: $v = t(u+v)/2$

"V" equation: $s = ut + (at^2)/2$

"T" equation: $v^2 = u^2 + 2as$

"U" equation: $s = vt - (at^2)/2$

Write a SUBROUTINE subprogram called SAVTU which has the

parameters DATA and CODES defined by:

        REAL DATA(5)
        INTEGER CODES(5)

Let the values in DATA be the values of distance, acceleration, final velocity, time and intial velocity. The values in CODES indicate which values are known and which are to be calculated. If CODES(I) is zero it means the value of DATA(I) is to be calculated by the subprogram and stored in DATA(I). If CODES(I) is 1, it means DATA(I) can be used in the calculation of the unknown values. Note that in any call to the subprogram, that at least three values in CODES must equal one. Use any method you like in the subprogram to calculate the unknown values. Test your subprogram on at least the ten different ways that three values of the five can be specified as known. If you wish, include in your subprogram a multiple return feature which will return to an error routine in the calling segment if fewer than three of the CODES values are 1.

Part II

OTHER TYPES OF VALUES

CHAPTER 11 OTHER TYPES OF VALUES - THE CONCEPTS

Questions Answered In This Chapter

1. What types of variables (other than REAL and INTEGER)
   can be used in WATFIV and what is the purpose of each?

2. What programming principles and concepts are common to
   these other types of variables?

11.1 Other Types Of Variables

Part I of this book has described the rules for writing
WATFIV programs which use REAL and INTEGER values. Almost
all problems which are solved with the aid of a computer can
be programmed using only these two types of values. In
WATFIV, however, there are three other types of values which
can be defined and manipulated using the statements
described in Part I of this book. The names given to these
other types are CHARACTER, LOGICAL and COMPLEX. Before
describing the purpose of each, you should know that WATFIV
also permits you to use two slightly different forms of REAL
and INTEGER values. These alternate forms are called
INTEGER*2 and Extended Precision Real values. These last two
types of values are described in Chapters 12 and 13
respectively.

CHARACTER Values

Suppose the sentence "ECOLOGY CONCERNS THE
INTERRELATIONSHIP OF MAN AND NATURE" has been punched on a
card. You are asked to write a program to determine the
number of words in the sentence. Could you do it using only
REAL and INTEGER variables? Probably not. It could be done
but the program would be very artificial. The solution of
this problem requires us to analyze a string of symbols. In
WATFIV, strings of symbols are called CHARACTER values. By
using CHARACTER variables, the algorithm for solving the
problem can be easily programmed. This is one example of a
problem in which the use of CHARACTER variables is almost a
necessity. Other uses and examples of CHARACTER variables
can be found in Chapters 16 and 21.

LOGICAL Values

Many problems deal with ideas and relationships which
are true or false. For example, "A.LE.B" can only have a

value of "true" or "false".   Quantities which can only have
one of these two values are called LOGICAL values in WATFIV.
By using LOGICAL variables, a programmer can manipulate
true-false values with relative ease. Note that the INTEGER
values of one and zero can also be used to represent true-
false quantities. By using LOGICAL variables and constants
however, the program is usually more readable and easier to
"debug".

COMPLEX Values

Many problems in mathematics and engineering require the
use of the square root of negative one in the solution of
the problem.   Pairs of   real numbers in which the second
number of the pair is assumed to be multiplied by the square
root of negative one are called COMPLEX numbers.   The
operations of   addition,   subtraction,   multiplication,
division and exponentiation of COMPLEX numbers are performed
according to well-defined rules. WATFIV permits programmers
to create and manipulate COMPLEX numbers easily. Any program
using COMPLEX numbers and variables however, could also be
programmed using REAL numbers and variables.   By using
COMPLEX numbers in a program,   the compiler,   not the
programmer, does the work in setting up the appropriate
machine language instructions to perform COMPLEX arithmetic.

11.2 The Concept of "Length".

In Chapter 2, the point was made that each REAL or
INTEGER value is represented in the memory of the computer
as a string of thirty-two ones and zeros. Thus we might say
that a REAL or INTEGER value has a "memory length" of
thirty-two bits. A more common unit of memory length is the
"byte". A byte is eight consecutive bits.   Thus we can
equivalently say that REAL and INTEGER values have a length
of four bytes. Throughout the remainder of the book, when we
speak of the length of a value, we shall mean the number of
bytes of memory used to store the value. For example,
assuming X is REAL, the values 2, X, and -3.567E02 each have
a length of four.

CHARACTER values in WATFIV can have lengths which vary
from one to 255.   This means that strings of symbols having
from one to 255 characters can be manipulated in WATFIV.
LOGICAL values have a standard length of four.   COMPLEX
values, which are, in effect, pairs of REAL values, have a
length of eight bytes (twice the length of a REAL value).

The fact that any value stored in the computer memory has a finite length means that there are a finite number of unique values which can be taken on by a value. This is the reason that INTEGER values are restricted to the range plus or minus 2.1 billion (roughly) and that REAL values have seven significant digits.

There are two circumstances in which a programmer might wish to change the standard length of a value. First, he might wish to _increase_ the length of a value in order to extend the range of values permitted by that particular type. This can be done for REAL and COMPLEX values. Secondly, he might wish to _decrease_ the length of a value in order to reduce the amount of memory space required to store the values used in the program. This can be done for INTEGER and LOGICAL values. The method for changing the standard length of each of the five types of values (REAL, INTEGER, CHARACTER, LOGICAL, COMPLEX) is described in the appropriate chapter.

Each of the next five chapters discusses a different type of value. Chapters 12 and 13 describe, respectively, INTEGER variables of length two and REAL values of length eight. Chapters 14, 15, and 16 are somewhat more extensive and deal with COMPLEX, LOGICAL and CHARACTER values in that order.

In each of these chapters, the following questions are answered.

How are the constants and variables defined?

How are the variables used in the statements available in WATFIV?

What happens when values of different types are combined in the same statement?

What built-in functions are available for processing the values?

How are the values input and output in format-free and formatted operations?

Chapter 17 discusses the use of non-REAL and/or non-INTEGER variables in several statements which are not used in most WATFIV programs. These are: EXTERNAL, IMPLICIT, ENTRY, COMMON, BLOCK DATA, DIMENSION, DATA and Statement Functions. Since the same principles apply in using these statements regardless of the type of values appearing in the statement, this discussion is presented in a single chapter for the reader who requires information on this topic.

Exercise 11.1

1 What are the five types of values which can be defined and manipulated in WATFIV programs? What is the purpose of each?

2. What is meant by the "length" of a value or variable?

3. What are the reasons for permitting a programmer to change the standard length of a variable?

11.3 Summary

1. Knowledge of REAL and INTEGER values and the rules for using them is sufficient to translate almost all algorithms into WATFIV. To make the programming of problems which involve strings of symbols, true-false quantities, and complex values much easier, CHARACTER, LOGICAL, and COMPLEX variables and constants are permitted in WATFIV.

2. A length is associated with each value stored in the computer's memory. The length of a value is the number of bytes used to store the value.

3. A programmer may modify the standard length of a variable in order to increase the precision of REAL or COMPLEX values and/or to reduce the memory required for storing INTEGER or LOGICAL values.

CHAPTER 12   INTEGER VARIABLES OF LENGTH TWO

Questions Answered In This Chapter

    1. What are INTEGER*2 variables?

    2. How are INTEGER*2 variables defined and used in
       WATFIV programs?

    Before studying the material of this chapter, the reader
should be familiar with the ideas in Chapter 11.

12.1 Purpose

    INTEGER variables have a standard length of four bytes.
This permits INTEGER values to range between -2147483648 and
+2147483647.   If one or more INTEGER variables used in
program are known to have values within the range -32768,
+32767, a saving in memory space can often be achieved by
declaring that these variables are to have a length of two.
INTEGER variables of length two are called Half-Word INTEGER
variables or INTEGER*2 variables.   The latter term
(INTEGER*2) will be used in this book.

12.2 Defining INTEGER*2 Variables

    The pair of statements below are equivalent.   Each
specifies that JACK and JILL are to be INTEGER*2 variables
and each assigns a value of 1 to JACK and -17 to JILL.

        INTEGER*2 JACK/1/,JILL/-17/

        INTEGER JACK*2/1/,JILL*2/-17/

Note that the length modifier may follow either the word
INTEGER or the variable name to which it applies.

    The statements below are equivalent.   Each defines TABLE
to be a table of INTEGER*2 variables having 100 rows and 90
columns. The initial values in the table are all zero.   Each
statement also specifies that AVG is to be an INTEGER
variable having the standard length of four.

        INTEGER*2 TABLE(100,90)/9000*0/,AVG*4

        INTEGER TABLE*2(100,90)/9000*0/,AVG

        INTEGER*4 TABLE*2(100,90)/9000*0/,AVG

The point being illustrated in this example is that if a length specification follows the word INTEGER, then that length is applied to all variables in the list unless a length specification follows a variable or array name. Note also that INTEGER and INTEGER*4 are equivalent.

INTEGER*2 variables can also be declared by using an IMPLICIT statement. This topic is discussed in Chapter 17.

12.3 Constants, Expressions, and Assignments

Constants

All INTEGER constants in WATFIV have a length of four. Only variables may be given the optional length of two.

Expressions

When evaluating expressions which involve INTEGER*2 variables, the value of the variable is expanded to the equivalent INTEGER value of length four before the operation is performed. This means that when INTEGER*2 variables are used in mixed-mode expressions, the type of result obtained is identical to the type and value of the result obtained had the variable been of length four.

Assignment Statements

When an INTEGER*2 variable appears on the left hand side of an Assignment statement, the value of the expression on the right is converted to an INTEGER*4 value (if it is not already in this form). Next, the digits represented by the bit pattern of the rightmost two bytes of this value are assigned to the INTEGER*2 variable. This means that if the value of the expression on the right lies within the range minus 32768 to +32767, then the "correct" value will be assigned to the INTEGER*2 variable. If the expression value lies outside this range, the value assigned to the variable will be incorrect. Since no warning message is printed, a programmer should satisfy himself that values assigned to INTEGER*2 variables in a program are within the permitted range. The example program below illustrates the facts described above.

```
INTEGER*2 H1/20/,H2/4/,H3/240000/,H4,H5
H4=H1**H2
H5=H1**H2/100
PRINT,H3,H4,H5
STOP
END
```

When executed, the values printed for H3, H4, and H5 are:

H3 = -22144   H4= 28928   H5= 1600

The reasons are as follows. The value of H3 (namely 240000) lies outside the permitted range of INTEGER*2 values. However the bit pattern of the rightmost two bytes of the INTEGER value 240000 represents an INTEGER*2 value of negative 22144. (See Appendix C for details). Consider H4. The value of 20**4 is greater than 32768. The value printed for H4 represents the INTEGER*2 value of the bit pattern of the rightmost two bytes of the result. Finally, in calculating the value of H5 (which equals H1**H2/100) the calculations are done using the INTEGER*4 equivalents of the values of H1 and H2. The value of the expression is 1600 which does lie within the permitted range. Even though H1**H2 is greater than 32768, the value of this part of the expression is left as an INTEGER*4 value.

12.4 Built-In Functions

There is only one built-in function for processing INTEGER*2 values. The function HFIX can be used to convert a REAL value to an INTEGER*2 value. For example, the statement "HW=HFIX(3.14)" causes HW to be assigned the value 3. The variable HW in this example is assumed to have been declared as an INTEGER*2 variable.

12.5 Input-Output Of INTEGER*2 Variables

An I-mask is used to input or output INTEGER*2 variables under format control. In format-free operations, the default mask is I12 for each INTEGER*2 variable appearing in an output list. In format-free input operations, the programmer should be careful that values assigned to INTEGER*2 variables lie within the permitted range.

12.6 Valid And Invalid Uses

INTEGER*2 variables may be used anywhere INTEGER variables are permitted with two exceptions. An INTEGER*2 variable may not be used as the index of an Assigned GO TO. For example, if HALF is an INTEGER*2 variable, then the statements "ASSIGN 6 TO HALF" or "GOTO HALF,(6)" are invalid. Secondly, an INTEGER*2 variable cannot be used in a READ or WRITE statement to store the device number. The following pair of statements, for example, is invalid.

```
INTEGER*2 DEVICE
READ(DEVICE,900) X
```

Exercise 12.1

1. What is the chief reason for using INTEGER*2 variables?
What is the most significant restriction on their use?

12.7 Summary

If memory space is at a premium and if a large number of
INTEGER variables are used in a program, a significant
reduction in memory requirements can be realized by using
INTEGER*2 variables instead of INTEGER variables. The only
disadvantages which result are: the values assigned to
these variables must lie in the range -32768 thru +32767;
INTEGER functions such as MAXO cannot be used; there may be
an increase in execution time. All INTEGER constants have a
length of four. Only variables may be given the optional
length of two.

12.8 Programming Problems

12.1 What triples of integer values (x, y, z) have the
property that $x^2+y^2=z^2$? A rigorous way of generating
such values is to choose any pair of values m and n such
that: m and n are relatively prime (one is not a
multiple of the other); m is even and n is odd or m is
odd and n is even. If m and n satisfy these conditions
then set

$$x = 2mn, \quad y = m^2 - n^2 , \text{ and } z = m^2 + n^2$$

For example, set m=2 and n=1. The values of x, y, and z
are x=4, y=3 and z=5. Note that $3^2+4^2=5^2$. Write a
program using INTEGER*2 variables for m, n, x, y and z
and generate all possible triples using values of m and
n of five or less which satisfy the given conditions.

12.2 A programming project. Suppose a fifty-by-fifty
matrix contains elements whose values are zero or one.
Suppose less than twenty percent of the elements have a
value of one and all the rest are zeros. Design any
scheme you like for reducing the memory required to
store the array values. Make sure your technique will
work for an arbitrary set of values and does not depend
on the array values having a particular pattern.

CHAPTER 13   EXTENDED PRECISION

Questions Answered In This Chapter

1. What are the three important reasons for using
   numbers having as many as 16 significant digits?

2. How are these "extended precision" values defined
   and used in WATFIV programs?

Before studying the material of this chapter,   the reader
should be familiar with the ideas in Chapter 11.

13.1 Extended Precision Values

Seven significant digits are stored for each REAL value
used in a WATFIV program. By doubling the amount of memory
used to   store a REAL number,   numbers with sixteen
significant digits can be stored in the computer memory.
Such numbers are called Extended Precision numbers.   The
terms DOUBLE PRECISION and REAL*8 are synonyms for Extended
Precision.   The significance of the   "*8" is that each such
value occupies eight bytes of memory.   In this book, the
words Extended Precision will be   used and   will be
abbreviated to "E.P." in this chapter.

What are the reasons for requiring numbers having as
many as sixteen significant digits? Three reasons are:

  i) To manipulate values which represent large
      sums of money.   For example,   the figure
      $10,473,126.52 has ten significant digits.

  ii) To manipulate integer values which lie outside
      the permitted range of INTEGER values,   eg:
      12345678901.

  iii) To reduce the degree of error associated with
      operations involving numbers in which the
      fractional portion of the number is a non-
      terminating string of binary digits.   For
      example, .2 in base two is .001100110011... .

13.2 E.P. Constants, Variables and Expressions

Constants

E.P.   constants may be defined with or without an
exponent. Examples of valid E.P. constants are:

123451234512345.1

-17.2D06   i.e: -17.2 x 10⁶

0.001425683415D-2   i.e: .001425683415 x 10⁻²

Examples of invalid E.P. constants are:

123,456,789.012   (commas not permitted)

1.0D-200   (exponent too large)

123451234512345123.   (more than 16 digits)

123.45   (a REAL constant but not an E.P. constant.
The equivalent value as an E.P. constant
would be 123.45D00 or 123.45000.)

Note that a "D" precedes the exponent value when an E.P. constant is written with an exponent. The D is used with E.P. numbers in precisely the same way that the E is used in writing REAL constants. The range of exponents permitted for E.P. values is the same as that for REAL values, namely the range between -78 and +76. A discussion of the bit pattern used to represent E.P. values can be found in Appendix C.

Variables

Each E.P. value occupies eight bytes of memory instead of the four bytes used for storing a REAL value. If variables used in a program are to be assigned E.P. values, the WATFIV compiler must be informed of this fact in order that it can reserve sufficient memory space for each such variable or function value. The two statements below each inform the compiler that the variables A,B, and C are to be assigned E.P. values.

REAL*8 A,B,C

DOUBLE PRECISION A,B,C

The statements above are equivalent. In the first, the length modifier of "*8" is added to the end of the word REAL. In the second, the words DOUBLE PRECISION are used to inform the compiler that the variables A, B, and C are to have E.P. values. In this chapter, the REAL*8 form of the declaration statement will always be used since it is somewhat more flexible as the examples below will show.

Each of the following statements defines a two-by-five table of E.P. variables which is initialized to zeros. MAX is declared as a REAL variable with an initial value of 7.

        REAL*8 TABLE(2,5)/10*0.D00/,MAX*4/7./

        REAL TABLE*8(2,5)/10*0.D00/,MAX/7./

        REAL*4 TABLE*8(2,5)/10*0.D00/,MAX/7./

The ideas illustrated by these statements are:

i) A length modifier of "*8" or "*4" may follow the word REAL. If omitted, "*4" is assumed.

ii) A length modifier of "*8" or "*4" may follow a variable or array name. If omitted, the length of the variable or array element is that associated with the word REAL.

iii) E.P. variables may be initialized at compile time. The initializing values must agree in number and type with the variables being initialized. The statements "REAL*8 A/1./" and "REAL*8 B/12.E04/" for example, are invalid.

The DIMENSION statement (Chapter 7, Section 9) can also be used to define sets of E.P. variables. The DATA statement (Chapter 7, Section 8) is an alternate method of specifying initial values for E.P. variables. These topics are discussed in Chapter 17.

Expressions

Expresssions which involve E.P. values are of two types: those which involve only E.P. values; and those which involve one or more other types of values as well as E.P. values.

When E.P. values are combined using any of the arithmetic operators + - * / **, the result is an E.P. value. Some examples are:

Expression	Result
2.0D00+3.25D00	5.25D00
-2.D00**3.D00	-8.0D00

$(-2.D00)**3.D00$ ERROR (negative base used
                                     with a REAL type exponent)

$1.D25-1.D25+1.D00$ $1.D00$

$1.D00+1.D25-1.D25$ $0.D00$ (only 16 digits are
                                     kept at each step when
                                     evaluating the expression)

In evaluating mixed-type expressions, the general rule
is that if an operation involves an INTEGER and an E.P.
value or a REAL and an E.P. value, the non-E.P. value is
converted to an E.P. value before the operation is
performed. The result is an E.P. value. Some examples are:

Expression	Result
$2.0D00 + 3.$	$5.0D00$
$6.0D00/3$	$2.0D00$
$(-.5D00)**(-3)$	$-8.0D00$ (the exception to the rule -- an INTEGER exponent is left unchanged)
$5/2*1.D00$	$2.D00$ (the division is done first)
$1.D00*5/2$	$2.5D00$ (the multiplication is done first)

Are the values of the three expressions below the same?

$.2D00+.2D00$ $.2D00+.2E00$ $.2E00+.2E00$

The answer is "No, they are all different.". Why? The
reason is primarily due to the fact that a value of two-
tenths has a non-terminating string of binary digits to the
right of the decimal point when written in the base two
number system. This means that the values of .2D00 and .2E00
which are stored in the computer's memory are only
approximations to the value .2. Furthermore, since E.P.
values have more significant digits, the value of .2D00 is a
better approximation than the value .2E00. If we label the
values of .2E00 and .2D00 as "good" and "better"
respectively, then the "quality" of the result in the three
cases is shown below.

.2D00 + .2D00	better + better	i.e: .400000000000
.2D00 + .2E00	better + good	i.e: .399999988079
.2E00 + .2E00	good + good	i.e: .399999976158

As you can see, the most accurate result is obtained by using the two E.P. values and the least accurate by using the two REAL values. The result obtained by using one of each type lies somewhere in between.

The foregoing discussion emphasizes the reason for using E.P. values in situations where numbers have fractional values and a high degree of accuracy is very important.

One further point. The relationship in the statement

IF (.2D00 .EQ. .2E00) ...

is false. The reason is as discussed above. That is, a comparison is being made between a good approximation and a better approximation -- but not the same approximation. The relationship (2.D00 .EQ. 2.E00) will always be true however, since the representation of whole numbers (and many fractional values) is exact. Thus, if two E.P. values A and B, say, must be tested for equality, it is wise to compare the absolute value of their difference to some very small value. The built-in function DABS can be used for this purpose. (This and other E.P. built-in functions are described in Section 4.) That is, the statement

IF (DABS (A-B) .LE. 1.D-1) ...

should be used intead of "IF (A.EQ.B) ...".

13.3 E.P. Assignment Statements

An E.P. Assignment statement has one of the following forms.

    i)   E.P. variable = E.P. expression

    ii) E.P. variable = non-E.P. expression

    iii) non-E.P. variable = E.P. expression

Case (i) is straightforward in that the value of the expression is simply assigned to the variable. In Case (ii), the value of the REAL or INTEGER expression is converted to an E.P. value before the assignment takes place. For example, if A is an E.P. variable, the statement "A=3" results in A being assigned the value 3.D00. The only situation in which unexpected results may occur is illustrated in the following example.

```
REAL*8 B/.2D00/
A=B
IF(A.EQ.B) PRINT,A,B
STOP
END
```

For the reasons discussed in the previous section, the values of A and B are different since they have been assigned different approximations of the value one-fifth.

In Case (iii), a non-E.P. variable is assigned the value of an E.P. expression. When this happens, the value of the expression is converted to the type required by the variable on the left of the equal sign before the assignment takes place. For example, "I=-2.7D00" results in I having a value of -2 . "X=.2D00" results in X having a value of .2E00.

Exercise 13.1

1. What is the value assigned to each variable in the following sets of statements?

a)
```
REAL*8 A,B,C,D/1.D00/
A=20.*D/1.D1
B=3.0D00**A
C=-A**3
```

b)
```
REAL*8 W(3)/3.D00,4.D00,5.D00/
INTEGER XX,YY,ZZ
YY=ZZ=10.D00/10.E3*W(1)
DO 1 XX=1,3
    W(XX)=W(XX)-W(MOD(XX+1,3)+1.D00)+YY/ZZ
1 CONTINUE
```

c)
```
REAL X*8/49.D00/,REAL/4./
INTEGER ASK/2/
ASK=ASK/(2*ASK)+X
REAL=REAL+SQRT(SQRT(FLOAT(ASK))+SQRT(REAL))
```

2. What is the error in each of the following?

a) REAL*8 A/2.E10/

    b)   REAL*4 B(5,8)/40*2.D3/
    c)   REAL XYZ*8(3)/1.0D05,-10.346D-8/
    d)   REAL A*8,B(2)*8

3. Answer true or false to each of the following.

    a) The number of memory locations used to store a REAL*8
       value is twice that used for a REAL*4 value.
    b) E.P. representations of whole numbers are exact.
    c) E.P. representations of many fractional values are
       exact.
    d) E.P. representations of all fractional values are
       exact.
    e) E.P. representations of some fractional values are
       better approximations to the value than the REAL*4
       representation of the same value.
    f) Same as (e) but replace "some" with "all".
    g) The number .1 is an E.P. constant.
    h) The number .000000001 is an E.P. constant.
    i) In any operation involving an E.P. value and a non-
       E.P. value, the non-E.P. value is always converted
       to an E.P. value before the operation is performed.
    j) The Assignment statements "A=.2D00" and "A=.2E00" are
       equivalent (i) when A is a REAL variable, and (ii)
       when A is an E.P. variable.

13.4 Extended Precision Built-In Functions

    The WATFIV language includes a large number of built-in
functions for processing E.P. Values. The table below lists
those which are commonly used. A complete list can be found
in Appendix J. In the table, the symbol "r8" denotes an E.P.
argument, the symbol "r4" denotes a REAL argument and "i"
denotes an INTEGER argument.

           TABLE OF E.P. BUILT-IN FUNCTIONS

Purpose	Name And Arguments	Definition	Result
Square Root	DSQRT(r8)	$\sqrt{}$	E.P.
Trigonometric Functions (angles in radians)	DSIN(r8) DCOS(r8) DTAN(r8) DCOTAN(r8)	sine cosine tangent cotangent	E.P. E.P. E.P. E.P.

Inverse trig Functions (result in radians)	DARSIN(r8) DARCOS(r8) DATAN(r8)	arcsine arccosine arctangent	E.P. E.P. E.P.
Logarithms	DLOG(r8) DLOG10(r8)	log (base e) log (base 10)	E.P. E.P.
Exponential	DEXP(r8)	e**argument	E.P.
Absolute value	DABS(r8)	|argument|	E.P.
Transfer of sign	DSIGN(r8,r8)	|arg1| sign(arg2) where, $sign = \begin{cases} +1 \text{ if } >0 \\ 1 \text{ if } =0 \\ -1 \text{ if } <0 \end{cases}$	E.P.
Truncation	IDINT(r8)	integer part of the argument	INTEGER
Modular Arithmetic	DMOD(r8,r8)	remainder of arg1/arg2	E.P.
Maximum and Minimum	DMAX1(r8,r8..) DMIN1(r8,r8..)	largest arg. smallest arg.	E.P. E.P.
Type	DFLOAT(i)	E.P. value of arg.	E.P.
Conversion	SNGL(r8)	REAL value of arg.	REAL
	DBLE(r4)	Adds zeros to REAL value to form an E.P. value	E.P.

There are several important points concerning the use of E.P. built-in functions.

   i) It is not necessary to declare a built-in function as having an E.P. value but no problems arise if this is done. For example, if the built-in functions DSQRT and DABS say are used in a segment, then the statement below could be used.

REAL*8 DSQRT,DABS

ii) The reasons for having the   type conversion
functions are:

a) Some Fortran compilers do not permit mixed-type
expressions. Thus in order to cause all terms in an
expression to have the same mode,   the functions
DFLOAT,SNGL and DBLE may be required.

b) Function arguments must be of the type specified
in the table. For example to obtain the square root
of an INTEGER variable   I correct to sixteen
significant   digits,   one   could   write
DSQRT(DBLE(FLOAT(I))).

13.5 Input-Output Of E.P. Values

Formatted Input-Output

A D-mask or F-mask is used to input or output E.P.
values under format control. The operation of a D-mask is
similar to that of an E-mask with the exception that as many
as 16 significant digits can be printed using a D-mask. The
general form of the D-mask is Dw.d where "w" denotes the
number of columns or print positions covered by the mask and
"d" denotes the number of digits to the right of the decimal
point. A few examples will illustrate its use.

Suppose the symbols "1.23456789D02" are punched in 13
columns covered by a D-mask. The value assigned to a
variable is shown for three different masks.

Mask	Value Assigned
D13.8	1.23456789D02
D13.3	1.23456789D02 (value of d is ignored)
F13.8	error ("D" is an invalid character when read under an F-mask)

Suppose the E.P. value of .123456789 is to be printed. The symbols printed for several masks are shown below.

Mask	Symbols Printed
D16.9	b0.123456789Db00 (b denotes a blank)
D15.9	0.123456789Db00
D13.6	b0.123457Db00
D14.9	**************
F11.9	0.123456789
F10.9	**********
F10.6	bb0.123457

Format-Free Input-Output

On input, values to be assigned to E.P. variables may be punched either with or without an exponent. If an exponent is used, a "D" should precede the exponent value.

On output, the mask used for printing E.P. values is D28.16.

13.6 Subprograms

The example program of this section illustrates the important points in writing subprograms which utilize E.P. values. The program determines the largest root of the equation $ax^2 + bx + c = 0$. The values of a, b and c are read from a card. The assumption is made that $b^2 - 4ac$ is positive. The FUNCTION subprogram BIGRUT is used to obtain the result.

```
C EXAMPLE 13.1 FIND LARGEST ROOT
      REAL*8 A,B,C,BIGRUT
      READ,A,B,C
      PRINT 1,BIGRUT(A,B,C)
    1 FORMAT('1LARGEST ROOT IS',D23.16)
      STOP
      END

      REAL FUNCTION BIGRUT*8(A,B,C)
      REAL*8 A,B,C,X,Y,DISC
      DISC=B*B-4.*A*C
      X=(-B+DSQRT(DISC))/(2.*A)
      Y=(-B-DSQRT(DISC))/(2.*A)
      BIGRUT=DMAX1(DABS(X),DABS(Y))
      RETURN
      END
  $ENTRY
```

Remarks

i) All E.P. arguments and parameters must be declared as such in the appropriate segment. Arguments and parameters should agree in number and type.

ii) The name of a user-defined E.P.-valued FUNCTION must appear in a suitable type declaration statement in the calling segment. (BIGRUT is declared as being REAL*8.)

iii) The first statement in the FUNCTION subprogram can be one of the following:

   REAL FUNCTION name*8 (parameter list)

   DOUBLE PRECISION FUNCTION name (parameter list)

   Note that in the first case, the length specification "*8" **must** follow the FUNCTION name. It cannot appear after the word REAL.

   Alternatively, the first statement of the subprogam can begin with the word FUNCTION provided that the function name is declared as having the type REAL*8 or DOUBLE PRECISION in a type declaration statement within the subprogram.

In SUBROUTINE subprograms, no value is assigned to the SUBROUTINE name. This means that rules (ii) and (iii) above do not apply to SUBROUTINE subprograms.

13.7 Other Statements Involving E.P. Values

1. Extended Precision variables may be used in the following WATFIV statements: IMPLICIT, EQUIVALENCE, and COMMON. Details can be found in Chapter 17.

2. E.P. Statement Functions can be defined and used in a program segment. The name of the function and any E.P. variables used in its definition must be declared as having E.P. values.

3. E.P. variables in COMMON Blocks may be initialized in BLOCK DATA subprograms.

4. E.P. FUNCTION subprograms may appear in EXTERNAL and ENTRY statements. This topic is discussed in Chapter 17, Section 10.

5. E.P. expressions may be used as subscripts. The subscript value is obtained by using the integer part of the value of the expression. For example, if X is an array, then X(1.99999D00) is equivalent to X(1).

6. A G-mask can be used to input or output E.P. values under format control. Its effect is similar to that obtained with REAL values.

7. A P-code can be used to modify E.P. values which are: input under an F-mask; output under a D-mask or F-mask.

13.8 Summary

1. Extended Precision values can be used in WATFIV programs. Each E.P. value occupies eight bytes (two words) of memory. The equivalent of sixteen decimal digits are stored for each E.P. value used.

2. The use of E.P. values should be considered when a program manipulates fractional values and a high degree of accuracy is important.

13.9 Programming Problems

In all of the problems which follow, use Extended Precision variables whenever appropriate.

13.1   In 1624 Peter Minuit bought Manhattan Island from the Indians for $24.00. Suppose the Indians had invested the money at 4% compounded annually. How much would their investment have been worth in 1969? Display the values of the investment at fifteen year intervals starting with 1624 and ending with 1969 as shown below. Use a mask of F20.2 to display each dollar amount.

YEAR	AMOUNT	YEAR	AMOUNT	YEAR	AMOUNT
1624	$ _____	1639	$ _____	1654	$ _____
1669	$ _____	1684	$ _____	1699	$ _____
etc.		etc.		etc.	

13.2   Repeat problem 5.5 using E.P. variables and constants. Stop further execution when the change in the two estimates is less than 1.D-12.

13.3   The value of the inverse sine of a value x is given
        by the following expression.

$$\sin^{-1} x = x + \frac{x^3}{2.3} + \frac{1.3}{2.4.5}x^5 + \frac{1.3.5}{2.4.6.7}x^7 + \ldots$$

Write a FUNCTION subprogram which calculates the inverse
sine of a value of .25.   (What angle is such that its
sine equals .25?)   Calculate your answer correct to
fourteen decimal places. Compare your result with that
obtained from the built-in function DARSIN.

13.4   A ladder of length L leans against a wall.   The top
        of the ladder is initially a distance H above the floor.
        The top of the ladder starts to slip down the wall.
        Calculate the position of the mid-point of the ladder
        when the top is .95H, .90H, .85H, ..., .05H above the
        floor. Read values of L and H from a data card.

13.5   Large values of factorial N can be approximated using
        Stirling's formula which is

$$N! \text{ is approximately } e^{-n} N^n \sqrt{2_\pi N}$$

Calculate the values of factorial 1, 2, 3, ..., 20 using
the approximation formula. Use E.P. variables, constants
and built-in functions in your program.

13.6   An approximate value of π can be calculated using one
        of several formulae. Two of these are:

$$\frac{\pi^2}{8} = 1 + \frac{1}{3^2} + \frac{1}{5^2} + \frac{1}{7^2} + \ldots$$

$$\pi = \sqrt{\frac{6}{1^2} + \frac{6}{2^2} + \frac{6}{3^2} + \frac{6}{4^2} + \ldots}$$

Write two different E.P.   FUNCTION subprograms to
calculate an approximate value of π using the given
formulae. Which formula requires the fewest terms to get
a good approximation to π?

13.7   Suppose a ball dropped from a height H rebounds to a
        height of .9H. (a) Write a program which determines the
        number of bounces which the ball must make before its
        maximum height is .1D-10.   (b) Add a feature to the

program for (a) to determine the total length of time
the ball is in the air.

13.8   Find the roots of $x^2-325678x-.02=0$ using first, REAL
       variables and secondly,   E.P.   values.   Explain the
       significant difference in the two results.

Questions Answered In This Chapter

1. What are COMPLEX values?

2. How are COMPLEX values defined and used in WATFIV programs?

Before studying the material of this chapter, the reader should be familiar with the ideas of Chapter 11.

14.1 Complex Numbers

In mathematics and engineering, a complex number can be considered to be a pair of real numbers which obey well defined rules of arithmetic. Suppose (a,b) and (c,d) are two pairs of real numbers. Then, by definition, the operations of addition, subtraction, multiplication and division of the complex numbers (a,b) and (c,d) are:

$$(a,b) + (c,d) = (a+c, b+d)$$

$$(a,b) - (c,d) = (a-c, b-d)$$

$$(a,b) * (c,d) = (ac-bd, ad+bc)$$

$$(a,b) / (c,d) = \left(\frac{ac+bd}{c^2+d^2}, \frac{-ad+bc}{c^2+d^2} \right)$$

The complex conjugate of a complex number (a,b) is defined as the number (a,-b). For any complex number (a,b), the first number of the pair is called the real component of the number and the second number of the pair is called the imaginary component of the number.

Complex numbers are sometimes written in the form "a+ib" where "i" denotes the square root of negative one. In this book, this method of writing complex numbers will not be used since WATFIV uses the the form (a,b) to represent complex numbers.

14.2 Constants, Variables, and Expressions

WATFIV permits a programmer to define and manipulate complex values. Numbers, variables, functions and expressions which have a complex value are called COMPLEX.

In WATFIV, a COMPLEX value is viewed as a pair of REAL numbers. This means each COMPLEX value occupies two words of memory. Operations on COMPLEX values are performed using machine language instructions generated by the WATFIV compiler. The circuits used to perform these calculations are the same as those used to do REAL arithmetic. Of necessity, more machine language instructions are required to add two COMPLEX values, for instance, than to add two REAL values.

Constants

COMPLEX constants are defined by enclosing a pair of REAL constants, separated by a comma, in brackets. Examples of valid COMPLEX constants are:

$$(2.,1.) \qquad (-3.257E+06,-5.2) \qquad (.0025E-1,.002E-20)$$

Some invalid constants are:

$(2.,1)$ (imaginary component is an INTEGER)

$(3.56E01 \ -2.1)$ (no comma)

$(-5.73,X)$ (X is not a constant)

$(2.*3.,-5.6789)$ (real component is an expression)

Since a pair of REAL values is stored for each COMPLEX value used, the real and imaginary components of a COMPLEX number may be only good approximations of the desired value. This will occur in cases where one or both of the components have a non-terminating binary representation.

Variables

COMPLEX variables are defined using a COMPLEX declaration statement. Each such variable occupies eight bytes (two words) of memory. The statement below declares U and V to be COMPLEX variables and defines ARRAY as a three by four table of COMPLEX variables, each having an initial value of zero.

COMPLEX U,V,ARRAY(3,4)/12*(0.,0.)/

The DIMENSION statement can also be used to define sets of COMPLEX variables. The DATA statement is an alternate method of defining initial values. An IMPLICIT statement can be used to specify a first-letter rule for COMPLEX variables. These topics are discussed in Chapter 17.

Expressions

Expressions which involve COMPLEX values are of two types: those which involve only COMPLEX values; those which involve some other type of value as well as one or more COMPLEX values.

Case (i) All values COMPLEX. When COMPLEX values are combined using any of the four arithmetic operators + - * /, the result is a COMPLEX value. Some examples are:

Expression	Result
(2.,-3.)+(5.,7.)	(7.,4.)
(1.,2.)*(0.,3.)	(-6.,3.)
(1.,0.)/(3.,1.)	(.3,-.1)

The operation of exponentiation is permitted only if the exponent is an INTEGER value. Thus "(1.,2.)**2" is valid whereas "(1.,0.)**2." and "(1.,0.)**(1.,0.)" are invalid.

In a COMPLEX expression, each COMPLEX item must be either a COMPLEX constant or a COMPLEX variable. A COMPLEX value cannot be created simply by putting one or two REAL variables or expressions inside a pair of brackets. For example, if X and Y are REAL variables, the following are invalid COMPLEX values.

(X, 1.)   (0.2,X)   (X,Y)

To create a COMPLEX value from a pair of REAL values, the built-in function CMPLX (discussed in Section 14.4) must be used.

Case(ii) Mixed type expressions. Other types of values and variables may be combined with COMPLEX values in an expression. In such cases, the operation is performed by converting the non-COMPLEX value to a COMPLEX value having an imaginary component of zero. The result of the operation is always a COMPLEX value. Some examples are:

Expression	Result
3. + (1.,5.)	(4.,5.)
2 * (-6.,7.)	(-12.,14.)
(1.,-8.)**3.	error - only INTEGER exponents allowed

    6/4*(12.,0.)   (12.,0.) (division is done first)

    (12.,0.)*6/4   (18.,0.) (multiplication is done first)

14.3 COMPLEX Assignment Statements

    A COMPLEX Assignment statement has one of the following
forms:

    i)   COMPLEX variable = COMPLEX expression

    ii) COMPLEX variable = non-COMPLEX expression

    iii) non-COMPLEX variable = COMPLEX expression

    Case (i) is straightforward. The value of the COMPLEX
expression is assigned to the variable.

    In Case (ii), the value of the expression is assigned to
the real component of the variable. The imaginary component
is given a value of zero. For example,

                    COMPLEX A
                    B=2.5
                    I=3
                    A=B*I

results in A having a value of (7.5,0.)

    In   Case (iii)   (non-COMPLEX   variable =   COMPLEX
expression), the imaginary component of the expression value
is ignored and the real component is assigned to the
variable on the left.   For example,

                    COMPLEX U/(10.125,-3.5)/
                    J=U
                    A=U

results in J having a value of 10 and in A having a value of
10.125.

14.4 COMPLEX Built-In Functions

    Several   built-in   functions   are   available   for
manipulating and creating COMPLEX values. In the following
table, "c" denotes a COMPLEX argument and "r" denotes a REAL
argument.

TABLE OF COMPLEX BUILT-IN FUNCTIONS

Purpose	Name and Arguments	Definition	Result
Square Root	CSQRT(c)	$\sqrt{}$	COMPLEX
Trigonometric functions	CSIN(c) CCOS(c)	sine cosine	COMPLEX COMPLEX
Exponential & logarithm	CEXP(c) CLOG(c)	e**arg log (base e)	COMPLEX COMPLEX
Absolute value	CABS(c)	$\sqrt{a^2+b^2}$ where c=(a,b)	REAL
Type Conversion	CMPLX(r1,r2)	forms a COMPLEX number from r1 and r2	COMPLEX
Component Extraction	REAL(c)	the real component of c	REAL
	AIMAG(c)	the imaginary component of c	REAL
Complex Conjugate	CONJG(c)	if c=(a,b), result is (a,-b)	COMPLEX

The example program below could be used to obtain the
roots of the equation ax²+bx+c=0.

```
C EXAMPLE 14.1 ROOTS OF QUADRATIC

        COMPLEX ROOT1,ROOT2
        READ,A,B,C
        X = -B/(2.*A)
        DISCR = B*B - 4.*A*C
        IF (ABS(DISCR) .LT. 0.000001) THEN
            ROOT1 = CMPLX(X,0.)
            ROOT2 = ROOT1
        ELSE
            Y = SQRT(ABS(DISCR))/(2.*A)
            IF (DISCR .LT. 0.) THEN
                ROOT1 = CMPLX(X,Y)
                ROOT2 = CONJG(ROOT1)
            ELSE
                ROOT1=CMPLX(X+Y,0.)
                ROOT2=CMPLX(X-Y,0.)
            END IF
        END IF
        PRINT,ROOT1,ROOT2
        STOP
        END
```

14.5 Input-Output Of COMPLEX Values

Formatted Input-Output

A pair of masks (F-masks, E-masks, or one of each) is
used to input or output COMPLEX values under format control.
The following program illustrates this point.

```
C EXAMPLE 14.2 FORMATTED I/O OF COMPLEX VALUES
        COMPLEX U,V,W
        READ 1,U,V,W
      1 FORMAT(2F3.1,E6.2,F7.0,2E10.3)
        PRINT 2,U,V,W
      2 FORMAT('1U=(',2F11.2,')',/,' V=(',2E11.3,
       *')',/,' W=(',E11.3,F11.2,')')
        STOP
        END
    $ENTRY
    2.0-.5.25E04 -1234.  1.000E00 -1.000E00

    F3.1 F3.1  E6.2   F7.0    E10.3    E10.3
```

When executed, the following lines are printed.

```
U=(        2.00        -0.50)
V=(    0.250E 04 -0.123E 04)
W=(    0.100E 01        -1.00)
```

Format-Free Input-Output

Each COMPLEX value which is read using a format-free READ statement must be punched as a valid COMPLEX constant. This means that the real and imaginary components must be separated by a comma and enclosed in brackets. A comma and/or blank column(s) are used to separate successive values on a card.

When using format-free output, each COMPLEX value appearing in the output list is printed using the following set of format codes.

```
'(',E16.7,' ,',E16.7,')'
```

The following example illustrates these points.

```
C EXAMPLE 14.3 FORMAT-FREE INPUT-OUTPUT
        COMPLEX U,V
        READ,U,V
        PRINT,U
        PRINT,V
        PRINT, +(2.,7.)
        STOP
        END
$ENTRY
    (2.5, 16.E00) , (-7.,3.5)
```

The lines printed are:

```
(  0.2500000E 01 ,   0.1600000E 02)
( -0.7000000E 01 ,   0.3500000E 01)
(  0.2000000E 01 ,   0.7000000E 01)
```

In the statement "PRINT,+(2.,7.)", the "+" sign is necessary. The reason, as you may recall, is that any element in an output list which begins with a left bracket must be an implied DO-loop.

14.6 Subprograms

The example program of this section illustrates the important points in writing subprograms which utilize COMPLEX values.

If U is a COMPLEX number, the equation U = 1 has N roots. The N roots are given by the formula below.

$$U = \left(\cos \frac{2K\pi}{N} \, , \, \sin \frac{2K\pi}{N}\right) \, , \text{ where } K=0,1,2, \ldots, N-1$$

The mainline segment of the following program reads in a value of N and uses the FUNCTION subprogram CROOT to obtain, in order, the N COMPLEX roots of unity.

```
C ROOTS OF UNITY              COMPLEX FUNCTION CROOT(K,N)
      COMPLEX CROOT,U          ANG = 2.*K*3.14159/N
      READ,N                   X = COS(ANG)
      DO 1 K=1,N               Y = SIN(ANG)
         U = CROOT(K,N)        CROOT = CMPLX(X,Y)
         PRINT,U               RETURN
    1 CONTINUE                 END
      STOP
      END
```

Remarks

i) All COMPLEX arguments and parameters must be declared as such in the appropriate segment. Arguments and parameters should agree in number and type.

ii) The name of a COMPLEX-valued FUNCTION must appear in a suitable type declaration statement in the calling segment. (CROOT is declared as COMPLEX in the example mainline.)

iii) The first statement in a FUNCTION subprogram should have the form:

COMPLEX FUNCTION name (parameter list)

Alternatively, the first statement of the subprogram can begin with FUNCTION provided that the function name is declared as having the type COMPLEX in a type declaration statement within the subprogram.

In SUBROUTINE subprograms, no value is assigned to the name of the SUBROUTINE. This means that remarks (ii) and (iii) above do not apply to SUBROUTINE subprograms.

Exercise 14.1

1. What is the value of each of the following expressions?

   a) $(3.,4.)+(2.E00,-8.)$
   b) $(2.,-3.)/(4.,-1.)$
   c) $(2.,1.)**2*(4./(1.,-1.)+(2.,-1.)/(1.,1.))$
   d) $((0.,1.) +(0.,1.) +(0.,1.))/(2-(0.,1.) +(0.,1.))$

2. If $u=(1,1)$, $v=(2,4)$, and $w=(3,-2)$, use the computer to evaluate:

   a) $u +2v-3$
   b) $|2v-3w|$ where $|x|$ denotes the absolute value of x
   c) $(u\bar{v}-v\bar{u})$ where $\bar{u}$ and $\bar{v}$ are the complex conjugates of u and v.

   d) $\dfrac{1}{2}\left(\dfrac{w+\bar{w}}{\bar{w}} - \dfrac{}{w}\right)$ where $\bar{w}$ is the complex conjugate of w

3. What is the last value assigned to each variable in the following sets of statements?

   a)   COMPLEX U/(1.,2.)/,V(3)/3*(1.,1.)/
           DO 1 I=1,3
              V(I) = V(I)+U*I
         1 CONTINUE

   b)   COMPLEX A,B,T/(1.,0.)/
           X = 2.
           Y = X*2
           A = CMPLX(X+AIMAG(T),Y)
           B = CMPLX(CABS(A),REAL(2*T))
           K = A+B

4. What is the error in each of the following?

   a) COMPLEX J/1/

   b) COMPLEX A,CSQRT
      A = CSQRT(3.,4.)

   c) COMPLEX B/(1.,0.)/
      J = B**2.

```
    d) COMPLEX AIMAG,U/(6.,8.)/,V,CMPLX
       V = CMPLX(CABS(U),AIMAG(U**2))

    e)        COMPLEX A,B
              READ,A,B
              .
    $ENTRY
       3.,4.        5.,6.
```

14.7 Extended Precision COMPLEX Values

In order to understand the material of this section, the reader should be familiar with the ideas in Chapter 13 (Extended Precision).

Since COMPLEX values are stored as a pair of REAL values and since the precision of REAL values can be increased to sixteen significant digits by doubling the amount of memory reserved to store each such value, it is only natural to permit the two components of a COMPLEX value to have Extended Precision (E.P.) values. This is done by declaring each E.P. COMPLEX variable to have a length of sixteen bytes. In this chapter, COMPLEX values in which the real and imaginary components are E.P. values will be called COMPLEX*16 values. The rules for defining, processing, reading and printing the real and imaginary components of a COMPLEX*16 value are those found in Chapter 13. A brief summary of the important points follows.

Constants

Each COMPLEX*16 constant is defined by a pair of E.P. constants enclosed in brackets. Examples are: (1.24D02, .0004D00), (123456789.,+123456.D-8).

A COMPLEX*16 value is also created (with a warning message) if one of the components is a REAL*4 value, for example (2.D00,5.) is a COMPLEX*16 constant.

Variables

Each of the following statements declares A to be a COMPLEX*16 variable with an initial value of (1.,0.), B as a "regular" COMPLEX variable, and C as a vector of COMPLEX*16 variables each having an initial value of zero.

```
COMPLEX*16 A/(1.D00,0.D00)/,B*8,C(10)/10*(0.D00,0.D00)/

COMPLEX*8 A*16/(1.D00,0.D00)/,B,C*16(10)/10*(0.D00,0.D00)/
```

COMPLEX A*16/(1.D00,0.D00)/,B,C*16(10)/10*(0.D00,0.D00)/

The points illustrated by these examples are:

    i) A length modifier of "*16" or "*8" may follow the word COMPLEX. If omitted, "*8" is assumed.

    ii) A length modifier of "*16" or "*8" may follow a variable or array name. If omitted, the length is taken from the length associated with the word COMPLEX.

    iii) Initial values (if present) must be of the same type as the variable(s) being initialized.

Expressions

When a COMPLEX*16 value is combined with other types of values in an arithmetic expression, the result is a COMPLEX*16 value. Some examples are:

Expression	Result
(3.52D00,2.0D00)+(1.,2.)	(4.52D00,4.D00)
(-1.D00,0.D00)-2.D0Q	(-3.D00,0.D00)
(4.D00,-1.D00)*2	(8.D00,-2.D00)
(20.D00,-1.D00)/2.	(10.D00,-.5D00)

A COMPLEX*16 value is also produced if an operation involves a REAL*8 value and a COMPLEX*8 value. For example, 2.D00*(3.,7.) has a value of (6.D00,14.D00).

Assignment Statements

There are two cases of interest.

    i) COMPLEX*16 variable = non-COMPLEX*16 value

    ii) non-COMPLEX*16 variable = COMPLEX*16 value

Consider Case (i). If the expression has a COMPLEX value, zeros are added to the right of the real and imaginary components to give each component sixteen significant digits. This value is then assigned to the COMPLEX*16 variable. If the expression is REAL (of either length) or an INTEGER value, the value of the expression is

assigned to the real component of the variable and the
imaginary component is set equal to zero.

Consider Case (ii). If the variable is COMPLEX, the real
and imaginary components of the value are truncated to seven
decimal digits. If the variable is REAL (of either length)
or INTEGER, the real component of the value is assigned to
the variable after any necessary truncation is performed.

Built-In Functions

Several built-in functions are available for processing
COMPLEX*16 values. In the following table, "c16" denotes a
COMPLEX*16 value and "r8" denotes an E.P. value.

Table of COMPLEX*16 Built-In Functions

Name and Arguments	Definition	Type of Result
CDSQRT (c16)	Square root	COMPLEX*16
CDSIN (c16)	Sine	COMPLEX*16
CDCOS (c16)	Cosine	COMPLEX*16
CDEXP (c16)	e**argument	COMPLEX*16
CDABS (c16)	Absolute value	REAL*8
DCMPLX (r8,r8)	forms a COMPLEX*16 value from two E.P. values	COMPLEX*16
DCONJG (c16)	complex conjugate	COMPLEX*16

Note that there are no built-in functions for extracting
the real and imaginary components of a COMPLEX*16 value. If
this is required, an EQUIVALENCE statement must be used to
overlay the COMPLEX*16 value with a pair of REAL*8
variables. An example is given in Chapter 17 (see
EQUIVALENCE).

Formatted Input-Output

A pair of D-masks, F-masks, or one of each can be used
to input or output C*16 values under format control.

Format-Free Input-Output

On input, each COMPLEX*16 value should be punched as a pair of E.P. constants, separated by a comma and enclosed in brackets. On output, the sequence of format codes used to print each COMPLEX*16 value is

'(',D28.16,' ,',D28.16,')'

Subprograms

Arguments and parameters may have COMPLEX*16 values. If a FUNCTION has a COMPLEX*16 value, then

i) The first statement of the FUNCTION subprogram must be
   COMPLEX FUNCTION name*16 (parameter list)

ii) The FUNCTION name must appear in a COMPLEX*16 declaration statement in the calling segment.

14.8 Other Statements Involving COMPLEX Values

1. COMPLEX variables may be used in statements such as COMMON, EQUIVALENCE, DIMENSION, etc. See Chapter 17 for details.

2. Subscript values may be COMPLEX. If so, the subscript value used is obtained by truncating the fractional part of the real component of the value.

3. G-masks can be used to input or output COMPLEX values. P-codes can be used to modify COMPLEX values which are input or output under one or more E-masks (D-masks if COMPLEX*16 values).

14.9 Summary

COMPLEX values can be used in WATFIV programs. Each COMPLEX value is stored as a pair of REAL values. Although the processing of complex numbers could be done using only REAL numbers and variables, the programming effort required is reduced if the COMPLEX values are used.

14.10 Programming Problems

The following ideas may be helpful in solving the problems which follow. A complex number (x,y) can represent a directed line segment (a vector) from the origin to the

point (x,y) in the xy plane. Two vectors having the same
length and direction but different initial points are
considered equal. Thus, in the diagram below, the vectors OP
and AB are considered equal.

14.1 One of the most famous equations ever discovered is

$$e^{i\pi} + 1 = 0$$

It involves five of the most fundamental quantities in
all of mathematics. Write a program to calculate the
value on the left hand side of the equation.

14.2 If several forces are acting on a body at rest, they
can be replaced by a single equivalent force. Suppose
each force is represented by a value (x,y) where the
magnitude of the force is given by the distance between
the origin and the point (x,y). The direction of the
force is represented by the angle between the x-axis and
the ray thru the origin and the point (x,y). Assume the
body upon which the forces are acting is at the origin.
The resultant force is simply the sum of the force
vectors. Write a program which reads a value of N and
then N pairs of REAL numbers representing the magnitude
and direction of the forces. Calculate the resultant
force and print its magnitude and direction.

14.3 In the following problem, use COMPLEX numbers to
represent the positions of the cat and dog. At time
zero, Fifi, the cat, is located at point (0,10) in the
xy plane. Fido, the dog, is at the origin. Fifi runs
parallel to the x-axis at a rate of 0.8 units per
second. Fido runs at a rate of 1 unit per second with
his head down in the direction of Fifi. At the end of
each second he lifts his head up, sees where Fifi is,
and runs in that direction during the next second. How
long, to the nearest second, does it take Fido to catch
Fifi? Print the positions of Fifi and Fido at one
second intervals during the chase.

14.4 A wooden equilateral triangle is used to hold balls on
a pool table. If the rack is positioned in the corner of

the pool table as shown in the following diagram, what is the distance X? Use any method you like to solve the problem.

14.5 The angle between a vector represented by the complex number (x,y) and the x-axis can be calculated from the following formula.

$$\cos^{-1}\left(\frac{x}{\sqrt{x^2 + y^2}}\right)$$

Write a FUNCTION subprogram called ANGLE to calculate this value. The subprogram will have only one parameter, a COMPLEX value.

14.6 Write a FUNCTION subprogram to calculate the angle between any two vectors. Use the subprogram written for problem five in the solution to the problem.

14.7 The dot (scalar) product of two complex numbers u and v is denoted by u•v and has a value of |u| |v| cos(x) where x is the angle between the vectors. The cross product of u and v has a value of |u| |v| sin(x). Write a pair of FUNCTION subprograms called DOT and CROSS to compute these values. Each will have two COMPLEX parameters. Two vectors in the xy plane are parallel if, and only if, their dot product is zero. They are perpendicular if, and only if, their cross product is zero. Write a mainline segment which reads the end coordinates of an unspecified number of pairs of vectors and for each, prints one of "PARALLEL", "PERPENDICULAR", or "OBLIQUE". Use the subprograms DOT and CROSS.

14.8 A man travels 24 miles northwest, 40 miles 35 degrees east of north and then 36 miles 20 degrees south of east. How far and in what direction is he from his starting point?

14.9 Write a FUNCTION subprogram called MEDIAN which has
      three COMPLEX variables A,B,C as its parameters where
      A,B and C represent the coordinates of the vertices of a
      triangle. The FUNCTION value should be the length of
      the median from the vertex A to the side BC.

CHAPTER 15   LOGICAL VALUES

Questions Answered In This Chapter

    1. What are LOGICAL values?

    2. How are LOGICAL values defined and used in WATFIV
       programs?

    Before studying the material in this chapter the reader
should be familiar with the ideas in Chapter 11.

15.1 LOGICAL Values

    In general, any statement is either true or false. For
example, "Two is less than three." is true; "August comes
before July." is false; "The point (3,4) lies outside the
circle $x^2+y^2=1$." is true, and so on. If one is writing a
program in which some of the variables have true-false
values it may be desirable to use LOGICAL variables,
constants and operators to represent and manipulate true-
false quantities. This chapter describes how.

15.2 LOGICAL Constants, Variables and Expressions

Constants

    There are only two LOGICAL constants. They are ".TRUE."
and ".FALSE.".   Each has a length of four (occupies four
bytes of memory).   Details of the bit patterns used to
represent the values of .TRUE. and .FALSE. can be found in
Appendix C.

Variables

    LOGICAL variables are those which can be assigned values
of .TRUE. and .FALSE.. A LOGICAL statement is used to define
LOGICAL variables and (optionally) specify initial values.
Consider the following two examples.

       i)   LOGICAL U,V/.TRUE./

      ii)   LOGICAL TF(80)/80*.FALSE./,X/F/,Y/T/

In example (i), the variables U and V are defined as LOGICAL
variables and V is given an initial value of .TRUE..   In
example (ii), TF is defined as a set of eighty LOGICAL
variables each of which has an initial value of .FALSE..

Furthermore, X and Y are simple LOGICAL variables with initial values of .FALSE. and .TRUE. respectively. Note that when specifying initial values for LOGICAL variables, it is sufficient to use "T" or "F" to indicate values of .TRUE. and .FALSE. respectively.

Expressions

The arithmetic operators are meaningless when applied to LOGICAL values. Dividing "true" by "false", for instance, is nonsense. There are three operators which do have meaning, however. They are ".AND.", ".OR.", and ".NOT.". They are called LOGICAL operators. The effect of each is as follows. "U.AND.V" is .TRUE. only if both U and V are individually .TRUE.. "U.OR.V" is .TRUE. if either or both of U and V is individually .TRUE.. Finally, ".NOT.U" is .TRUE. if U is .FALSE. and ".NOT.U" is .FALSE. if U is .TRUE.. That is, the operator .NOT. changes the "truth value" of the value on which it operates.

The priority of the LOGICAL operators (in the absence of brackets) is

.NOT.

.AND.

.OR.

Within each priority level the expression is evaluated left to right. For example,

.TRUE..OR..FALSE..AND..NOT..FALSE.

is evaluated as if written with the following sets of brackets.

.TRUE..OR.(.FALSE..AND.(.NOT..FALSE.))

By working from the innermost brackets outwards the expression is found to have a value of .TRUE.

LOGICAL operations are performed only after all other types of operations have been completed. This means that the complete set of priorities in evaluating WATFIV expressions is as follows.

1. Evaluation of functions

2. Brackets

3. Arithmetic operations (**, *, /, +, -)

4. Relational operations (.LE., .LT., .EQ., etc.)

5. Logical Operations (.NOT., .AND., .OR.)

"Truth Tables" can often be used to create a LOGICAL expression having desired properties. A Truth Table can also be used to evaluate a complex LOGICAL expression and perhaps replace it with a simpler but equivalent expression. For example, suppose A and B are LOGICAL variables. What is the value of "(A.OR.B).AND.(.NOT.(A.AND.B))"? The truth table for this expression is shown below.

Truth Table For (A.OR.B).AND.(.NOT.(A.AND.B))

A	B	C=(A.OR.B)	D=(.NOT.(A.AND.B))	C.AND.D
T	T	T	F	F
T	F	T	T	T
F	T	T	T	T
F	F	F	T	F

There are four rows in the table because there are four possible combinations of truth values of A and B. For each combination, columns three and four indicate the truth value of a part of the expression and column five indicates the overall value of the expression for the combination being evaluated. An expression which has the truth values indicated in the foregoing table is often called the "exclusive or" of A and B. That is, it is .TRUE. if exactly one but not both of A and B is .TRUE..

Two identities known as DeMorgan's Laws are frequently useful in writing LOGICAL expressions. These are:

.NOT.(A.AND.B)   =   (.NOT.A).OR.(.NOT.B)

.NOT.(A.OR.B)   =   (.NOT.A).AND.(.NOT.B)

15.3 Assignment Statements and Comparisons

Assignment Statements

A LOGICAL Assignment statement has the general form:

LOGICAL variable = LOGICAL value

The value on the right may be a LOGICAL constant, variable or expression.

Suppose U and V are LOGICAL variables and X and Y are REAL variables. Examples of LOGICAL Assignment statements are:

$$U = .NOT.V.OR..TRUE.$$

$$V = X.LE.Y$$

Note that the use of a relational operator produces a LOGICAL value.

Comparisons

Relational operators cannot be used to compare LOGICAL quantites. Instead, the LOGICAL operators are used in conjunction with an IF-THEN-ELSE construct or a Logical IF statement. Consider the following examples. Assume X and Y have LOGICAL values.

Requirement	Solution
Test X for a value of .TRUE.	IF(X) ...
Test X for a value of .FALSE.	IF(.NOT.X) ...
Test X and Y for equality	IF(X.AND.Y) ... IF(NOT.(X.OR.Y)) ...
Test X and Y for being different	IF(X.AND..NOT.Y) ... IF(Y.AND..NOT.X) ...

15.4 Built-In Functions

There are no LOGICAL built-in functions. If a particular LOGICAL expression is frequently required, a Statement Function may be useful in reducing programming time. Statement Functions having non-REAL and non-INTEGER values are discussed in Chapter 17. A SUBROUTINE or FUNCTION subprogram may also be useful in performing frequently required LOGICAL operations. Subprograms are discussed in Section 6.

15.5 Input-Output of LOGICAL Values

Formatted

An L-mask is used to input and output LOGICAL values under format control. Its general form is "Lw" where "w" denotes the number of card columns or print positions covered by the L-mask.

On input, the L columns covered by the mask are scanned left to right. The first occurence of a "T" or "F" results in the input variable being assigned a value of .TRUE. or .FALSE. respectively. If no "T" or "F" is found, the error message "IMPROPER CHARACTER SEQUENCE OR INVALID CHARACTER IN INPUT DATA" is generated.

On output, values of .TRUE. and .FALSE. are indicated by the appearance of "T" or "F" respectively in the rightmost print position reserved by the L-mask. As with other masks, any unused print positions are left unchanged.

The following program illustrates formatted input-output of LOGICAL values.

```
C FORMATTED I/O OF LOGICAL VALUES
      LOGICAL A,B,C
      READ 900,A,B,C
  900 FORMAT(3L4)
      PRINT 901,A,B,C
  901 FORMAT('1',L3,2L1)
      STOP
      END
$ENTRY
FLATHATSHALF
```

When this program is executed, The symbols "FTF" appear in print positions four thru six at the top of a page.

Format-Free

When reading LOGICAL values using a format-free READ
statement, successive data items are separated by a comma
and/or one or more blank card columns. The first "T" or "F"
encountered as the data item is scanned left to right
results in the input variable being assigned a value of
.TRUE. or .FALSE. respectively. If no "T" or "F" is found,
an error message is generated, as with formatted input. The
following example illustrates format-free input of LOGICAL
values.

```
            LOGICAL U,V,W,X
            READ,U,V,W,X
            ...
            ...
        $ENTRY
            .TRUE.  HALT, AFTER  .FALSE.
```

When the READ statement is executed, U and V are each
assigned a value of .TRUE. and W and X are assigned a value
of .FALSE..

In format-free output operations the mask used for each
LOGICAL value in the output list is "L8". This means a "T"
or "F" is printed in the rightmost print position of the
eight reserved by the mask. The symbols "UUUUUUUU" will be
printed for any LOGICAL variable which has not been assigned
a value. The symbols "   J" could also appear if a
logical variable had inadvertently been assigned a numeric
value. (Section 17.7 describes how this could happen.)

15.6 Subprograms

LOGICAL values may be used as arguments for a
subprogram. The corresponding parameter will normally be a
LOGICAL variable or an array. If a FUNCTION subprogram is to
have a LOGICAL value, the FUNCTION name must be declared as
being LOGICAL in the calling segment. The first statement of
the subprogram will have the general form

            LOGICAL FUNCTION name (parameter list)

Alternatively, the first statement of the subprogram can
begin with the word FUNCTION provided that the function name
is declared as having the type LOGICAL in a type declaration
statment within the subprogram.

The following subprogram could be used to determine if a
point with coordinates (A,B) lies inside the circle $x^2+y^2=1$.

```
      LOGICAL CIRCLE,S          LOGICAL FUNCTION CIRCLE(X,Y)
      READ,A,B                  Z=SQRT(X*X+Y*Y)
      S=CIRCLE(A,B)             CIRCLE=Z.LE.1.
      IF(S)PRINT,'INSIDE'       RETURN
      IF(.NOT.S)PRINT,'OUTSIDE' END
      STOP
      END
```

15.7 LOGICAL*1 Variables

Each LOGICAL variable has a default length of four. If a large number of LOGICAL variables are used in a program, a considerble saving in memory space can be achieved by specifying that some or all of the LOGICAL variables are to have a length of one. This is done in the same way that optional lengths are specified for REAL and INTEGER variables.

The following three statements are equivalent. Each specifies that that U and V are LOGICAL variables of length one and that X is an array of twenty LOGICAL variables of length four. Initial values are provided for U and X.

   i)   LOGICAL U*1/.TRUE./,V*1,X(20)/20*F/

   ii)   LOGICAL*1 U/.TRUE./,V,X*4(20)/20*F/

   iii) LOGICAL*4 U*1/.TRUE./,V*1,X(20)/20*F/

The points illustrated by these statements are:

   i) A length modifier of "*1" or "*4" may follow the word LOGICAL. If omitted, "*4" is assumed.

   ii) A length modifier of "*1" or "*4" may follow a variable or array name. If omitted, the length of the variable is that associated with the word LOGICAL.

   iii) Initial values may be specified for LOGICAL variables. They can be any of: ".TRUE.", ".FALSE.", "T", or "F".

The LOGICAL constants .TRUE. and .FALSE. have a length of four.

LOGICAL*1 variables can be used anywhere that LOGICAL variables are used. An operation involving a LOGICAL*1 value and a LOGICAL*4 value has a result of length four.

Exercise 15.1

1. For each of the following, determine the last value
   assigned to every variable used in the sequence.

   a)   LOGICAL U/.TRUE./, V/.FALSE./, T, Z
          T=U.AND..NOT.V
          IF(U.AND.T) Z=V.OR.T

   b)   LOGICAL U,V,W,X,F/F/
          U=V=F
          W=.NOT.U.OR.V.OR..NOT.F
          IF(.NOT.F.OR.U.AND..NOT.W) X=.TRUE.

   c)   LOGICAL T/F/,F/T/,TF,Z   LOGICAL FUNCTION TF(T,F)
          I=A=2.7   LOGICAL T,F
          B=I**(-1)   TF=.NOT.T.OR.F
          Z=TF(T,F)   F=T
          IF(A*B.EQ.1) Z=TF(F,T)   T=F
          STOP   RETURN
          END   END

   d)   LOGICAL TRUE/F/,FALSE/T/,AND,OR,NOT
          AND(OR,NOT)=.NOT.NOT.AND.OR.OR.TRUE.
          OR(NOT)=AND(NOT,NOT).OR.NOT
          FALSE=OR(.NOT.TRUE).AND.AND(FALSE,TRUE)

2. For each of the following LOGICAL expressions, write
   another LOGICAL expression which will have the opposite
   truth value regardless of the values of the variables
   appearing in the expression.

   a)   .NOT.A
   b)   3.GE.X
   c)   B.LT.C.OR.C.GT.D
   d)   .NOT.B.AND.NOT.C
   e)   .NOT.(A.AND.B).AND.A.OR.B
   f)   3..EQ.X.AND..NOT.X.NE.Y.OR.Z

3. a) Construct a truth table for the expression below.

      A.AND.B.AND..NOT.C.OR.B.AND.C.AND..NOT.A

   b) Use the truth table to assist in writing a simpler
      expression which is equivalent to the one given.

4. The truth table below has eight rows.   Each row
   represents   one   of   the   eight possible different
   combinations of truth values of A, B, and C.   The five
   remaining columns are labelled (a), (b), (c),   (d), and

(e).   For each of (a) thru (e),   write a LOGICAL
expression which   would give the   truth values   shown in
that column   for all   the corresponding   combinations of
values of A, B,   and C.   Five different expressions are
required.

A	B	C	(a)	(b)	(c)	(d)	(e)
T	T	T	F	T	F	F	T
T	T	F	F	F	T	T	F
T	F	T	F	F	F	T	F
T	F	F	F	F	T	F	T
F	T	T	F	T	T	T	T
F	T	F	T	F	T	F	F
F	F	T	F	F	T	F	F
F	F	F	F	F	T	F	F

15.8 Summary

   LOGICAL operations (those involving the manipulation of
true-false quantities)   can be performed in a meaningful way
by using LOGICAL   constants and   variables in   a program.
Using LOGICAL values   instead of the INTEGER   values of zero
and one   offers several advantages   the most   significant of
which is ease of understanding the program logic.

15.9 Programming Problems

15.1 Consider   the two circles defined by the pair of
     equations $x^2+y^2=9$ and $(x-2)^2+(y-4)^2=16$.   Write a program
     which reads values   of x and y   and prints a "T" if the
     point (x,y) lies inside both circles and "F" otherwise.
     Test the program on the following points: $(1,1)$, $(1,-1)$,
     $(2,-.5)$, $(0,1)$, $(0,-2.5)$.

15.2 Suppose each student's answers to a true-false test of
     ten questions have been punched on cards.   On   each
     student card, columns one to six contain the student's
     ID number; columns seven to ten are blank and columns
     eleven thru twenty contain "T's" and "F's" indicating
     the student's answers. Assume twelve students took the
     test.   Preceeding the first student card is a card
     containing the correct answers. This answer card has an
     ID number of zeros and the correct answers in columns
     eleven thru twenty. Write a program which:

a) Lists each student's answers and calculates the percentage of right answers.
b) Calculates the average mark on the test.
c) Prints the percentage of right answers for each question.
d) Determines how many students answered both of questions 3 and 7 correctly.
e) Determines those questions for which the students in the bottom half of the class did as well as students in the top half of the class.

The foregoing problem should be solved making the assumption that each student answered all questions. Suppose now that a blank in an answer column means that the student did not answer the question. Explain why this makes the programming problem more difficult. Can you solve the problem with this new assumption?

15.3 The game of Tic-Tac-Toe is well known. Suppose the elements of a three-by-three matrix called BOARD contain values of -1, 1, or 0 where: -1 indicates Player One has chosen the square; +1 indicates Player Two has chosen the square; 0 indicates neither player has chosen the square. Write a program which reads values for BOARD and prints one of "PLAYER ONE WINS", "PLAYER TWO WINS", or "UNDECIDED".

15.4 On the island of Ho, there are two races -- the Good Guys who always tell the truth, and the Bad Guys who always lie. On my last visit to the island, I met three villagers named Tom, Dick and Zack. I asked each of them one question. Their answers are shown in brackets.

Q: Tell me Tom, is Dick a Good Guy? (yes)
Q: Dick, do Tom and Zack belong to the same race? (no)
Q: Zack, what about Dick, is he a Good Guy? (yes)

Write a program to determine the races of the three villagers. To solve this problem, generate the eight possible combinations of race-to-people assignments using three DO-loops. Check each combination to see if they would answer the questions in the manner described. This can be done using as few as three IF statements. Remember that the computer cannot think or reason and you must find the implications of each answer under the assumption that the speaker was first of all, a Good Guy, and secondly, a Bad Guy. The results of this analysis will permit you construct the appropriate IF statements.

CHAPTER 16   CHARACTER VALUES

Questions Answered In This Chapter

1. What are CHARACTER values?

2. How are CHARACTER values defined and used in WATFIV programs?

3. How can one define and use non-standard symbols in WATFIV programs?

4. What methods are available for manipulating the patterns of ones and zeros used to represent values of variables used in a WATFIV program?

Before studying the material of this chapter, the reader should be familiar with the ideas presented in Chapter 11.

16.1 CHARACTER Values

Strings of symbols can be defined and manipulated in WATFIV programs. You and I regard "1234" as both a number on which arithmetic operations can be performed and as a string of four symbols. In WATFIV, a distinction is made. If "1234" is to be treated as a number, it will appear in a REAL or INTEGER expression. If the symbols are of interest, it must be defined as a CHARACTER value.

What symbols can be used in CHARACTER values? The standard set of CHARACTER values in WATFIV consists of the following forty-eight symbols.

letters: ABCDEFGHIJKLMNOPQRSTUVWXYZ

digits: 0123456789

special symbols: +-*/,.'()=$ blank

What of the other symbols which appear on a keypunch? Can they be defined, input and/or output under control of a WATFIV program? The answer is yes -- and in fact, many other symbols which do not appear on a keypunch can often be used. Section 16.12 describes how.

16.2 Constants, Variables, and Expressions

Constants

A CHARACTER constant consists of a string of symbols enclosed in single quotes. Examples are: 'FEBRUARY 8, 1942', 'K96', and 'AVERAGE='. The length of a CHARACTER constant is simply the number of symbols (including blanks) between the quote signs. The maximum number of symbols permitted in a CHARACTER constant is 255. One byte of memory is used to store each symbol in the constant. Hence the length of a CHARACTER constant is the number of symbols it contains. This means that four symbols can be stored in the amount of memory used to store each REAL or INTEGER value. If a quote sign is one of the symbols in the constant, a pair of successive quote signs is used to indicate this fact to the compiler. For example, the CHARACTER constant "IT'S" is defined as 'IT''S'. The length of 'IT''S' is four, however, since the second quote of any successive pair is not stored in the computer's memory.

Variables

Variables which take on CHARACTER values can be defined and assigned initial values. Unless declared otherwise, each CHARACTER value has a length of one. That is, each CHARACTER variable is capable of storing only one symbol. If more than one symbol must be stored in a CHARACTER variable, the compiler must be informed of this fact as illustrated in the following examples.

  i) CHARACTER A,B*2

 ii) CHARACTER*4 TUF, BAKER*2,LENGTH*6/'LENGTH'/

iii) CHARACTER MONTH*4(4)/'JAN.','FEB.','MAR.','APR.'/

 iv) CHARACTER*3 X/'A'/,Y/'ABCDE'/

In example (i), the variable A is defined as a CHARACTER variable of length one (one is the default length). Because a length modifier of "*2" follows the variable name B, B is a CHARACTER variable of length two (capable of storing two symbols).

In example (ii), a length modifier of "*4" has been appended to the word CHARACTER. This means that all variables appearing in the list will have a length of four unless declared otherwise. In particular, BAKER has a

length of two and LENGTH a length of six with an initial
value of 'LENGTH'.

In example (iii),   MONTH is declared as being a set of
four CHARACTER variables, each of length four. The values of
the elements of MONTH are initialized to the abbreviations
of the first four months of the year.

In example (iv),   X and Y are defined as CHARACTER
variables, each of length three.   Since the initial value
assigned to X has only one symbol, two blanks are added to
the right of the constant 'A' to give the initializing
constant a length of three.   Thus the initial value of X is
'A '.   Since the initial value for Y has more than three
symbols, two of the symbols must be truncated. O.K. -- which
ones? In an assignment operation, the rightmost symbols are
truncated. Thus the initial value for Y is 'ABC'.

The points illustrated by these examples are:

i) A length modifier of "*1" thru "*255" may follow
   the word CHARACTER. If omitted, a length of one is
   assumed.

ii) A length modifier of "*1" thru "*255" may follow a
    variable or array name. If omitted, the length of
    the variable is taken from the length associated
    with the word CHARACTER.

iii) Initial   values may be   assigned to CHARACTER
     variables.   Initializing   constants which   are
     shorter than the length of the variable are padded
     on the right with blanks.   Initializing constants
     which have too many symbols are truncated beginning
     with the rightmost symbol. A warning message is
     printed in this latter case.

Expressions

There are no operators for manipulating CHARACTER
values.   It is meaningless, for instance, to multiply
'SEPTEMBER' by 'HAMBURGER'.

16.3 Comparison of CHARACTER Values

In some programs it may be necessary to compare one or
more strings of symbols. For example, if X and Y are
CHARACTER variables of length ten, the statement

        IF(X.EQ.Y) ...

could be used to test the strings for equality. If two
CHARACTER values of different lengths are compared, blanks
are added to the right of the shorter value before the
comparison is made. This means the values 'A' and 'A ' are
considered equal if they are compared using a relational
operator.

The other five relational operators can also be used to
compare CHARACTER values. For example, the following
expressions are all true.

        'A'.LT.'B'   '2'.LT.'9'

        'A'.LE.'B'   '9'.GE.'2'

        'C'.NE.'4'   ')'.GT.'('

The "dictionary" order of the standard set of forty-eight
WATFIV symbols is as follows.

    blank .(+$*)-/,'= A thru Z   0 thru 9

This means that: any letter is "less than" any number; any
special character is "less than" any letter and hence "less
than" any number, etc. The sequence of symbols above is
often called the "collating sequence of CHARACTER values of
length one". If strings of length two or longer are
compared, the comparison proceeds left to right as you would
expect. Thus, since "." is less than "-", '.A93' is less
than '-A93'. The constant '*Z)K' is greater than '*A)K',
etc.. If the strings being compared have different lengths,
the shorter string is padded on the right with blanks before
the comparison is made. For example, '/Z3' is greater than
'/Z' since '3' is greater than a blank.

16.4 CHARACTER Assignment Statements

A CHARACTER Assignment statement has the form

    CHARACTER variable = CHARACTER value

The value on the right may be a CHARACTER constant or a
CHARACTER variable. No problem arises if the variable on the
left and the value on the right have the same length. If
the lengths are different, we need an apt reminder of what
happens. Here it is.

In the word "APT", the letters "P" (for padding) and "T" (for truncation) appear to the right of the letter "A" (for Assignment).

To illustrate the use of the APT rule, suppose the variable "CHAR" has a length of three. Consider the three statements:

i) CHAR='ABC'   ii) CHAR='A'   iii) CHAR='ABCDEF'

In (i), CHAR is given the value 'ABC'. In (ii), the value of 'A' must be padded with two blanks to give it a length of three. Using the APT rule, padding occurs on the right. Thus CHAR is given the value 'A '. In (iii), three symbols must be truncated. The APT rule says truncate on the right. Thus CHAR is assigned the value 'ABC'. Note that the APT rule also describes how initial values are assigned to CHARACTER variables at compile time. Extended Assignment statements for CHARACTER variables are not allowed.

16.5 Built-In Functions

There are no built-in functions for manipulating CHARACTER values in WATFIV. Most computing centers however, have a library of SUBROUTINES for manipulating and analyzing CHARACTER values. Routines for determining the length of a string, the positions of a set of symbols within a string, or creating a long string from a pair of shorter strings, are often available.

16.6 Input-Output of CHARACTER Values

Formatted Input-Output

An A-mask is used to input or output CHARACTER values under format control. The general form of an A-mask is "Aw" where "w" denotes the number of card columns or print positions covered by the mask. Suppose X is a CHARACTER

variable of length three. The following table shows the
results when different A-masks are used to input a value of
X under format control.

Mask	Symbols In Columns Covered By Mask	Value Assigned To X (length 3)
A3	PQR	'PQR'
A1	P	'P '
A6	PQRSTU	'STU'

How about a tip to help remember where padding and
truncation occur during input operations? Here it is.

In words, the TIP rule says: "On an input operation, if the
mask covers fewer columns than the length of the variable,
padding occurs (blanks are added) on the right. If the mask
covers more columns than the length of the variable,
truncation occurs beginning with the leftmost symbol covered
by the mask.".

For formatted output operations,   the word "POT" should
be remembered. That is,

To illustrate the POT rule, consider the following pair of statements.

```
        PRINT 999,'ABC','DEF','GHI'
    999 FORMAT ('1',A3,A5,A1)
```

The effect is to print the symbols

```
    ABC  DEFG
```

```
    A3  A5  A1
```

at the top of a page. Note that on output, padding occurs on the left and truncation occurs on the right. This is just the opposite of the padding-truncation effect on input.

Format-Free Input-Output

CHARACTER variables may appear in an input list used with a format-free READ statement. The data values to be assigned to the variables must be punched as CHARACTER constants and separated by a comma and/or one or more blank columns. When using format-free input for CHARACTER variables, the TIP rule describes where padding and truncation occur.

In format-free output operations, WATFIV assigns a mask of "Aw" to each CHARACTER value in the output list. The value of "w" used is one more than the length of the value being printed. Because of the POT rule, a blank appears to the left of the leftmost symbol in the value. The following example program illustrates format-free input and output of CHARACTER values.

```
        CHARACTER*4 X,Y,Z
        READ,X,Y,Z
        PRINT,X,Y,Z
        STOP
        END
    $ENTRY
    'ABCD',   'EF'   'GHIJKL'
```

When the program is executed, the values assigned to the variables, and hence the values printed are: X='ABCD', Y='EF ', Z='IJKL'.

16.7 Subprograms

CHARACTER values may be used as arguments for a subprogram. The corresponding parameter will normally be a CHARACTER variable or array having the same properties. If the argument is an array, the parameter array should be of the same length or shorter than the argument array. Rules of correspondence are the same as those for other types of values.

Suppose a sequence of symbols is read from a card and it is desired to know if the symbols "THE" appear. The following FUNCTION subprogram could be used to indicate the last card column in which the first symbol of "THE" appears. A FUNCTION value of zero means "THE" does not appear.

```
C  EXAMPLE 16.1                 INTEGER FUNCTION TEST(X)
       INTEGER TEST             CHARACTER X(80)
       CHARACTER COL(80)        TEST=0
       READ 99,COL              DO 1 N=1,78
   99  FORMAT(80A1)                IF(X(N).EQ.'T' .AND.
       PRINT,TEST(COL)       *       X(N+1).EQ.'H' .AND.
       STOP                  *       X(N+2).EQ.'E') TEST=N
       END                    1 CONTINUE
                                RETURN
                                END
```

Does this program determine which card column contains the last occurence of the beginning of the word "THE"? If you think so, suppose the mainline read a card containing the words "GATHER THERE TO BATHE". What would the output be?

Note that any arguments and parameters which take on CHARACTER values must be defined with an appropriate length in the segment in which they are used.

CHARACTER valued FUNCTION subprograms are not permitted in WATFIV. A statement such as

        CHARACTER FUNCTION INDEX*3(A,B)

will result in a compile time error.

One feature which can be used to great advantage is the following. If an argument is a simple CHARACTER value, the corresponding parameter can be an array provided the total length of the parameter array does not exceed the length of the argument value. For example, if X is a CHARACTER variable of length ten then the following program structure is permissible.

```
      CHARACTER*10 X            SUBROUTINE LOOK(STRING,N)
      READ,X                    CHARACTER STRING(N)
      ...                       ...
      CALL LOOK(X,10)           ...
      ...                       ...
      END                       END
```

The advantage of passing a CHARACTER variable to a parameter array is that the subprogram can be used to analyze the individual symbols stored in the variable.

16.8 Two Example Programs

Example 1

The following program could be used to print whatever is punched in a deck of data cards.

```
      C EXAMPLE 16.2 PRINT DATA DECK
            CHARACTER*80 CARD
      C     READ LOOP
          1 READ(5,2,END=4) CARD
          2    FORMAT(A80)
               PRINT 3, CARD
          3    FORMAT(' ',A80)
               GO TO 1
          4 STOP
            END
      $ENTRY
```

The foregoing program is sometimes called an "80-80 List". That is, eighty columns of each card are read and the symbols in all eighty columns are printed.

Example 2

Suppose a sentence has been punched on a card. The problem is to count the number of words of length 1,2,3,...,15 in the sentence. The method used in the following program is simply to determine the locations of blank card columns. The length of the word between the blanks is then one less than the difference of the positions of the blanks.

```
C EXAMPLE 16.3 WORD LENGTHS
      CHARACTER COLUMN(80),BLANK/' '/
      INTEGER LENGTH(15)/15*0/,POS1/0/,DIFF
      READ 900,COLUMN
  900 FORMAT(80A1)
C
      DO 20 I=1,80
         IF(COLUMN(I).EQ.BLANK) THEN
            DIFF=I-POS1
            IF(DIFF.GT.1) THEN
               LENGTH(DIFF-1)=LENGTH(DIFF-1)+1
            END IF
            POS1=I
         END IF
   20 CONTINUE
C
C     CHECK TO SEE IF COLUMN 80 IS BLANK
C     IF SO, TAKE CARE OF LAST WORD
      IF(POS1.NE.80) THEN
         LENGTH(81-POS1)=LENGTH(81-POS1)+1
      END IF
C
      PRINT 901,'COUNT OF WORDS AND THEIR LENGTHS'
     *          ,'LENGTH','COUNT'
  901 FORMAT('1',A32,/,5X,A6,5X,A5)
      PRINT 902,(I,LENGTH(I),I=1,15)
  902 FORMAT('0',I10,5X,I5)
      STOP
      END
```

16.9 Storing Format Codes In CHARACTER Arrays

Aside from a statement number and the word "FORMAT", a FORMAT statement contains a string of codes enclosed in brackets. In WATFIV, the brackets and the codes enclosed by them can be stored in the first element of a CHARACTER array and subsequently referenced by formatted READ, WRITE or PRINT statements. Consider the following example.

```
C EXAMPLE 16.4 FORMAT CODES AS CHARACTER VALUES
      CHARACTER*9 FMT(1)/'(I4,F7.2)'/
      J=301
      X=1.75
      PRINT FMT,J,X
      STOP
      END
```

In this example, the array name "FMT" follows the word
"PRINT". This means that the formatting information is to be
found in the first element of the array "FMT".
Consequently, the PRINT statement in this example produces
output which is identical to that which would be obtained
using the following pair of statements.

```
            PRINT 999,J,X
        999 FORMAT(I4,F7.2)
```

The statement "WRITE(6,FMT) J,X" could have been used
instead of the the PRINT statement shown.

   The rules for storing and using format codes assigned to
CHARACTER variables are as follows.

   i) The format codes stored in a CHARACTER variable must
      begin with a left bracket and end with a right
      bracket.

   ii) The CHARACTER variable containing the start of the
       codes to be used must be the first element of an
       array.

   iii) In a formatted input or output statement, the
        statement number of a FORMAT statement may be
        replaced by the name of an array containing the
        codes. The codes are assumed to be found starting
        in the first element of the array.

   Why must the codes be stored in an array element? Why
not a simple CHARACTER variable? The reason in that some
Fortran languages do not allow CHARACTER variables. Instead,
CHARACTER values, and hence format codes, must be stored in
an INTEGER, REAL or some other type of array. To be
consistent across all types of variables, the rule is that
codes must be stored in an array. Further details can be
found in Chapter 17, Section 12.

   Why store format codes in a CHARACTER array instead of
using a FORMAT statement? Because CHARACTER values can be
read from a card, this means that different format
information can be made available at execution time. For
example, the following program structure reads in format
information for a report heading which it then passes to a
subprogram called report.

```
      C EXAMPLE 16.5 EXECUTION TIME FORMAT CODES
            CHARACTER*33 HEADER(1)
            READ 2, HEADER
          2 FORMAT(A33)
            ...
            CALL REPORT(HEADER,...)
            ..
            END

            SUBROUTINE REPORT(LINE1,...)
            ...
            PRINT LINE1
            ...
            END
      $ENTRY
      ('1SPECIAL REPORT FOR J.B.SMITH')
```

A second situation in which storing format codes as CHARACTER values may be useful is found in the following example. Suppose several numbers from one thru six are punched as INTEGER values, one per card. The problem is simply to read in each value and print a "*" in the print position specified by the number on the card. The following program could be used.

```
      C EXAMPLE 16.6 FORMAT CODE SELECTION
            CHARACTER*4 FMT(6)/'(A2)','(A3)','(A4)',
          * '(A5)','(A6)','(A7)'/,CODES(1)
      C     READ LOOP
          1 READ(5,*,END=2) N
                CODES(1)=FMT(N)
                PRINT CODES,'*'
            GO TO 1
          2 STOP
            END
```

The reason for using the array CODES in the foregoing program is to satisfy the requirement that the start of the format codes must be in the first element of an array.

Suppose now that INTEGER values of one thru one-hundred were permitted for the foregoing problem. Using the approach found in the example would mean that one-hundred different codes of the type '(An)' would have to be defined, simply because we have no way (as yet) of making the value of "w" in a mask such as "Aw" a variable quantity. It would be nice, for instance, to use a sequence of statements such as the following.

```
      READ,N
      PRINT 1,'*'
    1 FORMAT (A (N+1))
```

In order to do something like this, it is necessary to convert the value of N from an INTEGER value to a CHARACTER value. The method for doing this is described in detail in Chapter 21.

Exercise 16.1

1. If the following sequence of statements is executed, what is the last value assigned to each variable?

```
      CHARACTER*3 X/'AC'/,Y/'DE'/,U*2,W*4/'ACDE'/
      U=X
      IF (U.EQ.X) Y=X
      IF (U.EQ.W) W=X
      IF (Y.NE.X) Y=X
```

2. Suppose an array T has been defined by

```
      CHARACTER*3 T (5)
```

Suppose the symbol "A" is punched in the even numbered columns of a card and the symbol "B" is punched in the odd numbered columns of the same card. What is printed in each of the following cases.

```
a)      READ 900,T                b)        READ 900,T
    900 FORMAT (5A2)                  900 FORMAT (5A2)
        PRINT 901,T                       PRINT 902,T
    901 FORMAT ('1',5A1)              902 FORMAT ('1',5A4)


c)      READ 903,T                d)        READ 903,T
    903 FORMAT (5A4)                  903 FORMAT (5A4)
        PRINT 904,T                       PRINT 905,T
    904 FORMAT ('1',5A1)              905 FORMAT ('1',5A4)
```

3. What is the error in each of the following?

```
a)      CHARACTER X*3/ABC/

b)      CHARACTER SET*256 (5) /5*' '/

c)      CHARACTER U*3/'111'/,V*3/'222'/
        IF(U+V.EQ.'333') STOP
```

```
   d)      CHARACTER W (5),S (5)
           READ,W
           S=W
           PRINT,S

   e)      CHARACTER*2 R/'3.3E02'/
           S=3.3E02
           PRINT 9,S,R
        9 FORMAT('0',2E10.3)

   f)      CHARACTER*10 A              SUBROUTINE OHOH (X)
           CALL OHOH (A)              CHARACTER X (10)
           PRINT,A                    IF (X.EQ.' ') RETURN
           STOP                       RETURN
           END                        END

   g)      CHARACTER U,F              CHARACTER FUNCTION F(T)
           READ,U                     CHARACTER T
           PRINT,F (U)                IF (T.EQ.'X') F=' '
           STOP                       F=T
           END                        RETURN
                                      END
```

4. Where are the APT, TIP and POT rules applied?

5. A synonym for "CHARACTER constant" is "literal". To print a CHARACTER constant, the value of the constant can appear as an item in an output list or as a literal in a FORMAT statement. Does one method have any advantages over the other?

6. Suppose the following sequence of statements appears in a program.

```
        CHARACTER*4 CYEAR
        READ 900,CYEAR,IYEAR,YEAR
    900 FORMAT(A4,T1,I4,T1,F4.0)
```

What is achieved during the input operation?

7. Suppose CHARACTER values are read from a card using a format-free READ statement. (a)   What is the maximum number of data values which can be punched on a single card?   (b) If each value in the input list has a length of three, what is the maximum number which can be punched on a card?

8. Suppose an unknown number of INTEGER values have been punched on a card. The values are separated by commas. It is necessary to know how many values have been

punched on the card. Explain why this problem cannot be
solved easily using our present knowledge. (A suitable
technique is described in Chapter 21.)

16.10 Hexadecimal Values

Occasionally, a WATFIV programmer wants to "get at the
bits". That is, he may want to do one or more of the
following.

    i) Assign a particular bit pattern to a variable.

    ii) Print out the bit pattern of a variable.

    iii) Manipulate the individual bits of a value.

Bit assignment and display are described in this section.
Bit manipulation is described in Section 16.11.

A byte consists of eight bits. In WATFIV, if one wishes
to assign a bit pattern or print a bit pattern stored in one
or more bytes of memory, it can be done by working with
groups of four bits at a time. A group of four bits is
called a hexadecimal value. The term hexadecimal is used
since there are sixteen possible patterns of four bits. The
sixteen patterns and the hexadecimal symbol used to identify
each is found in the following table.

Bit Pattern	Hexadecimal Value	Bit Pattern	Hexadecimal Value
0 0 0 0	0	1 0 0 0	8
0 0 0 1	1	1 0 0 1	9
0 0 1 0	2	1 0 1 0	A
0 0 1 1	3	1 0 1 1	B
0 1 0 0	4	1 1 0 0	C
0 1 0 1	5	1 1 0 1	D
0 1 1 0	6	1 1 1 0	E
0 1 1 1	7	1 1 1 1	F

The following table shows some bit patterns and how to decribe them using hexadecimal symbols.

Bit Pattern	Length (in bytes)	Hexadecimal Representation
00001111	1	0F
10101100	1	AC
0011001100110011	2	3333
1111000111000011	2	F1C3

Note that two hexadecimal digits are required to describe the bit pattern of one byte.

The use of hexadecimal values in WATFIV programs is restricted to the following four situations.

   i) Compile time initialization of variables

  ii) Formatted input operations

 iii) Format-free input operations

  iv) Formatted output operations

Compile Time-Initialization

Suppose a CHARACTER variable K of length two is to be assigned the bit pattern shown below.

Bits   0101 1001 1101 0000

Hexadecimal   5   9   D   0

A statement to achieve this result is

        CHARACTER*2 K/Z59D0/

Note that the initializing constant is preceded by the letter "Z".   Since two hexadecimal digits are required to represent the bit pattern of one byte, the initializing constant must have four hexadecimal symbols.   If fewer symbols are provided than necessary, hexadecimal zeros are added on the left. If the initializing constant contains a surplus of symbols, the leftmost symbols are truncated and a warning message is printed. For example, the following pair of statements are equivalent.

```
          INTEGER A/ZABCD/,B/Z12345678AB/

          INTEGER A/Z0000ABCD/,B/Z345678AB/
```

Formatted Input-Output (The Z-mask)

The general form of the Z-mask is "Zw" where "w" denotes the number of card columns or print positions covered by the mask. The following example illustrates the use of Z-masks.

```
     C EXAMPLE 16.7 HEXADECIMAL INPUT-OUTPUT
          READ 1,A,B,C
        1 FORMAT(Z8,Z5,Z11)
          PRINT 2,A,A,A
        2 FORMAT('1',Z8,Z5,Z11)
          STOP
          END
     $ENTRY
     123456789ABCDEF0 12345678
     ‿‿‿‿‿‿‿  ‿‿‿‿‿  ‿‿‿‿‿‿‿

        Z8       Z5       Z11
```

Since A, B, and C are REAL variables, each has a length of four bytes. Since each hexadecimal digit represents the bit pattern of one-half byte (four bits), eight hexadecimal symbols are required to define the bit pattern for a REAL (or INTEGER) value. In the example, the READ statement causes A, B and C to have the following hexadecimal values.

    A: 12345678,   B: 0009ABCD,   C: 12345678

The value of A printed with the three Z-masks produces:

```
     1234567845678bbb12345678
     ‿‿‿‿‿‿‿ ‿‿‿‿‿ ‿‿‿‿‿‿‿

        Z8       Z5       Z11
```

Format-Free Input

Hexadecimal values can be read using a format-free READ statement. Consider the following example.

```
          READ,A,I,K
          ...
     $ENTRY
       Z12345678, Z12    Z123456789
```

When the data card is read, the hexadecimal values are:

    A: 12345678,   I: 00000012,   K: 23456789

Padding and truncation of hexadecimal values occurs on the left for initialization, input, and output.

16.11 Bit Assignment And Manipulation

Bit Assignment

By using the hexadecimal features available in WATFIV, any desired bit pattern can be assigned to a variable of any type and the bit pattern of any value can be displayed on the printer using a Z-mask. In what follows, two types of bit manipulation operations will be discussed. These are single bit manipulation and bit shifting operations.

Single Bit Manipulation

Since a bit has one of two values -- zero or one, we can: turn a bit "off" (set it equal to zero); turn a bit "on" (set it equal to one); "flip" a bit (set it equal to zero if one, and to one if zero); test a bit to see if it has a particular value. To perform operations of the type suggested above, the built-in functions "AND", "OR", "EOR" and "COMPL" can be used. Each has a REAL value.

These functions are very similar to the LOGICAL operators ".AND.", ".OR.", and ".NOT." which were discussed in Chapter 15. The essential difference is that the LOGICAL operators work with the LOGICAL values .TRUE. and .FALSE. whereas the functions AND, OR, COMPL and EOR work with bit patterns of REAL values. The correspondences appear in the following table.

Usual Name Given	LOGICAL Operator	Bit Function (X&Y are 32 bits each)	Value of ith Bit In The Result
and	X.AND.Y	AND(X,Y)	1 if X_i and Y_i are 1
or	X.OR.Y	OR(X,Y)	1 if X_i or Y_i is 1
not	.NOT.X	COMPL(X)	1 if X_i is 0, 0 if X_i is 1
exclusive or	(X.OR.Y).AND. .NOT.(X.AND.Y)	EOR(X,Y)	1 if $X_i \neq Y_i$

Note when using these functions that: (i) any type of argument can be used provided it has a length of four bytes; (ii) The function value is REAL. If it is desired to use any of the functions AND, OR, COMPL, or EOR as an INTEGER value, an EQUIVALENCE statement should be used as is illustrated in the following program.

```
C EXAMPLE 16.8 USE OF THE FUNCTION "AND"
        EQUIVALENCE (J,X)
        X=AND(243,-571)
        PRINT,J
        STOP
        END
```

The statement "J=AND(243,-571)" could not be used since it would drastically alter the bit pattern of the function value in converting it from a REAL to an INTEGER value.

Examples Of Bit Manipulations

a) Turn the ith bit off. Solution: AND the value with a second value which has a zero in the ith position and ones elsewhere. For example, to turn the leftmost bit off and leave the others unchanged --

```
        REAL OFFLEF/Z7FFFFFFF/
        READ,A
        A=AND(A,OFFLEF)
        ...
```

b) Turn the ith bit on. Solution: OR the value with a second value which has a one in the ith position and zeros elsewhere. For example, to turn the rightmost bit on and leave the others unchanged --

```
        REAL ONRITE/Z00000001/
        READ,A
        A=OR(A,ONRITE)
        ...
```

c) Flip (change) the value of the ith bit. Solution: EOR the value with a second value which has a one in the ith position and zeros elsewhere. For example, to flip the value of the second leftmost bit --

```
        REAL SECOND/Z40000000/
        READ,A
        A=EOR(A,SECOND)
        ...
```

d) Extract the value of the ith bit. Solution: AND the
value with a second value having a one in the ith
position and zeros elsewhere. For example, to test
the second rightmost bit for a value of zero --

```
REAL RIGHT2/Z00000002/,ZERO/Z00000000/
READ,A
B=AND(A,RIGHT2)
IF(B.EQ.ZERO) ...
...
```

e) Flip all bits. Solution: COMPL the value.   For
example, to flip all bits --

```
READ,A
A=COMPL(A)
```

In performing bit operations it is often desirable to
generate two sets of thirty-two values such that the ith
variable in the first set has ones everywhere except in the
ith leftmost bit position and the ith variable in the second
set has zeros everywhere except in the ith leftmost
position.   In the following program OFF(J) has only the Jth
leftmost bit off and ON(J) has only the Jth leftmost bit on.
The program takes advantage of the fact that an INTEGER
value of 2**N for N=0,1,2,...,30 has a one in the (N+1)th
rightmost bit position and zeros elsewhere.

```
C EXAMPLE 16.9 CREATE BIT PATTERNS
      SUBROUTINE CREATE(ON,OFF)
      REAL ON(32),OFF(32),ONLEFT/Z80000000/
      EQUIVALENCE (X,IPOWER)
      INTEGER IPOWER/1/
      ON(32)=X
      OFF(32)=COMPL(X)
      DO 1 K=1,30
         IPOWER=IPOWER*2
         ON(32-K)=X
         OFF(32-K)=COMPL(X)
    1 CONTINUE
      ON(1)=ONLEFT
      OFF(1)=COMPL(ONLEFT)
      RETURN
      END
```

The reason for the special attention given to ON(1) and
OFF(1) is that a one bit in the leftmost position indicates
a negative number and not a positive power of two.

Bit Shifting Operations

The bit pattern "11011100" shifted two bits to the left is "01110000"; shifted three positions to the right is "00011011". Multiplication and division of non-negative INTEGER values by 2 can be used to shift a pattern one bit to the left and right respectively. Recommended procedures are as follows.

a) Shift left N positions. Solution: Multiply the value by $2**N$. Note that the bit pattern to be shifted must be an INTEGER value.

b) Shift right N positions. Solution:
   If the pattern represents a non-negative integer then divide the value by $2**N$.
   If the pattern represents a negative integer
   then i) Set the leftmost bit to zero.
        ii) Divide the value by $2**N$.
       iii) Set the bit in the (S+1)th position from the left equal to 1 where S denotes the magnitude of the shift.

```
C EXAMPLE 16.10 READ VALUES OF A AND B,
C SHIFT A LEFT 5 BITS AND SHIFT B RIGHT 3 BITS
C 'CREATE' IS THE SUBROUTINE IN EXAMPLE 16.9
      INTEGER LSHIFT/5/,RSHIFT/3/
      REAL ON(32),OFF(32)
      EQUIVALENCE (A,M),(B,N)
      CALL CREATE(ON,OFF)
      READ,A,B
      NEGSW = 0
      IF(B.LT.0) THEN
         NEGSW = 1
         B=AND(B,OFF(1))
      END IF
      M=M*2**5
      N=N/2**3
      IF(NEGSW.EQ.1) THEN
         DO 1 I=1,3
            B=AND(B,OFF(I))
    1    CONTINUE
         B=OR(B,ON(RSHIFT+1))
      END IF
      PRINT 900,A,B
  900 FORMAT(' A=',Z8,' B=',Z8)
      STOP
      END
 $ENTRY
   Z12FD8790 ZFFFFF037
```

Exercise 16.2 (Hexadecimal and Bit Manupulation)

1. For each of the following define an appropriate variable
   and initialize the variable with a hexadecimal constant
   to cause the variable to be assigned the bit pattern.

   a) 0000 0000
   b) 1111 0000 1111 0000 1111 0000 1111 0000
   c) 1011 0011 1000
   d) 0111 1000 0011 1100 0001 1110 0000 1111

2. Write statements to print out the hexadecimal representation of the following constants: '2000', 2000, 2000.0.

3. A programmer wants to "turn on" the rightmost bit of an
   INTEGER value assigned to the variable J and then print
   the resulting INTEGER value. He writes the following
   sequence of statements.

                INTEGER K/Z00000001/,J/27436/
                K=AND(J,K)
                PRINT,K

   a)   Why do these statements not produce the correct
   result?
   b) How can the desired result be obtained?

4. Each of the following asks you to suppose one of the
   built-in functions "AND", "OR", "COMPL" was not available
   but that the other two along with "EOR" was available.
   In each case write a subprogram to achieve the same
   effect as the (supposedly) missing function by using the
   built-in functions suggested.

   a) Use OR and COMPL to achieve the same effect as AND.
   b) Use AND and COMPL to achieve the same effect as OR.
   c) Use AND and OR to achieve the same effect as EOR.

5. Assign the hexadecimal value "A2B3C4D5" to an INTEGER
   variable. Write a sequence of statements to perform each
   the following manipulations in the order shown.

   a) Turn the second leftmost bit off.
   b) Turn the fourth and eighth rightmost bits on.
   c) Test the middle two bits and: if "00" shift the
      pattern left three bits; if "01" shift the pattern
      right three bits; if "10" shift the pattern left
      five bits;   if "11" shift the pattern right five
      bits.

d) Flip the value of every second bit starting with the
   leftmost bit.

16.12 Other Symbols In WATFIV

Occasionally a program must be written in which one or
more of the non-standard WATFIV symbols are required to be
read, defined and/or printed. For example, in a library
application, it may be necessary to use the lower-case
letters of the alphabet. In order to do something like this
(define and display lower-case letters) the printer to be
used must have an appropriate "print train". That is, it
must have a rotating set of metal slugs containing the
symbols which are required. Secondly, since the symbol
printed at any particular position along the print line
depends on the bit pattern which the programmer has assigned
to the print position, it is necessary to know what bit
pattern produces what symbol for the print train being used.
Finally, if the bit pattern for each printed symbol is
known, then we must be able to read or define symbols which
have the appropriate pattern.

In brief, the sequence of events is as follows.

holes in a   bit pattern in   symbol on print
   card column   a byte   line

Hole patterns are described by specifying which of the
twelve positions in a column are to be punched. Hole
positions are labelled (beginning from the top) 12, 11, 0,
1, 2, 3, 4, 5, 6, 7, 8, and 9.   The pattern 11-4-9 for
instance means holes are punched the second, seventh and
bottom positions of the column starting from the top.
Appendix A describes how to punch any desired hole pattern
in a column.   Appendix A also has a chart showing the bit
pattern produced in a byte for any valid hole pattern.
Chapter 23 describes a second method of inputting bit
patterns.

If a bit pattern for a non-standard symbol must be
defined within a program, CHARACTER constants, initialized
with the appropriate hexadecimal digits, should be used. For
example, the bit patterns for the lower-case letters "b" and
"c" can be assigned to the variables BEE and CEE using the
following statement.

CHARACTER BEE/Z82/ , CEE/Z83/

If this is done, a statement pair such as

```
     PRINT 99,BEE,CEE
  99 FORMAT('0',A1)
```

would cause the symbols "b" and "c" to be printed on separate lines (provided an appropriate print train was used).

A feature not previously mentioned, available on some printers, is the "Universal Character Set Feature". In effect, it permits you to define the correspondences between bit patterns and the type slugs on any print train. This feature would only be required in very unusual circumstances.

If you have a requirement for using special symbols, check with your computing center to find out what types of print trains are available. Some of the most frequently used print trains and the bit pattern corresponding to each slug on the train are described in Appendix D.

16.13 Other Statements Involving CHARACTER Values

The use of CHARACTER values and variables in statements such as IMPLICIT, COMMON, EQUIVALENCE, Statement Functions, BLOCK DATA subprograms, EXTERNAL, ENTRY, DATA and DIMENSION statements is described in Chapter 17.

CHARACTER values may be used as subscripts. The value of the subscript is that obtained by using the bit pattern in the leftmost byte of the CHARACTER value as a base two number. For example, if VEC is a set of variables then VEC('0') is equivalent to VEC(240) since the value '0' has a bit pattern of "11110000" which, in the base two number system, represents a value of 240. This feature can be useful in translating one set of bit patterns to another.

16.14 Summary

Strings of symbols can be defined and manipulated in WATFIV programs. This is done by using CHARACTER variables and CHARACTER constants. Each symbol in a CHARACTER value occupies one byte of memory.

CHARACTER arrays can be used to store format codes. This permits some degree of flexibility in changing format codes at execution time.

Bit strings can be defined, manipulated and displayed. They are defined by using hexadecimal values. Each hexadecimal value represents a pattern of four bits. By using hexadecimal values, non-standard symbols can be defined, input and output. Bit manipulations can be done by using the built-in functions AND, OR, EOR and COMPL. Shifting operations can be done by multiplying and dividing by powers of two.

CHARACTER variables can also be used to simulate input and output devices. Because of the importance of this application, it is discussed in a separate chapter (Chapter 21).

16.15 Programming Problems

16.1 Write a program to count the number of occurences of each letter of the alphabet in a sentence which is punched on a data card.

16.2 Example program 16.3 was used to count the number of words having different lengths in a sentence. Modify the program to take into account that a comma or period as well as a blank can indicate the end of a word.

16.3 Write a program which scans a string of symbols looking for left and right brackets. The program should check that there are equal numbers of each and that at any point during the scan that at least as many left brackets have been encountered as right brackets.

16.4 Write a program which reads in several words punched one per card and determines which are valid variable names.

16.5 Write a program which counts the number of occurences of the word "THE" in a sentence. Test the program on the following sentence. "THE PROBLEM OF FAT THEODORE GOETHE IS THE ACCURATE PRONUNCIATION OF THE WORD THE".

16.6 Write a SUBROUTINE called "CONCAT" which could be used to "concatenate" (join together) two strings of symbols. For example, the concatenation of 'JONES' and '63R' is 'JONES63R'. The values to be concatenated and the result should be stored in separate arrays. The first statement in the SUBROUTINE will be:

SUBROUTINE CONCAT(A1,L1,A2,L2,R)   where

A1 is the array containing the first value
L1 is the number of symbols to be used in the first
   value
A2 is the array containing the second value
L2 is the number of symbols to be used in the second
   value
R is the array containing the concatenated string

16.7 Write a program which reads in twenty words punched one
per card and prints them in alphabetical order. Write a
SUBROUTINE to do the sort.

16.8 Suppose a sentence on a card occupies less than fifty
card columns and contains N words (where N is determined
by the program).   Write a program which reads in the
sentence and prints it N times such that on the first
line the first word starts in print position 60, on the
second line the second word starts in print position 60,
etc..   For example, if the sentence is "PROGRAMMING IS
EASY", the following output would be produced.

$$\downarrow T60$$

PROGRAMMING IS EASY
     PROGRAMMING IS EASY
     PROGRAMMING IS EASY

16.9 a) Write a FUNCTION subprogram which will convert an
       array of five CHARACTER constants of length one to
       its equivalent INTEGER value. Assume each symbol is
       one of the digits zero thru nine.

     b) Explain why the reverse   operation (INTEGER to
        CHARACTER) is more difficult. (A method of doing
        this easily is described in Chapter 21.)

16.10 Draw a circle. Write the letters of the alphabet and a
blank around the outside of the circle in a clockwise
direction.   Write a program which reads in a value of N
and then a sentence.   (a) Translate the sentence into a
coded message by replacing each symbol in the sentence
by the symbol which is N positions clockwise around the
circle. Print the coded message.   (b) Print the original
message by decoding the message produced in part (a).

CHAPTER 17   MIXED-TYPE STATEMENTS -- A SUMMARY

Questions Answered In This Chapter

1. What are the statements in which more than one type of variable can appear?

2. What are the rules of use of these "mixed-type" statements?

This chapter summarizes those statements in which more than one type of value or variable may be used. It discusses the use of non-INTEGER and non-REAL values in statements such as COMMON, EQUIVALENCE, DATA, DIMENSION, ENTRY and mixed-type Assignment statements.

17.1 Allowed Types And Length of Variables

The table below indicates the standard and optional length(s) of the different types of variables which can be used in WATFIV programs.

Type	Standard Length (bytes)	Optional Length (bytes)	Usual Name(s) Given To Optional Length Variable(s)
INTEGER	4	2	INTEGER*2 or Half-Word INTEGER
REAL	4	8	REAL*8 or Double Precision or Extended Precision
LOGICAL	4	1	LOGICAL*1
COMPLEX	8	16	COMPLEX*16 or Extended Precision Complex or Double Precision Complex
CHARACTER	1	2-255	CHARACTER*n

INTEGER and LOGICAL constants have no optional lengths. Both types of constants have a length of four. REAL, COMPLEX and CHARACTER constants may be given the optional length(s).

17.2 Specification Of Variable Type

There are three ways the type of a variable may be specified. These are:

i) Default or first-letter rule. This rule applies unless changed using (ii) or (iii). Variables beginning with any of I, J, K, L, M, or N are INTEGER variables; Those begining with A thru H, O thru Z or a "$" are REAL variables.

ii) IMPLICIT Typing. (See also Chapter 2, Section 5.) An IMPLICIT statement is used to change all or part of the first-letter rule. If present, its specifications apply unless overridden for specific variables by a type declaration statement. Its general form is:

        IMPLICIT type*L(x,y,...), type*L(x,y,...)...

where,
   "type" is one of INTEGER, REAL, COMPLEX, LOGICAL,
      CHARACTER or DOUBLE PRECISION
   "*L" is a length modifier (optional); It is not
      allowed if "type" is "DOUBLE PRECISION".
   "x", "y", etc. are one of the following
      - a letter of the alphabet or a "$"
      - a pair of letters separated by a hyphen

Example. The statement

        IMPLICIT CHARACTER*10(M,N),REAL*8(A-D,$),
      * COMPLEX(Z), LOGICAL(H-J)

specifies that variables beginning with

      A thru D are REAL*8
      E thru G are REAL (first-letter rule)
      H thru J are LOGICAL
      K and L are INTEGER (first-letter rule)
      M and N are CHARACTER*10
      O thru Y are REAL (first-letter rule)
      Z are COMPLEX
      $ are REAL*8

There are two important rules regarding the IMPLICIT statement. These are that only one IMPLICIT statement is permitted in any segment and, if present, it must be the first statement in the mainline segment or the second statement in a subprogram segment.

iii) Explicit Type Declaration Statement. The type declaration statement is used to override the first-letter rule and/or IMPLICIT statement for specific variables. Its general form is:

    type*L name1*L1(D1)/V1/,name2*L2(D2)/V2/,...

where,

"type" is one of INTEGER, REAL, COMPLEX, LOGICAL, CHARACTER or DOUBLE PRECISION

"*L" is optional and specifies one of the permitted lengths for the type used. ("*L" is not permitted if "DOUBLE PRECISION" is used to specify the type.) If omitted, the standard length is assumed.

"name1", "name2", etc. are names of variables or arrays.

"*L" following a name is optional and specifies the length of the variable or array elements. If omitted, the length of the variable(s) is (are) that associated with the "type".

"(D1)", "(D2)", etc. are optional and describe the dimensions of an array. Each "Di" represents one to seven unsigned positive INTEGER constants separated by commas.

"/V1/", "/V2/", etc. are optional and specify initial values to be assigned to variables specified by "name*L". The initial values must be constants and must agree in number and type with the variable(s) being initialized. If the "name" refers to an array, values are assigned with the rightmost subscript varying least rapidly. A repeat factor of the form "r*v" in a list of initializing constants indicates that the value "v" is to be repeated "r" times. "r" must be a positive INTEGER constant.

17.3 Defining Arrays

An array can be defined using any <u>one</u> of: an explicit type declaration statement as described in the previous section; a COMMON statement (see Chapter 10, Section 4 and Section 8 of this chapter); a DIMENSION statement (see Chapter 7, Section 9).

If a COMMON statement is used to define an array, the type of variable in the array must have been specified by a previous statement or, if not, its variables must have a length which is the same as that obtained from first-letter rule (or IMPLICIT statement, if used). (See also Section 17.13 on "Ordering Of Statements".)

17.4 Specification Of Initial Values

Values can be assigned to variables of any type at compile time using either an explicit type declaration statement (Section 17.2) or a DATA statement (See Chapter 7, Section 8.). Occasionally a DATA statement must be used (See Section 17.13 on ordering of statements.)

An example of a DATA statement used to initialize three different types of variables is shown in the following sequence.

```
COMPLEX Z(4,2)
REAL*8 A(3)
LOGICAL LOG
DATA (Z(I,1) I=1,4)/4*(0.,0.)/,A(1),LOG/0.D00,T/
```

17.5 Mixed-Type Expressions And Statements

Arithmetic Expressions

If two variables or constants of different types are involved in an arithmetic operation, the type of value resulting from the operation is that of the higher of the two types in the following list.

```
COMPLEX*16
COMPLEX
REAL*8
REAL
INTEGER
INTEGER*2
```

For example, "2.5D-6 * 2" equals 5.0D-6 because REAL*8 values appear higher in the list. There are two exceptions to the hierarchy of values appearing in the list. First, an operation involving two INTEGER*2 values produces an INTEGER value of length four. Second, if an operation involves a COMPLEX value and a REAL*8 value, the result is a COMPLEX*16 value. In any operation between a COMPLEX value of either length and a non-COMPLEX value, the non-COMPLEX value is considered to be a complex value with an imaginary component of zero for purposes of performing the operation.

Two facts about exponentiation should be recalled. First, COMPLEX numbers may only be raised to INTEGER powers. Second, if the base and exponent are REAL, then the base must be positive. For example, the expression "(-2.)**4." is invalid.

Logical Expressions

Logical expressions involve LOGICAL values and/or expressions which use the six relational operators .LE., .EQ., etc.. Logical expressions may be combined using the Logical operators .AND., .OR. and .NOT.. The relational operators may only be used to compare

i) Two numeric values, neither of which is COMPLEX

ii) Two CHARACTER values of any length

Priorities

A complete summary of priorites of operations and the order in which they are performed is shown in the following list.

```
┌─────────────────────────────────────────────────────────────┐
│                                                               │
│                   Priority of Operations                     │
│                                                               │
│    1. Functions (right to left)                               │
│                                                               │
│    2. Brackets (innermost first)                              │
│                                                               │
│    3. Arithmetic operations                                   │
│         a) Exponentiation (right to left)                     │
│         b) Multiplication and division (left to right)        │
│         c) Addition and subtraction (left to right)           │
│                                                               │
│    4. Relational operations                                   │
│         All six have equal priority and are processed         │
│           left to right.                                      │
│                                                               │
│    5. Logical operations                                      │
│         a) .NOT. (left to right)                              │
│         b) .AND. (left to right)                              │
│         c) .OR. (left to right)                               │
│                                                               │
└─────────────────────────────────────────────────────────────┘
```

Assignment Statements

In an Assignment statement,   the permitted combinations of variables on the left and values on the right are:

Type of Variable	Type of Value
numeric	numeric
LOGICAL	LOGICAL
CHARACTER	CHARACTER

All other combinations are invalid.   In the foregoing table, numeric means INTEGER,   REAL or COMPLEX (in   each case,   of either length).

17.6 Subscript Values

If a subscript value is numeric and non-INTEGER (REAL or COMPLEX of either length),   the   subscript value used is that obtained   by applying IFIX or   its equivalent   to the   REAL value (the real component of a COMPLEX value).

If a   subscript is   a LOGICAL   or CHARACTER   value,   the subscript value used is that   obtained by evaluating the bit pattern of   the leftmost   byte of   the value   as a   base two number.   For example, suppose X is an array of three-hundred variables. Then,

i) X(.TRUE..AND..NOT..FALSE.)   is equivalent   to X(255) since the leftmost byte used to store ".TRUE.   (the expression value)   has the bit   pattern "11111111" which, in the base two number system,   represents a value of 255.

ii) X('A$2Z')   is   equivalent to   X(193)   since   the bit pattern used to represent   'A' is "11000001" which, in the base two number system has a value of 193.

CHARACTER subscripts can be useful   when translating one set of bit   patterns to another.   The program   below translates each of the letters in the alphabet to the one following it. "Z" is translated to "A" and a blank is left unchanged.

```
C EXAMPLE PROGRAM 17.1 BIT TRANSLATION
      CHARACTER TABLE(255)/255*' '/
      CHARACTER DATA(80)
      READ 1,(TABLE(I),I=193,201),(TABLE(I),I=209,
     * 217),(TABLE(I),I=226,233)
    1 FORMAT(26A1)
      READ 2, DATA
    2 FORMAT(80A1)
      PRINT 3, DATA
    3 FORMAT('1ORIGINAL DATA ',80A1,/)
      DO 4 I=1,80
          DATA(I)=TABLE(DATA(I))
    4 CONTINUE
      PRINT 5,DATA
    5 FORMAT('1TRANSLATED DATA ',80A1)
      STOP
      END
$ENTRY
BCDEFGHIJKLMNOPQRSTUVWXYZA
THIS MESSAGE WILL BE TRANSLATED
```

Appendix A decribes the bit patterns for CHARACTER values.

17.7 Shared Storage Within A Segment(EQUIVALENCE)

The rules covering the use of an EQUIVALENCE statement and some of its most frequent uses are described in Chapter 10 Section 7. Any type of variable may be used in an EQUIVALENCE statement. Only one additional rule is required. This is that the length of any variable used in an EQUIVALENCE statement must not subsequently (by some later statement) be given a length which is different from that assumed at the time the EQUIVALENCE statement was compiled. The examples below illustrate this rule.

Valid   Invalid

```
REAL*8 A                       EQUIVALENCE (A,B)
EQUIVALENCE (A,B)              REAL*8 A
```

The following paragraphs describe three situations in which EQUIVALENCEd variables of different types may be useful.

First, since there are no built-in functions for extracting the real and imaginary components of a COMPLEX*16 value, the following approach could be used.

```
COMPLEX*16 Z
REAL*8 CMPNT(2),ZREAL,ZIMAG
EQUIVALENCE (Z,CMPNT,ZREAL),(ZIMAG,CMPNT(2))
```

Second, if pairs of numbers must be tested for equality, a saving in execution time may result by Equivalencing the pair to a variable having a length equal to the total length of the pair. For example, suppose you are searching for a particular author-title combination where authors and titles are represented by INTEGER values. The program below reads in pairs of authors and titles and then scans the list to find out if author 2401 and title 3379 appear in the list.

```
C EXAMPLE PROGRAM 17.2 EQUIVALENCE
        INTEGER DATA(2,1000),PAIR(2),NPAIRS/0/
        REAL*8 ATPAIR(1000),ATTEST
        EQUIVALENCE (DATA,ATPAIR),(ATTEST,
      * PAIR(1),AUTHOR),(PAIR(2),TITLE)
        INTEGER AUTHOR/2401/,TITLE/3379/
C       READ THE AUTHOR-TITLE PAIRS
        DO 1  I=1,1000
            READ(5,*,END=2) DATA(1,I),DATA(2,I)
            NPAIRS=NPAIRS+1
      1 CONTINUE
C       SEARCH FOR THE PAIR 2401-3379
      2 DO 3 I=1,NPAIRS
            IF(ATTEST.EQ.ATPAIR(I))GO TO 4
      3 CONTINUE
        PRINT,'AUTHOR-TITLE NOT FOUND'
        STOP
      4 PRINT,'AUTHOR-TITLE FOUND'
        STOP
        END
```

In the foregoing program, the array DATA must be defined as having two rows and one-thousand columns and not vice-versa because storage for two-dimensional arrays is reserved column-by-column.

This idea (Equivalencing a pair of INTEGER variables to a REAL*8 variable) could be extended to Equivalencing groups of eight INTEGER*2 variables to a single COMPLEX*16 variable. The procedure is recommended only if a test for equality between groups of values is being made. The use of ".LE.", ".LT.",".GT.", or ".GE." would produce meaningless results except in very unusual circumstances. Keep in mind that this use of EQUIVALENCE is simply to reduce execution time. It is not a necessity.

A third reason for Equivalencing variables of different types would be to use the bit pattern of one variable as the bit pattern, and hence the value, of a different type of variable. This use was illustrated when using the built-in functions AND, OR, EOR and COMPL. Example programs 16.8 thru 16.10 all used the EQUIVALENCE statement for this purpose.

Three additional points about EQUIVALENCE are as follows. First, the total number of bytes used by all variables appearing in or implicated by EQUIVALENCE statements is included in the statistic "ARRAY AREA=XXX BYTES" which is printed following completion of the job. Second, if a LOGICAL variable is EQUIVALENCEd to some other type of variable and if, during the execution of the program, a bit pattern which is not a representation of .TRUE. or .FALSE. is stored in the variable, then any format-free printout of the LOGICAL variable will cause "   J" to be printed instead of "ꞍꞍꞍꞍꞍꞍꞍꞍ". Third, because of the nature of the internal memory structure of computers which process WATFIV jobs, it is much more efficient to EQUIVALENCE variables in order of decreasing length. For example,

```
REAL*8 R81,R82,R1*4,R2*4
CHARACTER A,B
EQUIVALENCE (R81,R82),(R1,R2),(A,B)
```

is much better than

```
REAL*8 R81,R82,R1*4,R2*4
CHARACTER A,B
EQUIVALENCE (A,B),(R1,R2),(R81,R82)
```

17.8 Shared Storage Among Segments(COMMON)

Different segments can assign variables to the same storage locations by defining a Common Block. By creating one or more Common Blocks, program segments can communicate with one another without using argument and parameter lists. The rules of use of the COMMON statement are described in Chapter 10 as are the rules for BLOCK DATA subprograms (used to initialize variables in labelled Common Blocks). Any type of variable may be put in a Common Block.

The elements in a Common Block should, whenever possible, be specified in order of decreasing length. This will make proper "boundary alignment" of the variables in the Block easy for the compiler to achieve. No errors will result if this procedure is not followed but execution time efficiency will likely be greatly reduced. Shown below are examples of good and bad ordering of items in a Common Block.

Good	Bad
REAL*8 A	REAL*8 A
INTEGER K	INTEGER K
CHARACTER*1 CHAR	CHARACTER*1 CHAR
COMMON A,K,CHAR	COMMON CHAR,K,A

One further point. The total number of bytes used by the Common Blocks in a program is included in the statistic "ARRAY AREA=XXX BYTES" which is printed following completion of a job.

17.9 Argument And Parameter Lists

Arguments and parameters may be of any type. Rules of correspondence are summarized in Section 10.3. Of special note is that an argument and its corresponding parameter must be of the same type only if the parameter is a simple variable. For example, the following structure is valid.

```
C MAINLINE SEGMENT          SUBROUTINE ROUT(Y)
      COMPLEX Z/(1.,2.)/     REAL Y(2)
      CALL ROUT(Z)           ...
      ...                    ...
      END                    END
```

In the foregoing program structure, the SUBROUTINE variables Y(1) and Y(2) would take on values of the real and imaginary components of the COMPLEX variable Z.

17.10 FUNCTION Subprograms

The function value in a FUNCTION subprogram may be of any type except CHARACTER. If the first-letter rule does not apply, the FUNCTION name must appear in a type declaration statement in the calling segment and the FUNCTION subprogram must begin with the statement

        type FUNCTION name*L (parameter list)

or, alternatively,

        FUNCTION name (parameter list)
        type name*L

where "L" is optional and if used denotes the length of the
FUNCTION value. (If "type" is "DOUBLE PRECISION", the length
modifier must be omitted.)

ENTRY Points (See also Chapter 10 Section 8)

An ENTRY point of a FUNCTION subprogram may have a type
of value other than that specified by the first-letter rule.
To do this, the FUNCTION name at the ENTRY point should
appear in an appropriate type declaration statement both at
the beginning of the subprogram and in the calling segment.
The following program structure illustrates this idea.

```
C MAINLINE                    FUNCTION X(...)
      LOGICAL HERE,NOW         LOGICAL HERE,PARAM
      .                        .
      NOW=HERE(.NOT.NOW)       ENTRY HERE(PARAM)
      .                        .
      END                      END
```

EXTERNAL SUBPROGRAMS (See also Chapter 10 Section 10)

Recall that an EXTERNAL statement is used when an
argument is the name of a subprogram or built-in function.
FUNCTION subprograms and built-in functions may be of any
type except CHARACTER. To specify the type of an EXTERNAL
function, the function name must appear in an appropriate
type declaration statement in both the calling and the
called segments. The following program structure illustrates
this idea.

```
C CALLING SEGMENT             SUBROUTINE R(DUMMY)
      EXTERNAL F               INTEGER DUMMY
      INTEGER F                .
      .                        END
      CALL R(F)
      .                        INTEGER FUNCTION F(...)
      .                        .
      .                        F=...
      .                        .
      END                      END
```

17.11 Input-Output

Format-Free Output

The table below summarizes the format codes used for
each type of value appearing in a format-free output list.

Type Of Value   Mask Or Codes

    INTEGER   I12
    INTEGER*2   I12
    REAL   F20.7
    REAL*8   D28.16
    COMPLEX   '(',E16.7,' ,',E16.7,')'
    COMPLEX*16   '(',D28.16,' ,',D28.16,')'
    LOGICAL   L8
    LOGICAL*1   L8
    CHARACTER*n   A(n+1)

Formatted Input-Output

Normally, I-masks, F-masks or E-masks, pairs of F-masks and/or E-masks, L-masks, and A-masks are used for INTEGER, REAL, COMPLEX, LOGICAL, and CHARACTER type values respectively. However, the following three masks can be used with any type of variable or value: A-masks, Z-masks, and G-masks. Section 13 of this chapter discusses the use of A-masks with non-CHARACTER values.

There are two additional facts concerning the use of P-codes (scale factors). First, the effect of a P-code on a D-mask is similar to that of a P-code on an E-mask. Second, if a P-code is applied to a G-mask its effect depends on whether or not the G-mask becomes equivalent to an F-mask or E-mask. (See Sections 5.16, 5.17, 6.10 and 6.11 for details of the G-mask and P-code.)

17.12 Storing CHARACTER Values In Other Variables

Any type of variable can be used to store a CHARACTER value. In fact, in most versions of Fortran, this is the only means of storing and manipulating strings of symbols. Recall that each symbol uses one byte of memory. Thus the number of symbols which can be stored in a variable, regardless of its type, is equal to the length of the variable. For example, four symbols can be stored in a REAL or INTEGER variable, sixteen symbols in a COMPLEX*16 variable, etc..

One method of assigning a CHARACTER value to a non-CHARACTER variable is to initialize the variable with the desired string of symbols. The initializing constant may be either a quote-type literal or an H-type literal. The following sequence of statements assigns "ABCD" to the variables J and K and "$ XXX.XX" to the variables A and B. Note that either a type declaration statement or a DATA statement can be used to specify initial values.

```
INTEGER J/'ABCD'/, K/4HABCD/
REAL*8 A/'$ XXX.XX'/,B
DATA B/8H$ XXX.XX/
```

Rules of padding and truncation during compile time
initialization are the same as those which apply when
CHARACTER values are used. That is, the "APT" rule (Chapter
16, Section 4) applies.

A CHARACTER value can also be assigned to a non-
CHARACTER variable by reading the value under control of an
A-mask. An A-mask is also used to print strings of symbols
stored in non-CHARACTER variables. The following program
reads a card and counts the number of blank columns in the
card. In this example, INTEGER variables are used to store
CHARACTER values.

```
C EXAMPLE 17.3 COUNT BLANK COLUMNS
      INTEGER BLANK/' '/,COUNT/0/,COL(80)
      INTEGER TITLE(7)/'NUMB','ER O','F BL','ANK ',
   *  'COLU','MNS ','IS'/
      READ 900,COL
900   FORMAT(80A1)
      DO 1 I=1,80
         IF(COL(I).EQ.BLANK) COUNT=COUNT+1
    1 CONTINUE
      PRINT 901,TITLE,COUNT
901   FORMAT('1',7A4,I3)
      STOP
      END
$ENTRY
BLANKS IN THIS CARD WILL BE COUNTED
```

The foregoing program illustrates how INTEGER variables can
be used to read, analyze and print CHARACTER values.
Because an INTEGER variable has a length of four, the
symbols in the title "NUMBER OF BLANK COLUMNS IS" must be
broken up into groups of four. Therefore seven INTEGER
variables are required to store the message. Note that COL
is a set of eighty variables and that a mask of A1 is used
for each. This causes each symbol in the card to be stored
in the leftmost (the TIP rule applies) byte of a unique
INTEGER variable. If more than one symbol was stored in a
variable, it would be difficult to determine the presence of
a blank. The POT (Section 6 of Chapter 16) rule describes
truncation-padding operations during output.

If non-CHARACTER variables are used to store CHARACTER
values, it is a good policy to consistently use one type of

variable for this purpose. Why? Well, for example, in the program statements below, the relationship "X.EQ.K" is not true.

```
REAL X/'ABCD'/
INTEGER K/'ABCD'/
IF(X.EQ.K) ...
```

The reason is simply that when an INTEGER value and a REAL value are compared, the bit pattern of the INTEGER value is converted to its equivalent REAL value before the comparison is made. This means the bit pattern for "ABCD" stored in the variable K is drastically altered before being compared with the bit pattern stored in the variable X. Therefore the relationship is false.

If non-CHARACTER variables are used to store strings of symbols, these variables should not participate in any arithmetic operations. After all, you wouldn't think of adding "ABCD" and "WXYZ" if they were stored in CHARACTER variables. It doesn't make any more sense if they are stored in non-CHARACTER variables.

Section 16.9 explained that format codes could be stored in CHARACTER arrays. Format codes can also be stored in non-CHARACTER arrays using the techniques described in preceding paragraphs. For example,

```
REAL*8 FMT(2)/8H('1VALUE,8H IS',I6)/
PRINT FMT, -71
```

is equivalent to

```
PRINT 900, -71
900 FORMAT('1VALUE IS',I6)
```

This section has described techniques which can be used to define and input-output strings of symbols without using CHARACTER variables. In some versions of Fortran it is the only set of techniques available.

17.13 Ordering Of Statements In Program Segments

Because the WATFIV compiler examines each statement only once, non-executable statements must be ordered in such a way that a statement does not contradict any assumption which the compiler had to make in compiling an earlier statement. No problems will arise if statements are ordered in the following sequence.

SUBROUTINE/FUNCTION/BLOCK DATA

IMPLICIT

type declaration statements which do not contain
    any initializing constants

DIMENSION statements

COMMON statements

EQUIVALENCE statements

DATA statements

Statement Function definitions

Executable statements and FORMAT statements

Comments can be placed anywhere. It is not necessary to
follow the above ordering. However, there are two errors
which are frequently made. First, the initial value for any
variable appearing in, or implicated by, a COMMON or
EQUIVALENCE statement must follow the COMMON or EQUIVALENCE
statement. Second, if a variable is Equivalenced, any
subsequent declaration of variable type must not change the
length assumed at the time the EQUIVALENCE statement was
compiled. The following sequence is in error because at the
time the EQUIVALENCE statement was compiled, the variable
"A" was assumed to have a length of four.

            EQUIVALENCE (A,B)
            REAL*8 A

17.14 Summary

Many statements in the Fortran language which are
acceptable to the WATFIV compiler permit more than one type
of variable or value to be used in the statement. This
chapter has described these "mixed-type" statements and has
summarized the rules for, and effects of, using these
statements. Several uses of mixed-type statements have been
discussed. Some of these are rather sophisticated and are
presented for the benefit of the experienced programmer.

Exercise 17.1

1. Describe the advantages and disadvantages of using COMMON
   Blocks to provide communication among subprograms versus
   transfer of values using argument and parameter lists.

2. Modify the program in Example 17.1 to decode the translated data string and thus produce the original.

Part III

OTHER TYPES
OF INPUT/OUTPUT

Questions Answered In This Chapter

    1. What is punched output?

    2. What statements are used in WATFIV programs to create
       and control punched output?

18.1 Punched Output

    Values used in a program can be punched into cards as
well as displayed on a printer. If punched output is
required, the programmer controls the appearance and
placement of values in much the same way as is done with
printed output. There are two distinct differences however.
First, there are eighty punch positions instead of the one-
hundred-and-thirty-three print positions available with most
printers. Second, the first punch position has no special
use as does print position one. The symbol stored in punch
position one is punched into card column one and is not used
to control the operation of the card punch.

    As with printed output, the formatting of the punched
values can be controlled by the programmer using format
codes or left up to the WATFIV program.

    The most common reason for punching data values into
data cards is to produce a set of values which will be used
as input data for another program. A second use is to
produce duplicate copies of programs or data cards.

    The table below describes the different forms of the
PUNCH and WRITE statements which are used to produce punched
output in WATFIV programs.

	Format-Free	Formatted
Output device assumed to be the card punch	PUNCH,list	PUNCH #,list # FORMAT(codes)
Card punch named as the output device	WRITE(7,*) list	WRITE(7,#) list # FORMAT(codes)

In the foregoing table, the symbol "#" refers to the number of the FORMAT statement which describes how the values are to be punched in the cards (the use of the card columns). The number 7 is frequently used as the device number of the card punch. If it is different from 7, the appropriate number should be used. The device number can also be assigned to an INTEGER variable. This is frequently a good idea when testing a complex program. During the testing phase a variable such as IOUT can be given a value of six which causes values in a WRITE list to be sent to the printer. Once the program is working properly, IOUT can be given a value of seven. The advantage of this approach should be obvious -- it permits output to be switched from the printer to the punch simply by changing one statement (one data card if the value of IOUT is read from a data card).

18.2 Formatted Punched Output

The FORMAT statement used to punch values into cards may contain masks, literals, and other codes. Since a card has eighty columns, format codes are positioned explicitly or implicitly in punch positions one thru eighty. Any attempt to reference a punch position outside this range is an error. All format codes are valid. Punch position one has no special use as it does with printed output. Each time the right bracket at the end of the format codes is reached, a card is punched which contains the symbols currently stored in the punch positions. After each card is punched, all positions are set to blanks. The following examples should make these ideas clear.

```
      PUNCH 900,2.,3.
  900 FORMAT(2F3.0)
```

Result: the symbols b2.b3. (b denotes a blank)
        are punched in columns 1 thru 6 of a card.

```
      WRITE(7,901) (J,J=1,4)
  901 FORMAT(/I3,T2,I3,'VALUES'/)
```

Result: Six cards are punched. The second card contains "12" in columns 3 and 4 and "VALUES" in columns 5 thru 10. The fifth card contains "34" in columns 3 and 4 and "VALUES" in columns 5 thru 10. The first, third, fourth and sixth cards are blank.

18.3 Format-Free Punched Output

If values are punched into cards using either of the two format-free statements shown in the table, values are positioned in the cards according to the default mask appropriate to each type of value. Format-free output is generally used when the values will be read back in using a format-free READ statement.

The PUNCH statement is considered invalid by most non-WATFIV compilers. For this reason, as well as the flexibility of using other device numbers, the WRITE statement is generally preferred by many programmers.

18.4 An Example Program

The following program could be used to reproduce a deck of data cards. The program also prints the number of cards punched. Such a program is often called an "80-80 Reproduce" because 80 columns are read and 80 columns are punched.

```
C EXAMPLE 18.1 80-80 REPRODUCE
      CHARACTER*80 CARD
      N = 0
C
C     READ LOOP
    1 READ(5,900,END=2) CARD
        N = N + 1
        WRITE(7,900) CARD
      GO TO 1
C
    2 PRINT,'NUMBER OF CARDS PUNCHED=',N
      STOP
  900 FORMAT(A80)
      END
```

Exercise 18.1

1. In each of the following, what symbol is punched in column 6?

a)   PUNCH 900,2.,3.
        900 FORMAT (F4.2,F4.1)

b)   PUNCH,-2.4536

c)   WRITE(7,900) 2,4.235
        900 FORMAT (T5,'HI',T1,I8,T4,F7.2)

2. How many cards are punched by executing each
   of the following?

   a)   PUNCH 900,A,B,C
            900 FORMAT(E10.2)

   b)   WRITE(7,901) (I,FLOAT(I),I=1,7)
            901 FORMAT(T6,2(3X,I2,/F7.4)/)

   c)   WRITE(7,902)(K+1,(J,J=3,10,3),K-1,K=1,5)
            902 FORMAT((//2I3,4X,T2,2(/I1),3(I2)//))

3. a) Can any set of values which are punched using a
      format-free PUNCH statement be read in using a
      format-free READ statement? Explain.

   b) Suppose the value of the variable AA is punched by
      the statements:

               WRITE(7,900) AA
           900 FORMAT(codes)

      Suppose the card which is punched is read in by the
      statement:
               READ 900,AA

      What restrictions, if any, are there on the codes
      used to punch AA if the READ statement is to cause
      AA to have its previously assigned value?

4. Given the statement

           PUNCH 900,123.123,456.456

   then for each of the following, write a single FORMAT
   statement which will cause a card or cards to have
   the symbols shown. A "b" denotes a blank. Assume the
   symbols start in column one.

   a) b123.123bb456.bbb456

   b) b123b456

   c) 123456.123456

   d) bbb123.123
       456.456

   e) 123.123456.
       456

f)   123.123456.
            456

g)   456.456456.456.

18.5 Summary

Output values can be punched in cards as well as printed. To do this a PUNCH statement or a WRITE statement specifying the punch is used in a program. Both formatted and format-free punching is permitted. Unlike output which is sent to a printer, no special significance is attached to the symbol stored in punch position one.

Punched output may be useful for creating a set of data cards which will be used as input data for some other program and for creating duplicate copies of program or data decks.

18.6 Programming Problems

18.1 Write a program which reads an unknown number of data cards and for each card read, replaces every group of two or more consecutive blanks with a single blank. The compressed data should then be punched into a card.

18.2 Input to the program consists of a set of name and address cards punched according to the following rules. Name cards have a name in columns 1-20. In an address card: line 1 appears in columns 1-20; line 2 in columns 21-40; line 3 in columns 41-60. Write a program which combines each name-address pair and punches it on a single card.

18.3 Modify example program 17.1 to produce N copies of an input deck where N is a value read from the first data card. Assume there are no more than 200 cards in the deck to be copied.

18.4 Recall that columns 73-80 of a statement or comment card can be used to punch sequencing or program identification information. Write a program to reproduce and punch sequence numbers in an existing source program according to the following specifications. The first data card contains a four-character program identifier ID in columns 1 thru 4 and two INTEGER values N1 and N2 in columns 5 thru 8 and 9 thru 12. The remaining data cards are the statements and comments in the program which is to be repunched. The output is to be an exact copy of the program read as

data but having the ID in columns 73-76 and a four-digit
sequence number in 77-80 of each card punched.   The
sequence numbers should begin at N1 and increase by N2
for each card.   Test your program by printing rather
than punching the output.

Questions Answered In This Chapter

1. What is magnetic tape and what are the characteristics of the devices used to record and read data stored on magnetic tape?

2. What statements are used to read and write data stored on magnetic tape?

19.1 Magnetic Tape And Magnetic Tape Units

A deck of punched cards is a suitable medium for recording small volumes of data. If it is necessary to process large volumes of data, a more suitable medium is a reel of magnetic tape. The strips of magnetic tape used by most computer systems are one-half inch wide and come in standard lengths of 300, 600, 1200 and 2400 feet. Each strip is wound on a plastic reel. One side of the strip is coated with a special material which can be magnetized. Data (ones and zeros) are recorded on the tape by creating little magnetic spots on its surface. Eight bits of data (one byte) can be written across the width of the tape. Usually 1600 bytes of data are recorded along one inch of tape.

In order to mark the two ends of the tape, short strips of a reflective material are stuck on the ends of the tape. These reflective markers are detected by photoelectric cells contained in the magnetic tape unit.

A Magnetic Tape Unit (MTU) is a device which reads data from and writes data on magnetic tape. It operates much the same as a standard tape recorder. That is, the tape containing the data to be read or on which data is to be written, comes off one reel, passes under a "read-write head", and is wound onto a second (take-up) reel. After the processing is completed, the tape is rewound on to the original reel.

If changes are required in data recorded on a magnetic tape, two separate MTUs should be used. One is used to read the original data -- the other to write the revised data. This operation is called "updating". The diagram on the following page illustrates this idea.

19.2 A First Example

Suppose a deck of one-hundred cards each contains ten INTEGER values. We want to read the one-hundred sets of ten numbers and record them on tape. Assume the reel of tape on which the values are to be recorded has been put on a MTU having a device number of two. (Recall the usual device number of a card reader is five.) The following program could be used.

```
C EXAMPLE 19.1 WRITE 100 SETS OF NUMBERS ON TAPE 2
      INTEGER SET(10)
      REWIND 2
      DO 1 I=1,100
         READ,SET
         WRITE(2) SET
    1 CONTINUE
      ENDFILE 2
      STOP
      END
```

In this example, three statements refer to the MTU. The first, "REWIND 2" causes the reel of tape on device 2 (which we have assumed to be a MTU) to be rewound to the reflective marker at the start of the tape. This insures that we are at the beginning of the tape before starting to write anything on it. The second reference to device 2 is in "WRITE(2) SET". Since there is no reference to a FORMAT statement, values will be written in an unformatted mode. Because there are ten elements in the array SET, ten values will be recorded on magnetic tape each time the WRITE statement is executed. Each set of ten values creates a "tape record" on the tape. The statement "ENDFILE 2" causes a special symbol called a tapemark to be written on the tape. The tapemark should be written after all data values have been recorded.

Since any data recorded on tape will presumably be read in at some later time, the purpose of the tapemark is simply to indicate the end of data has been reached during the reading operation.

There are five statements which reference Magnetic Tape Units. These are:

```
REWIND i

BACKSPACE i

ENDFILE i

READ (i, ...)

WRITE (i, ...)
```

In each statement, the symbol "i" specifies the device number associated with the MTU being used. The value of "i" can be an INTEGER constant or assigned to an INTEGER variable. In some computing centers, device numbers 1, 2, 3, 4 are reserved for Magnetic Tape Units. If you are planning to use magnetic tape, check with your computing center to find out which device numbers can be used. Job Control Statements are available for causing specific MTUs to have a particular device number. See for example, the IBM publication "Fortran H User's Guide".

Suppose device numbers 2 and 3 were MTUs and we wanted to read from 2 and write on 3. The following program structure could be used.

```
C EXAMPLE 19.2 DEVICE ASSIGNMENTS
      INTEGER TAPIN/2/, TAPOUT/3/
      .
      .
      REWIND TAPIN
      REWIND TAPOUT
      .
      .
      READ(TAPIN ...) ...
      WRITE(TAPOUT ...) ...
      .
      .
      ENDFILE TAPOUT
      REWIND TAPIN
      REWIND TAPOUT
      .
      END
```

There are several important questions which must be answered if we are to avoid serious errors in using magnetic tape. With respect to the example problem, these are:

a) Are there spaces on the tape <u>between</u> each set of ten values written on the tape?

b) Are there spaces on the tape <u>within</u> each set of ten values written on the tape?

c) If I tried to read the data written on the tape, would I get the first number recorded, the first set recorded, or all 100 values?

There are two very important differences between unformatted and formatted input-output operations with magnetic tape. <u>Unformatted is not the same as format-free</u> which is dealt with in section 19.5. In particular, when reading data previously written on magnetic tape, the same type of statement (unformatted or formatted) should be used almost without exception. The chart below makes this idea clear.

Method Data Was Written	Type Of READ Statement Used	
	Unformatted	Formatted
Unformatted	O.K.	See note
Formatted	See note	O.K.

Note: You better know what you're doing!

19.3 Unformatted Input-Output

The allowed forms of the unformatted READ and WRITE statements are:

        READ(i) list

        READ(i,END=n) list

        READ(i,ERR=m) list

        READ(i,END=n,ERR=m) list

        WRITE(i) list

Since data must be written on magnetic tape before it can be read from magnetic tape, the WRITE statement will be considered first.

Unformatted Write - (WRITE(i))

Each time an unformatted WRITE statement is executed:

a) Each value in the output list is written on the tape _exactly as it is stored in the memory of the computer._

b) There are no gaps between the values recorded.

c) Together the set of values in the output list form a single tape output record which is separated from adjacent tape records by a gap. The gap is necessary to allow the tape motion to be stopped.

d) The length of the tape record (in bytes) is the sum of the lengths of the values in the output list. See Chapter 11 for information on the length of any type of value.

e) By convention, all tape records must be at least sixteen bytes long.

The following example illustrates these ideas. Assume device number one is a MTU.

```
C EXAMPLE 19.3 UNFORMATTED WRITE
      REAL X(20),Y(50)
      REWIND 1
C     READ VALUES FOR X AND Y FROM CARDS
      READ, X, Y
C     WRITE VALUES ON TAPE
      WRITE(1) X
      WRITE(1) Y
      WRITE(1) X, Y
      ENDFILE 1
      STOP
      END
```

Recall that the length of a REAL value is 4 bytes. With respect to the preceding program, what are the answers to the following questions? How many tape records are written? What is the length of each? What value is recorded in bytes 17 thru 20 of the first record?

A picture of what has been recorded on tape is shown below.

Motion of tape

Answers

a) Four tape records are written. Three data records, one for each WRITE statement, and a tapemark record. The records are separated from each other by a gap.

b) The output list of the first WRITE statement has twenty values. Since each value has a length of four, the first tape record will be 20x4 or eighty bytes long. Similarly, the second and third records will be 50x4 and (20+50)x4 bytes long respectively.

c) The ones and zeros recorded in bytes 17 thru 20 of the first record will be the ones and zeros which represent the value of the variable X(5). Bytes one thru sixteen of the first record contain the values of the variables X(1), X(2), X(3) and X(4).

It is important to note that when values are written on tape using an unformatted WRITE statement, there is no such thing as a default mask. Instead the bit patterns of the values are simply copied onto tape.

Unformatted READ Statements

There are four forms of the unformatted READ statement which are valid. They are listed at the beginning of this section. One of them should be used to read data which was written using an unformatted WRITE statement. The parameters "END=" and "ERR=" are optional. Either or both may be included.

Executing the statement "READ(i,END=n) list" will cause control to transfer to statement "n" if a tapemark record is read. This is the normal way of dectecting the end of recorded data. The value of "n" must be the statement number of an executable statement.

The "ERR=m" feature allows a program to specify that control should be transferred to statement number "m" if it is impossible to execute the READ successfully because of

some error condition on the tape or tape unit. Dust on the
surface or weak magnetic spots are two possibilities. In
example program 19.4, the ERR=m parameter is used.

Each form of the READ statement contains a list of the
variables to be assigned values by executing the READ
statement. Suppose the lengths of (number of bytes of memory
reserved for) the variables in the input list are L1, L2,
L3, ... Then, when the statement "READ (i) list" is
executed:

a) One tape record is read.

b) The bit pattern in the first L1 bytes of the record
   is assigned to the first variable in the list. The
   bit patterns of the next L2, L3, etc. bytes of the
   record are assigned to the second, third etc.
   variables in the list.

c) Any unused bytes of data in the record are ignored
   and cannot be accessed by a subsequent READ
   statement.

d) Any attempt to access bytes beyond the end of the
   record is an error and the job will be terminated.

The following program illustrates these ideas. The
program reads in six sets of REAL values having a varying
number of elements in each set and writes the six sets on
tape. Next the tape is rewound and the the sets are re-read
(this time from tape and not cards).   During the re-read,
the average of values in each set is computed. As you may
guess, this isn't the most efficient way to solve the
problem!

```
C EXAMPLE 19.4 UNFORMATTED READ
      REAL X(100)
C     REWIND 4, THEN READ AND STORE VALUES ON TAPE
      REWIND 4
      DO 1 I=1,6
         READ,N,(X(J),J=1,N)
C        CHECK FOR FEWER THAN 3 VALUES IN THE SET
         IF (N .LT. 3) GO TO 5
         WRITE(4) N,(X(J),J=1,N)
    1 CONTINUE
      ENDFILE 4
      REWIND 4
```

```
      C
      C       READ LOOP - READ TAPE,SUM VALUES
            2 READ(4,END=3,ERR=4) N,(X(I),I=1,N)
                  SUM = 0
                  DO 10 J=1,N
                     SUM = SUM + X(J)
           10     CONTINUE
                  AVG = SUM/N
                  PRINT,'AVERAGE=',AVG
               GO TO 2
      C
            4 PRINT,'ERROR TRYING TO READ TAPE'
              STOP
      C
            5 PRINT,'INSUFFICIENT DATA VALUES TO MAKE A',
              *        ' TAPE RECORD OF 16 BYTES'
      C
            3 STOP
              END
```

The following two points should be noted.   The reason for
the IF statement "IF(N.LT.3)GO TO 5" is to insure that the
length of each tape record written is at least sixteen bytes
long (the permitted minimum). If a set contains fewer than
three REAL elements (recall that one INTEGER element is also
stored),   then control is transferred to statement 5 which
prints an appropriate message. The problem could be overcome
by adding sufficient zeros to a short set to make it have
three elements. In order to obtain the correct average the
number of zeros added would have to be known and written on
tape along with the data values. Problem 1 asks you to do
this.   The second point is simply that when the END= and
ERR= parameters are present in a READ statement, it makes no
difference in which order they appear.

<u>Bypassing Records</u> (Unformatted Input-Output)

     Recall that a gap (an area of blank tape) is present
between each pair of records written and between the last
data record and the tapemark record. It is possible to cause
the tape to move to the next gap in either a forward or a
backward direction without reading or writing any data. The
following example illustrates how records can be bypassed.

```
      C EXAMPLE 19.5 SKIPPING OVER RECORDS
            REAL A(20)/20*0./
            REWIND 3
      C     WRITE 10 RECORDS ON MTU 3
            DO 1 I=1,10
               WRITE(3) A
          1 CONTINUE
      C      MOVE TO THE START OF RECORD 6 AND READ IT
            DO 2 I=1,5
               BACKSPACE 3
          2 CONTINUE
            READ(3) A
      C     SKIP RECORDS 7 THRU 10 AND WRITE A TAPEMARK
            DO 3 J=1,4
               READ(3)
          3 CONTINUE
            ENDFILE 3
      C     BACKSPACE TO THE BEGINNING OF THE LAST DATA
      C     RECORD AND READ IT. NOTE: WE MUST FIRST
      C     BACKSPACE PAST THE TAPEMARK
            BACKSPACE 3
            BACKSPACE 3
            READ(3) A
      C     END OF EXAMPLE
            STOP
            END
```

To summarize. "BACKSPACE" causes the tape to move backward to the gap preceding the last record read. A READ statement with an empty input list cause the tape to move forward to the next gap.

19.4 Formatted Input-Output

Most computer systems provide only one high speed printer for displaying program output. Occasionally, a program could effectively use additional printers to print two or more reports during the execution-phase of the job. One solution is to print one report on the available printer and write the other reports on separate magnetic tape units. At the end of the run, the tapes containing the lines in the other reports can be rewound one-at-a-time and the records on them displayed on the printer. This is the most common use of formatted magnetic tape output. Formatted output is not recommended for writing intermediate results which will not be printed directly since formatting is a relatively slow operation. The use of tape files to store "print-line images" is discussed in more detail in Chapter 21. The following information assumes the reader is familiar with unformatted output on magnetic tape.

If formatted values are to be written on tape, it is done in the normal way. That is, the WRITE statement has a pointer to format information containing the codes which control the appearance and placement of the values. The general form of the WRITE statement is therefore

                    WRITE(u,fmt) list

where "u" represents the device number of the tape unit on which records are to be written and "fmt" is a pointer to format information. The following two points are important.

  a) Each time the end of the format codes is reached or a slash code is encountered, a tape record is written. The length of the record is determined by the maximum number of bytes used by the format codes processed up to the time the record is written. Note that the width of the format code denotes the number of bytes written.

  b) Each record written must be at least sixteen bytes long. This means: a) Two consecutive slash codes cannot be used; b) A slash cannot be either the first or the last code in a FORMAT statement.

The following three examples should make these ideas clear. Assume that 4 is the device number of a MTU.

  i)   WRITE(4,900) X,Y,Z
     900 FORMAT(3E16.7)

  Result: One tape record is written. The length of the record is 48 bytes. Values of X, Y, and Z are each formatted according to the mask E16.7 and each E16.7 mask requires 16 bytes.

  ii)   WRITE(4,901) X,Y,Z
     901 FORMAT(2E16.7)

  Result: Two tape records are written. The first has a length of 32 and contains the formatted values of X and Y. The second has a length of 16 and contains the formatted value of Z.

  iii)   WRITE(4,902) X, Y, Z
     902 FORMAT(2(E16.7,/),E16.7)

  Result: Three tape records are written. Each has a length of 16 and they contain the formatted values of X, Y, and Z respectively.

d)   WRITE(4,903) V,W,X,Y,Z,P
   903 FORMAT(T6,F11.0,/,2(10X,E10.3))

Result: Four tape records are written. Their lengths and
    contents are as follows.

record	length	value(s)
1	16	V - positions 6 thru 16
2	40	W, X - positions 11-20, 31-40
3	40	Y, Z - positions 11-20, 31-40
4	20	P - positions 11-20

Formatted Input

If data has been written on tape under format control,
it should be read under format control. The allowable forms
of the READ statement are:

```
READ(u,fmt) list
READ(u,fmt,END=n) list
READ(u,fmt,ERR=m) list
READ(u,fmt,END=n,ERR=m) list
```

In the foregoing, "u" is the device number of a magnetic
tape unit; "fmt" is a pointer to format information; "n" and
"m" are statement numbers of executable statements to which
control will be transferred when an end-of-data or error
condition occurs respectively. The END= and ERR= parameters
are used in precisely the same way as with unformatted
input.

Bypassing Records (Formatted Input-Output)

When reading records under format control, a slash code
causes the next, tape record to be read immediately.   This
means slash codes can be used to bypass those records which
are not needed by the program.   An unformatted READ with no
input list achieves the same result. Thus, the following
are equivalent. Each causes four records to be skipped.

```
     READ(4,900)           DO 1 I=1,4
900 FORMAT(///)          1 READ(4)
```

Recall that the first left bracket in a FORMAT statement can
be thought of as causing a record to be read.

Regardless of how records have been written "BACKSPACE
u" is used to move back to the beginning of the previous
record.

An example. The following program: writes five records
on tape; writes a tapemark; backspaces to the beginning of
the second record; reads the second and fifth records.

```
        EXAMPLE 19.6 FORMATTED INPUT-OUTPUT
            INTEGER ARRAY(5) /5,4,3,2,1/
            REWIND 2
            WRITE(2,900) ARRAY
        900 FORMAT(I20)
            ENDFILE 2
            DO 1 I=1,5
                BACKSPACE 2
          1 CONTINUE
            READ(2,901) J,K
        901 FORMAT(I20,///,I20)
            PRINT,J,K
            STOP
            END
```

When the foregoing program is executed, the values printed
are 4 and 1.

19.5 Format-Free Input-Output

The "*" (format-free) forms of READ and WRITE statements
can be used with magnetic tape. They are not as efficient as
the non-* forms described in Section 3 of this chapter. The
allowed forms are:

```
        READ(u,*) list

        READ(u,*,END=n) list

        READ(u,*,ERR=m) list

        READ(u,*,END=n,ERR=m) list

        WRITE(u,*) list
```

If the format-free form of the WRITE statement is used: (a)
Exactly one record is written; (b) Each value in the output
list is formatted using the default mask appropriate to the
type of value;   (c) The length of the record is the sum of
the mask widths used when writing the values.

If one of the "*" forms of the READ statement is used,
sufficient tape records are read to find a value for each
variable in the input list. The data values in the record
must agree in type with the elements of the input list.

Any record written using the format-free form of the WRITE statement should be read using one of the "*" forms of the READ statement.

19.6 Other Topics

There are several topics related to the use of magnetic tape which are beyond the scope of this book. Control over the factors described below is accomplished by control cards which are not processed by the WATFIV compiler. For the interested reader, a discussion of these topics can be found in a reference such as the IBM manual "Fortran H Programmer's Guide".

a) The assignment of device numbers to specific MTUs attached to the system.

b) The creation of "blocked" records to reduce the number of gaps between data records thus increasing the efficiency of tape usage and improving (usually) reading and writing time.

c) The use of a single reel of tape to store more than one data file.

d) The creation of "header" and "trailer" labels to identify, describe and protect a set of tape records.

e) The use of magnetic tape to store programs as well as data.

19.7 Summary

Values may be written on and read from magnetic tape. Each WRITE statement generates one or more tape records which are separated by gaps. Each READ statement reads one or more tape records. Records can only be accessed sequentially in either a forward or backward direction. Data can be written or read with or without format control. Regardless of how the data has been written, it is the programmer's responsibility to know the method, placement, type and number of values recorded in each record. The most significant differences in the two methods are shown below.

	Unformatted	Formatted
Chief use	To store data for use later in the program or by some other program	To create formatted records which will be printed
Appearance of values	The internal represen- tation of the value	The formatted value
Length of Record	Sum of lengths of the values	Depends on format codes
Records written by a WRITE	Exactly one	Depends on format codes
Records read by a READ	Always one	Depends on format codes

The statements which control the reading and writing of data on magnetic tape are: READ, WRITE, BACKSPACE, REWIND and ENDFILE.

Exercise 19.1

1. For each of the following, determine the length of the tape record which is written and the values in the record.   Assume "A" has been defined by "REAL A(8)/1., 2., 3., 4., 5., 6., 7., 8./" Assume device 1 is a tape unit.

   a) WRITE(1) A
   b) WRITE(1) (A(I),I=1,7,2)
   c) WRITE(1) (J,J+A(J),J=1,8)
   d) WRITE(1) ((A(K),K=I,8),I=1,8)

2. Making the same assumptions as in question 1, suppose the record which is written in (a) thru (d) above is read by the corresponding READ statement below. What values are assigned to the variables in the input list?

   a) READ(1) X,Y,Z
   b) READ(1) (A(I),I=3, 8, 3),Z
   c) READ(1) (M,A(9-K),K=1,8)
   d) READ(1) ((A(J),J=1,I),I=1,8)

3. Suppose a set of ten data records have been written on

MTU 3 and is followed by a tapemark. What is the last record read after executing the following sequence of statements?

```
          REWIND 3
    C
    C         READ LOOP
        1 READ(3,END=2)
          GO TO 1
    C
        2 BACKSPACE 3
          DO 3 I=1,6,4
             BACKSPACE 3
             BACKSPACE 3
             READ(3,END=4)
        3 CONTINUE
          READ(3)
        4 STOP
          END
```

4. What will cause a program error when
   a) writing records in an unformatted mode?
   b) reading records in an unformatted mode?

5. State two important differences between unformatted tape output and formatted tape output.

6. How many records are written by each of the following and what is the length of each? Assume 3 is a magnetic tape unit.

```
    a)          WRITE(3,900) I,J,K
            900 FORMAT(2I12,/,I20)


    b)          WRITE(3,901) (A,J=1,20)
            901 FORMAT(3X,F7.4,4(T12,2F3.0),/,E16.7)
```

7. What values are assigned to the variables in the input list in each of the following?

```
    a)          WRITE(2,900) 3.5,7,60.
            900 FORMAT(F8.3,2X,I4,E12.2)
                BACKSPACE 2
                READ(2,900)X,J,B


    b)          WRITE(2,901) .1234567,1234567
            901 FORMAT(T10,F8.6,T1,I7)
                BACKSPACE 2
                READ(2,902) I,A,L
            902 FORMAT (I6,F4.2,4X,I3)
```

19.8 Programming Problems

19.1   Modify example program 19.4 to permit sets of two or fewer values to be processed. A method of doing this is suggested in the discussion which follows the example.

19.2   Write a program which reads a set of twenty INTEGER values; sorts them into increasing order of magnitude; and writes them in four groups of five values each on a MTU. Repeat this process for a second set of values and write the output on a different MTU. Using these two sets of values as input, perform a merge (explained below) of the two sets of values to produce one string of forty non-decreasing values. Write the merged set on a third MTU in records of four values per record. Print the values in the original sets and in the merged set. An example of a merged string of values obtained from two strings of five and four values respectively is shown below.

Direction Of Tape Motion

String A: 10 9 7 4 3   Merged String

10 9 8 7 6 4 3 2 1

String B: 8 6 4 2 1

19.3   Prepare a deck of twenty-five data cards each of which has the following information.

card columns	item
1-5	student number
6	year of studies (1,2,3 or 4)
7-9	mark in course 1 (format F3.0)
10-12	mark in course 2
13-15	mark in course 3
16-18	mark in course 4
19-21	mark in course 5

a) Arrange the cards in order of increasing student number and write them on tape -- one tape record per student. Call this the student master file.

b) Read the student master file and: (i) print the student number, marks, and average of each student. (ii) While reading the data from tape, accumulate statistics required to print the report shown below. Print the report at the end of the run. One page should be printed for each year. Assume a pass requires a 60% average.

PASS/FAIL REPORT

	YEAR OF STUDIES				
	1	2	3	4	OVERALL
NUMBER OF STUDENTS	XX	XX	XX	XX	XX
% WHO PASSED	XX.X	XX.X	XX.X	XX.X	XX.X
% WHO FAILED	XX.X	XX.X	XX.X	XX.X	XX.X
AVERAGE MARK	XX.X	XX.X	XX.X	XX.X	XX.X

19.4   Prepare several cards of each of the following types. Each of the cards is either an "add" or "delete" card which refers to the student master file created in problem 3 above. Add cards have the same data as the student cards described in problem 3 but in addition, have a "1" in column 80. Delete cards have a student number in columns 1-5 and a "0" in column 80. Arrange the add/delete cards in order of increasing student number. The inputs to the program are the student master file and the set of add/delete cards. The output is a new student master file (written on a tape which is different from the old student master file). The new master file should reflect the changes specified by the add/delete cards. The program should detect and print error messages for the following conditions: an attempt to delete a student record which is not on the old student master file; an attempt to add a student who is already on the old student master file; an add or delete card which is out of sequence -- the student number on the add/delete card is less than the student number on the previous add/delete card. Once the new student master file has been written, rewind the tape and print the same two reports described in problem 3.

19.5   Read an unspecified number of pairs of INTEGER and REAL numbers from cards and write each pair on tape using the format codes (I10,F10.2). Print the REAL values according to the following rules. The first is the REAL number in the first record. The second and subsequent values are in the record whose number is the INTEGER value in the record just read. That is, the first number in each pair is a pointer to the next record to read. Stop reading and printing the REAL values when the pointer has a value of 99.

Use the following pairs to test your program.

1.	3	2.7
2.	9	3.85
3.	7	9.
4.	6	824.
5.	2	1.
6.	8	62.
7.	5	25.
8.	99	3.
9.	10	10.
10.	4	56.

For this example the values printed should be 2.7,   9.,
25., 1., 3.85, 10., 56., 824., 62., 3.

Questions Answered In This Chapter

    1. What is direct access input output?

    2. What statements are available for creating,   changing
         and reading files of direct access data?

20.1 Direct Access Concepts

    Large volumes of data can be recorded on direct access
devices.   The words "direct access" means that the time
required to locate a particular item or items of data is
largely independent of the position of the data item(s) on
the device. A card reader or a device for processing a reel
of tape is not a direct access device since each record of
data (each card) must be read in sequence. A direct access
card reader, if such a thing existed,   would permit a
programmer to use statements such as: "Read card number 50";
"Read card number 417"; etc..   By recording punched card
data on a direct access device so that each card's data is
recorded as a separate record, statements such as: "Read
record 50"; "Read record 417"; can be used to obtain the
data in any desired order.

    The most common type of direct access device is called a
magnetic disk unit. Data is recorded on the top and bottom
surfaces of a set of circular disks which together form a
"disk pack".   The disk pack is placed on a rapidly rotating
spindle in a disk drive. Reading and writing of data is
accomplished by "read-write heads" located on the tips of a
comb-like mechanism which moves back and forth between the
disk surfaces.   A typical disk pack can store as much data
as 600,000 punched cards. The average time to locate an item
of data recorded on the pack is approximately a tenth of a
second. The chief advantage of direct access is that any
particular collection of data (any data record) can be read
or written simply by specifying a record number along with a
list of variables and, optionally, a pointer to formatting
information.

20.2 Direct Access In WATFIV

    The WATFIV compiler recognizes statements which create
and process direct access files of data. A "file" is a
collection of records. A "record" is the amount of data
normally read or written in a single READ or WRITE
statement. For example, there might be one record in a

payroll file for each employee. For each direct access file, the compiler must know certain facts such as the file number and the length of each record in the file. All records must have the same length. READ and WRITE statements are used to input and output direct access records. Each READ or WRITE contains at least a file number and a record number. Because there are significant differences between unformatted and formatted operations, they will be discussed separately.

20.3 Unformatted Direct Access Input-Output

Suppose one-hundred cards each contain ten INTEGER values. The values are to be read and stored on a direct access file. The ten values on card one are to constitute record one; those in card two, record two; etc.. Once the cards have been read and the data written in the file, additional cards are to be read each of which contains a single INTEGER value. If the value is K, the total of the values in the Kth and (K+1)th records is to be calculated and printed. The following program solves the problem. It illustrates the most important features of unformatted input-output.

```
C EXAMPLE 20.1 UNFORMATTED DIRECT ACCESS I/O
C DEFINE THE DIRECT ACCESS FILE - FILE #8, 100
C    RECORDS OF 10 VALUES EACH USING FORMAT-FREE
C    INPUT-OUTPUT STATEMENTS
      DEFINE FILE 8(100,10,U,NEXT)
      INTEGER SET(10)
C
C     READ AND WRITE THE 100 SETS OF DATA
      DO 1 I=1,100
         READ,SET
         WRITE(8'I) SET
    1 CONTINUE
C
C     READ LOOP - READ CARD,GET A VALUE OF K
C
    2 READ(5,*,END=5) K
         ISUM=0
C
C        READ THE KTH DATA RECORD AND
C           FIND THE TOTAL
         READ(8'K) SET
         DO 3 I=1,10
            ISUM=ISUM+SET(I)
    3    CONTINUE
C
```

```
C           READ AND ADD THE VALUES IN
C              THE NEXT RECORD
C
            READ(8'NEXT) SET
            DO 4 I=1,10
               ISUM=ISUM+SET(I)
       4    CONTINUE
C
            PRINT,'SUM OF VALUES IN SETS',K,'AND',
      *        K+1,'IS',ISUM
          GO TO 2
C
       5 STOP
         END
```

Remarks

1. The statement which defines the direct access file is

    DEFINE FILE 8 (100,10,U,NEXT)

In this statement:

"8" is the "file number". A different file number should be used for each direct access file in a program. Check with your computing center to find out what device numbers refer to direct access files.

"100" is the number of records in the file. Any attempt to reference a record beyond 100 would result in an error.

"10" is the length of each record. For unformatted records, this length must be stated in "words". Since each INTEGER value occupies one word (4 bytes) of memory, the length of each record is ten words.

"U" indicates that unformatted READ and WRITE statements will be used to read and write the records in the file.

"NEXT" is called the "associated variable". Following execution of any READ or WRITE it has a value which is one more than the record number of the record used in the READ or WRITE statement.

2. The statement "WRITE(8'I) SET" causes the ten values in SET to be written in the space reserved for record I in file 8. Note that a single quote separates the file number and the record number. Since there is no pointer to format information, the operation is unformatted. This means that a copy of the bit patterns of the ten INTEGER values in SET is written into record I.

3. The statement "READ(8'K) SET" causes a copy of the first ten words of the Kth record in file 8 to be stored in the ten words of memory reserved for SET. Since NEXT is the associated variable, following execution of this statement, the value of NEXT will automatically be K+1.

4. The statement "READ(8'NEXT) SET" is similar to the previous READ statement. It illustrates the use of the associated variable. If the program had attempted to assign a value to NEXT, an error would have occured.

20.4 Summary Of Unformatted Input-Output

1. The general form of the DEFINE FILE statement is

   DEFINE FILE file# (number of , length of , U , assoc.)
                        records   record   var

   where: the file# must be in the range 1 thru 99

          the length of a record is stated in words

          the associated variable is an INTEGER variable

2. The READ statement has the general form

            READ (file# ' record#) list

   where: "file#" is an INTEGER constant or variable indicating the file from which data is to be read

          "record#" is an INTEGER constant, variable or expression indicating which record is to be read. Its value must be positive and not greater than the number of records in the file.

"list" is optional and, if present, indicates the
    variables to be assigned a value by executing
    the READ statement.   The bit patterns found
    in the record   are assigned sequentially
    (byte-by-byte)   to   the memory locations
    reserved for variables in the list.   The
    total length of the input list must not
    excede the record length.

3. The WRITE statement has the general form

        WRITE (file# ' record#)list

   where: "file#" is as above.

        "record#" is as above and indicates which record
            is to contain the values in the output list.

        "list" describes the values which are to be
            written into the record. If the total length
            of the values in the output list is less than
            the length of the record, the unused portion
            of the record is filled with zero bits. If
            the length of the values in the output list
            excedes the length of the record,   an error
            occurs.

4. A FIND statement (Section 20.8)   can be used with
   unformatted direct access files.

    Unformatted direct access files should be used for
temporary storage of data values. That is,   when the data
will be used as input later in the program or perhaps by
some other program.

20.5 Formatted Input-Output

    The rules and use of formatted direct access files will
be presented using two example problems. A summary of the
rules can be found in Section 20.6.

Problem 1

    Suppose the XYZ Company maintains records of how much
money is owed by each of its 1700 customers. The information
is currently punched on cards. The problem is to store the
data on a direct access file. Assume that each customer has
a customer number in the range 1 thru 2000. Input to the

program consists of 1700 cards each of which contains the
following information.

columns	mask	data
1-4	I4	customer number
5-24	A20	customer name
25-32	F8.2	amount owing
33-38	I6	date of last change (DDMMYY)

   The following program reads the cards and records the
information about customer N in the Nth record of direct
access file 27. Further comments follow the program.

```
C EXAMPLE 20.2 FORMATTED DIRECT ACCESS
C DEFINE A FILE OF 2000 RECORDS OF LENGTH 50
        DEFINE FILE 27(2000,50,E,IVAR)
        INTEGER CUSTNO,DATE
        CHARACTER*34 DATA
C       READ EACH CARD AND WRITE THE DATA IN THE FILE
        DO 1 N=1,1700
            READ(5,900,END=2) CUSTNO, DATA
900         FORMAT(I4,A34)
            WRITE(27'CUSTNO,901)DATA
901         FORMAT(A34)
      1 CONTINUE
      2 STOP
        END
```

Remarks

1. The statement which defines the direct access file is

        DEFINE FILE 27 (2000 , 50 , E , IVAR)

   In this statement:

   "27" is the file number. A different file number
       should be used for each direct access file.

   "2000" is the number of records in the file. Since
       customer numbers can be as large as 2000 and
       since the data for customer N is to be in the
       Nth record, the file contains 2000 records
       even though not all records will be used.

   "50" is the length of each record in bytes. Aside
       from the customer number, there are 34 bytes
       of data about each customer. The length was

chosen as 50 to allow additional information to be kept if needed in the future.

"E" indicates that formatted READ and WRITE statements will be used to process the records in the file.

"IVAR" is the associated variable. Following any READ or WRITE its value is automatically set to the next higher record number. IVAR was not used in this program.

2. Consider the statement pair

```
        READ(5,900,END=2) CUSTNO,DATA
    900 FORMAT(I4,A34)
```

When reading the symbols in the cards, the information in columns 1-38 is of interest. Specifically, columns 1-4 contain the customer number and columns 5-38 the information about the customer. Since our purpose is simply to store the data in the file, it is not necessary to separate the name, amount and date information.

3. The statements

```
        WRITE(27'CUSTNO,901)DATA
    901 FORMAT(A34)
```

cause the 34 symbols stored in DATA to be stored in the first 34 positions of record number CUSTNO of direct access file 27. The remaining 16 bytes of the record are automatically set to blanks.

Problem 2

In order to keep its set of customer records up to date, changes are necessary in records of the direct access file created to solve problem one. In particular, suppose change cards have the following information.

columns	mask	item
1-4	I4	customer number
5-12	F8.2	dollar amount
13-18	I6	date (DDMMYY)

Suppose an unspecified number of change cards have been keypunched and are in no particular order with respect to customer number. The problem is simply to read the cards and: add the amount value in the card to the amount value in the customer record (assume a negative amount represents a payment); change the date in the record to the date in the card. The following program could be used.

```
C EXAMPLE 20.3 UPDATE CUSTOMER FILE
      INTEGER CUSTNO,DATE,CDATE
      CHARACTER*20 NAME
      DEFINE FILE 27(2000,50,E,MMM)
C
C     READ LOOP - READ A CHANGE CARD
    1 READ(5,900,END=2)CUSTNO,CAMNT,CDATE
  900    FORMAT(I4,F8.2,I6)
C        READ THE RECORD FROM THE FILE
         READ(27'CUSTNO,901) NAME,AMT,DATE
  901    FORMAT(A20,F8.2,I6)
         AMT=AMT+CAMNT
         DATE=CDATE
C        WRITE THE REVISED RECORD
         WRITE(27'CUSTNO,901) NAME,AMT,DATE
      GO TO 1
C
    2 STOP
      END
```

Remarks

1. The DEFINE FILE statement is identical to the one used when the file was created.

2. The statements

```
      READ(27'CUSTNO,901) NAME,AMT,DATE
  901 FORMAT(A20,F8.2,I6)
```

cause NAME, AMT and DATE to be assigned a value using information stored in record number CUSTNO of file 27. Why is NAME an element of the input list? Why not leave it out since no change is being made in the name? The answer has nothing to do with the READ statement but a great deal to do with the WRITE statement. If the value of NAME is not obtained at READ time, it would be impossible to know what to put in the name area of the record at WRITE time. That is, a WRITE statement replaces the entire contents of a record.

3. The statement "WRITE(27'CUSTNO,901)NAME,AMT,DATE" causes the contents of record number CUSTNO to be replaced with the values of NAME, AMT, and DATE according to the format codes in statement 901.

20.6 Summary Of Formatted Input-Output

1. The DEFINE FILE statement has the general form

DEFINE FILE file# (number of , length of , E , assoc.)
                   records   a record   var.

where: "file#" is a constant in the range 1-99

"number of records" is the number of records in the file

"length of a record" is the length of each record in bytes.

"E" indicates that formatted input-output statements will be used to process the records in the file.

"associated variable" is an INTEGER variable which has a value one greater than the number of the record most recently read or written.

2. The READ statement has one of the following forms:

READ(file#'record#, fmt) list

READ(file#'record#, fmt,ERR=m) list

where: "file#" is the number of the direct access file from which data is to be read. An INTEGER variable can be used to store the file# value.

"record#" is an INTEGER constant, variable or expression whose value indicates which record within the file is to be read. The value must be positive and not greater than the number of records in the file.

"fmt" is a reference to the set of format codes to be used when reading the data.

"ERR=m"   indicates   that   control   is   to   be
transferred   to   statement   number   m   if   an
equipment   problem   occurs when   reading   the
record.

"list" is a list of variables to be assigned a
value by executing the READ statement.

3. The WRITE statement has the form

WRITE(file#'record#, fmt) list

where: "file#", "record#" and "fmt" have the same use as
when present in a READ statement.

"list" is optional and contains the values which
are to be stored in the record by executing
the WRITE statement.

A WRITE statement causes the entire contents of a record
to be   replaced.   All   positions   skipped   over or
unreferenced by the format codes will contain blanks.
All positions covered by masks or literals will contain
the symbols appropriate to the use of the particular
code.

4. Executing a single READ or WRITE statement may cause more
than one record to be read or written. It depends on the
format codes. If it is necessary to recycle format codes
because there are fewer masks than items in the input or
output list,   the   record   number   is automatically
increased by one each time the end of the format codes
is reached. A slash code can be used in an input
operation to cause the next record to be read.   On
output, a slash code causes: a record to be written
before the end of the format codes is reached;   the
record number to be increased by one. Care should be
used in the use of recycling and slash codes on input
operations since any attempt to read a record in which
nothing has previously been written is an error.

5. The symbol "E" in a DEFINE FILE statement also permits
the "*" (format-free) forms of READ and WRITE statements
to be used. The allowed forms are:

READ(file#'rec#,*)...

READ(file#'rec#,*,ERR=m)...

WRITE(file#'rec#,*)...

If the "*" form of the WRITE statement is used, each
item in the output list is written according to the
default mask appropriate to the type of value.   On
input, WATFIV routines scan successive records beginning
with the one whose record number appears in the READ
statement.   Values in the records are assumed to be
separated by a comma or blanks. As many records will be
read as is necessary to find a value for each item in
the input list.

20.7 Input-Output Using A Mix Of Statements

When using a direct access file, the same type of
statement (unformatted or formatted) is normally used for
all READ and WRITE statements used to process records in a
particular file.   If it is necessary to use a mixture of
unformatted and formatted input-output statements then:

i) In the DEFINE FILE statement, an "L" is used
instead of an "E" or "U" to indicate that a mix of
statement types may be used.

ii) The length of each record is stated in bytes.

iii) All format-free READ and WRITE statements are
processed according to the rules in Section 4 of
this chapter.

iv) All formatted READ and WRITE statements are
processed according to the rules in Section 6 of
this chapter.

A word of caution. It is extremely unlikely that a
format-free WRITE statement and a formatted READ statement
(or vice-versa) would ever be used to process the same
record in a file.

20.8 The FIND Statement

The FIND statement has the general form

FIND (file# ' record#)

where "file#" and "record#" indicate the direct access file
and record within that file which is to be "found".

There are two delays which occur when locating a record
to read or write. The names given to these delays are "seek
time delay" and "rotational delay". By issuing a FIND for a

record before it is read or written, the first of these two
delay times _may_ be reduced thus speeding up the overall
execution-time of the job.   The program structure below
illustrates the use of a FIND statement.

```
          C EXAMPLE 20.4 USING A FIND STATEMENT
                DEFINE FILE 8 (...)
                    .
                    .
                FIND (8'i)
                    .
                    .
                READ(8'i,...) ...
                    .
                END
```

     After the execution of a FIND statement, the associated
variable has a value equal to the record number which
appeared in the FIND statement.

20.9 Other Topics

     Several direct access files can be defined in a single
DEFINE FILE statement.   The information about each file is
separated by a comma. For example:

     DEFINE FILE 8 (100,34,E,IVAR1), 9 (60,10,U,IVAR2)

defines two direct access files.   File 8 contains 100
formatted records of 34 bytes each and file 9 contains 60
unformatted records of 10 words each. IVAR1 and IVAR2 are
the names of the associated variables.

     There are several topics related to the use of direct
access files and devices which are beyond the scope of this
book.   Control over the factors outlined below is
accomplished by cards which are not processed by the WATFIV
compiler. Information can be found in a publication such as
the IBM manual "Fortran H Programmer's Guide".

     a) The assignment of file numbers to specific devices.

     b) Selection of efficient record lengths and the use of
        blocked records.

     c) The creation of labels to identify and protect data
        files.

     d) Techniques for converting record identifiers to
        record numbers for use in locating data.

Exercise 20.1

1. For each of the following,   write a suitable DEFINE FILE
   statement to define the file characteristics.

   a) Records in the file will be read and   written using
      unformatted READ and WRITE statements.   Each record
      will have 20 INTEGER values. Assume the file number
      is 20 and the associated variable is NEXT.

   b) Direct access file 12 is to be a set of 137 records
      some of which may require as many as 200 characters
      of data. Formatted READ and WRITE statements will
      be used to process the records.   No use is expected
      to be made of the associated variable.

   c) Records in file 17 may be read with or without format
      control.   ION is to take on the value of the next
      higher record number following execution of any
      input-output statement.   As many as 10000 records
      may be needed and the largest records will have to
      store the values in 12 by 5 matrix of REAL numbers.

2. What is the output of the following program?

```
                DEFINE FILE 25(10,8,U,NEXT)
                INTEGER VEC(8),NUM(4)
        C
                DO 1 I=1,4
                    READ,VEC
                    WRITE(25'VEC(1)) (VEC(J),J=2,8,2)
                1 CONTINUE
        C
                2 READ,IREC
                    READ(25'IREC) NUM
                    IF(NUM(3) .EQ. 0)    STOP
                    PRINT,NUM
                GO TO 2
        C
                END
        $ENTRY
                3 8 0 2 5 6 1 10
                6 0 3 5 1 0 2 0
                8 9 0 0 6 1 8 0
                1 0 3 5 7 8 4 6
                8
                3
                6
                1
```

3. What is the output of the following program?

```
        DEFINE FILE 16(16,16,E,J)
        REAL A(3)/2.,4.5,7.3/,I(3)/12,2,5/
C
        WRITE(16'1,900)(A(K),I(K),K=1,3)
900 FORMAT(F3.1/I6)
C
        READ(16'2,901)X,Y,Z
901 FORMAT(F6.2)
        PRINT,X,Y,Z
C
        READ(16'J,902)M,N
902 FORMAT(I1,1X,I6)
        PRINT,M,N,J
C
        STOP
        END
```

20.10 Summary

Data can be recorded on, and read from, direct access devices. All records in a direct access file must have the same length. A DEFINE FILE statement is used to specify the characteristics of a direct access file. A WRITE statement replaces the entire contents of a record.

If unformatted READ and WRITE statements are used to process records,

- The length of each record is specified as being a number of words.

- Exactly one record is read by any READ statement.

- Exactly one record is written by any WRITE statement.

If formatted READ and WRITE statements are used to process records,

- The record length is stated in bytes.

- The number of records which are read or written in an input-output operation depends on the format codes which are used.

Proper use of a FIND statement may reduce the time necessary to locate a record on a direct access device.

20.11 Programming Problems

20.1 Assume that each of twelve students takes two courses -- math and English. Prepare a deck of twelve cards containing the following data.

cols.	item
1-2	student number (range 01-99)
3-24	student name
25-26	math mark (F2.0)
27-28	English mark (F2.0)

Write a program which reads the twelve cards and records the information on a direct access file so that the information about the student having a student number of K is found in the Kth record of the file. On a second direct access file write a single record containing the twelve valid student numbers in order of increasing magnitude. Display the contents of each card for future reference.

20.2 Using the data files created in problem one, print a report which, for each student, displays the student number, name, math mark, English mark, and average. Rewrite each student's record to include his average in the information kept in the file.

20.3 Using the data created in problem two as input to the program, write a program which prints the names and averages of the twelve students in order of decreasing standing in the class based on the student's average.

20.4 Write a program which will store the elements of a matrix on a direct access file. Each row of values in the matrix should be recorded as a separate record in the file. The file should be large enough to accommodate matrices having as many as 500 rows and 200 columns. Input to the program consists of the number of rows and columns in the matrix followed by the values in the matrix -- row by row. Once the values have been read and stored in the file, use the file information as input to determine: (a) which column of elements contains the longest sequence of decreasing values; (b) the number of non-decreasing sequences of values in each row.

20.5 Create two direct access files each of which contains twenty records of one INTEGER value each. The values in each set should be in order of non-decreasing

magnitudes. Using these files as input, determine how
many values are present in both sets. Use an algorithm
such that each record needs to be read only once. Use
format-free input-output.

CHAPTER 21   CHARACTER "DEVICES"

Questions Answered In This Chapter

  1. How are CHARACTER variables used as the source of
     data in a READ statement? What are the reasons for
     wanting to do this?

  2. How can CHARACTER variables be used to store the
     output of a WRITE operation? How is this technique
     useful in creating "print-line images" and
     modifying FORMAT codes at execution time?

21.1 Concepts And Uses Of CHARACTER Devices

     Consider the following simple problem. An unknown number
of REAL values have been punched on each of several cards.
Each card contains from one to ten values and the values on
any card are separated by commas.   The problem is to
determine the average of the values punched on each card. So
you say "What's so hard about that?". O.K.   -- write a
program to solve the problem! The difficulty results from
the following chain of implications. (1) Commas are used to
separate the data values and so a format-free READ statement
must be used. (2) Given that a format-free READ statement
must be used, then the input list in the READ statement must
have the same number of variables as there are values
punched on the card. (If there are more variables than
values, more than one card would be read. If there are fewer
variables than values, some numbers would not be read since
we can't read the same card twice.) (3) The problem then is
we must know how many values are on each card before we read
it and yet we can't find this out until we read it.

     The solution to the problem is essentially the
following. Read each card and store the symbols in the card
in a set of eighty CHARACTER variables. Determine the number
of values in the card by counting the number of commas in
the card.   Set up an input list (using an implied DO-loop)
in a format-free READ statement which has the appropriate
number of variables.   "Read" the values using the CHARACTER
variable(s) as the source of input. A suitable program can
be found later in the Chapter.

     A second problem.   Suppose INTEGER values in the range
one thru one-hundred are being read in, one value per card.
For each value read, a line is to be printed which contains
a "*" in the print position specified by the number on the

card. To solve this problem a brute force approach could be used which would involve writing 100 FORMAT statements and perhaps a DO CASE or Computed GO TO with 100 values in the statement number list. What we would like however, is to be able to use a sequence of statements such as

```
         READ,N
         PRINT 900
     900 FORMAT(' ',TN,'*')
```

Unfortunately, variables and expressions cannot be used in a string of format codes.

    We can look at format codes as simply strings of symbols. Therefore, if there were some way of converting the INTEGER value which we read, into its equivalent CHARACTER value, the problem would be solved.

    The two preceding problems can be easily programmed if there was some way of converting CHARACTER values to non-CHARACTER values and vice-versa. This is the subject of this chapter. When converting CHARACTER values to non-CHARACTER values, the basic idea is to consider a CHARACTER variable or array as being a "dummy card reader" from which data can be read. To convert non-CHARACTER values to CHARACTER values, a CHARACTER variable is treated as though it were a single print line.

21.2 CHARACTER Variables Used As Input Devices

How To Do It

    Suppose the variable SYMBLS has been defined by

         CHARACTER*4 SYMBLS/'1234'/

The problem is to convert the constant '1234' to the INTEGER value 1234 and to the REAL value 1234. If J and A are the two variables which are to have the converted values, statements such as

```
         J=SYMBLS
         A=SYMBLS
```

will cause errors since a CHARACTER value cannot be assigned to a non-CHARACTER variable. The following statements do the job.

```
      C CONVERT THE SYMBOLS TO AN INTEGER VALUE
            CHARACTER*4 SYMBLS/'1234'/
            READ(SYMBLS,900) J
        900 FORMAT(I4)
      C
      C CONVERT THE SYMBOLS TO A REAL VALUE
            READ(SYMBLS,901) A
        901 FORMAT(F4.0)
```

In both READ statements the source of data (the input "device") is the CHARACTER variable SYMBLS. The input list contains the variables which are to be assigned a value as a result of executing the READ statement. The FORMAT statement serves its usual purpose -- to describe the locations within the source of data which are to be scanned when looking for a value to be assigned to each variable in the list.

Why use a READ statement? Why not have a built-in function or library subprogram to perform the conversion? The answer is that by using a READ statement, the programmer can take advantage of the tremendous power of formatting. Consider the following examples.

```
    i)        CHARACTER*4 SYMBLS/'1234'/
              READ(SYMBLS,900) J,A
          900 FORMAT(I4,T1,F4.0)

        Result: J=1234 and A=1234.

   ii)        CHARACTER STRING*12/'-2.73E01589.'/
              READ(STRING,901) A,B,K
          901 FORMAT(E8.2,2X,F2.0,T1,I2)

        Result: A=-27.3, B=9., K= -2

  iii)        CHARACTER VEC(5)/'1','2','3','4','5'/
              READ(VEC,902) I,J,K,L,M
          902 FORMAT(I1)

        Result: I=1, J=2, K=3, L=4, M=5
          That is, each element of the array is treated
          as a separate "card".

   iv)        CHARACTER DATA*8/'1234 678'/
              READ(DATA,*) I,J

        Result: I=1234, J=678
```

v)   Two examples of errors.

a)   CHARACTER*10 ARRAY(3)/'1', '2', '3'/
         READ(ARRAY,903) J,K,L,M
     903 FORMAT(I10)

   Error: Four input variables and only three vari-
          ables in ARRAY. The "END=" parameter should
          be used.

b)   CHARACTER*3 DATA/'123'/
         READ(DATA,904) K
     904 FORMAT(I4)

   Error: Length of format codes exceeds length of
          variable. (Similar to attempting to read
          beyond column 80 in a card.)

To summarize. A READ statement in which the the input
"device" is a CHARACTER variable or CHARACTER array or array
element is permitted in WATFIV. All forms of format-free and
formatted READ statements are permitted. The source of data
(the CHARACTER variable(s)) can be thought of as an internal
card reader in which:

a) The number of cards in the card reader equals the
   number of variables specified by the CHARACTER
   device.   That is: 1 if a simple variable; N if the
   name of an array having N elements; (N-I+1) if the
   Ith element of an array of N elements is specified
   as the source of data.

b) The length of each "card" is the length of the
   CHARACTER variable or array element used as the
   source of data.

21.3 Use Of CHARACTER Input Devices

A CHARACTER variable or array must be used as an input
device when the input data contains information which is
essential to properly read the data. The information may
indicate what format codes should be used and/or which and
how many variables should be in the input list.   This means
the program must be able to select or construct appropriate
format codes and/or an input list by examining the symbols
found in the data. Once this has been done, the data can be
re-read using the CHARACTER variable(s) as the source of
data. The determination of suitable format codes or input
list may be a simple or a very complex problem.   The
following problem is simple.

A First Example

Suppose a data deck contains two types of cards -- name cards and wage cards. Name cards contain an employee number in columns 1-5, the person's name in columns 6-30 and a "1" in column 80. Wage cards contain an employee number in columns 1-5, a wage rate in columns 6-10 (F5.2), the number of hours worked in columns 11-15 (F5.2) and a "2" in column 80. Assume that the cards are arranged in order of increasing employee number and that a wage card follows the name card. Although there is a name card for every employee, there may or may not be a wage card for each employee since some employees did not work during the period for which the payroll is to be calculated. The problem is to read the data cards and print the pay of those employees having a wage card following their name card. The following program solves the problem.

```
      C EXAMPLE 21.1 PAYROLL REPORT
            INTEGER CDTYPE,NAMNUM,WAGNUM
            CHARACTER*79 DATA,NAME*25
      C
      C       READ LOOP
          1 READ (5,900,END=4) DATA,CDTYPE
        900     FORMAT(A79,I1)
      C         DETERMINE IF A NAME OR WAGE CARD
                IF(CDTYPE.EQ.1) THEN
      C             PROCESS NAME CARD
                    READ(DATA,901) NAMNUM,NAME
        901         FORMAT(I5,A25)
                ELSE
      C             PROCESS WAGE CARD
                    READ(DATA,902)WAGNUM,RATE,HOURS
        902         FORMAT(I5,2F5.2)
      C             CHECK FOR MATCH ON EMPLOYEE NUMBER
                    IF(WAGNUM .EQ. NAMNUM) THEN
                        PAY=HOURS*RATE
                        PRINT 903,WAGNUM,NAME,PAY
        903             FORMAT('0',I5,2X,A25,F8.2)
                    ELSE
                        PRINT,'WAGE AND NAME CARD MISMATCH'
                        PRINT,'THE WAGE CARD HAD THE DATA:'
                        PRINT,WAGNUM,RATE,HOURS
                    END IF
                END IF
            GO TO 1
      C
          4 STOP
            END
```

A Second Example

The problem which introduced the material in this chapter was that of calculating the average of an unknown number of REAL values punched in each of several data cards. The values on each card are separated by commas. This means a format-free READ statement is required. Because the READ statement must be format-free, the program must know how many items are on the card in order to set up an appropriate input list. Unfortunately this value can only be determined after the card has been read.

In the following program, the symbols in the card are read and stored in a set of eighty CHARACTER variables. Then commas are counted and finally the required number of values are read using the CHARACTER variable as the source of data.

```
C EXAMPLE 21.2 READING FROM A CHARACTER VARIABLE
      CHARACTER SCAN(80),CHDEV*80,COMMA/','/
      REAL VALUE(20)
C
C     READ A CARD AND STORE ITS SYMBOLS AS A GROUP
C         OF 80 AND AS 80 GROUPS OF 1
    1 READ (5,900,END=4) CHDEV,SCAN
  900     FORMAT (A80,T1,80A1)
C
C         COUNT COMMAS BY TESTING ELEMENTS OF SCAN
          NVALS=1
          DO 2 I=2,79
              IF(SCAN(I).EQ.COMMA)NVALS=NVALS+1
    2     CONTINUE
C
C         READ THE NVALS VALUES USING CHDEV AS THE
C             SOURCE OF DATA
          READ(CHDEV,*) (VALUE(I),I=1,NVALS)
C
C         COMPUTE THE AVERAGE AND PRINT IT
          SUM=0.
          DO 3 I=1,NVALS
              SUM = SUM+VALUE(I)
    3     CONTINUE
          AVG=SUM/NVALS
          PRINT,'AVERAGE OF',NVALS,'VALUES IS',AVG
      GO TO 1
C
    4 STOP
      END
```

Some remarks:

Note that the symbols are stored in both SCAN and CHDEV. SCAN is necessary so that each symbol in the card can be checked for a comma. CHDEV (length 80) is necessary when the data is read using the CHARACTER variable as the source of the input. The statement "READ(SCAN,*)list" could not be used since it would be treated as an input device of 80 "cards" of one column each instead of one card of 80 columns. (SCAN and CHDEV could have been EQUIVALENCEd to achieve the same effect.)

Is it really necessary to count commas? No. If one assumes there are twenty or fewer values in any card, the following approach could have been used:

(a) Read a card and store its symbols in CHDEV.
(b) Set all elements of VALUE to zero.
(c) Attempt to assign a value to all elements of VALUE by reading from CHDEV using format-free input and the "END=" parameter.
(d) Count backwards from VALUE(20) to find the first non-zero value in VALUE and thus determine the number of values in the card.
(e) Calculate the average and continue with the next card.

Problem 21.2 asks you to use this algorithm.

Exercise 21.1

1. For each of the following, determine the last value assigned to each variable.

a)
```
            CHARACTER*8 STR/' 123 56.8'/
            READ(STR,*) I,A
            READ(STR,900) B,C,K
        900 FORMAT(2F3.0,1X,I1)
            READ(STR,901) M,E,L,D
        901 FORMAT(I2,2(F1.1,I1))
```

b)
```
            CHARACTER*3 STR(6)/2*'1',4*'2'/,STR2*2(6)
            CHARACTER*2 STR3(3)
            INTEGER SET1(6),SET2(6)
            READ(STR,901) STR2
        901 FORMAT(A2)
            READ(STR,902) STR3
        902 FORMAT(/A2)
            READ(STR,*) SET1
            READ(STR,903) SET2
        903 FORMAT(I3)
```

2. What is printed by the following program?

```
          CHARACTER*79 CARD
          DO 1 I=1,5
             READ 900, ICODE,CARD
900          FORMAT(I1,A79)
             IF(ICODE.EQ.1) THEN
2               READ(CARD,903) A1,A2
903             FORMAT(F5.2,F3.1)
                PRINT,A1,A2
             ELSE
                READ(CARD,902) N1,N2
902             FORMAT(3X,I2,I2)
                PRINT,N1,N2
             END IF
        1 CONTINUE
          STOP
          END
    $ENTRY
    123456789
    223456789
    12.456.89
    12.456 89
    2.        .
```

3. Suppose the symbols "1234" are punched in the first four columns of a card. These symbols can, of course, be read three times in the same READ statement by the following statements.

```
          CHARACTER*4 SYMS
          READ 900, SYMS, A,M
      900 FORMAT(A4,T1,F4.0,T1,I4)
```

Under what circumstances could a T-code not be used to re-read card columns? Give an example.

4. Below are four READ statements. In each, the "?" is one of the following: a CHARACTER variable; an INTEGER constant; an implied DO-loop; an array containing format codes; an element of a CHARACTER array. Indicate which of the foregoing could be substituted for the question mark. Also indicate whether the READ statement is formatted or format-free.

```
    a)   READ, ?, list
    b)   READ(?) list
    c)   READ ?, list
    d)   READ, +(?), list
```

21.4 CHARACTER Variables As Output "Devices"

In formatted output operations, a CHARACTER variable or array can be used an an output "device". To do this, a WRITE statement is used in which a CHARACTER variable, array or array element replaces the reference to a printer, card punch, tape unit or direct access file. When the WRITE statement is executed, the symbols stored in the CHARACTER element(s) are those which would normally have been sent to the output device. A simple example is the following.

```
          CHARACTER*8 RECEVE
          WRITE(RECEVE,900) 12345678
      900 FORMAT(I8)
```

Result: The symbols "12345678" are stored in RECEVE

Why use CHARACTER variables as output devices? One important application is to perform "dynamic formatting". Dynamic formatting allows you to change format codes under program control at execution time. This application is described in Section 6 of this chapter. A second important application is in the preparation of "print-line images". This latter application is useful when a program needs to print two or more reports and only one printer is available. This application is discussed in Section 5 of this chapter.

How To Do It

Recall that there are 133 print positions in a line of printing. When values in the output list of a PRINT or WRITE statement are sent to the printer, symbols are stored in the print positions according to format codes or default masks. The same principles apply when a CHARACTER element is used as the output device. That is, each CHARACTER variable used as an output device can be viewed as a print line with a length equal to the length of the variable. However, the first symbol stored in each variable has no special use as it does when output is sent to the printer. Rules of use follow the examples below.

Example 1 - The output device is a simple variable

```
          CHARACTER*14 B
          WRITE(B,900) 'VALUE IS',-9.99
      900 FORMAT(A8,F6.2)
```

Result: The variable B contains "VALUE IS -9.99"

Example 2 - The output device is an array

```
        CHARACTER*5 X(4), Y*3/'ABC'/
        WRITE(X,901) Y,Y,Y,Y
    901 FORMAT(A3)
```

Result: Each of the four elements of X contains the
        symbols "bbABC" ("b" denotes a blank). Since
        there is only one one mask, each time the end
        of the format codes is reached, the codes are
        recycled and apply to the next variable in
        the array.   The blanks precede rather than
        follow the "ABC" because of the POT rule.

Example 3 - The output device is an array element

```
        CHARACTER*6 Y(8)/8*'ZZZZZZ'/
        WRITE(Y(3),902)  (J,J=1,4)
    902 FORMAT(2I3)
```

Result: Y(1) and Y(2) are unchanged
        Y(3) contains "bb1bb2"
        Y(4) contains "bb3bb4"
        Y(5) thru Y(8) are unchanged

The use of an array element allows you to begin the
write operation at a variable other than the first
element of an array. Otherwise it is the same.

Example 4 - Typical errors

a)   CHARACTER*5 X
        WRITE(X,904) 123
    904 FORMAT(I8)

Reason: The format codes exceed the length of
        the CHARACTER variable.

b)   CHARACTER*4 X(3)
        WRITE(X,905) 1, 2, 3, 4
    905 FORMAT(I4)

Reason: Since there is only one mask, four vari-
        ables or more are required for the device.
        X has only three.

Summary of Rules

1. The WRITE statement can be used to store symbols in
   CHARACTER variables. The allowed forms are:

                WRITE (char, fmt) list

                WRITE (char, *) list

    where: "char" is a CHARACTER variable, array or
           array element;

           "fmt" is any valid format reference. The
           "*" denotes format-free.

           "list" is a set of values which will be
           converted to symbols and stored in the
           CHARACTER variable(s) specified by
           "char". The list is optional.

2. When the WRITE statement is executed:

    a) The first variable specified by "char" is is set
       to blanks.

    b) If a formatted WRITE statement is used, the
       format codes are processed left to right in
       normal fashion. That is, as each mask is
       encountered, the next item in the output list
       is converted to symbols and stored in the
       CHARACTER variable. Slash codes and recycling
       can cause successive elements of an array to
       contain elements from the output list of a
       single WRITE statement. Before any symbols are
       stored in a variable, the variable is set to
       blanks.

    c) Variables in "char" which are unaffected by the
       format codes are left unchanged.

3. The total width of the format codes must not exceed the
   length of the variable to which they apply. The maximum
   number of recycling operations or slash codes is limited
   by the number of variables specified by "char".

21.5 Print-Line Images

Suppose two or more printed reports must be produced by the same program. If only one printer is available, one solution would be to run the job twice and print a different report on each run. A much better approach is to print one of the reports on the printer and write "print-line images" of the second report on an intermediate storage device such as magnetic tape or a direct access file. A print-line image is simply a string of 133 symbols (for the typical printer) stored in a CHARACTER variable and which contains the control character and symbols which will eventually appear on a printed line. The following problem and subsequent program illustrates the use of print-line images.

Suppose a deck of cards has data in the following format.

columns	data	mask
1-20	name	A20
21-50	address	A30
51	sex (M or F)	A1
52-53	age	I2
54-55	height in inches	I2
56-58	weight in pounds	I3

Two reports are to be printed. Report 1 is simply a name and address list. Report 2 is to show the sex, age, height and weight of each person. The reports are to appear as shown below.

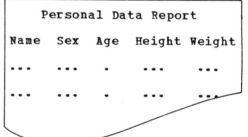

In the following program, the SUBROUTINE TAPRNT is used to print the lines in the Personal Data Report. The print-line images for this report are written on device 3 which is assumed to be a magnetic tape unit.

```
C EXAMPLE 21.3 PRINT-LINE IMAGES
      INTEGER TAPE/3/,AGE, HEIGHT, WEIGHT
      CHARACTER IMAGE*133, NAME*20,ADDRSS*30,SEX
      REWIND TAPE
C     PRINT HEADINGS FOR REPORT 1
      PRINT 900
  900 FORMAT('1',10X,'NAME AND ADDRESS REPORT'//)
C     WRITE HEADING FOR REPORT 2 INTO IMAGE AND
C            THEN ON TAPE
      WRITE(IMAGE,901)
  901 FORMAT('1',10X,'PERSONAL DATA REPORT')
      WRITE(TAPE)IMAGE
C
C READ CARDS AND PRINT APPROPRIATE DATA FOR EACH
C  REPORT - PERSONAL DATA GOES ON TAPE
C
    1 READ(5,902,END=2) NAME,ADDRSS,SEX,AGE,
     *                  HEIGHT,WEIGHT
  902     FORMAT(A20,A30,A1,2I2,I3)
C         PRINT LINES FOR REPORT ONE
          PRINT 903,NAME,ADDRSS
  903     FORMAT('0',A20,/,5X,A30)
C         CREATE PRINT-LINE IMAGE FOR REPORT 2
          WRITE(IMAGE,904)NAME,SEX,AGE,
     *                    HEIGHT,WEIGHT
  904     FORMAT('0',A20,A3,3I8)
C         WRITE PRINT-LINE IMAGE ON TAPE
          WRITE(TAPE) IMAGE
      GO TO 1
C
C     END OF CARD DATA PROCESSING
C
    2 ENDFILE TAPE
C     CALL SUBROUTINE TO PRINT REPORT 2
      CALL TAPRNT(TAPE)
      STOP
      END

      SUBROUTINE TAPRNT(I)
      CHARACTER*133 LINE
      REWIND I
C
C     READ AND PRINT TAPE RECORDS
    1 READ(I,END=2) LINE
      PRINT 900,LINE
      GO TO 1
C
  900 FORMAT(A133)
    2 RETURN
      END
```

Comments about the preceding program: In the mainline segment, each line of Report 2 is written into the variable IMAGE and then IMAGE is written on tape.   Note that an appropriate vertical control character is stored in the first symbol of IMAGE. Why not write the lines of Report 2 directly on tape?   This certainly could be done.   The only advantage in using the variable IMAGE is that all tape records written will be the same length.   That is,   if a formatted WRITE statement was used to produce the tape records, the length of each record would depend on the total length of the format codes used.   Since IMAGE is a simple variable,   it means that no slash codes or recycling is possible when writing into IMAGE. The use of slash codes or recycling would be O.K. if IMAGE was an array but this would add unnecessary complexity.

The only information needed in the subprogram is the device number of the tape on which the print-line images have been written.   Because of this, the subprogram TAPRNT could be used in different programs or at different points in the same program. In fact, a mainline as simple as

```
      READ, ITAPE
      CALL TAPRNT(ITAPE)
      STOP
      END
```

could be used to print any report previously written in the form of print-line images on tape.

The general procedure to create and use a tape (or direct access file) of print-line images is:

1. Rewind the tape
2. For each line, write the print-line symbols into a CHARACTER variable of length 133.
3. Write the variable on tape (format-free).
4. Write a tapemark record (ENDFILE).

To use the tape:

1. Rewind the tape.
2. Read each tape record (format-free) and print it using a mask of A133.

The use of print-line images allows

a) More than one report to be printed in a run.
b) A copy of a report to be kept for later use.

21.6 Execution-Time Formatting

This section illustrates and summarizes the different methods of using and changing format codes at execution time. In this section, a PRINT statement will be used for output which is sent to the printer. A WRITE statement will be used for all non-printed output operations.

On output, format codes are used to control the appearance and positioning of of program data. During an input operation, format codes are used to describe the usage of card columns in the cards read by executing a READ statement. In formatted statements such as

```
READ fmt, list
READ(...,fmt) list
PRINT fmt, list
WRITE(..., fmt) list
```

the "fmt" is either the statement number of a FORMAT statement or the name of an array containing format codes. The use of CHARACTER arrays to store format codes is described in Chapter 16 Section 9. The use of non-CHARACTER arrays to store format codes is described in Chapter 17 Section 12. It is assumed the reader is familiar with this material. As a brief review, the following pairs of statements are equivalent.

```
CHARACTER*10 FMT(1)/'(''0HELLO'')'/
PRINT FMT

PRINT 900
900 FORMAT('0HELLO')
```

Recall that two successive quotes are necessary to define a single quote as part of a Quote-type literal.

Method 1 - Reading Format Data From An Input Device

a) Reading An Entire Set Of Codes

If format codes need to be changed for different runs of the same program, the entire set of codes can be read from an input device. The following example illustrates this technique.

```
        CHARACTER*20 FMT(1)
        READ 900, FMT
    900 FORMAT(A17)
          .
          .
          .
        PRINT FMT, X, I
          .
          .
    $ENTRY
    ('1',F11.5,2X,I3)
```

Recall that format codes must be stored in an array and that
the array name is used in the READ, PRINT or WRITE statement
in place of a statement number of a FORMAT statement.

b) Reading Only Literal Data

If a literal of either type (Quote or H-type) appears in
a set of format codes used by a READ statement, the symbols
in the card columns covered by the literal replace the
symbols in the literal. For example, the following program
prints "FEBRUARY 8,1979" at the top of a page.


```
        READ 900
        PRINT 900
    900 FORMAT('THIS IS CHANGED ')
        STOP
        END
    $ENTRY
    1FEBRUARY 8,1979
```


This method of changing a literal in a set of format codes
is infrequently used because it implies the same set of
format codes would be used for both input and output -- a
situation which does not frequently occur.

Method 2 - Changes Made By Statements Within The Program

Each symbol in a set of format codes is stored as a
CHARACTER value. Thus the problem of modifying format codes
is that of modifying the appropriate symbols. The most
powerful technique is to "write" the approprate symbols into
the CHARACTER variable(s) used to store the codes.

Example 1

In the following, the codes

                    (nX , I8)

are used. The "n" denotes a value which is assigned to an
INTEGER variable N in the program.

```
          C EXAMPLE 21.4 EXECUTION TIME FORMATTING
                CHARACTER*8 FMT(1)
                DO 1 N=1,5
                    WRITE(FMT,900) N
          900       FORMAT('( ',I1,'X,I8)')
                    PRINT FMT,N
              1 CONTINUE
                STOP
                END
```

In this example, the WRITE statement is used to put the
appropriate value of "n" in the format codes.   The PRINT
statement simply displays the value of N using the format
codes set up by the WRITE statement. In words, the statement
"WRITE(FMT,900)N" says "Store the value of N in the
CHARACTER array FMT according to the format codes in
statement 900.".   The format codes in the statement

          900 FORMAT('(', I1, 'X,I8)')

consist of two literals and one I-mask. Note that "I8" is
not a mask but simply two of the symbols in the literal
"'X,I8)'".   This means that when N has a value of 3 for
example, that the eight symbols stored in FMT(1) are:

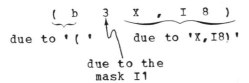

          (b   3   X , I 8)
    due to '('   due to 'X,I8)'

            due to the
            mask I1

The result of executing the program is to display the values
one thru five on five lines with successive values appearing
in print positions 9 thru 13 respectively.

An alternate way of achieving the same result would be
to put the two literals in the output list of a WRITE
statement and use A-masks to position them within FMT(1).
This is done in the statements below.

```
            WRITE(FMT,901) '(', N, 'X,I8)'
        901 FORMAT(A1,I1,A5)
```

This second approach is not as frequently used as the first.
The remaining examples will use the first approach.

Example 2

    Suppose we want to print the letter "V" using asterisks
in the print positions shown below.

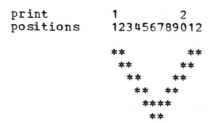

```
        print            1        2
        positions     123456789012

                      **          **
                       **        **
                        **      **
                         **    **
                          ****
                           **
```

To solve the problem, we need a set of format codes of the
type

                (Tm , '**' , Tn , '**')

where "m" and "n" change by +1 and -1 respectively each time
a line is printed. The following program could be used.

```
        C EXAMPLE 21.5 THE BIG "V"
                CHARACTER*21 CODES(1)
                M=10
                N=22
                DO 1 I=1,6
                  M=M+1
                  N=N-1
                  WRITE(CODES,901) M, N
        901       FORMAT('(T',I2,','' **''',T',I2,','' **'')')
                  PRINT CODES
              1 CONTINUE
                STOP
                END
```

Note that there are five format codes in statement 901.
These include three literals which define the non-varying
symbols used to print each line and an I-mask for each of
the values M and N.

Example 3 - Plotting

      A graph of the function y=(x-4)**2 for integer values of
x in the range 1 thru 14 is to be printed.   First,   we can
calculate   and store   the x-y   coordinates   of the   fourteen
points to   be plotted   in a   table called   POINT.   If   a " *"
symbol is used to indicate a   point on the graph,   our first
reaction might be to have the output appear as shown below.

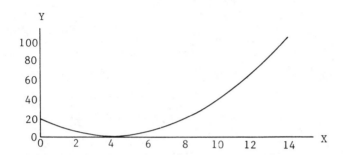

There are two disadvantages to this approach. First, on some
printed lines more   than "*" will have to   be printed.   This
means changes would have to be made in both the position and
number of format   codes required   by   the PRINT   statement.
Second,   since the graph is printed   from the top down,   the
set   of data   points would   have to   be sorted   in order   of
decreasing   magnitude   of   function   values.   These   two
disadvantages can   be overcome by   turning the graph   on its
side as shown in the following diagram.

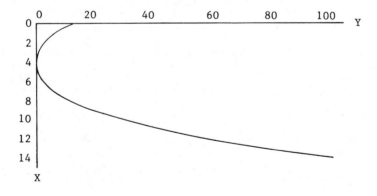

The following program solves the problem. It also prints axes for the graph.

```
      C EXAMPLE 21.6 PLOT OF Y=(X-4)**2 FOR X=1,2,...,14
            INTEGER POINT(14,2)
            CHARACTER*18 FCODES(1)
      C     CALCULATE X-Y COORDINATES OF THE DATA POINTS
            DO 1 I=1,14
                POINT(I,1)=I
                POINT(I,2)=(I-4)**2
          1 CONTINUE
      C     DISPLAY HEADING AND POINTS TO BE PLOTTED
            PRINT 900,POINT
        900 FORMAT('1GRAPH OF THE POINTS'//' X VALUES-',
           * 14I4,' Y VALUES-',14I4,//)
      C     DRAW Y-AXIS WITH LABELS
            PRINT 901,(I-1,I=1,106,5)
        901 FORMAT(' ',22I5)
            PRINT 902,'  0',('*',I=1,106),' Y'
        902 FORMAT(A3,106A1,A2)
      C
      C     DRAW GRAPH USING VALUES IN POINT
      C
            DO 2 I=1,14
      C         PUT VALUE OF N IN "(I3,' *',TN,'*')"
      C           WHERE THE FIRST "*" IS FOR THE X-AXIS
      C           AND THE SECOND FOR THE DATA POINT
            WRITE(FCODES,903) POINT(I,2)+5
        903     FORMAT('(I3,''*'',T',I3,',''*'')')
            PRINT FCODES, I
          2 CONTINUE
      C     PRINT "X" TO LABEL X-AXIS AND GO TO NEW PAGE
            PRINT 904
        904 FORMAT(T5,'*'/T5,'X'/'1')
            STOP
            END
```

In this example, the asterisks which represent the X-axis are located in print position five. This is the reason that five is added to each function value in order to determine the position of the data point in each line.

Execution-Time Formatting Rules - A Summary Of The Method

1. Define a CHARACTER array to store the format codes. The length of the array element(s) should be sufficient to contain all the symbols in the set of codes which will be used at print time.

2. WRITE the value(s) of the INTEGER(s) which vary from one line to the next into the array under control of a FORMAT statement. The FORMAT statement will contain literals (for those symbols which do not change) and an I-mask for each value which does change.

3. Print the required line using the format codes stored in the array.

Exercise 21.2 CHARACTER Variables As Output Devices

1. Assume VAR has been defined by "CHARACTER*20 VAR". Describe the symbols stored in VAR or explain why an error occurs.

a)
```
        WRITE(VAR,900) 245
    900 FORMAT(I20)
```

b)
```
        WRITE(VAR,901) (FLOAT(J)+.5,J=1,4)
    901 FORMAT(4F5.2)
```

c)
```
        WRITE(VAR,902) ('$12',I=3,16,3)
    902 FORMAT(T4,3A3,2A2)
```

d)
```
        WRITE(VAR,903) 3, 7, 2
    903 FORMAT('(I',I1,',''X'',T',I1,',',I2,'A3)')
```

e)
```
        WRITE(VAR,904) -2.35E-17,3.
    904 FORMAT(E16.7)
```

f)
```
        WRITE(VAR,905) ((I+J,J=1,4),I=1,3)
    905 FORMAT(3I3,T2,4I4,T4,5I5)
```

2. Assume CODES has been defined by "CHARACTER*20 CODES(1)". Describe the printed output.

a)
```
        WRITE(CODES,900) 3
    900 FORMAT('(I',I1,')')
        PRINT CODES, 8
```

b)
```
        DO 1 N=1,5
          WRITE(CODES(1),901) N
    901   FORMAT('(''0'',',I1,'I3)')
          PRINT CODES, (J,J=1,N)
        1 CONTINUE
```

c)   DO 2 I=1,4
            WRITE(CODES,902) 20-4*I, I
     902   FORMAT(' (T',I2,',',I2,'I4)')
            PRINT CODES, (I,J=1,I)
          2 CONTINUE

3. Suppose X is a CHARACTER array containing a single
   variable. For each of the following, assign X some
   initial value so that the statement shown can be
   executed without an error.

   a)   PRINT X, X
   b)   WRITE(X,X)
   c)   WRITE(X,X) X

4. State the use of "X" in the four statements shown below.
   In each case, select from the following list those
   things which are permitted for X: CHARACTER constant;
   CHARACTER variable; CHARACTER array; CHARACTER array
   element; non-CHARACTER variable, constant or expression;
   implied DO-loop.

        a)   PRINT X, list
        b)   PRINT, X, list
        c)   PRINT,'X', list
        d)   PRINT,(X), list

21.7 Summary

1. One or more CHARACTER variables may be used as an
   internal "card reader" in which: the number of "cards"
   equals the number of variables specified as the input
   device; the length of each "card" is the length of the
   variable(s) specified as the device. The use of
   CHARACTER variables as input devices means that it is
   possible to read and process "self-descriptive" data.
   That is, the data itself contains information which is
   essential to properly read the values present in the
   card.

2. One or more CHARACTER variables may be used as an
   internal "printer". The length of the print-line equals
   the length of the variable being used as the output
   device. The number of print-lines available equals the
   number of variables used as the output device. The two
   most important uses of CHARACTER output devices are:

   a) To create print-line images

   b) To create appropriate sets of format codes at

execution time.

3. Both formatted and format-free input-output operations are allowed when CHARACTER variables are specified as the device in a READ, PRINT or WRITE statement.

21.8 Programming Problems

21.1 Each data card which is read by the program contains either one REAL value or one INTEGER value. The program should read the cards and print the sum of the REAL values and the sum of the INTEGER values. Note: a REAL value will have a decimal point as one of the symbols in the value.

21.2 Modify example program 21.2 so that the card need not be scanned for commas. A suggested algorithm is found in Remark (ii) following the program. Under what circumstances would putting a zero in each element of VAL (step 2 of the algorithm) cause the average to be incorrect? How could this problem be overcome?

21.3 Write a FUNCTION subprogram called ICNVRT which converts a CHARACTER value whose symbols are digits to an equivalent INTEGER value. Test the subprogram using the following mainline.

```
CHARACTER*80 X/'123456'/
I=ICNVRT(X)
PRINT,I
STOP
END
```

21.4 Add a second parameter called ICODE to the subprogram ICNVRT of Problem 3. The subprogram should assign ICODE a value of zero if the symbols in the CHARACTER value represent a valid INTEGER constant. If invalid, set ICODE equal to one. Test the subprogram using a mainline which prints each CHARACTER value along with the word "VALID" or "INVALID".

21.5 Modify example program 20.1 to permit an employee to have multiple wage cards.

21.6 Write a program which reads in an INTEGER value representing a number of cents. Calculate the smallest number of coins required to pay this amount using quarters, dimes, nickels and cents. Display the output as shown in the following example.

46 CENTS REQUIRES 1 QUARTER, 2 DIMES, 0 NICKELS, 1 CENT

Use only one FORMAT statement in your program. Note: the program **must** use the plural or singular (e.g. DIMES or DIME) depending on the number of coins required.

21.7 Modify programming problem 21.6 so that zero values are suppressed. For example, the output for 46 cents would appear as

46 CENTS REQUIRES 1 QUARTER, 2 DIMES, 1 CENT

21.8 Write a SUBROUTINE to display the status of a Tic-Tac-Toe playing surface at any stage of the game. The SUBROUTINE will have a single parameter -- a three-by-three matrix of INTEGER values. The value of the (i,j)th element of the matrix will be : "-1" if Player One has selected that position; "0" if neither player has selected the position; "+1" if Player Two has selected that position. Display the playing surface using an "X" to indicate Player One's moves and an "O" to indicate Player Two's moves. Unused squares should be left blank. Use only one FORMAT statement to print the lines containing the X's and O's.

21.9 Write a program which reads a set of twenty-five INTEGER values of varying magnitudes and prints them using as few lines as possible. Do not print any symbols to the right of print position thirty.

21.10 Use execution time formatting to produce the following four patterns.

```
    ****        ****        *               *
    ***         ***         **             **
    **          **          ***           ***
    *           *           ****         ****
```

21.11 Write a program which reads a value of N and then N more INTEGER values. Print the N values as shown below.

X (1) = ___   X (2) = ___   ...   X (n) = ___

21.12 Suppose each of several data cards contains 5 INTEGER values in columns 11 to 80 of the card. Columns 1 thru 10 contain the format codes to read the required values in columns 11-80. Using the information in columns 1 to 10 read and print the values in each card.

Questions Answered In This Chapter

1. What is NAMELIST input-output?

2. How and why is the DUMPLIST statement used in WATFIV programs?

22.1 NAMELIST Output

Format-free output statements are   not allowed   in some members of the Fortran family of languages.   Instead,   the NAMELIST statement   is used to provide format-free-like output. Consider the following simple example.

```
C EXAMPLE 22.1 NAMELIST OUTPUT
        INTEGER NUM(3)/1,2,3/, NEG20/-20/
        REAL A/31.5/,BSET(2)/-5.,-7./
        COMPLEX Z/(1.,2.)/
        NAMELIST /LIST1/NUM,NEG20,A,BSET,Z
        WRITE(6,LIST1)
        PRINT LIST1
        STOP
        END
    $ENTRY
```

Result: Two sets of the two lines below are printed.

```
    &LIST1
    NUM= 1, 2, 3, NEG20= -20,A= 0.3150000E 02,
    (continued) BSET= -0.5000000E 01, -0.7000000E 01,
    (continued) Z=( 0.1000000E 01, 0.2000000E 01), &END
```

The following points should be noted.

a) In the NAMELIST statement, a name enclosed in slashes is used to identify a list of variables or array names which are to be output using the NAMELIST feature. In the example, "LIST1" was the name given to the list. Any valid WATFIV name can be used.

b) The WRITE or PRINT statement used to display the values of variables and array elements contains a NAMELIST name instead of a reference to formatting information.

c) The printed output consists of two or more lines for each list printed. Each begins in print position

two.   The first line contains the list name
preceded by a "&.";.su on The second and subsequent
lines consist of the names in the list followed by
the value(s) currently assigned to the variable(s).
Values of array elements appear in storage order
(rightmost subscript varying least rapidly). Values
are printed using the normal default mask for the
particular type of value.   The symbols "&END"
follow the last value.

<u>General Form And Rules Of NAMELIST Output</u>

a) The general form of a NAMELIST statement is

        NAMELIST /name1/ list1 /name2/ list2 etc.

where: "name1", "name2", etc. are any valid WATFIV
names and are used to identify the list which
follows the name; "list1", "list2", etc. are lists
of simple variables or array names which are
separated by commas. A variable or array name can
appear in more than one list.

b) A NAMELIST statement is a non-executable statement.
It should follow any declaration statements which
are required to define the type or dimensions of
elements in a list.   Subprogram parameters may not
appear in a NAMELIST list.

c) To create NAMELIST output one of the following two
statements should be used.

        WRITE(device,name)
        PRINT name

where: "device" specifies the output device on
which the data is to be written (e.g. "6" for the
printer); "name" is a NAMELIST name.

d) The statements

        NAMELIST /name/var1,var2,var3,...
        PRINT name

produce the same output as

    PRINT,'&name'
    PRINT,'var1=',var1,',var2=',var2, ...,',&END'

e) More than one NAMELIST statement is permitted in a
   segment. For example,

   NAMELIST /LIST1/X,Y /LIST2/T,U,X

is equivalent to
      NAMELIST /LIST1/ X,Y
      NAMELIST /LIST2/ T,U,X

22.2 NAMELIST Input

For non-NAMELIST input operations, the question "What
variables are to be assigned a value?" is answered by
including an input list in the READ statement.   In NAMELIST
input operations, the variables which are to be assigned a
value as well the values themselves are found on the data
cards. There are definite rules for kepunching the name-
value pairs. Any variable which is permitted to be assigned
a value in this way must belong to a NAMELIST list. Consider
the following example.

```
      C EXAMPLE 22.2 NAMELIST INPUT
            INTEGER NUM(3), K
            REAL A(5), B
            NAMELIST /INLIST/ NUM, K, A, B
            READ(5, INLIST)
      C     NOTE: "READ INLIST" COULD ALSO HAVE BEEN USED
            STOP
            END
      $ENTRY
       &INLIST NUM(2)=3, B=-7.24E03, A=1., 2., 3*-400.
            &END
```

Results: NUM(2) has a value of 3; NUM(1) and (NUM(3)
         are left unchanged.
         B has a value of -7240.
         A(1)=1; A(2)=2; A(3) thru A(5) each equal -400.
         The value of K is left unchanged.

General Form And Rules Of NAMELIST Input

a) One or more NAMELIST statements are used to specify
   lists of non-subscripted variables and arrays whose
   values may   be assigned in a   NAMELIST input
   operation.   Rules of the NAMELIST statement are
   those found in the preceding section (NAMELIST
   Output).

b) A READ statement used for NAMELIST input has one of
   the following forms.

```
        READ name
        READ(device, name)
        READ(device, name, END=n)
        READ(device, name, ERR=m)
        READ(device, name, END=n, ERR=m)
```

where: "name" is a NAMELIST name and "device" is a reference to the input device on which the input data is located (e.g. "5" for the card reader).

c) Keypunching NAMELIST Data

i) Column 1 of each data card read by a NAMELIST READ statement must be blank.

ii) The first data card read by a NAMELIST READ should have a "&" in column 2 and the NAMELIST name beginning in column 3. The NAMELIST name must be followed by at least one blank column.

iii) Each variable-value pair is punched as follows: variable name followed by "=" followed by the value. In the case of an array having more than one element, the sequence is array name followed by "=" followed by the values which are separated by a comma. The constants must agree in type with the variables to which they are assigned. Commas should be used to separate variable-value pairs and array-values data items. "&END" follows the last data item.

iv) If the data is punched on more than one card, variable names, array names and constants cannot be split onto two cards. That is, the first symbol following column 1 (which must be blank) must be the beginning of a variable name, array name or constant.

v) LOGICAL constants may be punched as "T", ".TRUE.", "F" or ".FALSE.".

4. The value of any element of a NAMELIST input list which is not assigned a value by the data cards is unchanged by the execution of a NAMELIST input operation.

5. Variable-value pairs on the data-cards can appear in
   any order. Each variable or array however, must be
   an element of the NAMELIST list specified in the
   READ statement.

6. If "&name" is not found starting in column 2 of the
   first card read, successive cards are read until it
   is found or until the end of data is reached.

7. NAMELIST input is not restricted to data stored on
   punched cards. Any valid input device can be used.

22.3 DUMPLIST Output

Occasionally, one would like to have NAMELIST-type
output only if a program terminates abnormally. This is the
purpose of the DUMPLIST statement. For this reason, the
DUMPLIST statement is often useful for debugging programs.
Values of the variables in all DUMPLIST statements are
printed automatically if a program terminates because of an
execution-time error.   Consider the   following simple
example.

```
C EXAMPLE 22.3 DUMPLIST OUTPUT
      INTEGER I/2/, J/0/
      DUMPLIST /LIST/I,J,K
      K=I/J
      STOP
      END
```

When the program is executed, the messages:

"***ERROR***   LIMIT EXCEEDED FOR FIXED-POINT DIVISION BY
ZERO"

and

"PROGRAM WAS EXECUTING LINE   3 IN   ROUTINE M/PROG   WHEN
TERMINATION OCCURRED"

are followed by the lines:

```
**** DUMPLIST FOR ROUTINE M/PROG FOLLOWS ****
&LIST
I=            2,J=            0,K=UUUUUUUUUUUU,&END
```

Note that the name of each variable in the DUMPLIST list is
printed followed by its value at the time the job was
terminated.   Any type of variable or array can be put in a
DUMPLIST list. The rules of DUMPLIST usage are identical to

those of NAMELIST output with the following four exceptions.

   i) The word "DUMPLIST" replaces the word "NAMELIST".

   ii) A DUMPLIST list name does not appear in a WRITE or PRINT statement.

   iii) A DUMPLIST statement has no effect if the program executes normally.

   iv) If a program terminates abnormally, the contents of all DUMPLIST lists are printed in the order in which they appear in the program.

22.4 Summary

NAMELIST output provides many of the features of format-free output with the bonus that the variable names are automatically printed ahead of the values which they have. NAMELIST output however, is not as "natural" to use as format-free output.

NAMELIST input permits the input data to answer (to a limited extent) the question "What variables are to be assigned values?". Its use is seldom required.

DUMPLIST output can be handy for debugging programs. It is easy to use and has no effect if the program runs without errors.

22.5 Programming Problems

22.1 Suppose students in a class take one or more of the following subjects: English, French, Math, Science, History. One card has been punched for each student in the class. Each card contains one or more subject abbreviation-mark pairs. For example, a typical card might contain

     ENG=79, HIST=92, MATH=58

Write a program which will read and process data cards of this type and print a report showing: (a) the number of students taking each subject; (b) the average mark of students taking each subject; (c) the class average. Use NAMELIST input in your program. Use one or more DUMPLIST statements to help during the debugging phase of the problem.

Questions Answered In This Chapter

1. What is Unformatted Input-Output?

2. How any why is it used?

3. What is the relationship between unformatted input-output and A-mask input-output?

23.1 Unformatted Input-Output

Unformatted input-output involves the direct transmission of bit patterns to and from devices attached to the computer. Unlike format-free or formatted input-output, the bit patterns are not tested, examined or altered in any way.

That is, there are essentially three different types of input-output operations -- formatted, format-free, and unformatted. With formatted and format-free the format codes and masks describing the appearance of the values are supplied by the programmer (formatted) or provided free by the WATFIV compiler (format-free). Unformatted input-output is somtimes called binary input-output. With unformatted, the number of bytes of data which is transferred during an input-output operation depends only on the total length of the items in the input or output list. The type of item (INTEGER, REAL, etc.) is of no consequence.

The allowed forms of unformatted READ and WRITE statements are:

        READ(u) list

        READ(u,END=n) list

        READ(u,ERR=m) list

        READ(u,END=n,ERR=m) list

        WRITE(u) list

In these statements, "u" is any valid reference to a device and "list" is optional.

Unformatted READ and WRITE statements for magnetic tape and disk devices were described in Chapters 19 and 20.

Consider the following example. Assume "5" refers to the card reader and "6" refers to the printer.

```
            READ(5) K,X
            WRITE(6) K,X
            PRINT,K,X
            STOP
            END
      $ENTRY
      234 67.
```

When this program is executed, two lines are printed. The first line contains " 234 67.". (The first blank is in print position 1.) The second line contains "1089663988" followed by "0.9647109E 00". Why? The statement "READ(5)K,X" is an unformatted READ statement. There are two items in the input list each of length four. This means the first four bytes of data sent from the card reader (the bit pattern produced by the symbols punched in columns one thru four) will be stored in the four bytes of memory reserved for the variable K. The four bytes of data produced by the hole patterns in columns five thru eight will be stored in the four bytes of memory reserved for X. The bit patterns produced by columns one thru eight and therefore those stored in the memory locations for K and X are:

cols. 1-4 " 234"   01000000 11110010 11110011 11110100

cols. 5-8 " 67." 01000000 11110110 11110111 01001011

Appendix A describes the bit pattern produced for any of the 256 valid hole patterns. It is important to note that the type of variable in the input list doesn't matter at all. Any symbols could be "assigned" to an INTEGER variable using an unformatted READ. The statement "WRITE(6)K,X" causes eight bytes of data to be stored in print positions one thru eight. The symbols represented by these eight bytes are then printed. The statement "PRINT,K,X" is a format-free output statement. It means "interpret" the bit patterns found in the memory locations for K and X as those of an INTEGER and REAL value respectively. Display those values on the printer using the (default) masks of I12 and E16.7.". Appendix C describes the correspondences between bit patterns and values.

23.2 Other Facts About Unformatted Input-Output

1. The effect of unformatted input-output is similar to that of formatted operations in which an A-mask is used for each item in the list. However, the width of each mask

must be the same as the length of the variable to which it applies. For example, the two sets of statements below are equivalent.

```
READ(5) A,B,C

READ(5,900) A,B,C
900 FORMAT(A4,A4,A4)
```

The differences occur when the length of an A-mask and the item to which it applies have different lengths. With the A-mask padding and truncation take place according to the TIP and POT rules described in Chapter 16. With unformatted input-output padding and truncation have no meaning. For example:

```
        READ(5) I
        PRINT, I
        STOP
        END
$ENTRY
1234
```

and

```
        READ(5,800) I
    800 FORMAT(A5)
        PRINT, I
        STOP
        END
$ENTRY
1234
```

Cause the values -235736076 and -218893248 to be printed respectively.

Unformatted input-output is faster than the equivalent formatted input-output.

2. If the total length of the input list exceeds the length of a record on the input device (80 bytes for card input), an error occurs.

3. If the total length of values in an output list exceeds the length of a record on the output device (133 for a printer), an error occurs.

4. Unformatted input-output may be useful for:

    a) Assigning a specific bit pattern to a variable.

b) Reducing the space required to store values on
   tape, direct access files, and punched cards.

c) Reducing the execution-time of input-output
   operations.

5. Unformatted input-output cannot be used when CHARACTER
   variables are used as the device in a READ or WRITE
   statement.

Exercise 23.1

1. Write a suitable READ statement and show the data card
   which would be read to cause the bit pattern

      11110000 01100000 11111001 11110110

   to be assigned to an INTEGER variable N using

      a) An unformatted READ statement
      b) A formatted READ statement with an A-mask
      c) A formatted READ statement with a Z-mask
      d) A format-free READ statement.

   Verify your answers by using an unformatted WRITE
   statement to print the results -- all four methods
   should produce the same output.

23.3 Summary

   In an unformatted READ operation, the number of bytes of
data transferred from the input device equals the total
length of items in the input list. The bytes of data are
stored sequentially in the memory locations reserved for
items in the list.

   In an unformatted WRITE operation, the number of bytes
of data transferred to the output device equals the total
length of items in the output list. The bytes of data are
sent sequentially from the memory locations reserved for
items in the list.

23.4 Programming Problems

   Solve any of the programming problems from Chapter 16
which require A-mask input. Where possible, use unformatted
READ and WRITE statements.

Part IV

APPENDICES
WITH WATFIV S

The standard punched card is 7.375 inches long and 3.25 inches wide. There are 960 positions in which holes can be punched in a card. These hole positions are arranged in a table of eighty vertical columns and 12 horizontal rows. The columns are numbered one thru eighty and the rows are called, beginning from the top, "row 12, row 11, row 0, row 1, row 2, row 3, ..., row 8, row 9. Although there are 4096 unique patterns of holes which could be punched in any column, only 256 of these patterns are acceptable to the card reader. Each valid hole pattern represents a different symbol and causes a unique pattern of eight bits (eight ones and zeros) to be stored in the computer memory. In the following table the hole patterns are numbered from zero thru 255. The hexadecimal (base 16) representation of the bit pattern, the bit pattern, and the keypunch symbol associated with the bit pattern is shown for each of the valid hole patterns. Those hole patterns for which no symbol is shown can be punched using the "multiple punch" key on the keyboard. Many references describe the operation of a keypunch. See for example the IBM publication "IBM 29 Card Punch".

Dec	Hex	Hole Pattern	Bits	Sym
0	00	12-0-9-8-1	0000 0000	
1	01	12-9-1	0000 0001	
2	02	12-9-2	0000 0010	
3	03	12-9-3	0000 0011	
4	04	12-9-4	0000 0100	
5	05	12-9-5	0000 0101	
6	06	12-9-6	0000 0110	
7	07	12-9-7	0000 0111	
8	08	12-9-8	0000 1000	
9	09	12-9-8-1	0000 1001	
10	0A	12-9-8-2	0000 1010	
11	0B	12-9-8-3	0000 1011	
12	0C	12-9-8-4	0000 1100	
13	0D	12-9-8-5	0000 1101	
14	0E	12-9-8-6	0000 1110	
15	0F	12-9-8-7	0000 1111	
16	10	12-11-9-8-1	0001 0000	
17	11	11-9-1	0001 0001	
18	12	11-9-2	0001 0010	
19	13	11-9-3	0001 0011	
20	14	11-9-4	0001 0100	
21	15	11-9-5	0001 0101	
22	16	11-9-6	0001 0110	
23	17	11-9-7	0001 0111	
24	18	11-9-8	0001 1000	
25	19	11-9-8-1	0001 1001	
26	1A	11-9-8-2	0001 1010	
27	1B	11-9-8-3	0001 1011	
28	1C	11-9-8-4	0001 1100	
29	1D	11-9-8-5	0001 1101	
30	1E	11-9-8-6	0001 1110	
31	1F	11-9-8-7	0001 1111	

Dec	Hex	Hole Pattern	Bits	Sym
32	20	11-0-9-8-1	0010 0000	
33	21	0-9-1	0010 0001	
34	22	0-9-2	0010 0010	
35	23	0-9-3	0010 0011	
36	24	0-9-4	0010 0100	
37	25	0-9-5	0010 0101	
38	26	0-9-6	0010 0110	
39	27	0-9-7	0010 0111	
40	28	0-9-8	0010 1000	
41	29	0-9-8-1	0010 1001	
42	2A	0-9-8-2	0010 1010	
43	2B	0-9-8-3	0010 1011	
44	2C	0-9-8-4	0010 1100	
45	2D	0-9-8-5	0010 1101	
46	2E	0-9-8-6	0010 1110	
47	2F	0-9-8-7	0010 1111	
48	30	12-11-0-9-8-1	0011 0000	
49	31	9-1	0011 0001	
50	32	9-2	0011 0010	
51	33	9-3	0011 0011	
52	34	9-4	0011 0100	
53	35	9-5	0011 0101	
54	36	9-6	0011 0110	
55	37	9-7	0011 0111	
56	38	9-8	0011 1000	
57	39	9-8-1	0011 1001	
58	3A	9-8-2	0011 1010	
59	3B	9-8-3	0011 1011	
60	3C	9-8-4	0011 1100	
61	3D	9-8-5	0011 1101	
62	3E	9-8-6	0011 1110	
63	3F	9-8-7	0011 1111	

Sym	Bits	Hole Pattern	Dec	Hex
¬	0110 0000	11	96	60
\	0110 0001	0-1	97	61
	0110 0010	11-0-9-2	98	62
	0110 0011	11-0-9-3	99	63
	0110 0100	11-0-9-4	100	64
	0110 0101	11-0-9-5	101	65
	0110 0110	11-0-9-6	102	66
	0110 0111	11-0-9-7	103	67
	0110 1000	11-0-9-8	104	68
	0110 1001	0-8-1	105	69
‚	0110 1010	12-11	106	6A
&	0110 1011	0-8-3	107	6B
%	0110 1100	0-8-4	108	6C
_	0110 1101	0-8-5	109	6D
>	0110 1110	0-8-6	110	6E
?	0110 1111	0-8-7	111	6F
	0111 0000	12-11-0	112	70
	0111 0001	12-11-0-9-1	113	71
	0111 0010	12-11-0-9-2	114	72
	0111 0011	12-11-0-9-3	115	73
	0111 0100	12-11-0-9-4	116	74
	0111 0101	12-11-0-9-5	117	75
	0111 0110	12-11-0-9-6	118	76
	0111 0111	12-11-0-9-7	119	77
	0111 1000	12-11-0-9-8	120	78
`	0111 1001	8-1	121	79
:	0111 1010	8-2	122	7A
#	0111 1011	8-3	123	7B
@	0111 1100	8-4	124	7C
'	0111 1101	8-5	125	7D
=	0111 1110	8-6	126	7E
"	0111 1111	8-7	127	7F

Sym	Bits	Hole Pattern	Dec	Hex
	0100 0000	no punches	64	40
	0100 0001	12-0-9-1	65	41
	0100 0010	12-0-9-2	66	42
	0100 0011	12-0-9-3	67	43
	0100 0100	12-0-9-4	68	44
	0100 0101	12-0-9-5	69	45
	0100 0110	12-0-9-6	70	46
	0100 0111	12-0-9-7	71	47
	0100 1000	12-0-9-8	72	48
	0100 1001	12-8-1	73	49
¢	0100 1010	12-8-2	74	4A
.	0100 1011	12-8-3	75	4B
<	0100 1100	12-8-4	76	4C
(	0100 1101	12-8-5	77	4D
+	0100 1110	12-8-6	78	4E
|	0100 1111	12-8-7	79	4F
&	0101 0000	12	80	50
	0101 0001	12-11-9-1	81	51
	0101 0010	12-11-9-2	82	52
	0101 0011	12-11-9-3	83	53
	0101 0100	12-11-9-4	84	54
	0101 0101	12-11-9-5	85	55
	0101 0110	12-11-9-6	86	56
	0101 0111	12-11-9-7	87	57
	0101 1000	12-11-9-8	88	58
	0101 1001	11-8-1	89	59
!	0101 1010	11-8-2	90	5A
$	0101 1011	11-8-3	91	5B
*	0101 1100	11-8-4	92	5C
)	0101 1101	11-8-5	93	5D
;	0101 1110	11-8-6	94	5E
¬	0101 1111	11-8-7	95	5F

Dec	Hex	Hole Pattern	Bits	Sym
160	A0	11-0-8-1	1010 0000	
161	A1	11-0-1	1010 0001	
162	A2	11-0-2	1010 0010	s
163	A3	11-0-3	1010 0011	t
164	A4	11-0-4	1010 0100	u
165	A5	11-0-5	1010 0101	v
166	A6	11-0-6	1010 0110	w
167	A7	11-0-7	1010 0111	x
168	A8	11-0-8	1010 1000	y
169	A9	11-0-9	1010 1001	z
170	AA	11-0-8-2	1010 1010	
171	AB	11-0-8-3	1010 1011	
172	AC	11-0-8-4	1010 1100	
173	AD	11-0-8-5	1010 1101	
174	AE	11-0-8-6	1010 1110	
175	AF	11-0-8-7	1010 1111	
176	B0	12-11-0-8-1	1011 0000	
177	B1	12-11-0-1	1011 0001	
178	B2	12-11-0-2	1011 0010	
179	B3	12-11-0-3	1011 0011	
180	B4	12-11-0-4	1011 0100	
181	B5	12-11-0-5	1011 0101	
182	B6	12-11-0-6	1011 0110	
183	B7	12-11-0-7	1011 0111	
184	B8	12-11-0-8	1011 1000	
185	B9	12-11-0-9	1011 1001	
186	BA	12-11-0-8-2	1011 1010	
187	BB	12-11-0-8-3	1011 1011	
188	BC	12-11-0-8-4	1011 1100	
189	BD	12-11-0-8-5	1011 1101	
190	BE	12-11-0-8-6	1011 1110	
191	BF	12-11-0-8-7	1011 1111	

Dec	Hex	Hole Pattern	Bits	Sym
128	80	12-0-8-1	1000 0000	
129	81	12-0-1	1000 0001	a
130	82	12-0-2	1000 0010	b
131	83	12-0-3	1000 0011	c
132	84	12-0-4	1000 0100	d
133	85	12-0-5	1000 0101	e
134	86	12-0-6	1000 0110	f
135	87	12-0-7	1000 0111	g
136	88	12-0-8	1000 1000	h
137	89	12-0-9	1000 1001	i
138	8A	12-0-8-2	1000 1010	
139	8B	12-0-8-3	1000 1011	
140	8C	12-0-8-4	1000 1100	
141	8D	12-0-8-5	1000 1101	
142	8E	12-0-8-6	1000 1110	
143	8F	12-0-8-7	1000 1111	
144	90	12-11-8-1	1001 0000	
145	91	12-11-1	1001 0001	j
146	92	12-11-2	1001 0010	k
147	93	12-11-3	1001 0011	l
148	94	12-11-4	1001 0100	m
149	95	12-11-5	1001 0101	n
150	96	12-11-6	1001 0110	o
151	97	12-11-7	1001 0111	p
152	98	12-11-8	1001 1000	q
153	99	12-11-9	1001 1001	r
154	9A	12-11-8-2	1001 1010	
155	9B	12-11-8-3	1001 1011	
156	9C	12-11-8-4	1001 1100	
157	9D	12-11-8-5	1001 1101	
158	9E	12-11-8-6	1001 1110	
159	9F	12-11-8-7	1001 1111	

Dec	Hex	Hole Pattern	Bits	Sym
192	C0	12-0	1100 0000	
193	C1	12-1	1100 0001	A
194	C2	12-2	1100 0010	B
195	C3	12-3	1100 0011	C
196	C4	12-4	1100 0100	D
197	C5	12-5	1100 0101	E
198	C6	12-6	1100 0110	F
199	C7	12-7	1100 0111	G
200	C8	12-8	1100 1000	H
201	C9	12-9	1100 1001	I
202	CA	12-0-9-8-2	1100 1010	
203	CB	12-0-9-8-3	1100 1011	
204	CC	12-0-9-8-4	1100 1100	
205	CD	12-0-9-8-5	1100 1101	
206	CE	12-0-9-8-6	1100 1110	
207	CF	12-0-9-8-7	1100 1111	
208	D0	11-0	1101 0000	
209	D1	11-1	1101 0001	J
210	D2	11-2	1101 0010	K
211	D3	11-3	1101 0011	L
212	D4	11-4	1101 0100	M
213	D5	11-5	1101 0101	N
214	D6	11-6	1101 0110	O
215	D7	11-7	1101 0111	P
216	D8	11-8	1101 1000	Q
217	D9	11-9	1101 1001	R
218	DA	12-11-9-8-2	1101 1010	
219	DB	12-11-9-8-3	1101 1011	
220	DC	12-11-9-8-4	1101 1100	
221	DD	12-11-9-8-5	1101 1101	
222	DE	12-11-9-8-6	1101 1110	
223	DF	12-11-9-8-7	1101 1111	
224	E0	0-8-2	1110 0000	
225	E1	11-0-9-1	1110 0001	
226	E2	0-2	1110 0010	S
227	E3	0-3	1110 0011	T
228	E4	0-4	1110 0100	U
229	E5	0-5	1110 0101	V
230	E6	0-6	1110 0110	W
231	E7	0-7	1110 0111	X
232	E8	0-8	1110 1000	Y
233	E9	0-9	1110 1001	Z
234	EA	11-0-9-8-2	1110 1010	
235	EB	11-0-9-8-3	1110 1011	
236	EC	11-0-9-8-4	1110 1100	
237	ED	11-0-9-8-5	1110 1101	
238	EE	11-0-9-8-6	1110 1110	
239	EF	11-0-9-8-7	1110 1111	
240	F0	0	1111 0000	0
241	F1	1	1111 0001	1
242	F2	2	1111 0010	2
243	F3	3	1111 0011	3
244	F4	4	1111 0100	4
245	F5	5	1111 0101	5
246	F6	6	1111 0110	6
247	F7	7	1111 0111	7
248	F8	8	1111 1000	8
249	F9	9	1111 1001	9
250	FA	12-11-0-9-8-2	1111 1010	
251	FB	12-11-0-9-8-3	1111 1011	
252	FC	12-11-0-9-8-4	1111 1100	
253	FD	12-11-0-9-8-5	1111 1101	
254	FE	12-11-0-9-8-6	1111 1110	
255	FF	12-11-0-9-8-7	1111 1111	

FLOWCHARTING

A program flowchart is a diagram of the steps which are
followed in solving a problem. There is a standard set of
symbols and connectors to represent different kinds of
operations (input-output,   computation, decision,   etc.).
These are listed below along with the type of statement
which is usually a translation of the logic represented by
the symbol.

Flowchart Symbol	Name	Statement(s)
	Terminal Operation	START, STOP, ENTRY, RETURN
	Input-Output	READ, WRITE, PUNCH, PRINT, BACKSPACE, ENDFILE, FIND, REWIND
	Compute	Assignment i.e: "=" EXECUTE, CALL
	Decision	IF, Computed or Assigned GO TO, WHILE
	Program Modification	Action which could cause a change in the order of execution. e.g: ASSIGN
	Predefined Process	To indicate a FUNCTION or SUBROUTINE is being used
	Comment	

Flowchart symbols are joined by straight lines. Arrowheads should be used on the connecting lines if the direction of flow is unclear. Flow is ususally assumed to be down and to the right. Connecting lines which cross have no logical interrelationship unless the arrowhead(s) indicate the nature of the relationship. Two types of connector symbols can be used to reduce the number of flowlines in a flowchart.

Onpage Connector

Used to identify an entry to, or an exit from, a point in the flowchart on the same page.

Offpage Connector

Used to identify an entry to, or an exit from, a point in the flowchart on a different page.

Special DO Symbol

If the logic shown in a flowchart will be converted to a Fortran-like program, a special symbol is frequently used to represent the logic of a DO statement. It has the following appearance.

An Example

Shown below is a flowchart which incorporates most of the symbols used in flowcharting. The program describes a procedure to calculate the sum of as many as N values of f(x) where only positive values of x are used. The procedure stops if the sum is negative before N values of x have been processed. A program which is a translation of the flowchart logic is shown on the right.

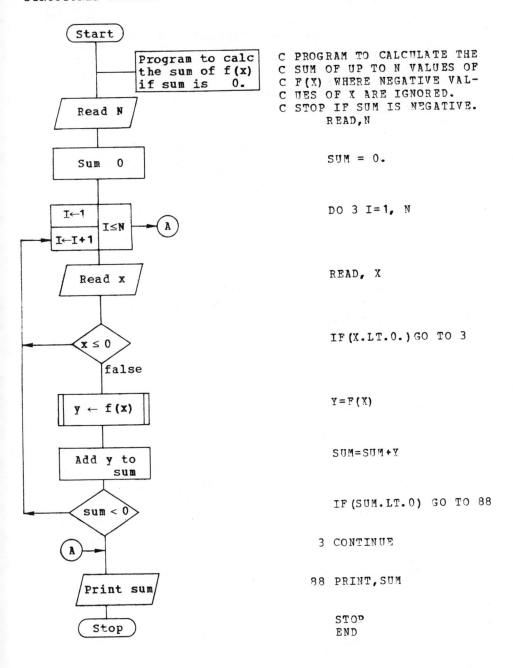

```
C PROGRAM TO CALCULATE THE
C SUM OF UP TO N VALUES OF
C F(X) WHERE NEGATIVE VAL-
C UES OF X ARE IGNORED.
C STOP IF SUM IS NEGATIVE.
      READ,N

      SUM = 0.

      DO 3 I=1, N

      READ, X

      IF(X.LT.0.)GO TO 3

      Y=F(X)

      SUM=SUM+Y

      IF(SUM.LT.0) GO TO 88

3     CONTINUE

88    PRINT,SUM

      STOP
      END
```

Conventions for Structured Programming Constructs

It is possible to describe any algorithm using only the three constructs: sequence, if-then-else and while-do. The flowchart symbols for these are:

1. Sequence block symbol

A sequence, process or function may contain other constructs within the logic block.

2. IF-THEN-ELSE

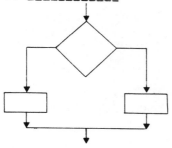

Either the left or right sequence block is executed.

3. WHILE-DO

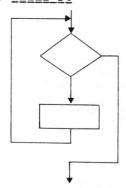

The sequence block is executed repeatedly as long as a relationship is true.

APPENDIX C   INTERNAL REPRESENTATION OF VALUES

1. Number Systems

In the decimal (base ten) number system, a value of three-hundred-and-forty-seven-and-a-quarter is written as "347.25". The value of each symbol is based on its position relative to the decimal point and the fact that we are using base ten. The value of 347.25 is arrived at as shown below.

$$3 \qquad 4 \qquad 7 \quad . \quad 2 \qquad 5$$

$$3 \times 10^2 + 4 \times 10^1 + 7 \times 10^0 + 2 \times 10^{-1} + 5 \times 10^{-2}$$

That is, to construct the value of the number, each digit beginning from the left, is multiplied by successively decreasing powers of ten (the base) and the values are added. The decimal point is a reference point which divides the non-negative and negative powers of ten. If the base were changed to eight, say, the value of 347.25 would be

$$3 \times 8^2 + 4 \times 8^1 + 7 \times 8^0 + 2 \times 8^{-1} + 5 \times 8^{-2} = 231.328125 \text{ (base 10)}$$

Frequently this equality is stated in the form shown below.

$$(347.25)_8 \quad = \quad (231.328125)_{10}$$

where the "8" and the "10" denote the bases used in determining the value of the number.

Note that N symbols are needed to represent all possible numbers in the base N number system. This allows the interval between two successive negative powers of the base to be split into N equally spaced subintervals simply by putting another symbol on the rightmost end of the number.

Most computer systems use the base two (binary) number system to represent all REAL and INTEGER values. The value of the base 10 number 347.25 in base two is $(101011001.01)_2$.

INTEGER Values

Each INTEGER value occupies one word (4 bytes or 32 bits) of the computer memory. The 32 bits are numbered, beginning from the left, 0, 1, 2, ..., 31. Bit zero indicates the sign of the number -- zero for positive, one for negative. Let V_i denote the value of bit i. Each V_i equals zero or one. The value of a positive INTEGER value is then:

$$V1 \times 2^{30} + V2 \times 2^{29} + V3 \times 2^{28} + \ldots + V31 \times 2^0$$

This means that positive INTEGER values can range from $(0111\ldots111)_2$ thru $(000\ldots0001)_2$. That is from 2147483647 down to one. (An INTEGER value of zero has all 32 bits equal to zero.)

A negative INTEGER value is stored in the "two's complement form" of the positive value. To get the two's complement form of any base two number: (a) write down the bit pattern of the positive value; (b) Change each zero to a one, each one to a zero; (c) Add one to the resulting number. For example, the internal representation of -156 can be obtained as follows:

a) +156 is   00000000000000000000000010011100
b) flip the bits   11111111111111111111111101100011
c) add one to get   11111111111111111111111101100100

Many references are available which describe how to do base two arithmetic. Any introductory book on computers would suffice.

For example: $(011)_2 + (1)_2 = (100)_2$. i.e: 3 + 1 = 4

Why are negative INTEGER values stored in two's complement form? The reason is simply that subtracting any base two value is the same as adding its two's complement. Consequently, only addition circuits are required to do INTEGER arithmetic.

If an operation involving two INTEGER values would produce a result which would require more than thirty-two bits to represent the value, only the rightmost thirty-two bits are used as the result. Because a "1" in the leftmost bit position indicates a zero and because negative numbers are stored in two's complement form, totally unexpected results may be obtained if you are not careful when working with large INTEGER values.

INTEGER*2 Values

Recall that all INTEGER constants are of length four. Only variables may be given the optional length of two. For each INTEGER*2 variable, a half-word of memory is used. The use of the sixteen bits is identical to that for length four INTEGER values. That is, the leftmost bit idicates the sign of the value; the other bits represent the value of the number in base two. Two's complement form is used for

negative values. Because only fifteen bits are used for the
value, INTEGER*2 values range from -2**15 thru (2**15-1).
That is between -32768 and +32767. This reduced range means
out-of-range conditions can be generated more easily.

REAL Values

One word (4 bytes or 32 bits) of memory is used to store
each REAL value. The bits are numbered, beginning from the
left, 0, 1, 2, ..., 31. The use of the bits is shown in the
following diagram.

```
                       1          2          3
    bit#    0 1234567 89012345678901234567 89 01

    sign 0     exponent     fraction (24 significant
         1      value             binary digits)
```

The decimal point precedes the first digit in the fraction.
If Vi denotes the value (one or zero) of bit i in a REAL
value, the value of the REAL number is

$$(V8 \times 2^{-1} + V9 \times 2^{-2} + V10 \times 2^{-3} + \ldots + V31 \times 2^{-24}) \times 2^{4(y-64)}$$

where: $y = V1 \times 2^6 + V2 \times 2^5 + \ldots + V7 \times 2^0$.

The number is positive if V0 is zero and negative if V0 is
one. The largest value of y is 127 and the smallest is of
course zero. This means that exponent values can range from
2**252 thru 2**(-256) or equivalently between 16**63 and
16**(-64)

This method of representing REAL numbers means that the
magnitude of the largest and smallest REAL values are:

Largest	Smallest
$(.11111...111) \times 2^{252}$	$(.00000...001) \times 2^{-252}$
or $(.7237005) \times 10^{76}$	or $(.0000051) \times 10^{-79}$

For reasons which are beyond the scope of this book,
fractional values are always "normalized". Normalized values
are such that at least one of the four leftmost bits in the
fractional value is one. This means that the magnitude of
the smallest REAL value which a programmer can define in a
WATFIV program without doing bit manipulation in the program
is approximately .5397605*10**(-78).

Exponent Errors and ON ERROR GO TO

If an arithmetic operation or a definition of a REAL constant requires an exponent value outside the permitted range, an error condition is generated. The terms "exponent overflow" and "exponent underflow" refer, respectively, to the conditions where the exponent value is too large or too small. Three subprograms are normally supplied with the WATFIV compiler which may be useful in handling overflow and underflow conditions. The names of these subprograms are "TRAPS", "ALLOW" and "OVERFL". Information about the three subprograms can likely be obtained from your computing center.

In addition, there is an "ON ERROR GO TO s" statement which will transfer control to statement "s" if any type of error occurs.

Extended Precision (REAL*8) Values

The reader should be familiar with the information about REAL values before reading this section.

Each Extended Precision value occupies a double-word (8 bytes or 64 bits of memory). The use of the sixty-four bits is shown in the following diagram.

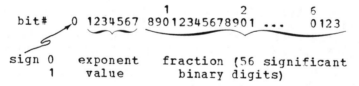

```
                        1           2        6
bit#   0  1234567  89012345678901 ...    0123

sign 0    exponent   fraction (56 significant
     1    value         binary digits)
```

The only difference between Extended Precision and REAL values is that Extended Precision values have 56 significant binary digits instead of 24 for REAL values. The range of exponent values is the same. Overflow and underflow conditions may occur and can be handled in the same way as for REAL values.

COMPLEX Values

A COMPLEX value occupies two consecutive words (8 bytes or 64 bits) of memory. Each of the words contains a REAL value. The value in the first word is the value of the real component of the complex number, that in the second, the value of the imaginary component of the complex number.

Extended Precision COMPLEX values (COMPLEX*16) each occupy two consecutive double-words of memory. The Extended Precision values in the first and second double words represent the values of the real and imaginary components of the number.

LOGICAL Values

LOGICAL values occupy one word (4 bytes or 32 bits) of memory. Only the leftmost byte is used to represent the value. If the leftmost byte contains "11111111" the value represented is .TRUE.. Eight zero bits in the leftmost byte represent a value of .FALSE.. Although four bytes are reserved for a LOGICAL value, only the leftmost byte of the four is affected by operations on the variable.

LOGICAL*1 variables each occupy one byte of memory. .TRUE. is represented by a string of eight one bits, .FALSE. by a string of eight zero bits.

CHARACTER Values

A CHARACTER value of length N occupies N consecutive bytes of memory. Since a byte has 256 possible bit patterns, there are 256 different "symbols" which any byte can represent. Appendix A contains a table showing the hole pattern which produces each possible bit pattern.

When a byte is sent to a printer, the symbol printed depends on the print "train" which is on the printer. Appendix D shows the symbol produced by a bit pattern for four of the more commonly used print trains.

Undefined Values

When a WATFIV program is compiled, any variable which is not assigned an initial value has bit pattern of "10000000" put in each byte of memory reserved for the value of the variable. When a statement references the value, a comparison is made to see if this bit pattern is still present. This is the method of detecting undefined variables. Using the "NOCHECK" feature described in Appendix E eliminates the test for the special bit pattern. Occasionally, the results of computation may accidentally generate the pattern. (The pattern represents an INTEGER value of -2139062144 and a REAL value of $-0.4335017E-77$.) If this is the case, the NOCHECK feature must be used to circumvent the problem.

APPENDIX D   SYMBOLS FOUND ON PRINT TRAINS

The tables which follow show the symbols printed by some commonly used print trains. The bit pattern which produces each symbol is specified as two hexadecimal digits. The first digit is the row label and the second, the column label. For example, on the TN Train the letter "c" is produced by the bit pattern "10000011" (hexadecimal "83").

PN Train

	0	1	2	3	4	5	6	7	8	9	A	B	C	D	E	F
0																
1																
2																
3																
4												.	<	(	+		
5	&											$	*	)	;	¬
6	-	/										,	%	_	>	?
7											:	#	@	'	=	"
8																
9																
A																
B																
C		A	B	C	D	E	F	G	H	I						
D		J	K	L	M	N	O	P	Q	R						
E			S	T	U	V	W	X	Y	Z						
F	0	1	2	3	4	5	6	7	8	9						

TN Train

	0	1	2	3	4	5	6	7	8	9	A	B	C	D	E	F
0																
1																
2																
3																
4											¢	.	<	(	+		
5	&										!	$	*	)	;	¬
6	-	/										,	%	_	>	?
7				†		`	?				:	#	@	⌐	=	"
8		a	b	c	d	e	f	g	h	i	{	≤	(	+	+	
9		j	k	l	m	n	o	p	q	r	}	□	)	±	▪	
A		¬	°	s	t	u	v	w	x	y	z	⌐	Γ	[	≥	•
B	0	1	2	3	4	5	6	7	8	9	⌐	¬	]	≠	─	
C		A	B	C	D	E	F	G	H	I						
D		J	K	L	M	N	O	P	Q	R						
E			S	T	U	V	W	X	Y	Z						
F	0	1	2	3	4	5	6	7	8	9						

APL Train

	0	1	2	3	4	5	6	7	8	9	A	B	C	D	E	F
0																
1																
2																
3																
4		..	‾	≤	≥	≠	∨	∧	÷	×	¢	•	<	(	+	|
5	ℰ	ω	∈	ρ	~	↑	↓	ι	○	←	!	$	*	)	;	¬
6	-	/	→	α	⌈	⌊	∇	∆	∘	⌷	[	,	%	_	>	?
7	]	⊂	⊃	∩	∪	⊥	⊤	\	◊	√	:	#	@	'	=	"
8	λ	a	b	c	d	e	f	g	h	i	⊣	{	A	B	C	D
9	⊢	j	k	l	m	n	o	p	q	r		}	E	F	G	H
A			s	t	u	v	w	x	y	z	I	J	K	L	M	N
B											O	P	Q	R	S	T
C		A	B	C	D	E	F	G	H	I	U	V	W	X	Y	Z
D		J	K	L	M	N	O	P	Q	R						
E			S	T	U	V	W	X	Y	Z						
F	0	1	2	3	4	5	6	7	8	9						

APPENDIX E   JOB CONTROL STATEMENTS

This Appendix describes the statements which can be used to control the appearance of output and the kinds of diagnostic messages printed. It also describes execution-time debugging aids -- the statement trace and the execution profiler. The last section of the appendix explains how to punch more than one statement on a card.

The two most important job control cards are the $JOB and the $ENTRY cards. They begin with a '$' in column 1 and are signals to begin compilation and execution respectively. The other control statements or cards begin with a 'C$' in columns 1 and 2. The 'C' is present so that if a WATFIV program is processed by another Fortran compiler which does not recognize the particular control card, it will be treated as a comment.

1. $JOB CARD

The $JOB card normally has the format shown below.

```
1        8        16
↓        ↓        ↓
$JOB    WATFIV   acct.#,options      comment
```

Options, if present, are separated by commas. The character following the first blank after the start of the option field indicates the beginning of the comment. The option list may extend to column 79. If an option appears more than once, the last specification will be used.

Any or all of the following options may appear on a $JOB card. Alternatives are separated by a '|'. The underlined value is the usual default value.

KP = 29 | 26

KP=29 indicates that a Model 29 keypunch was used to punch the source program; KP=26 that a Model 26 was used.

TIME = s | (m) | (m,s) | (3)

Used to specify an upper limit on execution-time in minutes (m) and/or seconds (s). "TIME" can be abbreviated to "T".

PAGES = n | 999

> Used to specify an upper limit on the number of pages of execution-time output that can be printed. "PAGES" can be abbreviated to "P".

LINES = n | 60

> Specifies the number of lines per page that will be printed both at compile time and execution time. If 0 is specified, all compile-time page ejects will be suppressed. "LINES" can be abbreviated to "L".

LIST | NOLIST

> LIST specifies that all statements between the $JOB and $ENTRY cards are to be printed at compile time. NOLIST suppresses this printout.

LIBLIST | NOLIBLIST

> LIBLIST causes the statements of subprograms retrieved from a subprogram library to be printed. NOLIBLIST suppresses this printout.

WARN | NOWARN

> NOWARN suppresses warning messages at compile time. WARN means they will be printed.

EXT | NOEXT

> EXT means messages identifying those features of WATFIV which are extensions of the standard Fortran IV language will be printed. NOEXT suppresses the printing of Extension messages.

CHECK | NOCHECK | FREE

> CHECK means that the compiler will insert statements to verify that a variable has been assigned a value before using it at execution time. NOCHECK bypasses this execution-time error-checking procedure. FREE means that if a normally fatal error occurs at execution time, an attempt will be made to continue execution past the point of the error.

SUB | NOSUB

>   SUB and NOSUB are options related to Pseudo-
>   Variable-Dimensioning (PVD). They refer to
>   subscript checking for arrays which appear as
>   parameters of subprograms. See comments
>   concerning Example 10.6 in Chapter 10 for a
>   detailed description.

PGM = name

>   If the mainline program to be executed is stored
>   in the WATFIV library, the compiler is informed
>   of this fact by putting its name after the "PGM="
>   keyword.

XREF | NOXREF

>   The XREF option produces a cross-reference of all
>   variables, subprogram names, statement numbers
>   and REMOTE BLOCKs used.

XREFP | NOXREFP

>   As for XREF but the output appears in a "packed"
>   format.

NARROW | NONARROW

>   NARROW causes the output of the PROFILER and XREF
>   options to be formatted into 80 character lines.

DECIMAL | DEC=f | DEC=fd | DEC=fw.d

>   When format-free output is used, the DECIMAL
>   option will cause REAL*4 values to be printed
>   with an F20.7 mask.
>   The second, third and fourth options
>   permit varying degrees of control of this default
>   mask. In the examples below, 'w' and 'd' denote
>   positive INTEGER values.

Option	Mask Used
DEC=E	E16.7
DEC=F	F20.7
DEC=G	G15.6
DEC=Ed	E16.d
DEC=Fd	F20.d
DEC=Gd	G15.d

                              DEC=Ew.d   Ew.d
                              DEC=Fw.d   Fw.d
                              DEC=Gw.d   Gw.d

If the option appears more than once in the source deck, the last specification will be the one in effect throughout the execution of the program.

S= n | <u>100000</u>

If more than n statements are executed, WATFIV will terminate the execution of the program (useful for catching infinite loops).

CCOMP=nnnn | CCOFF=nnnn

CCOMP is short for "Conditional Compilation". The string "nnnn" specifies a series of digits. Each card in the program (following this option) which has "Cn" in columns 1 and 2 will be treated as a normal Fortran statement rather than a Comment Card. (i.e. the "Cn" will be blanked-out). "CCOFF nnnn" turns the option off. This feature is useful for "turning-on" debugging PRINT statements, for selecting certain initialization statements, etc.

Profiler options:

The following four options are used to specify the type of statistics to be accumulated by the WATFIV Profiler. They are used in conjuction with the control cards "C$PROFON" and "C$PROFOFF" which are described in section 5.

PROFC | NOPROFC

PROFC means a count of the number of times selected statements are executed will be kept. NOPROFC suppresses this count.

PROFP | NOPROFP

PROFP causes a histogram of the relative frequencies of execution of selected statements to be printed. The frequencies are expressed in percentages. NOPROFP suppresses this histogram.

PROFA | <u>NOPROFA</u>

> PROFA causes a histogram of the absolute frequencies of execution of selected statements to be printed. NOPROFA suppresses the printing of this histogram.

PROF | <u>NOPROF</u>

> PROF is equivalent to specifying PROFC, PROFP, PROFA (all available types of statistics). NOPROF is equivalent to specifiying NOPROFC, NOPROFP, NOPROFA.

2. <u>$ENTRY</u>

> The $ENTRY causes compilation to end and execution to begin. "$ENTRY" appears in columns 1 to 6.

3. <u>C$OPTIONS</u>

> One or more of the options present on a $JOB card (either explicitly or by default) can be changed by using a C$OPTIONS card at points in the program where option changes are desired. All options except "PGM=" and the XREF options can be specified. "C$OPTIONS" appears in columns 1 to 9 and the option list begins in column 11. For example, following the appearance of

> C$OPTIONS NOWARN,KP=26,PROF,LINES=40

> the four options described would be in effect until the end of the program or until replaced by those on a subsequent C$OPTIONS card.

4. <u>Alternative Ways of Specifiying Some Options</u>

> Several of the options which can be specified on a $JOB or C$OPTIONS card can also be specified using a separate 'C$' control card. The left side of the table below shows the options as they appear on a $JOB or C$OPTIONS card. The corresponding pair of 'C$' control cards is shown on the right. These C$ control cards were used in earlier implementations of WATFIV. Use of the C$OPTIONS card is recommended.

Option List Key Words		Equivalent Control Card	
WARN	NOWARN	C$WARN	C$NOWARN
EXT	NOEXT	C$EXT	C$NOEXT
CHECK	NOCHECK	C$CHECK	C$NOCHECK
LIST	NOLIST	C$PRINTON	C$PRINTOFF
XREF	NOXREF	C$XREFON	C$XREFOFF

5. C$PROFON and C$PROFOFF

       Pairs of these two control cards are used
to enclose the groups of statements for which
profile (execution frequency) statistics are to be kept.
The kind of statistics to be kept is indicated by use of
the keywords PROFC, PROFP, PROFA or PROF on the $JOB
or C$OPTIONS cards. (These keywords were described
previously in section 1.)

       The statistics accumulated by the Profiler
feature are printed following other execution-time
output. If any difficulty is encountered interpreting
this output, a detailed explanation can be found in
the WATFIV Users' Guide located at your computing center.

       Profiler output is valuable for at least the
following two reasons. First, it is a debugging aid
in that it will indicate statements which were not
executed in a run. It is therefore a way of determining
if all parts of the program logic have been checked out.
Secondly, because it shows which statements have
a high execution frequency, it indicates where a
programmer should concentrate on improving program efficie

6. C$ISNON and C$ISNOFF

       A list of the program or Internal
Statement Numbers (ISNs) in the order in
which they are executed can be obtained by enclosing
one or more groups of source statements within a pair
of C$ISNON and C$ISNOFF statements. At least one
executable statement must precede the $ISNON statement.
Each time a statement within the pair is executed,
its statement number is printed. This tracing
feature can be very helpful in debugging complex program l

7. C$EJECT and C$SPACE n

C$EJECT causes the next line of compiler output to be printed at the top of the next page.

C$SPACE n (n is a positive integer, default 1.) causes n blank lines to be left before printing the next line of compiler output.

8. C$COPY membername

This card causes a member from the WATLIB library to be copied into the input stream.

Multiple Statements Per Card

More than one WATFIV statement can be punched on a card. Use of this feature is especially advantageous if source decks are stored on an auxilliary medium such as tape or disk since fewer storage locations are used and therefore fewer operations are required to access the program.

When punching more than one statement on a card the following rules must be followed.

a) A semicolon is used to indicate the end of a statement.

b) Statements are punched in columns 7 thru 72.

c) Column six is used in the normal way -- to indicate a continuation of the statement on the previous card.

d) Statement numbers may be punched in columns 1 thru 5. If a statement number is required in columns 7 thru 72, a colon must follow the statement number. A statement number cannot be split onto two cards.

e) Comment cards and FORMAT statements should be punched in the ususal way.

f) A comment may appear on a statement card. To do this, a "zigamorph" is punched preceding the comment. The hole pattern for a zigamorph is 12-11-0-7-8-9. The symbols following the zigamorph and preceding either a semicolon or column 73 are considered to be a comment. The comment is printed on the compiler listing. No symbol is printed for the zigamorph.

Two special subroutines called FIVPAK and UNPACK are distributed with the WATFIV system. FIVPAK takes a "standard" source program and punches an equivalent program in condensed format. UNPACK takes a condensed format source program and expands it to one having one statement per card. If FIVPAK is used, all literals containing one or more blanks should be defined within single quotes rather than by means of the H-code. Shown below are example job streams for the two subroutines.   Assume the reader is unit 5 and the punch is unit 7.

```
    $JOB                              $JOB
        CALL FIVPAK(5,7)                  CALL UNPACK(5,7)
        STOP                              STOP
        END                               END
    $ENTRY                            $ENTRY
        .                                 .
        . standard deck                   . condensed deck
        .                                 .
```

APPENDIX F   WATFIV - FORTRAN COMPARISONS

There are many varieties of Fortran. Because the alternative to using WATFIV in many computing centers is to use IBM's Fortran G or Fortran H, the comparisons in this Appendix will be limited to these languages. Detailed specifications of the IBM Fortrans can be found in IBM publications.

The material is divided into four sections. The first describes features in WATFIV which are not acceptable to the Fortran G and H compilers. These features could be considered extensions of the Fortran language. The second section describes incompatabilities between WATFIV and IBM Fortran. That is, situations in which the same source statements may produce different results. The third section describes features in "Extended Fortran H" which are not acceptable to the WATFIV compiler. Finally some suggestions are made for when each of the three languages should be used. No claim is made that the information in this appendix is complete. Only important differences are described.

Fortran "Extensions" Present In WATFIV

1. CHARACTER Values. See Chapter 17, Section 12 for methods of proccessing strings of symbols without using CHARACTER variables.

2. Multiple Assignment statements.

3. Expressions in output lists. Note that expressions may not begin with a left bracket. "PRINT,(A+B)/C" is invalid whereas "PRINT,+(A+B)/C" is valid.

4. Variables in an unlabelled Common Block may be initialized in a type declaration statement or a DATA statement. Variables in a labelled Common Block can only be initialized in a BLOCK DATA subprogram. The name of a Common Block cannot also be used as a variable name.

5. Implied DO-loops may be used to create a list of variables in a DATA statement.

6. Subscripted variables may be used in Statement Function definitions.

7. Subscripts may be LOGICAL, COMPLEX or CHARACTER values.

8. If the object of a DO is a Logical IF statement, the trailer can be any executable statement other than a DO, Logical IF, IF-THEN, WHILE, WHILE EXECUTE or DO CASE.

9. Multiple statements per card. (See Appendix E.)

10. Comments following a statement are permitted in WATFIV. (See Appendix E.)

11. Because WATFIV is a "one-pass" compiler, there are certain restrictions on the ordering of statements which are not restrictions in IBM Fortran. (See Chapter 17.)

12. DO-loops may be nested to any depth. Not more than 255 DO-loops are permitted in any one segment.

13. Format-free input-output is not allowed for card input and/or printed and punched output in IBM Fortran.

14. All the structured constructs. Thus all of the following statements are invalid.

```
WHILE( )      END WHILE
IF( )THEN     ELSE      END IF
DO CASE       CASE      IF NONE      END CASE
AT END        END AT END
REMOTE BLOCK      END BLOCK
EXECUTE       WHILE EXECUTE
```

15. The DUMPLIST and ON ERROR GO TO statements are not present in IBM Fortran.

16. Pseudo-Variable Dimensioning is not allowed in IBM Fortran.

Incompatabilities (No compile time differences but may cause execution time differences)

1. Input-Output

   a) In WATFIV, REAL*4 values are printed with seven significant digits. If the format code specifies that more than seven decimal places are to be displayed, zeros are added on the right.

   b) When using any of the format codes I, F, E, D, G or A, only non-blank symbols are stored in the print positions covered by the code. This may cause differences in the appearance of output if T-codes are used to overprint data previously stored in print positions.

c) In WATFIV, commas are not required between format codes if their omission does not cause any ambiguity.

d) In WATFIV there is no numeric limit on the number of continuation cards which can be used for a single FORMAT statement.

e) WATFIV does not allow group counts and/or repetition factors to be zero.

f) The symbol "+" on both the Model 26 and the Model 29 keypunch is an acceptable vertical control character in WATFIV.

2. Only the leftmost byte of a LOGICAL*4 value is moved in an assignment operation. Thus if U and V are LOGICAL variables, the statement "U=V" causes one byte to be moved.

3. Comment cards may precede a continuation card in WATFIV. Any number of comment cards can be used.

4. In WATFIV, a Function having a type of value other than that which can be assumed from the first-letter rule must have its type declared in an appropriate declaration statement.

5. In WATFIV, many REAL-valued built-in functions are evaluated in Extended Precision and the result truncated to a REAL value of length four.

6. In WATFIV, control of the number of lines printed per page depends on the "LINES=" parameter on the $JOB card.

7. In WATFIV, "FORMAT(" cannot be the first seven characters of a statement. "FORMAT(I)=2.5" is invalid whereas "X=FORMAT(I)" is acceptable.

8. In WATFIV a "$" cannot be punched in column one of a data card. It will be interpreted as being a WATFIV control card.

9. In other compilers the C$OPTIONS cards, the C$... cards and the "Cn" cards (used with the CCOMP option) may be treated simply as COMMENT cards.

Extended Fortran H Features Not Supported In WATFIV

1. REAL*16 and COMPLEX*32. A Q-mask is used for these types of values.

2. A "&" preceding a function name in an EXTERNAL statement means the user-supplied routine is to be used instead of any library function having the same name.

3. Asynchronous input-output statements. A feature exists which permits input-output operations and computations to proceed simultaneously.

4. By using a GENERIC statement, it is not necessary to use a unique name for the built-in functions which differ only in the type of value produced. For example, "SIN" includes DSIN, CSIN and CDSIN.

Use Of WATFIV And Fortran G and H

The following suggestions are based on the ideas found in the following table. They are not intended to be rules.

	WATFIV	Fortran G	Fortran H
Compile speed	best	better	good
Execute speed	good	better	best
Compile must precede execution	yes	no	no
Diagnostic messages	best	good	good

1. Small, one-shot programs should be written, debugged and executed using WATFIV.

2. Small programs which will be run many times should be written and debugged in WATFIV and run using a Fortran H object deck.

3. Large programs, especially those that will be run several times should be written and debugged in WATFIV; debugged in Fortran G to remove incompatabilities; executed using a Fortran H object deck.

APPENDIX G DEBUGGING HINTS,EFFICIENCY,GENERALITY

Debugging Hints

1. Echo your input data. That is, print the input values from cards as soon as they are read.

2. Use meaningful variable names.

3. Use statement numbers which increase or decrease from start to finish.

4. Use lots of comments.

5. Use the DUMPLIST statement. (See Chapter 22.)

6. Use "ON ERROR GO TO __" (See Appendix C.)

7. Print intermediate results until you are sure that the program logic is correct.

8. Use a LOGICAL variable called "DEBUG" and statements of the type "IF(DEBUG) PRINT,..." . Alternatively, use the CCOMP facility -- see Appendix E.

9. Carefully check your program logic after the program has been written and before it is keypunched. Carefully check your keypunching before the job is submitted.

10. Use $ISNON and $ISNOFF to trace through very complex sequences of statements. See Appendix E for details.

11. Use the profiler options to check that all parts of the program logic have been tested.

12. If you make a change in program logic, satisfy yourself that it will not affect other parts of the program.

13. During the debug phase, print any values which will eventually be sent to some other output device to insure that the correct values are being generated.

14. What not to do. Don't plan. Assume your logic is correct. Assume your input data is correct. If an error occurs, don't make any changes -- put the deck in again -- it must have been the computer's mistake.

15. Use structured constructs (especially WHILE and IF-THEN-ELSE). Avoid GO TO's of all types.

16. Indent the program statements to clearly show the logical structure of the program.

Program Efficiency

What is meant by an efficient program? Efficiencies can be achieved in the following areas: memory requirements; compile time; execution time; programming and keypunching time. Usually however, there is a tradeoff. That is, efficiency in one area means inefficiencies result in another area. The following list is not suggested as being complete. The suggestions in the list will generally decrease the execution time of a WATFIV program. Compile time is not usually a significant factor in running WATFIV jobs. In other types of Fortran, it may be very significant.

1. DO-loops

    a) Implied DO-loops are inefficient.

    b) A subscripted variable which is used more than once in the range of a loop should be assigned to a simple variable.

    c) To reduce the number of times the decision to repeat the loop must be made, processing two or more subscript values within the loop may be desirable. For example,

```
    DO 1 I=1,999,2                          DO 1 I=1,1000
      X(I)=0.        is better than            X(I)=0.
      X(I+1)=0.                             1 CONTINUE
    1 CONTINUE
```

    d) If possible, nested loops should have the innermost loops with the most repetitions. For example:

```
    DO 2 I=1,10                             DO 2 J=1,100
      DO 1 J=1,100   is better than           DO 1 I=1,10
        .                                         .
    1     CONTINUE                          1     CONTINUE
    2 CONTINUE                              2 CONTINUE
```

2. Subscripted Variables

    a) Avoid using arrays having many dimensions.

    b) Assign subscripted variables used more than once in a DO-loop to a simple variable.

3. Branching (Conditional Control)

   a) In a Logical IF statement, choose a relational
      operator which makes the most likely result
      .FALSE..

   b) Logical IFs are faster for two-way branches than
      Arithmetic IFs.

   c) A Computed GO TO is faster than a sequence of Logical
      IFs.

   d) An Assigned GO TO is faster than a Computed GO TO.

   e) Use a LOGICAL*1 variable for any "on-off" program
      switch.

4. Expressions

   a) Use INTEGER exponents instead of REAL exponents.

   b) Avoid mixing two types of values. "X+2." is better
      than "X+2".

   c) Addition is usually faster than multiplication. "X+X"
      is better than "2.*X".

   d) Use SQRT(X) instead of "X**.5".

   e) To evaluate a polynomial such as $Ax^3 + Bx^2 + Cx + D$, write
      it as (D+X*(C+X*(B+X*A))).

5. Boundary Alignment

   a) Order type declaration statements so that the
      variables having the longest length(s) are defined
      before those of lesser length(s).

   b) In Common Blocks, arrange the variables in the list
      in order of decreasing length.

   c) When Equivalencing two or more variables, put the
      variable with the longest length first.

6. Input-Output

   a) A single READ is better than two separate READs.

   b) Temporary tape and direct access files should use
      format-free READ and WRITE statements.

c) Unformatted input-output is the fastest.

d) Implied DO-loops are inefficient. For example:

<u>Bad</u>   <u>Best</u>

```
INTEGER SET(100)              INTEGER SET(100)
READ,N                        COMMON N
READ,(SET(I),I=1,N)           READ,N
STOP                          CALL READ(SET)
END                           STOP
                              END

                              SUBROUTINE READ(SET)
                              COMMON N
                              INTEGER SET(N)
                              READ,SET
                              RETURN
                              END
```

d) Read and write "blocks" of records when using tape and direct access files. For example:

<u>Bad</u>   <u>Better</u>

```
INTEGER SET(20)              INTEGER SET1(20),SET2(20)
DO 1 I=1,100                 DO 1 I=1,99,2
   READ,SET                     READ,SET1,SET2
   WRITE(2) SET                 WRITE(2) SET1,SET2
1 CONTINUE                   1 CONTINUE
```

e) Formatting is slow. Use format-free if it doesn't matter much.

7. <u>Subprograms</u>

a) Use COMMON instead of parameter lists.

b) Avoid subprograms for small repeated tasks.

c) Use Statement Functions if a function value can be calculated in a single expression.

8. <u>Memory Requirements</u>

a) Use INTEGER*2 and LOGICAL*1 variables.

b) Use NOCHECK for debugged parts of a program.

c) Use call by location instead of call by value.

d) Use EQUIVALENCE if variables are not required at the same time.

9. Miscellaneous

a) Avoid DATA statements. Use type declaration statements to specify initial values.

b) Use PRINTOFF to save paper and reduce print time.

10. Pinpointing Potentially Inefficient Blocks of Code

Use the profiler options to determine which parts of the program have high usage.   Concentrate your efficiency improvements in these areas.

Generalization Hints

A generalized program is one which can be used to solve a wide variety of problems without making changes in the program. This is usually done by reading in information from cards which define the characteristics of the problem to be solved.   A generalized program will solve many problems and it will also permit someone with no programming knowledge to use the program simply by preparing an appropriate set of input data. Some generalization hints are:

1. Check for error conditions which although not present in the problem for which the program was written, could be present using a different set of data.

2. Use execution time dimensioning of parameter arrays.

3. Use execution time formatting.

4. Use statements which are acceptable to almost all Fortran compilers.

5. Use INTEGER variables for device assignments.   For example, "INPUT=5; READ(INPUT,...)...".

6. Read the number of problems to be solved from a data card.

7. Read DO-loop parameter values.

Other Hints

1. Large programs should have a tree-like structure as shown in the following diagram.

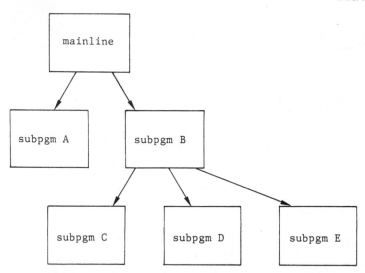

Don't make program segments too large. About 30 to 70 statements per segment is a reasonable range.

2. Documentation. The beginning of the program and/or each segment should have comment cards which describe: the purpose of the segment; error conditions; inputs and outputs; computation methods used; meaning of variable names; etc..

3. Style. Use meaningful variable names. Arrange the program logic in blocks. Don't jump back and forth all over the place. Use sequential statement numbers with a definite step size. Be consistent in the use of statement numbers and the placement of FORMAT statements.

Beginning on this page is a list of the messages which
may be produced at compile time or execution time when
running WATFIV jobs.

'MESSAGES FOR ACCOUNTING'
AC-5   'THE NUMBER OF STATEMENTS TO BE EXECUTED HAS BEEN
        EXCEEDED'

'ASSEMBLER LANGUAGE SUBPROGRAMMES'
AL-0   'MISSING END CARD ON ASSEMBLY LANGUAGE OBJECT DECK'
AL-1   'ENTRY-POINT OR CSECT NAME IN AN OBJECT DECK WAS
        PREVIOUSLY DEFINED.FIRST DEFINITION USED'

'BLOCK DATA STATEMENTS'
BD-0   'EXECUTABLE STATEMENTS ARE ILLEGAL IN BLOCK DATA
        SUBPROGRAMS'
BD-1   'IMPROPER BLOCK DATA STATEMENT'

'CARD FORMAT AND CONTENTS'
CC-0   'COLUMNS 1-5 OF CONTINUATION CARD ARE NOT BLANK.
        PROBABLE CAUSE:STATEMENT PUNCHED TO LEFT OF COLUMN 7'
CC-1   'LIMIT OF 5 CONTINUATION CARDS EXCEEDED'
CC-2   'INVALID CHARACTER IN FORTRAN STATEMENT.A'$' WAS
        INSERTED IN THE SOURCE LISTING'

CC-3   'FIRST CARD OF A PROGRAM IS A CONTINUATION CARD.
        PROBABLE CAUSE:STATEMENT PUNCHED TO LEFT OF COLUMN 7'
CC-4   'STATEMENT TOO LONG TO COMPILE (SCAN-STACK OVERFLOW)'
CC-5   'A BLANK CARD WAS ENCOUNTERED'
CC-6   'KEYPUNCH USED DIFFERS FROM KEYPUNCH SPECIFIED ON
        JOB CARD'
CC-7   'THE FIRST CHARACTER OF THE STATEMENT WAS NOT
        ALPHABETIC'
CC-8   'INVALID CHARACTER(S) ARE CONCATENATED WITH THE
        FORTRAN KEYWORD'
CC-9   'INVALID CHARACTERS IN COLUMNS 1-5.STATEMENT NUMBER
        IGNORED PROBABLE CAUSE:STATEMENT PUNCHED TO LEFT OF
        COLUMN 7'
CC-A   'CONTROL CARDS MAY NOT BE CONTINUED'
CC-B   'CONTROL CARDS MUST BE IN PROGRAM SEGMENT'

'COMMON'
CM-0   'THE VARIABLE IS ALREADY IN COMMON'
CM-1   'OTHER COMPILERS MAY NOT ALLOW COMMONED VARIABLES TO
        BE INITIALIZED IN OTHER THAN A BLOCK DATA SUBPROGRAM'
CM-2   'ILLEGAL USE OF A COMMON BLOCK OR NAMELIST NAME'

'FORTRAN TYPE CONSTANTS'
CN-0   'MIXED REAL*4,REAL*8 IN COMPLEX CONSTANT;REAL*8
        ASSUMED FOR BOTH'
CN-1   'AN INTEGER CONSTANT MAY NOT BE GREATER THAN
        2,147,483,647 (2**31 -1)'
CN-2   'EXPONENT ON A REAL CONSTANT IS GREATER THAN 2
        DIGITS'
CN-3   'A REAL CONSTANT HAS MORE THAN 16 DIGITS.IT WAS
        TRUNCATED TO 16'
CN-4   'INVALID HEXADECIMAL CONSTANT'
CN-5   'ILLEGAL USE OF A DECIMAL POINT'
CN-6   'CONSTANT WITH MORE THAN 7 DIGITS BUT E-TYPE
        EXPONENT,ASSUMED TO BE REAL*4'
CN-7   'CONSTANT OR STATEMENT NUMBER GREATER THAN 99999'
CN-8   'AN EXPONENT OVERFLOW OR UNDERFLOW OCCURRED WHILE
        CONVERTING A CONSTANT IN A SOURCE STATEMENT'
'COMPILER ERRORS'
CP-0   'COMPILER ERROR - LANDR/ARITH'
CP-1   'COMPILER ERROR.LIKELY CAUSE:MORE THAN 255 DO
        STATEMENTS'
CP-2   'COMPILER ERROR'
CP-4   'COMPILER ERROR - INTERRUPT AT COMPILE TIME,RETURN
        TO SYSTEM'

'CHARACTER VARIABLE'
CV-0   'A CHARACTER VARIABLE IS USED WITH A RELATIONAL
        OPERATOR'
CV-1   'LENGTH OF A CHARACTER VALUE ON RIGHT OF EQUAL SIGN
        EXCEEDS THAT ON LEFT. TRUNCATION WILL OCCUR'
CV-2   'UNFORMATTED CORE-TO-CORE I/O NOT IMPLEMENTED'

'DATA STATEMENT'
DA-0   'REPLICATION FACTOR IS ZERO OR GREATER THAN 32767.
        IT IS ASSUMED TO BE 32767'
DA-1   'MORE VARIABLES THAN CONSTANTS'
DA-2   'ATTEMPT TO INITIALIZE A SUBPROGRAM PARAMETER IN A
        DATA STATEMENT'
DA-3   'OTHER COMPILERS MAY NOT ALLOW NON-CONSTANT
        SUBSCRIPTS IN DATA STATEMENTS'
DA-4   'TYPE OF VARIABLE AND CONSTANT DO NOT AGREE.
        (MESSAGE ISSUED ONCE FOR AN ARRAY)'
DA-5   'MORE CONSTANTS THAN VARIABLES'
DA-6   'A VARIABLE WAS PREVIOUSLY INITIALIZED.THE LATEST
        VALUE IS USED CHECK COMMONED AND EQUIVALENCED
        VARIABLES'
DA-7   'OTHER COMPILERS MAY NOT ALLOW INITIALIZATION OF
        BLANK COMMON'
DA-8   'A LITERAL CONSTANT HAS BEEN TRUNCATED'
DA-9   'OTHER COMPILERS MAY NOT ALLOW IMPLIED DO-LOOPS IN
        DATA STATEMENTS'

DA-A   'MORE THAN 255 CONSTANTS IN A DATA STATEMENT SUBLIST'

'DEFINE FILE STATEMENTS'
DF-0   'THE UNIT NUMBER IS MISSING'
DF-1   'INVALID FORMAT TYPE'
DF-2   'THE ASSOCIATED VARIABLE IS NOT A SIMPLE INTEGER
         VARIABLE'
DF-3   'NUMBER OF RECORDS OR RECORD SIZE IS ZERO OR GREATER
         THAN 32767'

'DIMENSION STATEMENTS'
DM-0   'NO DIMENSIONS ARE SPECIFIED FOR A VARIABLE IN A
         DIMENSION STATEMENT'
DM-1   'THE VARIABLE HAS ALREADY BEEN DIMENSIONED'
DM-2   'CALL-BY-LOCATION PARAMETERS MAY NOT BE DIMENSIONED'
DM-3   'THE DECLARED SIZE OF ARRAY EXCEEDS SPACE PROVIDED
         BY CALLING ARGUMENT'

'DO LOOPS'
DO-0   'THIS STATEMENT CANNOT BE THE OBJECT OF A DO-LOOP'
DO-1   'ILLEGAL TRANSFER INTO THE RANGE OF A DO-LOOP'
DO-2   'THE OBJECT OF THIS DO-LOOP HAS ALREADY APPEARED'
DO-3   'IMPROPERLY NESTED DO-LOOPS'
DO-4   'ATTEMPT TO REDEFINE A DO-LOOP PARAMETER WITHIN THE
         RANGE OF THE LOOP'
DO-5   'INVALID DO-LOOP PARAMETER'
DO-6   'ILLEGAL TRANSFER TO A STATEMENT WHICH IS INSIDE THE
         RANGE OF A DO-LOOP'
DO-7   'A DO-LOOP PARAMETER IS UNDEFINED OR OUT OF RANGE'
DO-8   'BECAUSE OF ONE OF THE PARAMETERS,THIS DO-LOOP WILL
         TERMINATE AFTER THE FIRST TIME THROUGH'
DO-9   'A DO-LOOP PARAMETER MAY NOT BE REDEFINED IN AN
         INPUT LIST'
DO-A   'OTHER COMPILERS MAY NOT ALLOW THIS STATEMENT TO END
         A DO-LOOP'

'EQUIVALENCE AND/OR COMMON'
EC-0   'EQUIVALENCED VARIABLE APPEARS IN A COMMON STATEMENT'
EC-1   'A COMMON BLOCK HAS A DIFFERENT LENGTH THAN IN A
         PREVIOUS SUBPROGRAM:GREATER LENGTH USED'
EC-2   'COMMON AND/OR EQUIVALENCE CAUSES INVALID ALIGNMENT.
         EXECUTION SLOWED.REMEDY:ORDER VARIABLES B DECREASING
         LENGTH'
EC-3   'EQUIVALENCE EXTENDS COMMON DOWNWARDS'
EC-4   'A SUBPROGRAM PARAMETER APPEARS IN A COMMON OR
         EQUIVALENCE STATEMENT'
EC-5   'A VARIABLE WAS USED WITH SUBSCRIPTS IN AN
         EQUIVALENCE STATEMENT BUT HAS NOT BEEN PROPERLY
         DIMENSIONED'

'END STATEMENTS'
EN-0   'MISSING END STATEMENT:END STATEMENT GENERATED'
EN-1   'AN END STATEMENT WAS USED TO TERMINATE EXECUTION'
EN-2   'AN END STATEMENT CANNOT HAVE A STATEMENT NUMBER.
        STATEMENT NUMBER IGNORED'
EN-3   'END STATEMENT NOT PRECEDED BY A TRANSFER'

'EQUAL SIGNS'
EQ-0   'ILLEGAL QUANTITY ON LEFT OF EQUALS SIGN'
EQ-1   'ILLEGAL USE OF EQUAL SIGN'
EQ-2   'OTHER COMPILERS MAY NOT ALLOW MULTIPLE ASSIGNMENT
        STATEMENTS'
EQ-3   'MULTIPLE ASSIGNMENT IS NOT IMPLEMENTED FOR CHARACTER
        VARIABLES'
EQ-4   'ILLEGAL QUANTITY ON RIGHT OF EQUALS SIGN'

'EQUIVALENCE STATEMENTS'
EV-0   'ATTEMPT TO EQUIVALENCE A VARIABLE TO ITSELF'
EV-1   'THERE ARE LESS THAN 2 VARIABLES IN AN EQUIVALENCE
        LIST'
EV-2   'A MULTI-SUBSCRIPTED EQUIVALENCED VARIABLE HAS BEEN
        INCORRECTLY RE-EQUIVALENCED.REMEDY:DIMENSION THE
        VARIABLE FIRST'

'POWERS AND EXPONENTIATION'
EX-0   'ILLEGAL COMPLEX EXPONENTIATION'
EX-1   'I**J WHERE I=J=0'
EX-2   'I**J WHERE I=0, J.LT.0'
EX-3   '0.0**Y WHERE Y.LE.0.0'
EX-4   '0.0**J WHERE J=0'
EX-5   '0.0**J WHERE J.LT.0'
EX-6   'X**Y WHERE X .LT. 0.0, Y IS NOT TYPE INTEGER OR
        .NE. 0.0'

'ENTRY STATEMENT'
EY-0   'ENTRY-POINT NAME WAS PREVIOUSLY DEFINED'
EY-1   'PREVIOUS DEFINITION OF FUNCTION NAME IN AN ENTRY IS
        INCORRECT'
EY-2   'THE USAGE OF A SUBPROGRAM PARAMETER IS INCONSISTENT
        WITH A PREVIOUS ENTRY-POINT'
EY-3   'A PARAMETER HAS APPEARED IN A EXECUTABLE STATEMENT
        BUT IS NOT A SUBPROGRAM PARAMETER'
EY-4   'ENTRY STATEMENTS ARE INVALID IN THE MAIN PROGRAM'
EY-5   'ENTRY STATEMENT INVALID INSIDE A DO-LOOP'

'FORMAT'
        SOME FORMAT ERROR MESSAGES GIVE THE CHARACTERS IN
        WHICH THE ERROR WAS DETECTED
FM-0   'IMPROPER CHARACTER SEQUENCE OR INVALID CHARACTER IN
        INPUT DATA'

FM-1   'NO STATEMENT NUMBER ON A FORMAT STATEMENT'
FM-2   'FORMAT CODE AND DATA TYPE DO NOT MATCH'
FM-4   'FORMAT PROVIDES NO CONVERSION SPECIFICATION FOR A
         VALUE IN I/O LIST'
FM-5   'AN INTEGER IN THE INPUT DATA IS TOO LARGE.
         (MAXIMUM=2,147,483,647=2**31-1)'
FM-6   'A REAL NUMBER IN THE INPUT DATA IS OUT OF MACHINE
         RANGE (1.E-78, 1.E+75)'
FM-7   'UNREFERENCED FORMAT STATEMENT'
FT-0   'FIRST CHARACTER OF VARIABLE FORMAT IS NOT A LEFT
         PARENTHESIS'
FT-1   'INVALID CHARACTER ENCOUNTERED IN FORMAT'
FT-2   'INVALID FORM FOLLOWING A FORMAT CODE'
FT-3   'INVALID FIELD OR GROUP COUNT'
FT-4   'A FIELD OR GROUP COUNT GREATER THAN 255'
FT-5   'NO CLOSING PARENTHESIS ON VARIABLE FORMAT'
FT-6   'NO CLOSING QUOTE IN A HOLLERITH FIELD'
FT-7   'INVALID USE OF COMMA'
FT-8   'FORMAT STATEMENT TOO LONG TO COMPILE (SCAN-STACK
         OVERFLOW)'
FT-9   'INVALID USE OF P FORMAT CODE'
FT-A   'INVALID USE OF PERIOD(.)'
FT-B   'MORE THAN THREE LEVELS OF PARENTHESES'
FT-C   'INVALID CHARACTER BEFORE A RIGHT PARENTHESIS'
FT-D   'MISSING OR ZERO LENGTH HOLLERITH ENCOUNTERED'
FT-E   'NO CLOSING RIGHT PARENTHESIS'
FT-F   'CHARACTERS FOLLOW CLOSING RIGHT PARENTHESIS'
FT-G   'WRONG QUOTE USED FOR KEY-PUNCH SPECIFIED'
FT-H   'LENGTH OF HOLLERITH EXCEEDS 255'
FT-I   'EXPECTING COMMA BETWEEN FORMAT ITEMS'
FT-J   'HOLLERITH STRING EXTENDS BEYOND END OF STATEMENT'
FT-K   'CHARACTERS FOLLOW CLOSING RIGHT PARENTHESIS FOR
         VARIABLE FORMAT'

'FUNCTIONS AND SUBROUTINES'
FN-1   'A PARAMETER APPEARS MORE THAN ONCE IN A SUBPROGRAM
         OR STATEMENT FUNCTION DEFINITION'
FN-2   'SUBSCRIPTS ON RIGHT-HAND SIDE OF STATEMENT FUNCTION.
         PROBABLE CAUSE:VARIABLE TO LEFT OF EQUAL SIGN NOT
         DIMENSIONED'
FN-4   'ILLEGAL LENGTH MODIFIER'
FN-5   'INVALID PARAMETER'
FN-6   'A PARAMETER HAS THE SAME NAME AS THE SUBPROGRAM'

'GO TO STATEMENTS'
GO-0   'THIS STATEMENT COULD TRANSFER TO ITSELF'
GO-1   'THIS STATEMENT TRANSFERS TO A NON-EXECUTABLE
         STATEMENT'
GO-2   'ATTEMPT TO DEFINE ASSIGNED GOTO INDEX IN AN
         ARITHMETIC STATEMENT'

GO-3   'ASSIGNED GOTO INDEX MAY BE USED ONLY IN ASSIGNED
        GOTO AND ASSIGN STATEMENTS'
GO-4   'INDEX OF AN ASSIGNED GOTO IS UNDEFINED OR OUT OF
        RANGE,OR INDEX OF COMPUTED GOTO OR CASE IS UNDEFINED'
GO-5   'ASSIGNED GOTO INDEX MAY NOT BE AN INTEGER*2
        VARIABLE'

'HOLLERITH CONSTANTS'
HO-0   'ZERO LENGTH SPECIFIED FOR H-TYPE HOLLERITH'
HO-1   'ZERO LENGTH QUOTE-TYPE HOLLERITH'
HO-2   'NO CLOSING QUOTE OR NEXT CARD NOT A CONTINUATION
        CARD'
HO-3   'UNEXPECTED HOLLERITH OR STATEMENT NUMBER CONSTANT'

'IF STATEMENTS (ARITHMETIC AND LOGICAL)'
IF-0   'AN INVALID STATEMENT FOLLOWS THE LOGICAL IF OR
        ATEND'
IF-1   'ARITHMETIC OR INVALID EXPRESSION IN LOGICAL IF OR
        WHILE'
IF-2   'LOGICAL,COMPLEX OR INVALID EXPRESSION IN ARITHMETIC
        IF'

'IMPLICIT STATEMENT'
IM-0   'INVALID DATA TYPE'
IM-1   'INVALID OPTIONAL LENGTH'
IM-3   'IMPROPER ALPHABETIC SEQUENCE IN CHARACTER RANGE'
IM-4   'A SPECIFICATION IS NOT A SINGLE CHARACTER.THE FIRST
        CHARACTER IS USED'
IM-5   'IMPLICIT STATEMENT DOES NOT PRECEDE OTHER
        SPECIFICATION STATEMENTS'
IM-6   'ATTEMPT TO DECLARE THE TYPE OF A CHARACTER MORE
        THAN ONCE'
IM-7   'ONLY ONE IMPLICIT STATEMENT PER PROGRAM SEGMENT
        ALLOWED. THIS ONE IGNORED'

'INPUT/OUTPUT'
IO-0   'I/O STATEMENT REFERENCES NON-FORMAT STATEMENT.
         PROBABLE CAUSE STATEMENT DEFINED AS NON-FORMAT'
IO-1   'A VARIABLE FORMAT MUST BE AN ARRAY NAME'
IO-2   'INVALID ELEMENT IN INPUT LIST OR DATA LIST'
IO-3   'OTHER COMPILERS MAY NOT ALLOW EXPRESSIONS IN OUTPUT
        LISTS'
IO-4   'ILLEGAL USE OF END= OR ERR= PARAMETERS'
IO-5   'INVALID UNIT NUMBER'
IO-6   'INVALID FORMAT'
IO-7   'ONLY CONSTANTS,SIMPLE INTEGER*4 VARIABLES,AND
        CHARACTER VARIABLES ARE ALLOWED AS UNITS'
IO-8   'ATTEMPT TO PERFORM I/O IN A FUNCTION WHICH IS
        CALLED IN AN OUTPUT STATEMENT'
IO-9   'UNFORMATTED WRITE STATEMENT MUST HAVE A LIST'

IO-A   'EXPECTING STATEMENT TO BE A FORMAT. PREVIOUSLY
           REFERENCED IN I/O STATEMENT'

'JOB CONTROL CARDS'
JB-0   'CONTROL CARD ENCOUNTERED DURING COMPILATION;
           PROBABLE CAUSE: MISSING C$ENTRY CARD'
JB-1   'MIS-PUNCHED JOB OPTION'

'JOB TERMINATION'
KO-0   'SOURCE ERROR ENCOUNTERED WHILE EXECUTING WITH
           RUN=FREE'
KO-1   'LIMIT EXCEEDED FOR FIXED-POINT DIVISION BY ZERO'
KO-2   'LIMIT EXCEEDED FOR FLOATING-POINT DIVISION BY ZERO'
KO-3   'EXPONENT OVERFLOW LIMIT EXCEEDED'
KO-4   'EXPONENT UNDERFLOW LIMIT EXCEEDED'
KO-5   'FIXED-POINT OVERFLOW LIMIT EXCEEDED'
KO-6   'JOB-TIME EXCEEDED'
KO-7   'COMPILER ERROR - EXECUTION TIME:RETURN TO SYSTEM'
KO-8   'TRACEBACK ERROR. TRACEBACK TERMINATED'
KO-9   'CANNOT OPEN WATFIV.ERRTEXTS. RUN TERMINATED'
KO-A   'I/O ERROR ON TEXT FILE'

'LOGICAL OPERATIONS'
LG-0   '.NOT. WAS USED AS A BINARY OPERATOR'

'LIBRARY ROUTINES'
LI-0   'ARGUMENT OUT OF RANGE DGAMMA OR GAMMA. (1.382E-76
           .LT. X .LT. 57.57)'
LI-1   'ABS(X) .GE. 175.366 FOR SINH,COSH,DSINH OR DCOSH OF
           X'
LI-2   'SENSE LIGHT OTHER THAN 0,1,2,3,4 FOR SLITE OR 1,2,3,
           4 FOR SLITET'
LI-3   'REAL PORTION OF ARGUMENT .GT. 174.673, CEXP OR
           CDEXP'
LI-4   'ABS(AIMAG(Z)) .GT. 174.673 FOR CSIN, CCOS, CDSIN OR
           CDCOS OF Z'
LI-5   'ABS(REAL(Z)) .GE. 3.537E15 FOR CSIN, CCOS, CDSIN OR
           CDCOS OF Z'
LI-6   'ABS(AIMAG(Z)) .GE. 3.537E15 FOR CEXP OR CDEXP OF Z'
LI-7   'ARGUMENT .GT. 174.673, EXP OR DEXP'
LI-8   'ARGUMENT OF CLOG OR CDLOG IS ZERO'
LI-9   'ARGUMENT IS NEGATIVE OR ZERO, ALOG, ALOG10, DLOG OR
           DLOG10'
LI-A   'ABS(X) .GE. 3.537E15 FOR SIN, COS, DSIN OR DCOS OF X
LI-B   'ABSOLUTE VALUE OF ARGUMENT .GT. 1, FOR ARSIN, ARCOS,
           DARSIN OR DARCOS'
LI-C   'ARGUMENT IS NEGATIVE, SQRT OR DSQRT'
LI-D   'BOTH ARGUMENTS OF DATAN2 OR ATAN2 ARE ZERO'
LI-E   'ARGUMENT TOO CLOSE TO A SINGULARITY, TAN, COTAN,
           DTAN OR DCOTAN'

LI-F   'ARGUMENT OUT OF RANGE DLGAMA OR ALGAMA. (0.0 .LT. X
        .LT. 4.29E73)'
LI-G   'ABSOLUTE VALUE OF ARGUMENT .GE. 3.537E15, TAN,
        COTAN, DTAN, DCOTAN'

'MIXED MODE'
MD-0   'RELATIONAL OPERATOR HAS LOGICAL OPERAND'
MD-1   'RELATIONAL OPERATOR HAS COMPLEX OPERAND'
MD-2   'MIXED MODE - LOGICAL OR CHARACTER WITH ARITHMETIC'
MD-3   'OTHER COMPILERS MAY NOT ALLOW SUBSCRIPTS OF TYPE
        COMPLEX,LOGICAL OR CHARACTER'

'MEMORY OVERFLOW'
MO-0   'INSUFFICIENT MEMORY TO COMPILE THIS PROGRAM.
        REMAINDER WILL BE ERROR CHECKED ONLY'
MO-1   'INSUFFICIENT MEMORY TO ASSIGN ARRAY STORAGE. JOB
        ABANDONED'
MO-2   'SYMBOL TABLE EXCEEDS AVAILABLE SPACE,JOB ABANDONED'
MO-3   'DATA AREA OF SUBPROGRAM EXCEEDS 24K -- SEGMENT
        PROGRAM'
MO-4   'INSUFFICIENT MEMORY TO ALLOCATE COMPILER WORK AREA
        OR WATLIB BUFFER'
MO-5   'INSUFFICIENT MEMORY TO PRODUCE CROSS REFERENCE.
        COMPILATION CONTINUING.'

'NAMELIST STATEMENTS'
NL-0   'NAMELIST ENTRY MUST BE A VARIABLE,NOT A SUBPROGRAM
        PARAMETER'
NL-1   'NAMELIST NAME PREVIOUSLY DEFINED'
NL-2   'VARIABLE NAME TOO LONG'
NL-3   'VARIABLE NAME NOT FOUND IN NAMELIST'
NL-4   'INVALID SYNTAX IN NAMELIST INPUT'
NL-6   'VARIABLE INCORRECTLY SUBSCRIPTED'
NL-7   'SUBSCRIPT OUT OF RANGE'
NL-8   'NESTED BLANKS ARE ILLEGAL IN NAMELIST INPUT'

'PARENTHESES'
PC-0   'UNMATCHED PARENTHESIS'
PC-1   'INVALID PARENTHESIS NESTING IN I/O LIST'

'PAUSE, STOP STATEMENTS'
PS-0   'OPERATOR MESSAGES NOT ALLOWED:SIMPLE STOP
        ASSUMED FOR STOP. CONTINUE ASSUMED FOR PAUSE'

'RETURN STATEMENT'
RE-1   'RETURN I, WHERE I IS OUT OF RANGE OR UNDEFINED'
RE-2   'MULTIPLE RETURN NOT VALID IN FUNCTION SUBPROGRAM'
RE-3   'VARIABLE IS NOT A SIMPLE INTEGER'
RE-4   'A MULTIPLE RETURN IS NOT VALID IN THE MAIN PROGRAM'

'ARITHMETIC AND LOGICAL STATEMENT FUNCTIONS'
        PROBABLE CAUSE OF SF ERRORS - VARIABLE ON LEFT OF =
        WAS NOT DIMENSIONED
SF-1   'A PREVIOUSLY REFERENCED STATEMENT NUMBER APPEARS ON
        A STATEMENT FUNCTION DEFINITION'
SF-2   'STATEMENT FUNCTION IS THE OBJECT OF A LOGICAL IF
        STATEMENT'
SF-3   'RECURSIVE STATEMENT FUNCTION DEFINITION:NAME APPEARS
        ON BOTH SIDES OF EQUAL SIGN.LIKELY CAUSE VARIABLE
        NOT DIMENSIONED.'
SF-4   'A STATEMENT FUNCTION DEFINITION APPEARS AFTER THE
        FIRST EXECUTABLE STATEMENT'
SF-5   'ILLEGAL USE OF A STATEMENT FUNCTION NAME'

'STRUCTURED PROGRAMMING BLOCKS'
SP-0   'AT END STATEMENT MUST FOLLOW IMMEDIATELY AFTER A
        READ'
SP-1   'AT END FOLLOWS CORE TO CORE, DIRECT ACCESS OR
        INVALID READ STATEMENT'
SP-2   'AT END NOT VALID WHEN 'END=' SPECIFIED IN THE READ
        STATEMENT'
SP-3   'MISSING OR INVALID DO CASE, WHILE, LOOP, GUESS, AT
        END, OR IF-THEN STATEMENT'
SP-4   'IMPROPER NESTING OF BLOCK OR CONSTRUCT'
SP-5   'IMPROPER NESTING OF DO-LOOP'
SP-6   'IMPROPER NESTING WITH DO-LOOP'
SP-7   'MISSING END CASE, END LOOP, END WHILE, END GUESS,
        END AT END, OR END IF STATEMENT'
SP-8   'OTHER COMPILERS MAY NOT ALLOW IF-THEN-ELSE, DO
        CASE, STRUCTURED LOOP, OR REMOTE BLOCK STATEMENTS'
SP-9   'IF NONE BLOCK ALREADY DEFINED FOR CURRENT DO CASE
        CONSTRUCT'
SP-A   'IF NONE BLOCK MUST FOLLOW ALL CASE BLOCKS'

SP-B   'ATTEMPT TO TRANSFER CONTROL ACROSS REMOTE BLOCK
        BOUNDARIES'
SP-C   'REMOTE BLOCK NOT PRECEDED BY A TRANSFER'
SP-D   'REMOTE BLOCK PREVIOUSLY DEFINED'
SP-E   'REMOTE BLOCK STATEMENT MISSING OR INVALID'
SP-F   'LAST REMOTE BLOCK NOT COMPLETED'
SP-G   'REMOTE BLOCK IS NOT DEFINED'
SP-H   'REMOTE BLOCK IS NOT REFERENCED'
SP-I   'ATTEMPT TO NEST REMOTE BLOCK DEFINITIONS'
SP-J   'MISSING OR INVALID REMOTE BLOCK NAME'
SP-K   'ATTEMPT TO EXECUTE A REMOTE BLOCK RECURSIVELY'
SP-L   'NUMBER OF REMOTE BLOCKS EXCEEDS 255'
SP-M   'RETURN STATEMENTS ARE INVALID WITHIN REMOTE BLOCKS'
SP-N   'CASE STATEMENT FOR FIRST CASE GENERATED'
SP-P   'ATTEMPT TO QUIT MORE LEVELS THAN CURRENTLY EXIST'
SP-Q   'QUIT LEVEL MUST BE A POSITIVE INTEGER'

'SUBPROGRAMS'
SR-0   'MISSING SUBPROGRAM'
SR-1   'SUBPROGRAM REDEFINES A CONSTANT, EXPRESSION,
         DO-PARAMETER OR ASSIGNED GOTO INDEX'
SR-2   'THE SUBPROGRAM WAS ASSIGNED DIFFERENT TYPES IN
         DIFFERENT PROGRAM SEGMENTS'
SR-3   'ATTEMPT TO USE A SUBPROGRAM RECURSIVELY'
SR-4   'INVALID TYPE OF ARGUMENT IN REFERENCE TO A
         SUBPROGRAM'
SR-5   'WRONG NUMBER OF ARGUMENTS IN A REFERENCE TO A
         SUBPROGRAM'
SR-6   'A SUBPROGRAM WAS PREVIOUSLY DEFINED. THE FIRST
         DEFINITION IS USED'
SR-7   'NO MAIN PROGRAM'
SR-8   'ILLEGAL OR MISSING SUBPROGRAM NAME'
SR-9   'LIBRARY PROGRAM WAS NOT ASSIGNED THE CORRECT TYPE'
SR-A   'METHOD FOR ENTERING SUBPROGRAM PRODUCES UNDEFINED
         VALUE FOR CALL-BY-LOCATION PARAMETER'
SR-B   'MAINLINE PROGRAM NOT IN LIBRARY'

'SUBSCRIPTS'
SS-0   'ZERO SUBSCRIPT OR DIMENSION NOT ALLOWED'
SS-1   'ARRAY SUBSCRIPT EXCEEDS DIMENSION'
SS-2   'INVALID SUBSCRIPT FORM'
SS-3   'SUBSCRIPT IS OUT OF RANGE'
SS-4   'SUBSCRIPTS EXCEED BOUNDS OF ACTUAL ARRAY'

'STATEMENTS AND STATEMENT NUMBERS'
ST-0   'MISSING STATEMENT NUMBER'
ST-1   'STATEMENT NUMBER GREATER THAN 99999'
ST-2   'STATEMENT NUMBER HAS ALREADY BEEN DEFINED'
ST-3   'UNDECODEABLE STATEMENT'
ST-4   'UNNUMBERED EXECUTABLE STATEMENT FOLLOWS A TRANSFER'
ST-5   'STATEMENT NUMBER IN A TRANSFER IS A NON-EXECUTABLE
         STATEMENT'
ST-6   'ONLY CALL STATEMENTS MAY CONTAIN STATEMENT NUMBER
         ARGUMENTS'
ST-7   'STATEMENT SPECIFIED IN A TRANSFER STATEMENT IS A
         FORMAT STATEMENT'

ST-8   'MISSING FORMAT STATEMENT'
ST-9   'SPECIFICATION STATEMENT DOES NOT PRECEDE STATEMENT
         FUNCTION DEFINITIONS OR EXECUTABLE STATEMENTS'
ST-A   'UNREFERENCED STATEMENT FOLLOWS A TRANSFER'
ST-B   'STATEMENT NUMBER MUST END WITH COLON. STATEMENT
         NUMBER WAS IGNORED'

'SUBSCRIPTED VARIABLES'
SV-0   'THE WRONG NUMBER OF SUBSCRIPTS WERE SPECIFIED FOR A
          VARIABLE'
SV-1   'AN ARRAY OR SUBPROGRAM NAME IS USED INCORRECTLY
          WITHOUT A LIST'
SV-2   'MORE THAN 7 DIMENSIONS ARE NOT ALLOWED'
SV-3   'DIMENSION OR SUBSCRIPT TOO LARGE (MAXIMUM 10**8-1)'
SV-4   'A VARIABLE USED WITH VARIABLE DIMENSIONS IS NOT A
          SUBPROGRAM PARAMETER'
SV-5   'A VARIABLE DIMENSION IS NOT ONE OF SIMPLE INTEGER
          VARIABLE,SUBPROGRAM PARAMETER,IN COMMON'
SV-6   'PSEUDO VARIABLE DIMENSIONING ASSUMED FOR ARRAY '

'SYNTAX ERRORS'
SX-0   'MISSING OPERATOR'
SX-1   'EXPECTING OPERATOR'
SX-2   'EXPECTING SYMBOL'
SX-3   'EXPECTING SYMBOL OR OPERATOR'
SX-4   'EXPECTING CONSTANT'
SX-5   'EXPECTING SYMBOL OR CONSTANT'
SX-6   'EXPECTING STATEMENT NUMBER'
SX-7   'EXPECTING SIMPLE INTEGER VARIABLE'
SX-8   'EXPECTING SIMPLE INTEGER VARIABLE OR CONSTANT'
SX-9   'ILLEGAL SEQUENCE OF OPERATORS IN EXPRESSION'
SX-A   'EXPECTING END-OF-STATEMENT'
SX-B   'SYNTAX ERROR'
SX-C   'EXPECTING '(' OR END-OF-STATEMENT'

'TYPE STATEMENTS'
TY-0   'THE VARIABLE HAS ALREADY BEEN EXPLICITLY TYPED'
TY-1   'THE LENGTH OF THE EQUIVALENCED VARIABLE MAY NOT BE
          CHANGED REMEDY: INTERCHANGE TYPE AND EQUIVALENCE
          STATEMENTS'

'I/O OPERATIONS'
UN-0   'CONTROL CARD ENCOUNTERED ON UNIT 5 AT EXECUTION.
          PROBABLE CAUSE:MISSING DATA OR INCORRECT FORMAT'
UN-1   'END OF FILE ENCOUNTERED (IBM CODE IHC217)'
UN-2   'I/O ERROR (IBM CODE IHC218)'
UN-3   'NO DD STATEMENT WAS SUPPLIED (IBM CODE IHC219)'
UN-4   'REWIND,ENDFILE,BACKSPACE REFERENCES
          READER,PRINTER,OR PUNCH'
UN-5   'ATTEMPT TO READ ON UNIT 5 AFTER IT HAS HAD
          END-OF-FILE'
UN-6   'AN INVALID VARIABLE UNIT NUMBER WAS DETECTED (IBM
          CODE IHC220)'
UN-7   'PAGE-LIMIT EXCEEDED'
UN-8   'ATTEMPT TO DO DIRECT ACCESS I/O ON A SEQUENTIAL
          FILE OR VICE VERSA POSSIBLE MISSING DEFINE FILE
          STATEMENT (IBM CODE IHC231)'

UN-9   'WRITE REFERENCES READER, OR READ REFERENCES PRINTER
        OR PUNCH'
UN-A   'DEFINE FILE REFERENCES A UNIT PREVIOUSLY USED FOR
        SEQUENTIAL I/O (IBM CODE IHC235)'
UN-B   'RECORD SIZE FOR UNIT EXCEEDS 32767,OR DIFFERS FROM
        DD STATEMENT SPECIFICATION (IBM CODES IHC233,IHC237)'

UN-C   'FOR DIRECT ACCESS I/O THE RELATIVE RECORD POSITION
        IS NEGATIVE,ZERO,OR TOO LARGE (IBM CODE IHC232)'
UN-D   'ATTEMPT TO READ MORE INFORMATION THAN LOGICAL
        RECORD CONTAINS (IBM CODE IHC213)'
UN-E   'FORMATTED LINE EXCEEDS BUFFER LENGTH (IBM CODE
        IHC212)'
UN-F   'I/O ERROR - SEARCHING LIBRARY DIRECTORY'
UN-G   'I/O ERROR - READING LIBRARY'
UN-H   'ATTEMPT TO DEFINE THE OBJECT ERROR FILE AS A DIRECT
        ACCESS FILE (IBM CODE IHC234)'
UN-I   'RECFM IS NOT V(B)S FOR I/O WITHOUT FORMAT CONTROL
        (IBM CODE IHC214)'
UN-J   'MISSING DD CARD FOR WATLIB.NO LIBRARY ASSUMED'
UN-K   'ATTEMPT TO READ OR WRITE PAST THE END OF CHARACTER
        VARIABLE BUFFER'
UN-L   'ATTEMPT TO READ ON AN UNCREATED DIRECT ACCESS FILE
        (IHC236)'
UN-M   'DIRECT ACCESS SPACE EXCEEDED'
UN-N   'UNABLE TO OPEN WATLIB DUE TO I/O ERROR; NO LIBRARY
        ASSUMED'
UN-P   'ATTEMPT TO WRITE ON A READ ONLY FILE'
UN-Q   'DIRECT ACCESS UNAVAILABLE IN DEBUG MODE'
UN-R   'NAME ON C$COPY CARD NOT FOUND IN LIBRARY'
UN-S   'MISSING OR INVALID NAME ON C$COPY CARD'
UN-T   'C$COPY CONTROL CARD OR 'PGM=' OPTION FOUND IN
        LIBRARY'
UN-U   'ATTEMPT TO DO UNFORMATTED (BINARY) I/O ON READER,
        PRINTER, OR PUNCH'

'UNDEFINED VARIABLES'
UV-0   'VARIABLE IS UNDEFINED'
UV-3   'SUBSCRIPT IS UNDEFINED'
UV-4   'SUBPROGRAM IS UNDEFINED'
UV-5   'ARGUMENT IS UNDEFINED'
UV-6   'UNDECODABLE CHARACTERS IN VARIABLE FORMAT'
UV-7   'VARIABLE UNIT NUMBER IS UNDEFINED'

'VARIABLE NAMES'
VA-0   'A NAME IS TOO LONG.IT HAS BEEN TRUNCATED TO SIX
        CHARACTERS'
VA-1   'ATTEMPT TO USE AN ASSIGNED OR INITIALIZED VARIABLE
        OR DO-PARAMETER IN A SPECIFICATION STATEMENT'
VA-2   'ILLEGAL USE OF A SUBROUTINE NAME'

VA-3   'ILLEGAL USE OF A VARIABLE NAME'
VA-4   'ATTEMPT TO USE THE PREVIOUSLY DEFINED NAME AS A
          FUNCTION OR AN ARRAY'
VA-5   'ATTEMPT TO USE A PREVIOUSLY DEFINED NAME AS A
          SUBROUTINE'
VA-6   'ATTEMPT TO USE A PREVIOUSLY DEFINED NAME AS A
          SUBPROGRAM'
VA-7   'ATTEMPT TO USE A PREVIOUSLY DEFINED NAME AS A
          COMMON BLOCK'
VA-8   'ATTEMPT TO USE A FUNCTION NAME AS A VARIABLE'
VA-9   'ATTEMPT TO USE A PREVIOUSLY DEFINED NAME AS A
          VARIABLE'
VA-A   'ILLEGAL USE OF A PREVIOUSLY DEFINED NAME'

'EXTERNAL STATEMENT'
XT-0   'A VARIABLE HAS ALREADY APPEARED IN AN EXTERNAL
          STATEMENT'

APPENDIX I CONVERSION TO NON-STRUCTURED FORTRAN

The purpose of this appendix is to describe ways of transforming WATFIV programs containing any of the structured language elements:

IF-THEN-ELSE and ELSEIF	REMOTE BLOCK
WHILE	AT END
DO CASE	WHILE-EXECUTE
GUESS and ADMIT	LOOP, QUIT, UNTIL

to equivalent Fortran programs which do not contain any of these special constructs. There are essentially two ways -- the subprogram TRANSL supplied with the WATFIV system, and manual conversion on a construct-by-construct basis.

1. Using the TRANSL Subroutine

The TRANSL subroutine reads a WATFIV program as _data_ and produces an equivalent (logic-preserving) program in standard Fortran. For example, to punch a standard Fortran deck from a WATFIV program deck you could run the following job.

```
$JOB WATFIV
      CALL TRANSL(5,7)
      STOP
      END
$ENTRY
   data (WATFIV deck to be translated)
```

The 5 and 7 are the usual device numbers of the card reader and card punch. Certain restrictions on the input accepted by TRANSL must be noted. The more important ones are:

1. Statement numbers in the range 90000-99999 and variable names beginning with '$' should not be used.

2. The names of REMOTE BLOCKs must be unique in their first 5 characters and all REMOTE BLOCK definitions must follow their references.

3. Do not use keywords such as WHILE or ELSE as variable names.

4. Check the printout! Some errors may not be detected and the translator might produce incorrect code.

2. Manual Conversion

a) IF-THEN-ELSE

The IF construct can be converted to non-structured Fortran using a Logical IF and unconditional GO TOs. An example using one ELSEIF is shown below.

<table>
<tr><td align="center">Before Conversion
(Structured)</td><td align="center">After Conversion
(Unstructured)</td></tr>
</table>

```
IF(logical expr1)THEN              IF(.NOT.(logical expr1))GOTO 10
  .)                                 .)
  .}     THEN group                  .}       THEN group
  .)                                 .)
  .                                GO TO 30
ELSEIF(log expr2)THEN         10 IF(.NOT.(log expr2)) GO TO 20
  .)                                 .)
  .}     ELSEIF group                .}       ELSEIF group
  .)                                 .)
  .                                GO TO 30
ELSE                          20 CONTINUE
  .)                                 .)
  .}     ELSE group                  .}       ELSE group
  .)                                 .)
END IF                        30 CONTINUE
```

The reader will realize that this is only one of several methods that could be used.

b) WHILE

The recommended transformation uses a Logical IF and an unconditional GO TO.

<table>
<tr><td align="center">Structured (Before)</td><td align="center">Non-Structured (After)</td></tr>
</table>

```
WHILE(logical expr.)          10 IF(.NOT.(logical expr.))GOTO 20
  .)                                 .)
  .}     statement(s)               .}     statement(s)
  .)                                 .)
END WHILE                        GO TO 10
                              20 CONTINUE
```

Depending on the nature of the changes in the loop counter or index, an equivalent DO-loop may sometimes be used. A WHILE construct may also be terminated by an UNTIL statement. in this case the statement "UNTIL(log.expr)" is replaced by "IF(.NOT.(log.expr))GO TO s" where s denotes the statement number of the WHILE statement.

c) LOOP-QUIT-END LOOP

The   translation   of   the   LOOP   construct   is
straightforward.

Structured (Before)   Non-Structured (After)

```
LOOP                           10 CONTINUE
 .                              .
 . ... QUIT                     . ... GO TO 20
 .                              .
END LOOP                          GO TO 10
                               20 CONTINUE
```

Had the loop definition been   terminated by an UNTIL
statement of the form 'UNTIL(log.expn)' the UNTIL statement
would   be   transformed   into   the   statement
'IF(.NOT.(log.expr))GO TO 10'.

d) DO CASE

For this conversion, the existence of the Computed GOTO
statement means conversion is relatively easy.

Structured (Before)   Non-Structured (After)

```
DO CASE i                      GO TO (10,20,30,...),i
   CASE                           .)
    .)                            . }     IF NONE block
    . } statement(s)              .)
    .)                            GO TO 100
   CASE                        10   CONTINUE
    .)                            .)
    . } statement(s)             . }     1st CASE block
    .)                            .)
    .                            GO TO 100
    .                         20   CONTINUE
    .                             .)
   IF NONE                       . }     2nd CASE block
    .)                            .)
    . } statement(s)             GO TO 100
    .)                            .
END CASE                       100 CONTINUE
```

The Assigned GOTO could also be used but its use is not as
natural as using a Computed GOTO.

e) GUESS and ADMIT

The transformation of an example structure containing one ADMIT group is shown below. The extension to multiple ADMITs is straightforward.

Structured (Before)	Non-Structured (After)
GUESS	CONTINUE
.	.
. ... QUIT	. ... GO TO 10
.	.
.	GO TO 20
ADMIT	10 CONTINUE
.	.
. ... QUIT	. ... GO TO 20
.	.
END GUESS	20 CONTINUE

That is, if control reaches the end of the GUESS group or the end of an ADMIT group without a QUIT being executed, then control transfers to the end of the construct.

f) REMOTE BLOCK

In most cases the simplest approach is to use a subprogram in place of a REMOTE BLOCK. If the REMOTE BLOCK uses a large number of variables however, it would mean that the argument and parameter lists would be extremely long. In such cases use of the ASSIGN and Assigned GO TO may provide the best conversion as shown in the example below.

Structured	Non-Structured
	ASSIGN 10 TO I
EXECUTE TEST	GO TO 500
.	10 CONTINUE
.	.
.	.
REMOTE BLOCK TEST	500 CONTINUE
.⎫	.⎫ REMOTE BLOCK
.⎬ statement(s)	.⎬ statements
.⎭	.⎭
END BLOCK	GO TO I,(10,...)

Use of this method requires a unique statement number for each location from which it is accessed. Hence the statement number list may become very lengthy. Both difficulties (long argument lists and long statement number lists can be overcome by putting the arguments in a named

COMMON Block and using a subprogram to descibe the logic. Execution of a QUIT within a REMOTE BLOCK causes transfer to the assigned GO TO in the non-structured equivalent above.

g) AT END

Use the "END=" option in a READ statement in place of the AT END. Two possibilities are shown below.

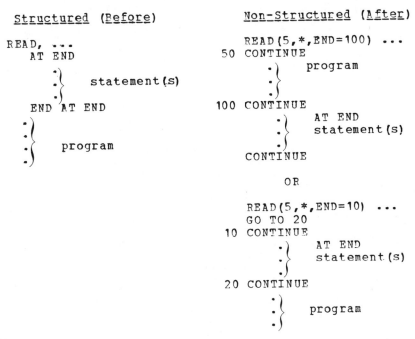

Structured (Before)

```
READ, ...
    AT END
        .⎫
        .⎬  statement(s)
        .⎭
    END AT END
.⎫
.⎬  program
.⎭
```

Non-Structured (After)

```
    READ(5,*,END=100) ...
 50 CONTINUE
        .⎫  program
        .⎬
        .⎭
100 CONTINUE
        .⎫  AT END
        .⎬  statement(s)
        .⎭
    CONTINUE

        OR

    READ(5,*,END=10) ...
    GO TO 20
 10 CONTINUE
        .⎫  AT END
        .⎬  statement(s)
        .⎭
 20 CONTINUE
        .⎫  program
        .⎬
        .⎭
```

Using an AT END statement instead of an AT END construct is equivalent to using a construct with a single statement.

h) WHILE-EXECUTE

To convert a WHILE-EXECUTE statement transform the logic to an equivalent WHILE loop and then use the techniques described in (b) and (f) above.

BUILT-IN FUNCTIONS

This appendix contains a list of built-in functions which can be used in source programs compiled by the WATFIV compiler. In the table:

   i2 denotes any INTEGER*2 expression

   i4 denotes any INTEGER*4 expression

   r4 denotes any REAL*4 expression

   r8 denotes any REAL*8 expression

   c8 denotes any COMPLEX*8 expression

   c16 denotes any COMPLEX*16 expression

These symbols also denote the type of function value produced.

If the function has only one argument, "a" represents its value. If a function has two arguments, "a1", and "a2" denote their values. If a function can have more than two arguments, dots ("...") indicate this fact.

TABLE OF BUILT-IN FUNCTIONS

PURPOSE	NAME AND ARGUMENTS	DEFINITION	TYPE OF RESULT
Square Root	SQRT (r4) DSQRT (r8) CSQRT (c8) CDSQRT (c16)	$\sqrt{a}$	r4 r8 c8 c16
Sine	SIN (r4) DSIN (r8) CSIN (c8) CDSIN (c16)	sin a (a in radians)	r4 r8 c8 c16
Cosine	COS (r4) DCOS (r8) CCOS (c8) CDCOS (c16)	cos a (a in radians)	r4 r8 c8 c16

Tangent	TAN (r4) DTAN (r8)	tan a (a in radians)	r4 r8
Cotangent	COTAN (r4) DCOTAN (r8)	cot a (a in radians)	r4 r8
Arcsine	ARSIN (r4) DARSIN (r8)	$x = \arcsin a$ $-\pi/2 \le x \le \pi/2$	r4 r8
Arccosine	ARCOS (r4) DARCOS (r8)	$x = \arccos a$ $-\pi/2 \le x \le \pi/2$	r4 r8
Arctangent	ATAN (r4) DATAN (r8)	$x = \arctan a$ $-\pi/2 \le x \le \pi/2$	r4 r8
	ATAN2 (r4,r4) DATAN2 (r8,r8)	$x = \arctan(a1/a2)$ $-\pi/2 \le x \le \pi/2$	r4 r8
Exponential	EXP (r4) DEXP (r8) CEXP (c8) CDEXP (c16)	$e{**}a$	r4 r8 c8 c16
Natural Logarithm	ALOG (r4) DLOG (r8) CLOG (c8) CDLOG (c16)	log a (base e)	r4 r8 c8 c16
Common Logarithm	ALOG 10 (r4) DLOG 10 (r8)	log a (base 10)	r4 r8
Hyperbolic Sine	SINH (r4) DSINH (r8)	sinh a	r4 r8
Hyperbolic Cosine	COSH (r4) DCOSH (r8)	cosh a	r4 r8
Hyperbolic Tangent	TANH (r4) DTANH (r8)	tanh a	r4 r8
Error Function	ERF (r4) DERF (r8)	$\operatorname{erf}(a) = \dfrac{2}{\sqrt{\pi}} \int_0^{} e^{-t^2}\, dt$	r4 r8
	ERFC (r4) DERFC (r8)	$1 - \operatorname{erf}(a)$	r4 r8

Gamma	GAMMA (r4) DGAMMA (r8)	$\Gamma(a) = \int_0^\infty t^{a-1} e^{-t} dt$	r4 r8
Function	ALGAMA (r4) DLGAMA (r8)	log (gamma (a)) (base e)	r4 r8
Absolute Value	IABS (i4) ABS (r4) DABS (r8)	$\lvert a \rvert$	i4 r4 r8
	CABS (c8) CDABS (c16)	$\sqrt{x^2 + y^2}$ for a= (x,y)	r4 r8
Complex Conjugate	CONJG (c8) DCONJG (c16)	(x,-y) for a= (x,y)	c8 c16
Transfer Of Sign	ISIGN (i4, i4) SIGN (r4, r4) DSIGN (r8, r8)	$\lvert a1 \rvert$*sign (a2) , where $sign (x) = \begin{cases} 1 & if\ x>0 \\ 1 & if\ x=0 \\ -1 & if\ x<0 \end{cases}$	i4 r4 r8
Truncation	INT (r4) AINT (r4) DINT (r8)	x*sign (a) where x is the largest integer $\leq \lvert a \rvert$	i4 r4 r8
Modular Arithmetic	MOD (i4, i4) AMOD (r4, r4) DMOD (r8, r8)	a1-a2*int (a1/a2)	i4 r4 r8
Largest Value	MAX0 (i4, i4, ...) MAX1 (r4, r4, ...) AMAX0 (i4, i4, ...) AMAX1 (r4, r4, ...) DMAX1 (r8, r8, ...)	max (a1, a2, ...)	i4 i4 r4 r4 r8
Smallest Value	MIN0 (i4, i4, ...) MIN1 (r4, r4, ...) AMIN0 (i4, i4, ...) AMIN1 (r4, r4, ...) DMIN1 (r8, r8, ...)	min (a1, a2, ...)	i4 i4 r4 r4 r8
Positive Difference	IDIM (i4, i4) DIM (r4, r4)	a1 - min (a1, a2)	i4 r4

Type Conversion	IFIX(r4) HFIX(r4)	convert from REAL to INTEGER	i4 i2
	FLOAT(i4) DFLOAT(i4)	convert from INTEGER to REAL	r4 r8
	SNGL(r8)	truncate REAL*8 to REAL*4	r4
	DBLE(r4)	pad REAL*4 value to make REAL*8 value	r8
	CMPLX(r4,r4) DCMPLX(r8,r8)	create COMPLEX value from 2 REAL values	c8 c16
	REAL(c8)	real component of a COMPLEX value	r4
	AIMAG(c8)	imaginary component of a COMPLEX value	r4

```
┌─────┐
│  E  │
└─────┘
```

┌─────┐
│ F │
└─────┘

```
 ┌───┐
 │ G │
 └───┘
```

```
 ┌───┐
 │ H │
 └───┘
```

```
 ┌─────┐
 ╎  Z  ╎
 └─────┘
```